The Vegetarian Gourmet

The Vegetarian Gourmet

Paul Southey

Marshall Cavendish

Editor's note: The average number of portions is stated at the head of each recipe, except in the case of breads, cakes, pastries and some puddings where the size of the portion depends on the appetite. We have calculated the calorie and protein values as accurately as possible and this accounts for the careful specification of weights in the lists of ingredients used. Please make allowances if you alter the proportions, vary the stated ingredients or add a sauce. A sauce has only been included in the count if it is an integral part of the dish. The Nutrition Tables beginning on page 212 will provide a basis for any extra calculation you may need to do. Spoon measures are level unless otherwise stated and the cooking times are intended to be a guide. The author is the speediest cook we have ever met, so we have adjusted the times to suit less nimble mortals!

Published by Marshall Cavendish Books Limited
58 Old Compton Street,
London W1V 5PA

First published in 1980
2nd printing 1982
3rd printing 1984

© Marshall Cavendish Limited 1980-1986

ISBN 0 85685 715 7

Printed and bound in Hong Kong by Dai Nippon Printing Company

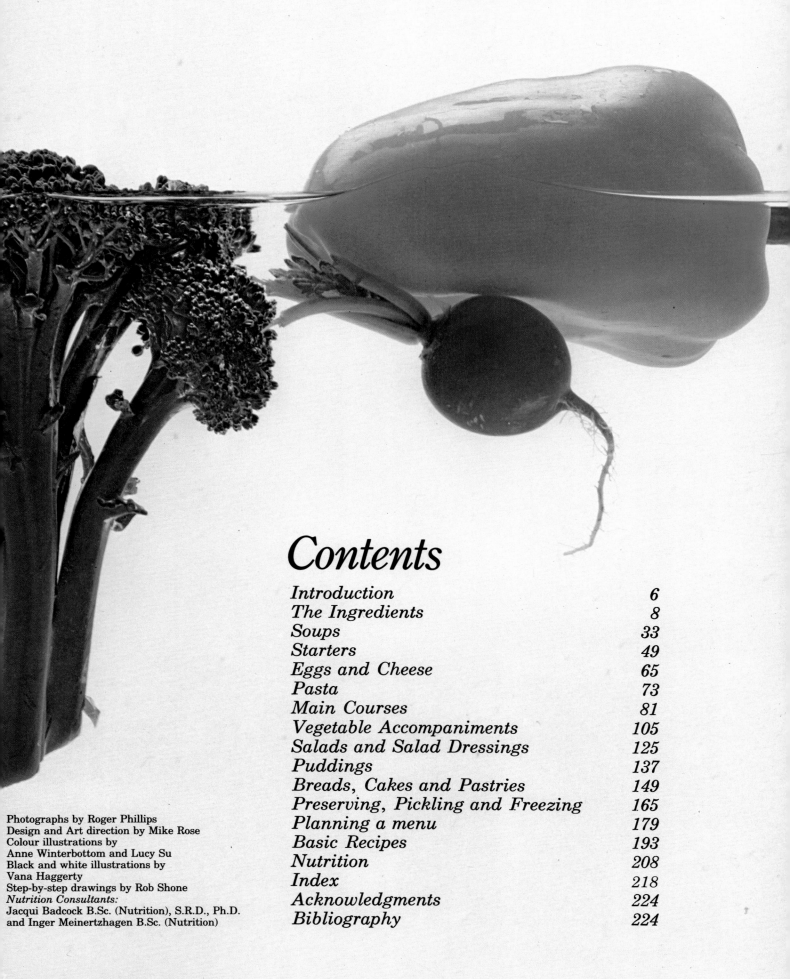

Contents

Photographs by Roger Phillips
Design and Art direction by Mike Rose
Colour illustrations by
Anne Winterbottom and Lucy Su
Black and white illustrations by
Vana Haggerty
Step-by-step drawings by Rob Shone
Nutrition Consultants:
Jacqui Badcock B.Sc. (Nutrition), S.R.D., Ph.D.
and Inger Meinertzhagen B.Sc. (Nutrition)

Introduction

What is vegetarianism? It is a belief in following a diet that includes no meat of any kind and therefore does not rely on the slaughter of animals for the provision of food. Vegetarianism is not a new discovery, nor is it a 'fad' or trend. At various times throughout our recorded history, people in many countries have successfully followed a vegetarian régime for economic, religious, cultural or ethical reasons. Philosophers down the ages have expounded on its virtues; writers and artists have followed its precepts; those who abhor cruelty to animals in any form have been converted to its princ-ciples and those to whom it represents a healthier way of life in stressful times have taken up its practice.

More and more, people seem to be looking towards vegetarianism as a partial solution to the approaching world food crisis – as the population increases. Medical authorities have some reason for believing that protein gained from natural food sources such as plants may be more easily assimilated in the body than that gained from animal sources, and is better for our health.

The aim of this book is to present a collection of recipes for vegetarians who include eggs, milk and milk products in their diet (it is not primarily intended for vegans, who eat no animal produce of any kind). I wanted to show that a vegetarian cuisine ranks among the best in the world and can be as varied and appetising as the more 'conventional' meat-orientated *haute cuisine*. The vegetarian need not rely solely on the produce of the kitchen garden; a whole variety of exciting foods – exotic fruits, vegetables, nuts, seeds, pulses, cereals from all over the world – is at his disposal to enrich his daily diet, and all the proteins, vitamins, minerals and trace elements necessary for a healthy, active, enjoyable life can be gained from these, as well as from eggs, milk, cream and a whole variety of cheeses.

Herbs and spices play their part in gourmet cooking and a little judicious tasting will soon tell you how

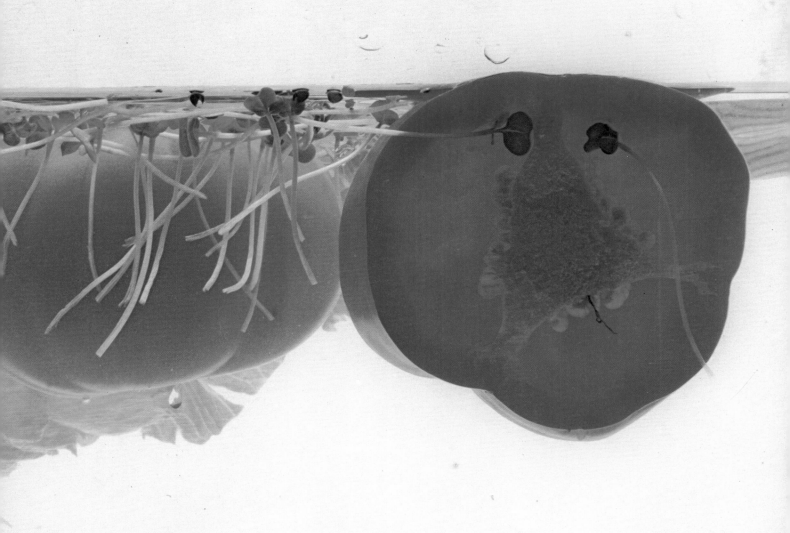

much or how little – and in what combination – best suits your palate. The very best cooks learn the art of experimentation early in life and treat recipes as a guide and not as a set of inflexible rules . . .

I am fond of wine, love entertaining, and enjoy the classic, four-course meal with the appropriate wines and side dishes. When I became a vegetarian, I saw no reason for giving up one of life's greatest pleasures. I have therefore worked out, tested, amended and created a number of recipes for the enterprising cook. Some of these can be used singly, or with a salad, as a simple supper or 'one-pot' meal; others can be combined into elaborate dinner party menus. The conscientious slimmer may find my use of eggs, cream, butter and olive oil excessive, but I am not suggesting that you over-indulge in rich food, or eat a five-course gourmet dinner every day!

When using my recipes for entertaining, I would suggest that you read through the complete recipe *before* beginning to cook. Check through the ingredients and weigh and measure them carefully before you start; by planning your cooking, you will accomplish more with less effort.

One of my main preoccupations on becoming a vegetarian was to calculate my daily intake of protein and to make sure I was eating enough. Accordingly, we have given – as accurately as is possible – the protein and the calorie content of each dish, in portions where this seemed sensible, to help you calculate your own menu without effort. A Table showing the recommended daily intake is given on page 208, and we have included further Tables, giving the protein and calorie content of many of the main foods in 100 gram and 1 ounce quantities to help you when compiling recipes.

Eat well, and enjoy your food, for as Talleyrand, that great French philosopher, said: 'Show me another pleasure like dinner, which comes every day and lasts an hour.'

The Ingredients
a visual glossary

No-one can begin to cook without the basic ingredients and on the following pages we present a visual glossary of many of the raw ingredients available to the vegetarian cook. It cannot pretend to be fully comprehensive; such an undertaking would be outside the scope of this book, but we have gathered together as many as possible over a considerable period of time and most of them are to be found in the recipes.

It is a fact of commercial practice that, as the supply of fruits and vegetables becomes more highly organised and efficient, our choice is becoming more and more limited to those varieties which are high-yielding, travel well and are convenient to use. The best way to enjoy greater variety is, of course, to grow your own. If this is not possible, do not be afraid to ask your supplier if you need a particular type – a cooking apple

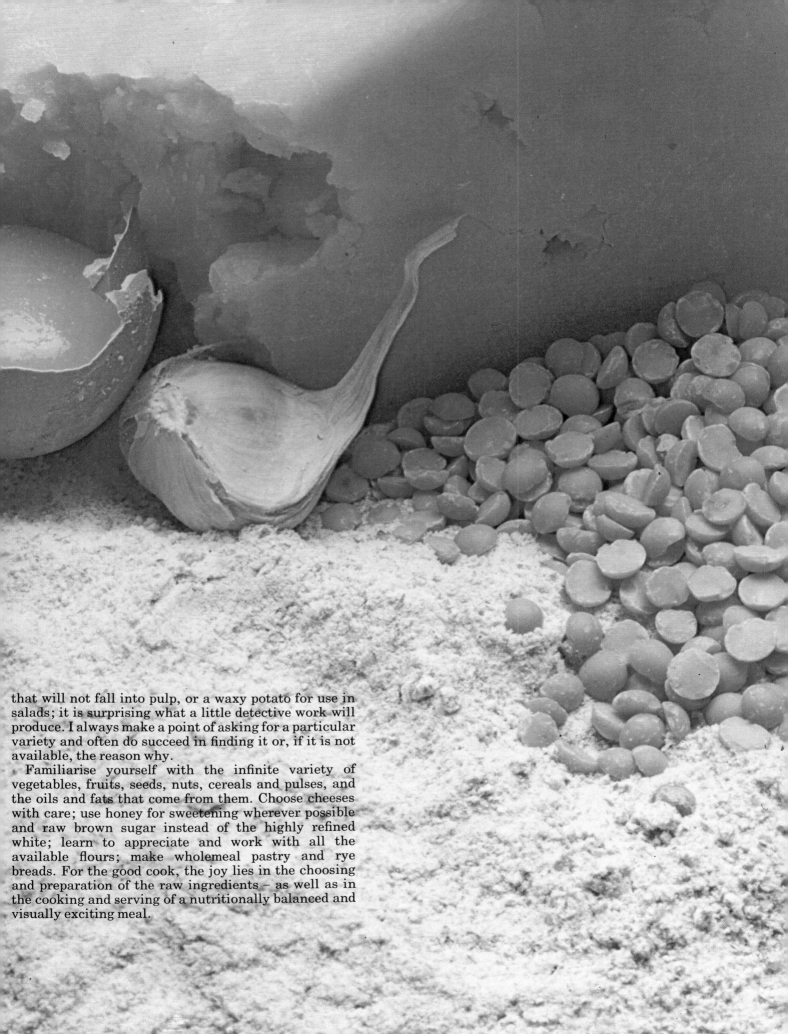

that will not fall into pulp, or a waxy potato for use in salads; it is surprising what a little detective work will produce. I always make a point of asking for a particular variety and often do succeed in finding it or, if it is not available, the reason why.

Familiarise yourself with the infinite variety of vegetables, fruits, seeds, nuts, cereals and pulses, and the oils and fats that come from them. Choose cheeses with care; use honey for sweetening wherever possible and raw brown sugar instead of the highly refined white; learn to appreciate and work with all the available flours; make wholemeal pastry and rye breads. For the good cook, the joy lies in the choosing and preparation of the raw ingredients – as well as in the cooking and serving of a nutritionally balanced and visually exciting meal.

ROOTS AND TUBERS

1 TURNIP *Brassica rapa*
Early ones available in summer
Maincrop available in autumn and winter
The staple food of northern and central Europe until the introduction of the potato in the sixteenth century, turnips contain sugar and starches. Early ones are best in taste and texture. Purée old roots.

2 SWEDE *Brassica napus*
var. *napobrassica*
Available from autumn to spring
Once known as 'swedish turnips', swedes are larger and sweeter than turnips, with orange-yellow flesh. Like most root vegetables, swedes store well.

3 SCORZONERA *Scorzonera hispanica*
4 SALSIFY *Tragopogon porrifolius*
Available mid autumn
These two different roots are similar in taste and the cooking method needed. Scorzonera has a nearly black skin: both have white flesh which discolours quickly, so cook them in water with lemon juice. Serve in a Béchamel or Tomato sauce.

5 GIANT RADISH *Raphanus sativus*
Available autumn and winter
Often sold under the name 'mooli', this radish can be grated for salad or cooked like turnip. (not shown)

6 HORSERADISH *Armoracia rusticana*
Available from autumn to early spring
Native to Europe, this peppery pungent root is grated raw for flavouring sauces.

7 CARROT *Daucus carota*
Early ones available from midsummer
Maincrop available all year round
Carrots are particularly rich in vitamin A. The tiny, early ones are the most delicious; scrape or peel the coarser maincrop carrots and use for soups and casseroles. Both are good to eat raw.

8 KOHLRABI *Brassica oleracea caulorapa*
Available from late summer through winter
Botanically related to the cabbage, kohlrabi is the enormously swollen base of the stem. It has a mild, sweet and rather nutty flavour. Cook small young kohlrabi unpeeled.

9 PARSNIP *Pastinaca sativa*
Available in autumn and throughout winter
Parsnips are rich in sugar and starch. Avoid roots with brown markings or woody tops. Remove very hard cores, if necessary, before cooking.

10 BEETROOT *Beta vulgaris*
Available all year round; at its best in late summer
Long-rooted beetroot are grown, but round ones are tenderer and more tasty. The smaller the root, the sweeter the flavour. Buy uncooked beetroot if possible, without bruises or broken skin, as these bleed when cooked.

11 CELERIAC *Apium graveolens*
var. *rapaceum*
Available from late autumn through winter
This rough-skinned root has creamy-white flesh with a pronounced celery flavour. Shred it raw and eat, tossed in a Vinaigrette dressing or Mayonnaise. Alternatively, cook and purée it.

12 JERUSALEM ARTICHOKE
Helianthus tuberosus
Available late autumn and winter
A relative of the sunflower and native to North America, this knobbly tuber has a slightly smoky flavour. It contains inulin a sugar substitute used by diabetics. Cook in acidulated water to prevent discoloration. Purée for soups or serve in a sauce.

POTATO *Solanum tuberosum*
Varieties available all year round
Once a luxury for the rich, the potato is now the staple diet of millions. As an important food crop, however, it is a relative new-comer, and has only been widely cultivated in Europe since the eighteenth century. There are a vast number of varieties, differing widely in flavour and texture. Larger, maincrop potatoes can be either waxy – good for slicing when cooked and for use in salads – or floury – best for puréeing, baking or roasting. Sadly, the choice of potatoes in the shops is limited to a few, high cropping varieties.

16 SWEET POTATO *Ipomoea batatas*
Available throughout the winter
Either red, white or purple skins enclose white or yellow, sweet-tasting flesh. Cook as you would ordinary potatoes, but boil in the skins. A native of America, sweet potatoes can also be served for dessert.

17 YAM *Dioscorea* (not shown)
Available in winter
The name 'yam' is loosely applied to any tropical root crop and, in America, to sweet potatoes. A true yam is one of the cultivated species of the *Dioscera* family. Yams store better than most tropical roots. They contain mainly starch. Boil, roast or fry them.

20 WHITE SKINNED ONIONS

21 PICKLING ONIONS
Available from mid summer to autumn
Known also as pearly or button onions, this variety is lifted before it is full size.

22 GARLIC *Allium sativum*
Available all year round
Strongest and most pungent member of the onion family, garlic is primarily used as a seasoning, in small amounts. It contains the antibiotic allicin. Garlic keeps well when stored in a dry place.

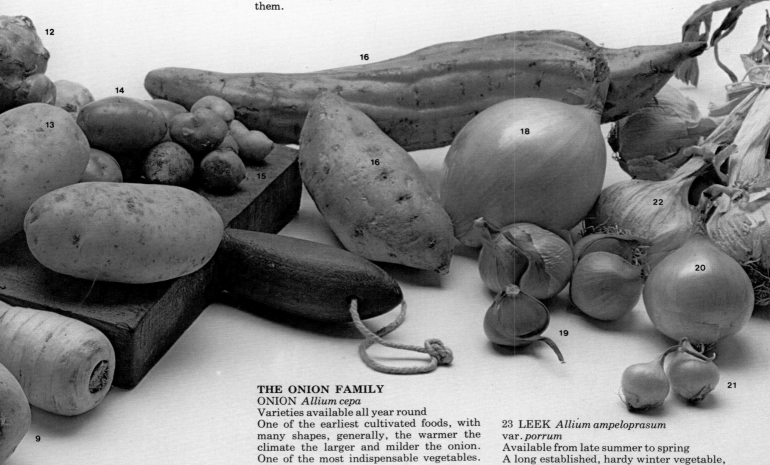

13 MAINCROP POTATOES
Available from late summer onwards
These are known as 'whites'; they store better than the tiny new potatoes, but should be kept in a cool, airy place. Avoid buying potatoes with green patches on the skin; these contain poisonous alkaloids. Reject potatoes with fungus marks. Smaller red-skinned potatoes are 14 King Edwards.

15 NEW POTATOES
Available in late spring and early summer
Freshly-dug new potatoes have an incomparable sweet, earthy taste and a crisp, juicy texture which diminishes with storage. Choose new potatoes the size of walnuts. After boiling or steaming, the skin should easily peel off in the fingers.

THE ONION FAMILY
ONION *Allium cepa*
Varieties available all year round
One of the earliest cultivated foods, with many shapes, generally, the warmer the climate the larger and milder the onion. One of the most indispensable vegetables.

18 SPANISH ONION
The largest and mildest in flavour – excellent and juicy for use in salads.

19 RED SKINNED SHALLOTS
Allium ascalonicum
Available autumn and early winter
Small and delicately-flavoured, use them in subtle sauces for a hint like garlic.

23 LEEK *Allium ampeloprasum*
var. *porrum*
Available from late summer to spring
A long established, hardy winter vegetable, cook the white blanched stems of leeks and use the green tops for soup.

24 SPRING ONION
Available from spring onwards
Originally the thinnings from the onion bed, spring onions are now cultivated for salads.

BRASSICAS AND LEAVES

1 CABBAGE *Brassica oleracea*
var. *capitata*
Varieties available all year round
Cabbages contain valuable amounts of vitamin C and minerals, but their nutritional value can be greatly lessened by overcooking. It is better to steam them or boil in a very little water and use any that may be left for stocks or soups. With all varieties, when choosing cabbage, look for firm hearted ones. See that the base of the stalk is not dry or withered, check that the outer leaves are not yellowed or limp and that there are no loose, curling leaves on the outside.

2 WINTER CABBAGE. Remember that it will not respond to over-cooking. Despite its tough texture when raw and its thick, crinkled leaves, it has a relatively mild flavour.

PURPLE SPROUTING BROCCOLI
(not shown)
Brassica oleracea var. *botrytis cymosa*

4 LARGE-HEADED BROCCOLI
Brassica oleracea botrytis
Available late winter and spring
The single purple head of Cape broccoli is shown, but the white-headed type is commoner. Choose heads with tight curds and fresh leaves, as for all types of broccoli. Broccoli goes well with cheese. Try it steamed or boiled.

6 SPRING CABBAGE or SPRING GREENS *Brassica oleracea* var. *capitata*
Available in early spring
These are young cabbages picked early in the season before the heart has a chance to develop. Choose greens with thick, firm leaves and cook them on the day you buy them as they wilt very quickly.

3 CALABRESE *Brassica oleracea*
var. *Italica*
Available in summer
The Italian sprouting broccoli, or calabrese, is a feathery palish green. These fronds grow after the first, tightly-packed head has been cut and are thought by many to be superior in flavour. Much sought-after during the summer months, it is not as easy to grow as the white or purple-sprouting types. Choose broccoli with firm, straight, juicy stems and tight-packed curds. It is delicious served on its own with a Butter sauce.

5 CAULIFLOWER *Brassica oleracea*
var. *botrytis cauliflora*
Available from late autumn to summer
After the pea, this is one of the most consistently popular vegetables. Winter cauliflowers have green leaves that curl tightly round the flower heads, or curds. Summer cauliflowers have leaves that are more spread out. If the leaves are limp, it is a sign that the vegetable has been too long out of the ground. Choose cauliflowers with firm, close-textured heads and no brown specks.

7 WHITE CABBAGE
Available late autumn and winter
Deliciously mild in flavour and good to eat either cooked, or shredded raw in salads such as coleslaw. The white cabbage is distinguished by its colour and very tightly packed leaves. Reject any with outward curling leaves or brown patches and do not be tempted to overcook or it will be limp and tasteless.

8 RED CABBAGE
Available autumn and early winter
This variety has a characteristic, slightly sour flavour. It takes much longer to cook than other varieties and is therefore especially suitable for braising, marinating and pickling. Try it sliced thinly in salads.

10 CHINESE CABBAGE
Brassica pekinensis
Another mild-tasting but non-hearting cabbage that is excellent when lightly cooked or, preferably, stir-fried. It looks rather like a paler variety of Cos lettuce and its crisp texture is much appreciated in salads.

12 GREENS
The leaves of many other plants, such as turnip (as shown here), beetroot, mustard greens and even dandelion are all good sources of vitamin C and minerals. Choose fresh-looking, tender young leaves and – once again – do not overcook them.

9 BRUSSELS SPROUTS *Brassica oleracea* var. *gemmifera*
Available in autumn and winter
Brussels sprouts look exactly like miniature cabbages and have a delicate, nutty flavour all their own. The smaller they are, the better they taste; large ones become coarse-textured. Choose firm, green, close-wrapped heads without any yellowing leaves or other obvious signs of wilting. Some say the flavour is improved by a touch of frost.

11 KALE (not shown) *Brassica oleracea* var. *acephala*
Available in winter
Kale is a variety of non-hearting cabbage that has no solid head. Its broad, curly leaves grow alternately from a thick central stalk and vary in colour from dark green to purple. The stalk and leaf ribs may have to be discarded if they prove too tough.

13 SPINACH *Spinacia oleracea*
Available all year round
The popular name of this plant is sometimes used to describe the leaves of Swiss chard or seakale as well as the true spinach. Summer spinach has round leaves, while the winter variety has leaves that are more spiky in shape. When buying, look for fresh, crisp leaves and handle them with extreme care as they bruise very easily. Do not wash them unless you are going to use them straight away, otherwise they will go limp. Spinach shrinks amazingly during cooking – it should be cooked with just the water left from rinsing clinging to the leaves – so buy twice as much as you think you will need. Spinach stalks make a welcome addition to the stock pot.

PODS AND SEEDS

1 FRENCH BEANS *Phaseolus vulgaris*
Available all year round
2 RUNNER BEANS *Phaseolus multiflorus*
Available summer and autumn
The pods of these are eaten before the bean itself is fully developed. Runner beans are larger, coarser in texture than French beans and usually darker in colour. If the pod is young and tender, it should break cleanly when snapped in half; French beans are sometimes called 'snap beans' for this reason. Some varieties are stringless.

3 SWEETCORN *Zea mays* var. *saccharata*
Available summer and autumn
Freshly picked corn is best to eat; a milky fluid should run from a seed when its skin is punctured. The leaves should be stiff, pale green and silky. Delicious boiled or steamed and simply served with melted butter.

4 OKRA *Hibiscus esculentus*
Available midwinter to early summer
Originally a native of the West Indies, usually eaten while still slightly under-ripe. It is glutinous in texture and therefore good for thickening casseroles. Choose pods that are less than 15 cm (6 in) long. Also known as ladies' fingers or gumbo.

5 SUGAR PEAS or MANGETOUT
Pisum sativum var. *saccharatum*
Available in spring
Called *mangetout* because these sweet-tasting young pods are eaten whole, sugar peas should be crisp and juicy. Delicious stir-fried.

6 PEAS *Pisum sativum* var. *hortense*
Available in spring and summer
At their very best in early summer, peas were the first vegetables ever to be canned or frozen; now much of the early crop goes to the frozen food industry. Early varieties are smooth-skinned; later ones are wrinkled. Both should have bright green, juicy pods without blemishes.

7 BROAD BEANS
Vicia faba vulgaris
Available spring through to autumn
Broad beans are a good source of protein and can be served in their pods if very young and small. Large ones are sold shelled and should be skinned after cooking. Look for bright green juicy pods and serve skinned beans with a herb butter.

STALKS AND SHOOTS

8 ASPARAGUS *Asparagus officinalis*
Available in early summer
A member of the lily family, the asparagus has been popular since Roman times. An immature shoot which is cut off early in the season, it quickly loses flavour once cut. Europeans prefer the thick-stalked white type, the British young green shoots. Avoid asparagus with thin or woody stems.

9 FLORENCE FENNEL *Foeniculum vulgare*
Available all year round
Also known by its Italian name, *finocchio*, this swollen stem base has a refreshing flavour halfway between celery and aniseed. Good to eat braised, or chopped raw in salads; choose fennel that is pale in colour, with a bulb that feels heavy for its size.

10 CELERY *Apium graveolens*
Available all year round; better in winter
One of the oldest-known 'medicinal' plants, its crisp stalks are white or green and the leaves of young shoots can be used to flavour casseroles, or eaten raw in salads. When buying, choose stalks that are fleshy and crisp.

11 GLOBE ARTICHOKE *Cynara scolymus*
Available all year round
The most suitable varieties for eating are those with slightly rounder tops to the leaves, making them less prickly to handle. It is the fleshy part at the base of each leaf that is scraped off and eaten, the choicest part being the heart (see page 111).

12 CHICORY *Cichorium intybus*
Available autumn and winter
A slightly bitter-tasting, succulent salad vegetable with broad, tightly packed silvery leaves. If the leaves are more green than white, it is likely to be very bitter. Good for braising, choose chicons that are plump and well-shaped.

13 WATERCRESS *Nasturtium officinale*
Available all year round

At its best from March to early summer, this small-leaved, peppery-tasting dark green leaved plant adds piquancy to salads and is often used as a garnish. The leaves should be a good, dark green, not yellowing.

14 MUSTARD AND CRESS
Sinapis alba/Lepidium sativum
Available all year round
Two of the easiest, most satisfying seeds to sprout (see page 201), they add a tang to any salad. Can be grown indoors.

15 BEAN SPROUTS (Mung beans or Alfalfa)
Available all year round
Try growing these indoors yourself (see page 201) to add crunchy-textured protein to your salads. A classic ingredient in Chinese cooking; low in calories so useful for slimmers – unless stir-fried.

16 RADISH *Raphanus sativus*
Available all year round
A peppery-tasting root vegetable popular in salads. This is the red type which adds a pleasing contrast in colour as well as texture. Also try the oval-shaped white European radish, sliced and salted.

LETTUCE *Lactuca sativa*
Available all year round, best in summer
The basic ingredient of most green salads; though soft-hearted hothouse varieties are available during winter they are so limp you should choose a more seasonal vegetable, such as chicory or endive. Look out, too, for Chinese cabbage (see page 13). Choose lettuce with crisp, fresh leaves, firm hearts – where appropriate – and reject any with brown or slimy patches.

17 COS LETTUCE
Easily recognisable by its long, spear-shaped leaves – a crisp and succulent type.

18 WEBBS WONDERFUL or ICEBERG
Pale green, tight leaved, crisp-hearted cabbage type with a crunchy texture.

19 TOM THUMB
A soft-leaved, round cabbage-type available in summer; early maturing and small.

20 ENDIVE *Cichorium endivia*
Available late autumn and winter
The endive has a very curly, rather tough leaf with a pleasant, slightly bitter taste.

FUNGI
MUSHROOMS

The best ones to find are the large, wild, field-grown mushrooms, but care must be taken if you are gathering them yourself. Some fungi are deadly poisonous. Either buy a definitive, illustrated book on the subject (see bibliography), or take an experienced picker with you.

1 FIELD MUSHROOMS *Agaricus campestris*
Available late summer and early autumn
Field mushrooms are the largest and coarsest in texture, but have the best and strongest flavour. They can be white or brown and, when fully opened, are flat-topped. Pick mushrooms with unwrinkled skins and stalks that are moist at the base and show no signs of withering. Fry or grill them on the day they have been picked – or bought.

2 MOREL *Morchella esculenta*
Available in spring
One of the best-flavoured of all edible fungi, the morel makes a superb garnish to most savoury dishes. It is not often seen in shops outside Europe, but if you are lucky enough to find this distinct, dark crinkly mushroom, you would be wise to keep the exact location to yourself

3 OYSTER MUSHROOM *Pleurotus ostreatus*
Available in winter
Another variety of edible mushroom, now more widely available in the shops. It is similar in flavour to the field mushroom, is paler in colour with a distinctive curling cap.

4 BUTTON MUSHROOM *Agaricus bisporus*
Available all year round
The commercially grown white variety, which is sold as button mushrooms when unopened, cap mushrooms when half-open and 'flats' when fully opened. Use them sliced raw in salads, marinated in French dressing, or cooked in dishes where the black spores of field mushrooms would spoil the appearance of the finished dish.

5 TRUFFLE *Tuber aestivum*
Something of a rarity and therefore very expensive, the truffle grows completely underground and has to be hunted out by specially trained dogs. The black truffle from Périgord is considered the finest; Italian truffles are a beautiful pale fawn inside. Both are used in sauces and for garnishing dishes.

THE VEGETABLE FRUITS
Back row from left to right:

6 PUMPKIN *Cucurbita pepo maxima*
Available late summer and autumn
A large winter squash with characteristic, bright orange flesh. Pumpkins can grow up to 45–50 kg (100 lb) in weight, but our British summers are not long enough for them to ripen fully. They contain more nourishment than the marrow and are often sold in sections because of their size and weight. Look for dense, non-fibrous flesh and firm outer skin. Pumpkin can be boiled, steamed, baked or roasted – or served in a traditional spiced dessert pie.

7 AUBERGINE *Solanum melongena* var. *esculentum*
Available all year round
Also widely known as the eggplant, because of its shape, this beautiful, exotic vegetable fruit has a tough, dark purple skin – occasionally you find white skinned ones – and yellow, mealy flesh. It should be sliced and sprinkled with salt to drain out any bitter juices before cooking. Aubergines can be baked, stuffed, fried, or dipped in batter and deep-fried. Choose vegetables with smooth, shiny skins that feel heavy for their size.

16

8 AVOCADO PEAR *Persea americana*
Available all year round
Not a pear in the dessert sense, but a rich-tasting vegetable fruit containing vitamins of the B complex and a high proportion of fat. The rather knobbly dark green or purplish skin encloses soft, smooth, pale green or yellow flesh surrounding a large stone. Best served on its own with a Vinaigrette dressing as a starter, or to contrast with sharper flavours in a salad. Test for ripeness by gently pressing the rounded end to see if it is soft. Reject avocadoes with dark patches or wrinkled skins.

9 PEPPER *Capsicum annuum*
Available all year round
A bright, tropical vegetable fruit full of vitamin C; the ripe ones are a glorious red or yellow, the unripe a rich and vibrant green. The pepper seems designed for holding a savoury stuffing. Ripe red peppers have a milder, sweeter flavour than the green ones and are good to use in salads. The crunchy, more pungent green ones give flavour to cooked dishes; if used raw, some people find them difficult to digest. Look for bright, firm, shiny fruits with no trace of dullness and no wrinkled patches on the skin.

10 TOMATO *Lycopersicon esculentum*
Available all year round
Originally grown as a decorative plant, the tomato has now become a favourite salad vegetable. The choice in the shops is limited to the commercially viable heavy-cropping varieties, though the large, eccentrically-shaped, coarse-fleshed European tomato can still be found. Look out, too, for the Italian plum-shaped variety; home growers should try the yellow tomatoes. Use the small green ones for pickling. Choose firm, unbruised tomatoes for salads; softer, riper ones will do for soups and purées.

11 SQUASH *Cucurbita pepo*, *maxima* and *moschata*
Varieties available in summer and winter
One of a variety of the small American marrows that are becoming more readily available here. Squashes vary greatly in shape and colour – from pale green to bright orange, yellow and cream, and have descriptive names such as golden, gem or crookneck. The seeds can be eaten as well as the flesh. Choose firm ones with tender skins and bake, boil or steam them.

12 MARROW *Cucurbita pepo* var. *ovifera*
Available summer and autumn
The larger the marrow, the coarser the texture of the flesh and the more insipid the flavour. A marrow is, after all, 99% water. However, like the pepper, it seems designed to hold a variety of savoury stuffings and be served with a richly flavoured sauce. Choose smaller marrows, if possible, those no more than 30 cm (12 in) long, which are heavy for their size, firm and straight.

13 COURGETTE
Available all year round
A type of baby marrow, specially bred and usually picked before it grows to 15 cm (6 in) in length. The smaller they are, the better the flavour. They are also widely known by their Italian name, zucchini. Some varieties need to be sliced and salted, like the aubergine, to drain away bitter juices before cooking. To test for this, cut off a slice and if it tastes bitter, give it the salt treatment.

14 CUCUMBER *Cucumis sativus*
Available all year round
There are two basic types of cucumber: the ridge type, with a knobbly skin, which is grown outdoors and usually considered to have a better flavour than the frame or hot-house cucumber, which is the one most usually grown commercially. Modern varieties have had the more indigestible qualities bred out of them. The small gherkin cucumber is used for pickling. Choose firm, straight, bright-skinned cucumbers not more than about 5 cm (2 in) in diameter.

HERBS

1 CHIVES *Allium schoenoprasum*
A member of the onion family, but now considered a culinary herb. Its thin, grasslike, mild-flavoured leaves go well with delicate egg dishes, curd or cottage cheese, and on salads. Use scissors for snipping over food.

2 ROSEMARY *Rosmarinus officinalis*
Spikes of rosemary give a most appetising fragrance to casseroles, soups and many vegetable dishes. If using fresh, make sure the spikes are very finely chopped, or tie in a muslin bag. Add rosemary when making scones or pastry.

3 DILL *Anethum graveolens*
The feathery leaves of dill, with their subtle flavour of caraway, can be used in salads, sauces and dishes where the stronger, more pungent dill seed (page 20) is not required.

4 OREGANO *Origanum vulgare*
This is related to marjoram, but much more powerful in flavour. Used in Italian dishes – add it to Tomato sauce for pasta, casseroles and the filling for Ravioli.

5 LEMON BALM *Melissa officinalis*
A perennial herb with a piercing aroma, used in tisanes and marinades. Try a leaf or two in your usual brew of tea.

6 BAY *Laurus nobilis*
An essential component of any *bouquet garni*, the bay leaf combines well with and complements many other flavours. Add bay leaves when cooking cabbage.

7 BERGAMOT *Monarda didyma*
This herb has attractive red flowers, the petals of which can be sprinkled on salads. Add the leaves to iced drinks or fruit cups. It is not to be confused with the Bergamot orange (*Citrus bergamia*) from which an aromatic oil is obtained.

8 APPLE MINT *Mentha rotundifolia*
One of the most fragrant members of the mint family; others worth investigating are eau-de-Cologne mint, peppermint, and spearmint (see right). Use with discretion in sauces, salads and vegetable dishes.

9 MARJORAM *Origanum majorana*
Marjoram and thyme are two of the best-known herbs and the one can be substituted for the other. Marjoram has the more delicate flavour, however, and goes well with egg dishes.

10 BORAGE *Borago officinalis*
A herb with a distinct, cucumber flavour, now only used in drinks. Its attractive blue flowers can be candied to decorate cakes.

11 ANGELICA *Angelica archangelica*
Often used to flavour liqueurs and fruit syrups; add angelica leaves when stewing apples or pears. The stems are candied and used to decorate cakes.

12 SAGE *Salvia officinalis*
The broad, flat, crinkled leaves of sage impart their unmistakeable flavour to any dish. Include sage in your stuffing mixtures, but try some in yeast dough too.

13 SAVORY *Satureia montana*
The spiky leaves of winter savory taste of rosemary and sage – with a dash of pepper; summer savory (*satureia hortensis*) has a similar but milder flavour. Both go well with bean dishes; I use them in my herb butters.

14 PARSLEY *Petroselinum crispum*
and FRENCH PARSLEY
Two types of our most familiar herb, used to garnish so many dishes and rich in vitamin C. An essential ingredient of Tabbouleh (page 133) and a perennial favourite.

15 TARRAGON *Artemisia dracunculus*
A welcome addition to most cream sauces and Mayonnaise or Béarnaise sauce – one cannot describe the aroma without going into the realms of fantasy! French tarragon has the best flavour.

16 THYME *Thymus vulgaris*
Another very familiar herb, much partnered by sage in flavourings, but similar itself to marjoram. Add it when cooking aubergines, mushrooms or carrots, or to a scone mixture.

17 SPEARMINT *Mentha spicata*
The most commonly grown variety of mint; use as for Apple mint.

18 LOVAGE *Levisticum officinale*
An uncommon herb which deserves to be better known. It has a celery-like flavour with a distinct spiciness – use in *bouquets garnis* or chopped and sprinkled over salads.

19 CHERVIL *Anthriscus cerefolium*
The flavour of these little leaves is fresh and spicy – use with watercress and parsley for an Omelette fines herbes. It goes well with egg dishes and in salads.

20 BASIL *Ocimum basilicum* or *minimum*
Sweet basil (as shown) has larger leaves than bush basil and its *rapport* with the tomato is well known. A basic ingredient of Pesto (page 75), try its sweet, pungent, aromatic flavour with other vegetables.

NOTE: If dried herbs are used, halve the quantity you would use for fresh herbs. Dried herbs have a much stronger flavour.

SPICES

1 MUSTARD SEED *Brassica alba*
Also found in a red or dark brown form. Whole mustard seed is not as pungent as when ground; try mixing red and yellow in varying proportions.

2 MACE *Myristica fragrans*
This is the lacy coating of the NUTMEG (shown left), both of which come from the same tropical tree, mace being fuller, stronger and sweeter than the nutmeg it encases.

3 CLOVES *Eugenia caryophyllata*
These are dried flower buds, pungent and spicy, used in mulled wine, stewed fruit – especially apples – and with caution in vegetable dishes.

4 CARAWAY SEEDS *Carum carvi*
The oil from this is used to make the German liqueur Kümmel (the German name for caraway); use the seeds in sponge cakes and to subtly flavour vegetable dishes and sauces.

5 CARDAMOMS *Amomum cardamomum*
One of the basic spices used in Indian cooking, and also popular in Scandinavia, the seeds are contained inside the fibrous shell.

6 CHILLIES
A variety of red, green and dried Mexican chillies, all from the *capsicum* family; used in curry powders, the seeds and fruit of *capsicum minimum* or *frutescens* are also ground cayenne (see below).

7 FENNEL
Foeniculum vulgare or *vulgare dulce*
Both the dried stalks (shown) and the seeds are used in European and Far Eastern cooking. They have a celery-like, aniseed flavour.

8 DILL SEED *Anethum graveolens*
The name comes from the Norse word 'to lull', and it is used to make dill water – good for the digestion. The seeds are used in making dill pickles; try them with potato salad, scrambled eggs or sautéed cabbage.

9 CURRY POWDER
Indian cooks always blend their own, varying the proportions of the spices to suit the dish (see Garam masala, page 200).

10 CUMIN *Cuminum cyminum*
The powder ground from the seeds, with fenugreek (right) gives commercial curry powder its flavour. Use with pulses.

11 PAPRIKA *Capsicum annuum*
A sweet, warm-tasting aromatic red pepper, it loses its flavour if stored for too long. Use it in salad dressings and beaten into curd cheese for filling baked potatoes.

12 CAYENNE PEPPER
Capsicum minimum or *frutescens*
A very hot pepper, to be used with extreme caution, made from a blend of dried chillies (see left). Use sparingly.

13 CINNAMON *Cinnamomum zeylanicum*
It comes from the bark of a tree of the laurel family; available in powdered or stick form. It does not keep its aroma long. Try it with apples, or to flavour your coffee.

14 GINGER *Zingiber officinale*
A powder made from the dried root – use a little in casseroles and composite dishes – and for flavouring cakes.

15 TURMERIC *Curcuma longa*
A bright yellow powder ground from the root, used in rice dishes or to give an exotic touch to simple vegetable dishes.

16 SAFFRON *Crocus sativus*
This comes from the orange stigmas of a mauve crocus – buy the filaments to be more sure of getting the genuine article. Use sparingly to flavour rice.

17 CORIANDER *Coriandrum sativum*
Seeds and leaves are both used in Middle Eastern cooking and Indian dishes.

18 ALLSPICE *Pimenta officinalis*
Also known as Jamaica pepper, allspice tastes like a blend of clove, cinnamon and nutmeg.

19 FENUGREEK *Trigonella foenum-graecum*
One of the ingredients used in commercial curry powders. Use very sparingly – the flavour is 'raw' and unsubtle.

20 WHITE PEPPERCORNS *Piper nigrum*
These are black peppercorns (see right) with the wrinkled outer layer removed. White pepper is sharper than black; use in dishes where black pepper would spoil the appearance of the finished dish.

21 JUNIPER BERRIES
Juniperus communus
A basic flavouring of gin, crushed juniper blends well with other spices.

22 BLACK PEPPERCORNS *Piper nigrum*
I always specify 'freshly ground pepper', as ready-ground pepper loses its flavour quickly, like most other spices.

23 STAR ANISEED *Pimpinella anisum*
Much used in Chinese cooking and to flavour alcoholic drinks.

24 POPPY SEEDS *Papaver somniferum*
Delicious when sprinkled on bread, cakes and buns when baking.

25 VANILLA PODS *Vanilla planifolia*
Store in a jar of castor sugar; use to infuse in milk for making custards, crushing the pods for a stronger flavour.

21

LEGUMES AND PULSES

Legumes and pulses – the dried peas, beans and lentils – play an important part in the vegetarian diet. An excellent source of protein, they are worth exploring in their amazing variety, from the soya bean – high in protein but so delicately flavoured that added herbs and spices are needed – to the distinctively flavoured red kidney bean, with an 'earthy' taste all its own. Pulses are relatively simple to prepare but, unless you have a pressure cooker, take quite a long time – varying from 2-3 hours to over-night – to soak and cook. A great deal depends on the type of bean, when it was harvested and how long it has been stored. Further details are given on page 123. It is best to adjust the seasoning towards the end of the cooking time, as protracted cooking tends to extract or lessen the added flavours. Some beans are delicious served cold in salads and make a vital contribution in this respect to summer dishes.

4 MUNG BEANS
Good for sprouting (page 201), extensively cultivated in Africa, China and the USA.

5 EGYPTIAN LENTILS
The basis of many spicy dishes, try them with butter and chopped parsley.

6 HARICOT BEANS
Use these with other beans in salads, soups or cooked with rosemary and garlic.

The eighteen varieties illustrated are:

1 BLACK BEANS
Extensively used in Caribbean dishes and in Chinese cooking – try them spiced with ginger or cumin; garlic and Tomato sauce.

2 WHOLE GREEN PEAS
Make 'mushy' peas to serve with other vegetables; cook them with onions, garlic or shallots.

3 SPLIT GREEN PEAS
These make good, thick soups and purées swirled with mint and cream – or make them into a traditional pease pudding.

7 ADUKI BEANS
Rather high in carbohydrate, these taste sweeter than other beans; good for sprouting as well as for cooking as a vegetable.

8 BROAD BEANS
These can be either white or brown and the skins must be removed after cooking as they are very tough – unless you buy them ready-skinned. Serve them puréed, hot or cold; if cold, season well and dress with lemon juice.

9 RED KIDNEY BEANS
These have an earthy 'country' quality. Serve them with rice and a Tomato sauce; hot in casseroles, or cold in salads.

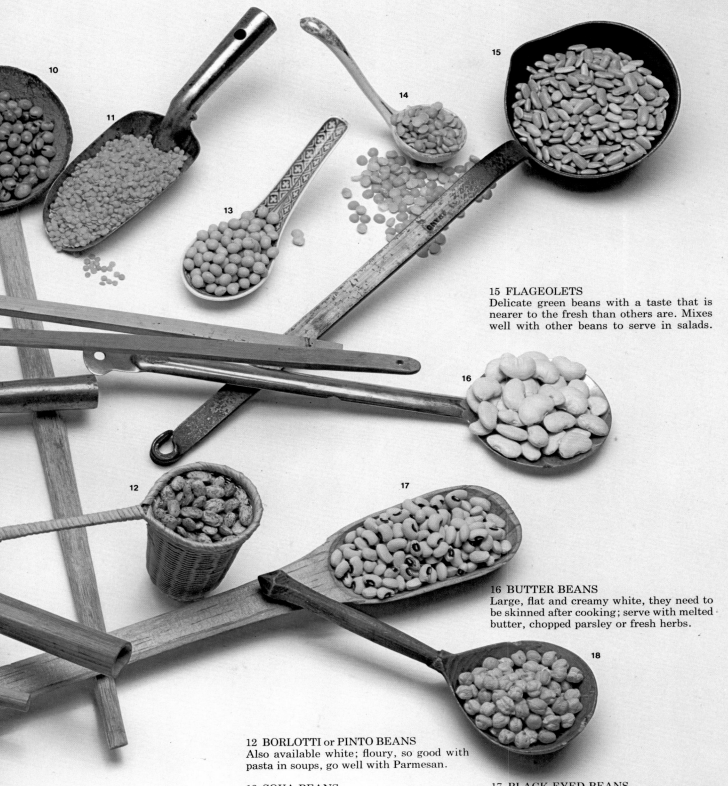

15 FLAGEOLETS
Delicate green beans with a taste that is nearer to the fresh than others are. Mixes well with other beans to serve in salads.

16 BUTTER BEANS
Large, flat and creamy white, they need to be skinned after cooking; serve with melted butter, chopped parsley or fresh herbs.

10 EGYPTIAN BROWN BEANS
The *ful medames* of Egypt; try them with lemon juice, oil, garlic and parsely.

11 RED LENTILS
Good for thickening soups, making dhal to accompany curries. Mild-flavoured, they purée quickly.

12 BORLOTTI or PINTO BEANS
Also available white; floury, so good with pasta in soups, go well with Parmesan.

13 SOYA BEANS
The high-protein food – mild-flavoured so use lots of spices. Coarse-crushed soya grits take much less time to cook.

14 SPLIT YELLOW PEAS
Also make good thickenings for soups – and a pease pudding; they can also be cooked, spiced and deep-fried as rissoles.

17 BLACK-EYED BEANS
The 'black-eyed peas' of the USA – a 'soul food' of the American South when cooked with onions and rice.

18 CHICK PEAS
Need the longest soaking and cooking of all the beans; eat them hot or cold, or make Hummus (page 64), the famous Greek 'dip'.

PASTA

Pasta – as its name implies – is made from a basic flour and water paste, sometimes with egg added to lighten the texture, add richness and – of course, protein. The best quality pasta is made from the hard durum wheat semolina flour, which itself contains a high proportion of protein and produces a firm pasta which does not break down in cooking. Wholemeal flour makes a thicker-textured but very tasty pasta, especially if made at home (see page 74). Pasta can be 'plain' or flavoured with spinach (pasta verde) and it comes in an amazing variety of shapes, a selection of which are illustrated here.

Illustrated here:

1 Durum wheat (semolina flour) spaghetti
2 Wholemeal spaghetti
3 Egg noodles
4 Nidi (nests) of plain tagliatelle and tagliatelle verde
5 Cannelloni
6 Wholemeal macaroni
7 Rigatoni
8 Tortiglioni
9 Farfalle (the smaller ones are called farfalletti)
10 Conchiglie (shells) and conchiglietti
11 Wholewheat anelli
12 Lasagne verde and wholemeal lasagne
13 Ravioli

CEREALS AND FLOURS

Top row from left to right:

WHOLEMEAL FLOUR
Fine-ground, for making cakes and pastry. I sift out the coarser bran and make up the quantity with extra sifted flour when making fine-textured cakes.

WHOLE WHEAT
The highly nutritious whole seed of the wheat itself. Rich in protein, vitamins and oils, it needs long, slow cooking.

UNBLEACHED WHITE FLOUR
I use this in preference to bleached white flour when making flavoured cakes (eg. coffee), as it masks the flavour less than wholemeal flour would do.

STONE GROUND WHOLEMEAL FLOUR
I use this flour when making bread and for other yeast cookery.

REFINED WHITE FLOUR
I prefer not to use this bleached flour.

CORNMEAL
Either yellow or white, depending on the colour of the wheat from which it was ground. Use it to make Corn bread rolls (page 152).

Second row from left to right:

COARSELY GROUND CORNMEAL
The kind you use for making Polenta (page 124) and dumplings for vegetable casseroles.

BUCKWHEAT or KASHA
Used extensively in Russia, where it is still eaten from the hand – it is very nutritious.

BUCKWHEAT FLOUR
Make Blinis (page 60) with this; much used in Russian cooking.

ROLLED OATS
The coarsest quality available, used for breakfast cereals; rolled oats make delicious sweet oatcakes (page 164). Sprinkle them on the tops of loaves before baking.

OATMEAL
Comes in varying grades – use this one for bread, scones and griddle cakes.

RYE FLOUR
This is light; the darker the colour, the stronger the taste of rye. I suggest mixing them when making bread as dark rye dough is sticky to handle.

Third row from left to right:

SOYA GRITS
Ground from the protein-rich soya bean (page 23), they take much less time to cook.

BURGHUL
Made by part-cooking wholewheat until the grains are about to burst, then dried and ground. Make sure you are not given cracked wheat instead, as this takes much longer to prepare. Use burghul for Tabbouleh (page 133).

COUSCOUS
Coarse-ground semolina made from wheat, it can also be made from millet. Much used in North Africa and Eastern Europe, it is steamed over a casserole.

BARLEY MEAL
Add a little to the mixed flours when making bread to give it a distinctive flavour.

SEMOLINA
Taken from the endosperm at the heart of the wheat, it is ground to varying grades; used fine for puddings, coarse for couscous.

MILLET
Usually thought of as bird seed, it can be ground and used in cooking. It is highly nutritious and has a nutty flavour.

Bottom row from left to right:

LONG GRAIN BROWN RICE
Use this unpolished rice whenever possible as it still has valuable vitamins, minerals and protein left. Long-grain is best for Indian, Chinese and Middle Eastern dishes, SHORT GRAIN for puddings, croquettes and sweet dishes.

CAROLINA (SHORT GRAIN) RICE
White, polished rice has the outer layers removed by milling. Used for puddings.

LONG GRAIN (BASMATI) RICE
The rice I favour for savoury dishes when the brown version is not available.

RICE FLOUR
Gluten-free, used by professional bakers to control the stickiness of their dough. Can be used for thickening soups, and for biscuits.

WILD RICE
Very expensive, but well worth it.

OILS AND FATS

Edible oils are the liquid form of fats which, in the vegetarian diet, are taken mainly from vegetables, cereals, nuts and seeds. Medical opinion is not in complete agreement about the possible connection between the consumption of fatty acids and the onset of cardio-vascular disease; as a general rule, nutritionists recommend that you watch your total intake of fats and edible oils. Those obtained from vegetable sources, containing polyunsaturated fatty acids, may be preferable to the saturated fatty acids from animal sources. The Basic Nutrition chapter, beginning on page 208 discusses this question in more detail.

Since it is impossible to avoid using fats and edible oils in my cooking, here are some of the most usual ones:
Above, from left to right:

1 WALNUT OIL
A delicious, highly flavoured oil, used in the south of France interchangeably with olive oil. Try it on your salads.

2 SUNFLOWER SEED OIL
This is often used in place of olive oil though it has, of course, a much blander flavour. Try soaking olives in it, so that it will acquire a slight olive flavour.

3 PEANUT OIL
A similar oil to sunflower seed oil, but with a more pronounced flavour – unless it is de-odorised in the processing.

4 SESAME SEED OIL
A beautifully-flavoured oil pressed from sesame seeds and greatly used in Oriental and Middle Eastern cooking.

5 TAHINA PASTE
This is made from sesame seeds and oil, and is a basic ingredient in the classic Hummus (page 64) found throughout the Middle East.

6 OLIVE OIL
This is the oil most often used in French and Italian cooking; I would use it for preference in most of my dishes – it has an incomparable flavour. The first pressing, known as 'huile vierge' is the strongest in flavour – and difficult to find!

7 ALMOND OIL
Mainly used in making confectionery, try a little for frying salted almonds.

8 SOYA BEAN OIL
An almost tasteless, refined oil pressed from the soya bean. It can be used both for cooking and for dressing salads.

9 SAFFLOWER SEED OIL
This, too, has very little flavour once it is refined. It is low in fatty acids.

10 CORN OIL
For me, this oil has a rather unpalatable flavour; many people prefer to use it for deep fat frying.

IMPORTANT: Never heat the oil used for deep fat frying to above 190°C (375°F), or it will spontaneously ignite. The danger signal is a blue haze over the pan. Sunflower seed oil should not be heated to above 185°C (360°F). A cube of dry bread should brown in 60 seconds at this temperature.

11 SHORTENING
A crumbly, white cooking fat made from vegetable oils and designed to be used in cakes; especially good for making the close-textured American cakes.

12 MARGARINE
A solid fat of varying degrees of firmness which can be used instead of butter, although the flavour of the finished dish will not be the same. Choose a margarine made from vegetable oils; some brands have added vitamins.

NUTS AND SEEDS

The term *nut* is used to describe a number of seeds, kernels or plants and fruit which, botanically speaking, are not all nuts. However, nuts can be divided for convenience into categories based on similarity of flavour. First we have the Brazils, hazelnuts, pecans and walnuts, all of which have a rich, oily flavour and firm texture. Then there are the pistachios and pine nuts, both of which have a slightly resinous taste. Almonds, cashews and chestnuts are

sweeter; chestnuts go floury after cooking.

Coconuts are in a class of their own, in flavour somewhere between Brazils and almonds but the nut is hollow and contains a sweet, vegetable milk.

Serve nuts whole, coarsely chopped or ground; add them to cooked dishes, sprinkle them over vegetables or salads as a garnish and you will be adding extra protein and nourishment to your diet; nuts generally have a high food value. Almonds are at the top of the league, followed by Brazils, walnuts and hazelnuts. Chestnuts come last, but are very popular, especially roasted.

If you can, beg *fresh* nuts from friends who have them growing in the garden. Many shop-bought nuts are kiln dried or roasted, and this alters their flavour – especially walnuts which can taste quite acrid if kiln-dried.

13 SUNFLOWER SEEDS
Best eaten raw – a good source of protein and vitamins; sprinkle over salads or cereals.

14 SESAME SEEDS
A valuable source of vitamins and minerals, e.g. magnesium, calcium and phosphorus.

15 CASHEW NUTS (unsalted and salted)
Sprinkle these sweet, crescent-shaped nuts over salads, or bake in a nut loaf (page 104).

16 WALNUTS
Pickle these in midsummer, before the shell has matured and hardened.

17 DESICCATED COCONUT
The dried, shredded meat of 27 COCONUT (*extreme right*), used in curries and sweet dishes and as a flavouring for cakes.

18 CHESTNUTS
These very popular nuts can be baked, boiled, mashed, made into flour, puréed, or served as a vegetable.

19 PISTACHIOS
A very sweet, rich-tasting nut which, when peeled is a characteristic pale green.

20 PECANS
An American relative of the walnut, it has a smooth shell and a milder flavour.

21 HAZELNUTS
Sometimes confused with the larger cob nut, hazelnuts are used in cakes; good toasted.

22 ALMONDS whole, shelled and green
Toast and salt them to eat as snacks; grind or shred and add to cakes.

23 PINE KERNELS or PIGNOLIAS
The aromatic nuts of certain pine trees, these are always sold shelled.

24 PEANUTS or GROUNDNUTS
Rich in fat content and protein, this nut is made into oil, butter or flour; serve as a vegetable, or ground in loaves.

25 WATER CHESTNUTS
Not strictly speaking, a nut, but with a crisp texture. Used in Chinese cooking.

26 BRAZIL NUTS
A large, meaty nut with a very hard shell.

EGGS

Apart from familiar white and brown HENS EGGS (*front right*), the eggs of some other birds can be eaten. A blue-tinged DUCK EGG (*far left*) should only be used in recipes in which it will be thoroughly cooked; a tiny spotted QUAIL'S EGG and a larger dark-shelled GULL'S EGG (*behind*) are both rich-tasting and considered delicacies. A GOOSE EGG (*behind right*) is strongly flavoured and very large!

Vegans, who eat no animal produce, will certainly not eat eggs, though they are high in protein and very nourishing. Free range eggs, from hens not kept in battery-type cages and accredited by a health food organisation, are best. Put an egg into a bowl of water. If it is fresh, it will lie flat; if aging, it will have a tendency to float as the bubble of air under the shell at the broad end enlarges.

Never place eggs straight from the refrigerator into boiling water, or the shell will almost certainly crack. The older the egg, the more likely the shell is to crack in any case. Store eggs pointed-end downwards, as they keep longer if the yolk is resting on the white and not on the bubble of air.

MILK

Milk makes a very valuable contribution to the diet, being rich in protein, vitamins, calcium and other minerals. It is, in fact, the most complete single food we know. Vegans do not drink milk, using instead the 'milk' that comes from nuts. The quality of any milk depends on the time of the year – summer pasture milk being traditionally the best – the breed of the animal and the type of fodder provided. Commercially available milk goes through varying processes to produce different 'grades' and to destroy harmful bacteria.

CREAM

This contains varying amounts of butterfat which is separated off the milk by centrifugal force. The higher the concentration of fat, the thicker the cream – double cream being the thickest you can buy.

When whipping thick cream, have the bowl and utensils chilled; when whipping very fresh cream, add a little lemon juice. If you overwhip cream, however, you are left with butter and buttermilk. Buttermilk is a very good source of protein and has a sour, slightly cheesy taste. Commercially soured cream is also available – delicious with fresh or cooked fruit, or in casseroles.

DRIED MILK

Skimmed powdered milk has had all the cream removed and therefore keeps longer than milk in its liquid form. Low in calories and good for anyone on a weight-reducing diet. 'Instant' dried milk has been processed to make it more soluble in beverages such as tea and coffee.

YOGHURT

This is made from milk, cows' or goats', which has been purposely soured by bacteria. Make sure, when buying yoghurt, that it has a fresh culture in it; some commercially available yoghurt has been sterilized. It is easy to make your own (page 200) – then you know it will be fresh!

CHEESE

Cheese poses a particular problem for the vegetarian as most contain animal rennet, which is used to curdle the milk or cream. Rennet-free Cheddar and Cheshire cheese are available from many health food stores, and there is a move afoot to use a vegetable based enzyme instead. Hard cheeses are highest in protein and generally lowest in calories, except for curd and cottage cheese. Here is a selection of the cheeses containing rennet:

1 PARMESAN
Strong-flavoured, hard Italian cheese that is matured for two years. Buy it in the piece and grate it as you need it.

2 RICOTTA
A very soft Italian cream cheese with a mild and pleasant flavour. Use for cooking.

BEL PAESE (not shown)
A popular Italian soft cheese with a mild, sweet flavour; goes well with fresh soft fruit at the end of a meal.

3 GORGONZOLA
Italy's most famous blue-veined cheese, ripe and sharp and very crumbly in texture.

4 CAMEMBERT and 5 BRIE
Two of France's best known soft cheeses, similar in flavour, Brie being slightly milder. At their best in early spring.

6 SWISS GRUYERE
The genuine article, with very small holes, unlike French Gruyère which closely resembles 7 SWISS EMMENTHAL a very similar cheese. Use any of these for making Fondue.

8 EDAM and 9 GOUDA
The two most familiar Dutch hard cheeses, the Edam being saltier, the Gouda having its characteristic red, waxy skin. Both these are excellent toasted.

10 DERBY SAGE and 11 RED WINDSOR, CHEESE
Just two of a number of locally produced specialities worth exploring. Green-veined Derby is flavoured with fresh sage, red with annatto berries.

12 CHEDDAR CHEESE
A most popular, rich-tasting cheese, made the world over under its original name. Its flavour deepens as it matures.

13 ROQUEFORT
The famous French blue-veined cheese, made from ewe's milk; the curds are mixed with breadcrumbs to give its characteristic veining. Use to flavour salad dressings.

14 BLUE STILTON
This has been called the 'King' of English cheeses. There is a white Stilton, too, which is younger, chalk-white and very crumbly. It naturally tastes milder than the blue.

15 GOATS' CHEESE
To represent the many varying 'members' of the Chèvre family of cheeses: this one is soft, chalky and sharp; yellower, smoother types tend to be sweeter in flavour.

16 MOZZARELLA
Originally made from buffalo milk, now from cows' milk! Mild-flavoured and good for cooking, though it is very stringy when heated.

17 COTTAGE CHEESE
Knobbly-textured, mild-flavoured and made from skimmed milk, therefore good for a weight-reducing diet. Sieve it before using it instead of curd cheese.

18 CURD CHEESE
Made from curdled milk – make your own by adding lemon juice and straining the soured milk through clean muslin. See page 200 for the Indian Chhanna and Panir.

19 CREAM CHEESE
Full-fat, soft and creamy; try flavouring it with fresh herbs or garlic. It can also be sweetened. With a little cream added it makes a delightful accompaniment to fresh summer berries.

20 FETA
Goats' cheese from Greece, feta is white firm and sharp-tasting. It is delicious sprinkled over salads.

A SELECTION OF FRUITS

1 APPLES *Malus*
Just three examples of the abundance of varieties that are available for dessert use and for cooking. Cooking apples can be divided into two types: those which fall rapidly to a pulp and those which hold their shape. Use tiny, sour crab apples for making jelly.

2 PEAR *Pyrus communis*
Again, many varieties are available, each with a slightly different flavour. Buy dessert pears when slightly under-ripe and allow them to ripen fully indoors to lessen the risk of bruising.

3 CHERRIES *Prunus avium* and *cerasus*
Both black and white (red-skinned) cherries make good dessert fruit. I use the slightly bitter Morellos for cooking and making jam.

4 PLUMS *Prunus domestica*
All dessert plums, whether red-, golden- or dark purple-skinned, should have a bloom on them. Types include the small, tart-tasting damson and the bright green-skinned gage; both are good for jam.

5 CRANBERRIES *Vaccinium macrocarpon*
These large American cranberries are also found in the British Isles. Their sharp, distinctive flavour makes delicious sweet or savoury jelly 'sauces'.

6 RASPBERRIES *Rubus idaeus*
The least juicy of soft fruits and slightly sharper in taste than the strawberry, raspberries are usually served with sugar and cream; they make superb sorbets, creamy ices and jam. Use fresh fruit on the day you buy.

7 LOGANBERRIES *Rubus loganobaccus*
A native of America and a cross between a raspberry and a blackberry, these are larger, softer and juicier than raspberries.

8 BLACKBERRIES *Rubus ulmifolius*
'Blackberrying' in autumn and blackberry and apple pies soften thoughts of the onset of winter for me! Cultivated blackberries are larger than wild ones. Blackberries make excellent jams and sorbets.

9 PEACH *Prunus persica*
Both yellow- and white-skinned varieties are commercially available, usually of the cling-stone type, with flesh that does cling firmly to its stone. Wash the velvety skins thoroughly, or peel them.

10 NECTARINE *Prunus persica* var. *nectarina*
A variety of smooth-skinned peach with a flavour best described as somewhere between a peach and a plum.

11 GOOSEBERRIES *Ribes grossularia*
These characteristically sharp-tasting green or pink-tinged berries make particularly good jams, pie fillings or fools.

12 BLACK and RED CURRANTS *Ribes nigrum* and *sativum*
Delicious in jams and jellies, ice creams or sorbets; cooked together, they make a delicious compote – use less blackcurrants as the flavour is much stronger.

13 APRICOTS *Prunus armeniaca*
Picked fresh, they have an incomparable flavour. Add a piece of vanilla pod when poaching the fruit and use the almond-flavoured kernel when making jam – add about 6 for each 450g (1lb) of fruit.

14 GRAPES *Vitis vinifera*
Both white and black grapes should have a bloom on them – choose large branches for preference, bearing juicy but not over-ripe fruit.

15 STRAWBERRIES *Fragaria*
The cultivated berries are large and well-flavoured, but for the gourmet there is nothing to touch the tiny, wild *fraises des bois*. A strawberry purée freezes well.

21 DATES *Phoenix dactylifera*
These fresh dates are moist and plump; as they dry, the sugar content becomes more concentrated and the flavour strengthens. Buy unstoned dates, if buying dried ones.

22 LYCHEE *Litchi chinensis*
A large-stoned fruit with a curiously brittle skin covering translucent, pink-tinged flesh; crisp and refreshing to eat.

23 GUAVA *Psidium guajava*
A rich-tasting tropical fruit, best cooked or canned as, eaten raw, its flesh can be unpleasantly sharp. It has pips rather like a tomato.

27 ORANGE *Citrus sinensis*
This is a cultivated variety with few seeds. Use the smaller, bitter Seville oranges for making marmalade. Blood oranges taste sweetest and have red-flecked flesh. Choose fruit with firm, oily skins.

28 LEMON *Citrus limon* and **LIME** *Citrus aurantifolia*
The lemon, like the smaller, green-skinned lime is an acid fruit with a strongly scented skin. Do wash the skins thoroughly before use in case they have been sprayed with preservative.

29 BANANA *Musa*
These are usually picked when green, then allowed to ripen in transit. The skin should be a rich, golden yellow, without bruising. Choose green ones for cooking.

30 PINEAPPLE *Ananas comosus*
In my opinion, one of the most delicious of all fruits; its flavour is the perfect balance between acid and sweet and the flesh is rich in vitamins A and C. Choose one with fresh-looking leaves and that 'gives' slightly at the opposite end when pressed.

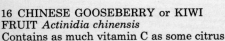

16 CHINESE GOOSEBERRY or KIWI FRUIT *Actinidia chinensis*
Contains as much vitamin C as some citrus fruits; it can be eaten in its skin, but this must be rubbed free of hairs first.

17 BLUEBERRIES *Vaccinium corymbosum*
A North American berry very like a large bilberry. Delicious as a pie filling, or just with brown sugar and thin cream.

18 RAMBUTAN *Nephelium lappaceum*
A native of Malaysia, this unusual tropical fruit has white flesh with a refreshing, sweet-sour taste. Can be eaten raw or cooked.

19 PASSION FRUIT *Passiflora edulis*
Its tough, wrinkled skin is a sign of ripeness! A juicy fruit full of seeds, which can be eaten – or strained off and the juice used to flavour moulded creams.

20 MANGOSTEEN *Garcinia mangostana*
Another unusual tropical fruit from Malaysia, its white, segmented flesh tastes rich and treacly. Best eaten fresh.

24 MANGO *Mangifera indica*
These large, yellow-skinned, red-tinged tropical fruits are widely grown in India. The fruit is fragrant and spicy. Choose fruit that is heavy with no brown spots.

25 GRAPEFRUIT *Citrus paradisi*
Two fine examples here – the more familiar yellow-skinned variety and the pink-tinged Texan grapefruit.

26 UGLI
A cross between a grapefruit and a tangerine, combining the best of both.

31 MELONS *Cucumis melo*
These belong to the same family as the cucumbers, marrows and squashes. Their flesh is fragrant, contains 94% water and about 5% sugar. Three varieties are shown: the round, ridged, green-tinged ogen melon, the oval, golden-skinned honeydew and the unmistakeable, seed-embedded red flesh of the water melon (*Citrullus vulgaris*). Tap lightly with the knuckles – a melon should sound hollow and resonant.

31

SWEETENERS AND LEAVENERS

1 CLEAR HONEY

2 THICK HONEY

3 HONEYCOMB

4 MOLASSES

5 RAW BROWN SUGAR

6 LIGHT BROWN SUGAR

7 GRANULATED WHITE SUGAR

8 ICING SUGAR

9 CASTER SUGAR

10 CORN SYRUP

11 MAPLE SYR

12 SEA SALT CRYSTALS

13 REFINED SAL

14 GLYCERINE

15 FRESH YEAST

16 BREWERS' YEAST

17 ACTIVE BAKING YEA

18 BAKING POWDER

19 BICARBONATE OF SODA

20 CREAM OF TARTAR

21 AGAR-AGAR

Soups

A good soup makes one of the best introductions to any meal, whether it is a well-flavoured clear consommé, a smooth-textured creamy soup, a warm, welcoming vegetable broth or a sophisticated chilled soup for a summer's evening.

Recipes for all of these are to be found in the following chapter. If substantial, such as a Minestrone or a Scotch broth, and served with chunks of freshly baked wholemeal bread, a soup can be a meal in itself.

With a blender, Mouli mill or sieve, it is a simple matter to make any number of nourishing soups using a selection of the best vegetables to hand, a good, rich vegetable stock and a little imagination. Try combining onion with beetroot and orange, or cabbage with apple and lemon . . .

Most cream and puréed soups are good served cold, but remember that chilled soups need to be a little more highly flavoured than if served hot. Triangles of thin toast spread with a Herb butter make a delicious accompaniment to vegetable soups: crisp Almond or Hazlenut biscuits are best with fruit soups.

Making Stocks

As a good vegetable stock is used as the basis of many of the soups in this chapter, here are two recipes to enable you to make your own.

Home-made stock does, of course, take time and effort to prepare, but the consequent improvement in taste does a great deal to enhance the quality of the finished soup.

Stocks are divided into two types, brown and white. Brown stocks are richly coloured because the ingredients are lightly fried to colour them well before liquid is added, while in white stocks the vegetables are fried, but not allowed to brown and are more delicate in colour and flavour.

When making stock, I tend to avoid using too many brassicas as I find their flavour too pronounced. However, the water in which they have been cooked can be used as part of the liquid.

It is important to remember that vegetable stock does not keep well beyond 24 hours and should therefore be made freshly for each soup, or made in advance and frozen. In this case, make 4 times the given quantity and freeze in convenient portions.

Of course, for emergencies, vegetarian bouillon cubes are available, but if you *are* using these, check the seasoning carefully as they tend to be salty.

Brown vegetable stock

CALORIES PER PORTION: 120 (502 kJ)
PROTEIN CONTENT PER PORTION: 5 grams
PREPARATION & COOKING TIME: 2 hours

2 tablespoons olive or sunflower oil
225 g (8 oz) finely chopped onions
225 g (8 oz) thinly sliced carrots
225 g (8 oz) tomatoes, cut in halves
    crosswise
450 g (1 lb) mixed green leaves (lettuce,
    cabbage, root tops, spinach) with any
    wilting leaves removed
900 ml (1½ pints) water
1-2 teaspoons yeast extract

Heat the oil in a deep thick-based pan over gentle heat. Add the onions and carrots and cook them gently for about 30 minutes, or until they are golden brown.

Meanwhile, grill the tomatoes until they are a good brown, then add them to the onions and carrots with the greens. Stir in the water, bring it to the boil, then lower the heat and simmer the stock gently for 1½ hours. Stir in the yeast extract. Measure the stock in a jug and add enough water to make it up to 900 ml (1½ pints). Strain through a sieve back into the pan, pressing the vegetables against the sides of the sieve to extract all the juices. The stock is now ready to use as directed.

This recipe makes 900 ml (1½ pints), enough for a first course of soup for 4.

Clear stock

If the recipe specifies a clear stock, leave it until cold, then whisk in 2 egg whites and bring slowly to the boil. When the egg coagulates and floats to the surface, turn down the heat and simmer for 1 minute, then strain the clarified stock through a piece of fine, clean muslin or cheesecloth.

White vegetable stock

CALORIES PER PORTION: 150 (615 kJ)
PROTEIN CONTENT PER PORTION: 2.5 grams
PREPARATION & COOKING TIME: 2 hours

2 tablespoons olive or sunflower oil
225 g (8 oz) finely chopped onions
225 g (8 oz) diced potatoes
50 g (2 oz) finely chopped celery
100 g (4 oz) thinly sliced parsnip,
    quartered first if large
100 g (4 oz) thinly sliced carrot,
    quartered first if large
100 g (4 oz) thinly sliced turnip,
    quartered first if large
2 bay leaves
900 ml (1½ pints) water

Heat the oil in a deep, thick-based pan, add the onions, potatoes and celery and cook over moderate heat for 10 minutes. Take care not to let the vegetables colour *at all*, and turn them over from time to time so that they cook evenly.

Add the remaining vegetables, the bay leaves and the water and stir well. Bring to the boil, lower the heat, then cover the pan and simmer gently for about 1 hour.

Measure the stock in a jug and make it up to 900 ml (1½ pints) with extra water. Strain twice through a sieve, pressing the vegetables against the sides of the sieve to extract as much flavour and goodness as possible, without actually rubbing the vegetables through. Discard the vegetables; the stock is now ready for use, and is enough to make soup for 4.

Consommé Basquaise

This classic consommé is also good served chilled.

Serves 4
CALORIES PER PORTION: 195 (820 kJ)
PROTEIN CONTENT PER PORTION: 6 grams
PREPARATION & COOKING TIME: 30 minutes

100 g (4 oz) finely diced red pepper
1 tablespoon butter
900 ml (1½ pints) clear brown
  vegetable stock
4 tablespoons boiled rice
salt
freshly ground pepper
4 teaspoons chopped chervil

Melt the butter in a pan over gentle heat, add the diced pepper and cook gently for 15 minutes, taking care that it does not burn. Meanwhile, pour the stock into a pan and bring to the boil.

Stir the hot stock into the cooked pepper, then add the rice and simmer for 5 minutes. Adjust the seasoning, pour into warmed soup bowls, sprinkle the chervil over and serve.

Consommé Brancas

Serves 4
CALORIES PER PORTION: 125 (515 kJ)
PROTEIN CONTENT PER PORTION: 5 grams
PREPARATION & COOKING TIME: 30 minutes

900 ml (1½ pints) clear brown
  vegetable stock, with at least 100 g
  (4 oz) fresh sorrel leaves included in
  the making
50 g (2 oz) finely shredded sorrel leaves
50 g (2 oz) finely chopped lettuce leaves
salt
freshly ground pepper

Pour the stock into a pan and bring to the boil. Add the sorrel leaves, the lettuce and salt and pepper to taste, then lower the heat and simmer for 15 minutes. Adjust the seasoning if necessary, pour into warmed soup bowls and serve hot with thin slices of freshly made wholemeal toast.

If sorrel is not easily obtainable, try this recipe using spinach instead.

Consommé Colbert

Serves 4
CALORIES PER PORTION: 205 (845 kJ)
PROTEIN CONTENT PER PORTION: 12 grams
PREPARATION & COOKING TIME: 15 minutes

900 ml (1½ pints) clear brown
  vegetable stock
salt
4 eggs
4 teaspoons finely chopped chervil

Pour the stock into a pan, bring it to the boil then keep it hot. Fill a separate shallow pan with water and bring it to the boil, then lower the heat to keep it just simmering. Add a little salt, then break the eggs carefully into the water one at a time, so that the yolks do not run.

After about 3-4 minutes, when the egg whites are set but the yolks are still soft, remove each egg with a draining spoon, trim neatly and place in the bottom of a warmed, shallow soup bowl. Pour in the hot stock slowly so as not to disturb the eggs, then sprinkle with chervil. Serve hot, with very thin slices of freshly made toast.

Consommé Crécy

Serves 4
CALORIES PER PORTION: 150 (632 kJ)
PROTEIN CONTENT PER PORTION: 5 grams
PREPARATION & COOKING TIME: 40 minutes

900 ml (1½ pints) clear brown
  vegetable stock
1 tablespoon butter
100 g (4 oz) diced carrot
salt
freshly ground pepper

Melt the butter over gentle heat, add the carrot and cook it over moderate heat for about 20 minutes, taking care not to burn or brown it. Bring the stock to the boil in a large saucepan (if not already prepared make the stock now).

When the carrot is tender, add it with its juices to the hot stock and simmer for a further 5 minutes. Adjust the seasoning, pour the consommé into warmed soup bowls and serve.

Okra consommé

Be sure to use freshly bought fennel seeds, otherwise the flavour of the soup will be impaired.

Serves 4
CALORIES PER PORTION: 170 (712 kJ)
PROTEIN CONTENT PER PORTION: 8 grams
PREPARATION & COOKING TIME (INCLUDING
  MAKING THE STOCK): 2 hours

100 g (4 oz) thinly sliced okra
900 ml (1½ pints) clear brown
  vegetable stock with 350 g (12 oz)
  coarsely chopped okra and ½
  teaspoon crushed fennel seeds in the
  making
salt
freshly ground pepper
4 tablespoons boiled rice
pinch of cayenne pepper

Strain the stock into a pan and season it well with salt and pepper. Add the okra and rice, stir well and bring the stock to the boil. Lower the heat and allow the soup to simmer for 10 minutes stirring occasionally to prevent the vegetables sticking and burning. Add the cayenne pepper before adjusting the seasoning, then pour into warmed soup bowls.

Mushroom soup

Serves 4
CALORIES PER PORTION: 420 (1765 kJ)
PROTEIN CONTENT PER PORTION: 7 grams
PREPARATION & COOKING TIME: 1 hour

450 g (1 lb) finely chopped mushrooms
generous 150 g (5 oz) butter
100 g (4 oz) finely chopped onion
1 tablespoon wholemeal flour
900 ml (1½ pints) brown vegetable
stock
100 ml (4 fl oz) dry red wine
1 teaspoon prepared French mustard
2 teaspoons yeast extract
salt
freshly ground pepper

Melt 75 g (3 oz) of the butter in a pan, add the onion and cook until golden brown. Add the mushrooms and continue cooking until the juices run and the mushrooms are dark and shiny. Work the remaining butter into the flour on a plate with a fork until it forms a smooth paste (kneaded butter or beurre manié). Add the stock to the mushrooms and bring to the boil, then lower the heat and add the kneaded butter, wine and mustard. Stir vigorously until the kneaded butter has dissolved, then continue cooking for a further 20 minutes, stirring occasionally.

Add the yeast extract, stir well and adjust the seasoning. Pour the soup into warmed bowls and serve garnished with croûtons.

Vegetarian Scotch broth

This is a thick, substantial soup and this recipe should be enough for 8.

CALORIES PER PORTION: 130 (538 kJ)
PROTEIN CONTENT PER PORTION: 3 grams
PREPARATION & COOKING TIME: 2 hours

4 tablespoons olive or sunflower oil
225 g (8 oz) finely chopped onion
225 g (8 oz) thinly sliced carrots,
quartered first if large
225 g (8 oz) diced turnips
225 g (8 oz) diced parsnips
50 g (2 oz) barley
1.6 litres (2¼ pints) water
½ teaspoon dried thyme
1 teaspoon salt
freshly ground pepper
2 teaspoons yeast extract
2 bay leaves
225 g (8 oz) leeks, halved lengthwise
then thinly sliced

Heat the oil and fry the onion and carrots over moderate heat until the edges are just beginning to brown, then add the rest of the ingredients except the leeks. Bring the soup to the boil, lower the heat and simmer very gently for 1 hour before adding the leeks. Simmer the soup for a further 30 minutes, adding a little more water during cooking.

Discard the bay leaves, adjust the seasoning if necessary, and serve with chunks of Wholemeal bread (page 151).

Three winter-warming soups – serve them all with chunks of freshly-made wholemeal bread. Top: Consommé Basquaise with rice, red peppers and fresh chervil; centre: a delicious Minestrone. Below: Mushroom soup is richly flavoured with onions and red wine

Brown lentil soup

Serves 4
CALORIES PER PORTION: 150 (627 kJ)
PROTEIN CONTENT PER PORTION: 6.5 grams
PREPARATION & COOKING TIME: 1½ hours

100 g (4 oz) brown lentils
2 tablespoons olive or sunflower oil
225 g (8 oz) thinly sliced onions
600 ml (1 pint) water
1 bay leaf
5 cm (2 in) stick of cinnamon
4 coarsely ground cloves
2 cloves of garlic, peeled and finely
chopped
salt
freshly ground pepper

Heat the oil in a pan and fry the onions over moderate heat until golden brown, stirring from time to time to prevent them sticking. Add the lentils with the water, the bay leaf, cinnamon stick, cloves and garlic. Increase the heat and let the soup simmer for 45 minutes, or until the lentils are tender and beginning to soften.

Remove the cinnamon stick and bay leaf, and work the lentils with their cooking liquid through a blender or Mouli mill, then rub through a sieve until they are puréed. Alternatively, rub them twice through a sieve.

Return the purée to a clean pan, make up the quantity to 900 ml (1½ pints) with extra water, if necessary, then adjust the seasoning and bring the soup to the boil. Serve with chunks of fresh Wholemeal bread (page 151).

Note: if you prefer a rough-textured soup, omit the sieving and puréeing and serve the soup as soon as the lentils are soft.

Minestrone

Serves 6
CALORIES PER PORTION: 200 (830 kJ)
PROTEIN CONTENT PER PORTION: 8 grams
PREPARATION & COOKING TIME: 1 hour

2 tablespoons olive or sunflower oil
225 g (8 oz) finely chopped onions
100 g (4 oz) thinly sliced carrots,
quartered if large
100 g (4 oz) sliced celery
225 g (8 oz) diced potatoes
225 g (8 oz) skinned tomatoes
225 g (8 oz) coarsely chopped green or
white cabbage
100 g (4 oz) shelled fresh or frozen peas
100 g (4 oz) green beans, cut into short
lengths
100 g (4 oz) cooked soya beans
200 ml (⅓ pint) dry red wine
2 litres (3⅓ pints) hot water
2 teaspoons yeast extract
4 cloves of garlic, peeled and finely
chopped
100 g (4 oz) stellette, or spaghetti
broken into very short pieces
salt
freshly ground pepper
100 g (4 oz) freshly grated Parmesan
cheese

Heat the oil in a large pan and fry the onions, carrots and celery until the vegetables are golden brown, stirring well so that they cook evenly. Add the rest of the ingredients except the salt, pepper and Parmesan and bring the soup to the boil. Lower the heat and let it simmer for 20-30 minutes, adding a little extra water if necessary, then season with salt and pepper. Serve with chunks of freshly made Wholemeal bread (page 151) and hand a bowl of Parmesan separately.

For a change, serve with Pesto (page 75) also handed separately.

Avgolemono (Greek lemon soup)

Serves 4
CALORIES PER PORTION: 220 (920 kJ)
PROTEIN CONTENT PER PORTION: 7 grams
PREPARATION & COOKING TIME: 20 minutes

900 ml (1½ pints) white vegetable stock
100 g (4 oz) boiled long-grain rice
salt
2 eggs
grated rind of ½ lemon
juice of 1-2 lemons, depending on size
freshly ground pepper

Bring the stock to the boil, add the cooked rice to the pan and bring the stock back to the boil before seasoning with salt. Lower the heat and simmer gently for 5 minutes. Break the eggs into a bowl and beat thoroughly with the lemon rind and juice, then add a little of the hot stock. Stir well, then pour this slowly back into the stock in the pan. Remove the pan immediately from the heat, or the eggs may curdle instead of blending into the soup. Stir until the mixture is well blended and smooth. Adjust the seasoning, pour into warmed soup bowls and serve with slices of Poppy seed plait (page 154) bread.

Carrot and orange soup

Serves 4
CALORIES PER PORTION: 310 (1302 kJ)
PROTEIN CONTENT PER PORTION: 5 grams
PREPARATION & COOKING TIME: 50 minutes

450 g (1 lb) coarsely shredded carrots
finely grated rind of 1 orange
4 tablespoons orange juice
75 g (3 oz) butter
50 g (2 oz) finely chopped onion
600 ml (1 pint) water
1 tablespoon wholemeal flour
300 ml (½ pint) milk
salt and freshly ground pepper

Melt two thirds of the butter in a pan over gentle heat, add the carrots and onion and cook them for about 5 minutes. Stir in the water, bring it to the boil, then cover the pan and let the soup simmer for 20 minutes.

Meanwhile, melt the remaining butter in a separate pan over gentle heat, sprinkle in the flour and cook for 1-2 minutes, stirring continuously. Take the pan off the heat and gradually stir in the milk. Return the pan to the stove and bring the sauce to the boil, stirring all the time until it thickens. Stand the pan in a larger pan almost filled with boiling water, or transfer the sauce to a double boiler to keep hot.

Rub the carrots, onion and their cooking liquid through a sieve, or work first in a blender and then rub through a sieve, so you have a completely smooth purée. Return this to a large, clean pan, add the orange rind and juice and bring the soup to the boil. Remove the pan from the heat, stir in the hot sauce, season with salt and pepper and serve — if you like — with a swirl of cream in each bowl.

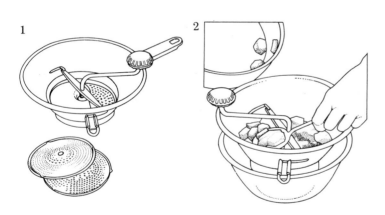

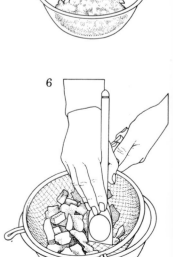

1. A vegetable mill or mouli-legumes has a choice of discs for coarse or fine purées. 2. Turn the vegetables, which are usually cooked, but can be raw if soft, into the container; do not fill more than half full. 3. Purée by turning the handle. 4. Stop occasionally to scrape the bottom of the plate clean with a spoon. 5. If you do not own a mill, or want a very fine purée, use a sieve. A sieve can also be used for vegetables that have already been blended or passed through a vegetable mill. 6. Press vegetables through the sieve into a bowl, using a wooden spoon.

Chinese cabbage, corn and mushroom soup

This soup is basically a clear consommé with a cabbage, corn and mushroom garnish. It is important that the cabbage should still be slightly crisp when the soup is ready.

Serves 4
CALORIES PER PORTION: 155 (640 kJ)
PROTEIN CONTENT PER PORTION: 7 grams
PREPARATION & COOKING TIME: 2¼ hours

*1-2 finely shredded Chinese cabbage
    leaves*
25 g (1 oz) sweetcorn kernels
25 g (1 oz) thinly sliced mushrooms
2½ tablespoons olive or sunflower oil
225 g (8 oz) finely chopped onions
225 g (8 oz) finely chopped turnips
100 g (4 oz) roughly chopped tomatoes
900 ml (1½ pints) water
¼ teaspoon star aniseed
2 teaspoons yeast extract
salt
freshly ground pepper
2 eggs, separated

Heat 2 tablespoons of the oil in a pan over gentle heat, add the onions and turnips and cook over gentle heat for about 15 minutes, stirring well, until the vegetables are just about to turn colour. Add the tomatoes and stir until reduced to a pulp. Pour in the water, add the aniseed and yeast extract and season with salt and pepper. Bring the soup to the boil before lowering the heat and simmering gently for about an hour.

Measure the stock and make it up to 900 ml (1½ pints) with extra water. Strain it through a sieve, pressing the vegetables against the sides to extract as much flavour and goodness as possible, without actually rubbing the vegetables through.

Leave the soup until slightly cooled, then clarify with the egg whites (see the instructions for this under Clear stock on page 34).

Meanwhile, heat the remaining oil in a separate pan, add the mushrooms and cook them until soft and shiny. Drain on absorbent kitchen paper. Add the sweetcorn to the soup, bring it to the boil then lower the heat and simmer for 5 minutes, before adding the mushrooms and cabbage. Beat the egg yolks to a smooth cream and stir them very slowly into the soup, then simmer it for a few moments until the egg yolks have set into fine strings. Adjust the seasoning, pour into warmed soup bowls and serve.

Sweetcorn, Chinese cabbage, mushroom and trailing egg soup

Serves 4
CALORIES PER PORTION: 865 (3620 kJ)
PROTEIN CONTENT PER PORTION: 30 grams
PREPARATION & COOKING TIME: 20 minutes

100 g (4 oz) cooked sweetcorn kernels
600 ml (1 pint) brown vegetable stock
*100 g (4 oz) thinly sliced button
    mushrooms*
1 tablespoon soya sauce
1 teaspoon lemon juice
*¼ teaspoon monosodium glutamate
    (optional)*
2 well-beaten eggs
*100 g (4 oz) finely shredded Chinese
    cabbage*
salt

Bring the stock to the boil, add the sweetcorn and mushrooms and simmer for 4 minutes. Stir in the soya sauce, lemon juice and monosodium glutamate (if using), then dribble the eggs very slowly into the boiling liquid, stirring continuously, so that they form thin shreds.

Add the Chinese cabbage and cook for a further 2 minutes, or until the cabbage is thoroughly hot and the soup has returned to the boil. Add a little salt, if necessary, and serve immediately.

Leek, tomato and potato soup with saffron

Serves 4
CALORIES PER PORTION: 205 (865 kJ)
PROTEIN CONTENT PER PORTION: 7 grams
PREPARATION & COOKING TIME: 45 minutes

*450 g (1 lb) washed leeks, halved
    lengthwise, then cut into thin slices*
*225 g (8 oz) coarsely chopped ripe
    tomatoes*
225 g (8 oz) diced potatoes
40 g (1 (generous 1½ oz) butter
2 tablespoons wholemeal flour
300 ml (½ pint) milk
300 ml (½ pint) water
*2 generous pinches of saffron strands,
    soaked in a little water for 10
    minutes to soften them*
salt
freshly ground pepper

Melt the butter in a saucepan over gentle heat, then put in the potatoes and cook for 5 minutes without allowing them to brown. Add the leeks and continue cooking for 10 minutes without allowing them to colour. Stir the vegetables from time to time — they should be gently 'stewed' in the butter rather than fried. Now sprinkle in the flour and stir well, then pour on the milk and the water. Bring the soup to the boil, stirring it frequently. Add the saffron in their soaking water, lower the heat and let the soup simmer for about 15 minutes.

Meanwhile, cook the tomatoes down to a pulp over low heat, adding a little water, if necessary. Strain the pulp through a sieve to remove the skin and seeds and keep the purée hot until the soup is ready to serve. Season it with salt and pepper, pour it into warmed soup bowls, swirl a little tomato purée into each bowl and serve.

Cream of asparagus soup

Use as much fresh asparagus in this recipe as you can — according to availability and price; 225 g (8 oz) is about the minimum.

Serves 4
CALORIES PER PORTION: 350 (1457 kJ)
PROTEIN CONTENT PER PORTION: 10 grams
PREPARATION & COOKING TIME: 45 minutes

450 g (1 lb) trimmed fresh asparagus (if available)
25 g (1 oz) butter
20 g (¾ oz) unbleached white flour
600 ml (1 pint) milk
salt
freshly ground pepper
150 ml (¼ pint) double cream (optional)

Melt the butter over gentle heat, then sprinkle in the flour. Cook until the mixture thickens, about 1 minute, stirring continuously, but do not allow it to brown. Remove the pan from the heat and gradually add the milk, stirring well between each addition. Return the pan to the stove, increase the heat and bring to the boil, stirring all the time until the sauce thickens. Stand the pan in a larger pan almost filled with boiling water, or transfer the soup to a double boiler. Cover the surface with a sheet of buttered greaseproof paper and cook over a gentle heat for about 20 minutes to let the soup mature.

Meanwhile, cook the asparagus (see page 59) in enough boiling, salted water to come halfway up the stems for 10-15 minutes, or until very tender. Drain off and measure the cooking water; make this up to 200 ml (¼ pint) with a little extra water, then stir this into the sauce in the pan.

Cut the tips off the 8 choicest asparagus spears and reserve them before stirring the rest of the asparagus into the sauce. Work the soup through a blender, then rub it through a sieve to make it really smooth. If you do not have a blender, mash the asparagus well with a fork before rubbing it through the sieve.

Return the soup to a clean pan to reheat, then season with salt and pepper and serve with 2 of the reserved asparagus tips on each bowl. Add a swirl of cream to each bowl before adding the asparagus tips, if desired.

Four deliciously creamy, filling soups.
From the left: Tomato and orange soup,
garnished with fresh basil leaves;
Cream of asparagus, also good served
chilled; Pumpkin soup flavoured with
cinnamon and Front: Corn chowder —
be sure to use freshly-bought fennel
seeds or the taste will be very bland

Pumpkin soup

Serves 6
CALORIES PER PORTION: 45 (190 kJ)
PROTEIN CONTENT PER PORTION: 1 gram
PREPARATION & COOKING TIME: 1 hour

450 g (1 lb) peeled pumpkin, cut into small, even chunks
25 g (1 oz) butter
100 g (4 oz) finely chopped onion
¼ teaspoon ground cinnamon
thinly pared rind of ¼ orange
900 ml (1½ pints) water
salt
freshly ground pepper

Melt the butter in a pan over gentle heat and add the pumpkin and onion. Cook the vegetables for about 10 minutes, stirring occasionally, until they are just beginning to brown, then sprinkle in the cinnamon. Add the orange rind and continue cooking for a few more minutes. Stir in the water and bring it to the boil, then lower the heat and let the soup simmer for 20-30 minutes, or until the pieces of pumpkin are soft and tender. Take out the orange rind, pour the soup into a blender and work it until smooth, then rub the purée through a sieve to remove any strings — or rub the soup twice through a sieve.

Return the soup to a clean pan, season with salt and pepper and bring back to the boil. Serve with slices of dark Rye bread (page 151).

Tomato and orange soup

Serves 4
CALORIES PER PORTION: 145 (602 kJ)
PROTEIN CONTENT PER PORTION: 2.5 grams
PREPARATION & COOKING TIME: 45 minutes

1 kg (2¼ lb) quartered ripe tomatoes
thinly pared rind of ¼ orange
4 tablespoons orange juice
50 g (2 oz) butter
100 g (4 oz) finely chopped onion
1-2 teaspoons chopped basil (optional)
1 small bay leaf
1 teaspoon raw brown sugar (optional)
salt
freshly ground pepper

Melt the butter in a pan over gentle heat, add the onion and cook until transparent but not browned. Add the tomatoes, orange rind and juice, the basil, if using, and the bay leaf. Bring the soup to the boil, lower the heat and simmer for 15 minutes, or until the tomatoes have turned into a pulp. Rub through a sieve and return the purée to a clean pan. Bring to the boil, add the sugar, if using, then season the soup with salt and pepper. Serve hot with freshly made wholemeal toast.

Note: If the tomatoes do not make quite enough pulp and juice, or if the purée is too thick, add enough water to make it up to 900 ml (1½ pints) before bringing the soup back to the boil.

Corn chowder

Serves 4

CALORIES PER PORTION: 410 (1715 kJ)
PROTEIN CONTENT PER PORTION: 18 grams
PREPARATION & COOKING TIME: 35 minutes

100 g (4 oz) frozen sweetcorn kernels
50 g (2 oz) butter
50 g (2 oz) thinly sliced onion
441 225 g (8 oz) diced potatoes
½ teaspoon fennel seeds
salt
freshly ground pepper
900 ml (1½ pints) milk
50 g (2 oz) dried skimmed milk
50 g (2 oz) grated Cheddar cheese

Melt the butter in a pan over gentle heat and cook the onion and potatoes for 5 minutes without letting them colour. Stir them occasionally to prevent them sticking. Add the fennel seeds and season with salt and pepper, then stir in the milk. Lower the heat and let the soup simmer for 20 minutes, stirring it occasionally. Put the soup through a blender and work until smooth. Add the dried milk and blend for a few moments longer until dissolved; otherwise, rub the soup through a sieve, then stir in the dried milk.

Return the purée to a clean pan, add the frozen corn kernels and bring it slowly back to the boil. Take the pan off the heat, sprinkle in the cheese and stir until it has melted. Serve in warmed soup bowls with wholemeal croûtons.

Cream of pea soup

Serves 4

CALORIES PER PORTION: 365 (1522 kJ)
PROTEIN CONTENT PER PORTION: 12 grams
PREPARATION & COOKING TIME: 30 minutes if using frozen peas; 1 hour if using fresh peas

450 g (1 lb) shelled fresh or frozen peas
100 g (4 oz) butter
100 g (4 oz) finely chopped onion
150 ml (¼ pint) water
600 ml (1 pint) milk
salt
freshly ground pepper

Melt the butter in a pan over gentle heat and add the peas, onion and water. Cook over moderate heat until the peas are just tender; the exact time will depend on whether fresh or frozen peas are used — fresh peas will take at least 25 minutes. Stir in the milk, salt and pepper, increase the heat and bring the soup to the boil, stirring all the time.

Pour the soup into a blender and work it to a smooth purée, or rub it through a sieve. Return the soup to a clean pan and bring to the boil again. Thin it down with a little extra hot milk if necessary to make it up to 900 ml (1½ pints). Adjust the seasoning and serve with wholemeal croûtons. Do not overcook this soup or the flavour will be spoilt.

Cream of leek soup

Serves 4

CALORIES PER PORTION: 385 (1615 kJ)
PROTEIN CONTENT PER PORTION: 10.5 grams
PREPARATION & COOKING TIME: 55 minutes

450 g (1 lb) leeks, washed, cut in half
  lengthways, then sliced
100 g (4 oz) butter
2 tablespoons wholemeal flour
900 ml (1½ pints) milk
salt and freshly ground pepper

Melt the butter over low heat, add the leeks and cook them very gently for about 15 minutes until they are just tender. Take care that they do not brown or this will spoil the flavour of the finished soup. Sprinkle in the flour and stir until the leeks are evenly coated.

Remove the pan from the heat and gradually add the milk, stirring well between each addition. Return the pan to the stove and bring the soup to the boil, stirring all the time until it thickens.

Pour the soup into a blender, and work until smooth, then rub it through a sieve to remove any remaining fibres, or mash the cooked leeks thoroughly before rubbing through the sieve. Return the soup to a clean pan and bring it back to the boil, then transfer it to stand in a larger pan almost filled with boiling water, or pour the soup into a double boiler.

Cover the surface with a sheet of buttered greaseproof paper and allow it to stand for 10 minutes before seasoning.

Artichoke soup

Serves 4

CALORIES PER PORTION: 125 (522 kJ)
PROTEIN CONTENT PER PORTION: 4 grams
PREPARATION & COOKING TIME: 45 minutes

450 g (1 lb) thinly sliced Jerusalem
  artichokes
25 g (1 oz) butter
100 g (4 oz) finely chopped onion
400 ml (¾ pint) water
400 ml (¾ pint) milk
salt and freshly ground pepper

Melt the butter over low heat, and cook the onion in it until transparent, taking care that it does not colour. Add the artichokes and cook them gently for about 5 minutes, then pour on the water, bring it to the boil, lower the heat and simmer the vegetables for 15 minutes. Pour the soup into a blender and work to a smooth purée, or rub the cooked vegetables through a sieve. Return the purée to a clean pan, add the milk and bring the soup back to the boil. Season with salt and pepper and serve with wholemeal croûtons.

Cream of cauliflower soup

Serves 6
CALORIES PER PORTION: 260 (1075 kJ)
PROTEIN CONTENT PER PORTION: 8 grams
PREPARATION & COOKING TIME: 45 minutes

*600 g (1¼ lb) cauliflower, broken into
    florets, and including the chopped
    stem and some of the leaves*
100 g (4 oz) butter
25 g (1 oz) finely chopped onion
900 ml (1½ pints) milk
2 egg yolks
salt
freshly ground pepper

Cook the cauliflower over gentle heat in about 1 cm (¾ in) water for about 15 minutes, or until just tender, adding a very little extra water if necessary. While it is cooking, melt the butter in a separate pan over gentle heat and fry the onion until transparent. Do not allow it to colour. Drain the cauliflower, reserving 2 tablespoons of the cooking water. Add this to the onion with the cooked cauliflower, stir well, then pour the vegetables into a blender

Add the milk and egg yolks and work until quite smooth; season with salt and pepper, then rub the soup through a sieve to remove any remaining fibres. If you do not have a blender, rub the vegetables through a Mouli mill or twice through a sieve.

Return the soup to a clean pan and reheat, stirring continuously, but do not allow it to boil or the egg yolks will curdle. As soon as the soup thickens, pour it into a warmed tureen or bowls and serve garnished with croûtons.

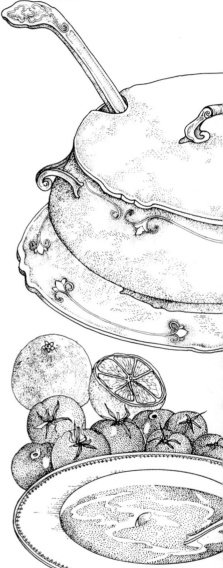

Chestnut soup

Serves 4
CALORIES PER PORTION: 435 (1815 kJ)
PROTEIN CONTENT PER PORTION: 5 grams
PREPARATION & COOKING TIME: 2 hours

*450 g (1 lb) whole chestnuts, to give
    about 350 g (12 oz) when prepared*
25 g (1 oz) butter
50 g (2 oz) finely chopped onion
900 ml (1½ pints) white vegetable stock
salt
freshly ground pepper
150 ml (¼ pint) cultured sour cream
a little freshly grated nutmeg

Slit the chestnuts down one side and bake them in a hot oven, 200°C (400°F) Gas 6, for 10-15 minutes until the skins are crisp. Carefully remove the skins and the membranes covering the nuts, holding the nuts in a kitchen cloth to protect your hands.

Melt the butter in a pan over gentle heat and cook the onion until just golden brown before pouring on the stock. Stir well, add the skinned nuts and simmer for 20-30 minutes, or until the nuts are tender. Rub them, with their cooking liquid, through a sieve or Mouli mill, or work to a purée in a blender. Rub this again through a sieve until it is really smooth, then season it with salt and pepper.

Reheat the soup a little and pour into warmed soup bowls. Swirl a little cultured sour cream in the centre of each and sprinkle with grated nutmeg just before serving.

Walnut soup

Serves 4
CALORIES PER PORTION: 350 (1455 kJ)
PROTEIN CONTENT PER PORTION: 6 grams
PREPARATION & COOKING TIME: 1¼ hours

100 g (4 oz) shelled fresh walnuts
25 g (1 oz) butter
50 g (2 oz) finely chopped onion
2 tablespoons wholemeal flour
900 ml (1½ pints) white vegetable stock
1 bay leaf
1 small strip of lemon rind
salt
freshly ground pepper
2 walnuts, halved

Put the walnuts in a pan, add enough water to cover, and bring it to the boil. Lower the heat and simmer the nuts for 5 minutes, then remove the pan from the heat. While they are still hot, carefully remove any traces of outer skin from the nut kernels, using a sharp-pointed knife.

If the nuts are still hot the skin is much easier to remove, so take them out of the pan one by one with a draining spoon as you peel them. Work the peeled nuts in a blender or nutmill until they are very finely ground.

Melt the butter over gentle heat, add the onion and cook until transparent, taking care that it does not colour. Sprinkle in the flour and continue cooking for 1-2 minutes, stirring continuously. Remove the pan from the heat and gradually add the stock, stirring well between each addition. Return the pan to the heat and bring the soup to the boil, stirring all the time until it thickens. Add the bay leaf and lemon rind, then lower the heat and simmer for about 10 minutes, removing the lemon rind if its flavour becomes too pronounced.

Add the walnuts and simmer for 10 minutes more, then rub the soup through a medium-meshed sieve. Season it with salt and pepper and serve; garnish each portion with a halved walnut, or croûtons.

To emphasize the walnut flavour, fry the croûtons in a mixture of walnut oil and butter. You need a blender or nutmill to make this soup.

Cheese and onion soup

Serves 4

CALORIES PER PORTION: 465 (1937 kJ)
PROTEIN CONTENT PER PORTION: 16 grams
PREPARATION & COOKING TIME: 40 minutes

*175 g (6 oz) Cheddar or Stilton cheese,
    crumbled or coarsely grated*
900 ml (1½ pints) white vegetable stock
50 g (2 oz) butter
100 g (4 oz) finely chopped onion
50 g (2 oz) wholemeal flour
1 bay leaf
salt
freshly ground pepper

Pour the stock into a pan and heat to just below boiling point. Melt the butter in a separate pan over gentle heat, add the onion and cook it until it is transparent. Sprinkle in the flour and stir until the onion is well coated, then cook for a further 1-2 minutes, stirring all the time. Add the cheese, stir until melted and well blended into the mixture, then gradually add the hot stock and continue stirring until the soup thickens.

Add the bay leaf, season with salt and pepper, then stand the pan in a larger pan and pour in boiling water almost to fill, or transfer the soup to a double boiler. Cover the surface with a sheet of buttered greaseproof paper, then cook the soup gently for about 20 minutes so that it matures. Discard the bay leaf, adjust the seasoning and serve with fresh wholemeal rolls or crisp toast.

Camembert soup

Serves 4

CALORIES PER PORTION: 295 (1237 kJ)
PROTEIN CONTENT PER PORTION: 12.5 grams
PREPARATION AND COOKING TIME: 45 minutes

*176 g (6 oz) mature but not over-ripe
    Camembert cheese, diced with the
    rind*
25 g (1 oz) butter
25 g (1 oz) wholemeal flour
600 ml (1 pint) white vegetable stock
*small clove of garlic, peeled and very
    finely chopped (optional)*
300 ml (½ pint) dry white wine
salt
freshly ground pepper
1-2 tablespoons chopped parsley

Melt the butter in a pan over gentle heat, then sprinkle in the flour. Cook for 1-2 minutes, stirring continuously, then remove the pan from the heat and gradually add the stock, stirring well between each addition. Return the pan to the stove and bring to the boil, stirring all the time until the sauce thickens.

Lower the heat, add the cheese with the garlic, if used, and stir briskly until the cheese has melted. Add the wine and simmer for about 10 minutes until the alcohol has evaporated and only the flavour of the wine is left. Season with salt and pepper, then strain the soup into a large bowl. Skim off any excess fat, pour the soup into warmed bowls, sprinkle with parsley and serve hot with wholemeal rolls.

Cream of tomato soup

Serves 4

CALORIES PER PORTION: 230 (953 kJ)
PROTEIN CONTENT PER PORTION: 7 grams
PREPARATION & COOKING TIME: 40 minutes

*450 g (1 lb) coarsely chopped ripe
    tomatoes*
50 g (2 oz) butter
100 g (4 oz) finely chopped onion
1 bay leaf
20 g (¾ oz) wholemeal flour
600 ml (1 pint) milk
salt
freshly ground pepper
*1-2 tablespoons chopped basil, or
    parsley, to garnish*

Melt half the butter in a pan over gentle heat, add the onion and cook until transparent, taking care not to let it colour. Add the tomatoes and bay leaf and cook the tomatoes down into a pulp.

Meanwhile, melt the rest of the butter in a separate pan, sprinkle in the flour and cook for 1-2 minutes, stirring continuously. Remove the pan from the heat and gradually stir in the milk, then return the pan to the stove, season, and bring to the boil, stirring all the time until the mixture thickens. Stand the pan in a larger pan almost filled with boiling water, or transfer the soup to a double boiler and cook gently for about 20 minutes.

Remove the pan containing the tomatoes from the heat, discard the bay leaf and work the pulp in a blender, or rub it through a sieve. Return the purée to a clean pan and bring it to the boil, then stir the bubbling purée into the gently simmering sauce. Adjust the seasoning, sprinkle with basil or parsley and serve at once.

Note: Do not allow this soup to stand for long before serving or it will separate and curdle. If it does, work it in a blender, or rub through a sieve, then reheat.

Cream of celery soup

Serves 4
CALORIES PER PORTION: 265 (1103 kJ)
PROTEIN CONTENT PER PORTION: 9 grams
PREPARATION & COOKING TIME: 1 hour

450 g (1 lb) chopped celery
50 g (2 oz) butter
100 g (4 oz) finely chopped onion
1 tablespoon wholemeal flour
900 ml (1½ pints) milk
salt
freshly ground pepper
150 ml (½ pint) double cream
a sprinkling of paprika

Melt the butter over gentle heat, add the celery and onion and cook for 20 minutes, stirring occasionally to make sure the vegetables cook evenly without browning. This should concentrate the flavours, rather than actually fry the vegetables. Sprinkle in the flour and cook for 1-2 minutes, stirring continuously until the vegetables are well coated.

Remove the pan from the heat and gradually add the milk, stirring well between each addition. Return the pan to the stove and bring to the boil, stirring all the time until the mixture thickens. Season with salt and pepper.

Stand the pan in another larger pan almost filled with boiling water, or transfer the soup to a double boiler. Cover the surface with a sheet of buttered greaseproof paper and cook very gently for at least 20 minutes to let the soup mature.

Pour the soup into a blender and work it until smooth, or mash the celery with a fork, then rub the soup through a sieve. Return the soup to the pan, adjust the seasoning and bring to the boil before serving with a swirl of cream and a sprinkling of paprika on each bowl.

Cream of onion soup

Serves 4
CALORIES PER PORTION: 270 (1120 kJ)
PROTEIN CONTENT PER PORTION: 9 grams
PREPARATION & COOKING TIME: 1 hour 10 minutes

225 g (8 oz) thinly sliced onions
50 g (2 oz) butter
20 g (¾ oz) wholemeal flour
900 ml (1½ pints) milk
1 bay leaf
pinch of freshly grated nutmeg
salt
freshly ground pepper

Melt the butter over gentle heat, add the onions and cook them until transparent, taking care that they do not brown. Sprinkle in the flour and cook for 1-2 minutes, stirring all the time until the onions are well coated. Remove the pan from the heat and gradually add the milk, stirring well between each addition. Return the pan to the stove, increase the heat and bring the soup to the boil, stirring all the time until it thickens. Lower the heat and cook the soup for about 5 minutes before pouring it into a blender and working it to a smooth purée, or rubbing through a sieve.

Return the soup to a clean pan and add the bay leaf, nutmeg and salt and pepper. Stand the pan in another larger pan almost filled with boiling water, or transfer to the soup to a double boiler. Cover the surface with a sheet of buttered greaseproof paper and cook over gentle heat for 20 minutes longer to allow the soup to mature. Discard the bay leaf, adjust the seasoning, pour into warmed bowls and serve with croûtons.

Jellied consommé

Serves 4
CALORIES PER PORTION: 150 (622 kJ)
PROTEIN CONTENT PER PORTION: 5 grams
PREPARATION & CHILLING TIME: 4¼ hours

900 ml (1½ pints) clear Brown
*   vegetable stock, including 100 g (4 oz)*
*   mushrooms in the making*
salt
freshly ground black pepper
1 tablespoon agar-agar
100 ml (4 fl oz) sherry (optional)
1-2 tablespoons chopped parsley
4 lemon wedges

Make up the stock, adjust the seasoning and allow it to cool, then sprinkle on the agar-agar. Bring the stock back to the boil, stirring briskly all the time, then lower the heat and allow the stock to simmer for 5 minutes. Put it aside to cool. Add the sherry, then chill the consommé until jellied. Chop it up or scoop out small chunks of Jellied consommé and pile it into four individual glass bowls. Sprinkle with parsley and serve with lemon wedges and thin brown toast.

Chilled avocado soup

Serves 4
CALORIES PER PORTION: 580 (2422 kJ)
PROTEIN CONTENT PER PORTION: 15 grams
PREPARATION & CHILLING TIME: 1½ hours

4 large avocados, weighing about 800 g
*   (1¾ lb)*
juice of 1 lemon
400 ml (¾ pint) white vegetable stock
400 ml (¾ pint) natural yoghurt, or
*   cold Béchamel sauce (page 196)*
salt
freshly ground pepper

Peel the avocados, cut them into chunks and mix them with the lemon juice. Put them, with the stock and the yoghurt or Béchamel sauce, into a blender and work to a smooth purée, or rub through a Mouli mill or nylon sieve. Season with salt and pepper and chill thoroughly before serving with thin slices of wholemeal bread and butter, or thin brown toast.

Note: The avocados will cause this soup to discolour slightly if it is left to chill for more than 2 hours, so don't be tempted to make this soup the night before. If the surface does discolour, stir well before serving.

Perfect for a summer's eve, chilled soups that are subtle and refreshing. Top: an Orange and lemon soup, served with thin Almond biscuits. Right: chilled Avocado soup – this can be made with a base of either yoghurt or Béchamel sauce. Below: Jellied consommé made from a rich Brown vegetable stock, garnished with lemon

Chilled orange and lemon soup

Serves 4
CALORIES PER PORTION: 60 (252 kJ)
PROTEIN CONTENT PER PORTION: 0.5 grams
PREPARATION & CHILLING TIME: 3 hours

225 g (8 oz) cooking apples
225 g (8 oz) pears
900 ml (1½ pints) water, plus 4
*   tablespoons*
5 cm (2 in) strip of lemon rind
5 cm (2 in) strip of orange rind
2 tablespoons wholemeal flour
½ teaspoon grated orange rind
2 tablespoons lemon juice
4 tablespoons orange juice
a little granulated sugar
4 thin orange slices

Peel the apples and pears and cut them into chunks. Put these with the cores in a pan with 900 ml (1½ pints) water. Bring to the boil, add the strips of lemon and orange rind, then lower the heat and simmer the soup for 20 minutes or until the fruit is tender and pulpy. Remove the pieces of rind and rub the soup through a sieve or a Mouli mill. Mix the flour with the remaining cold water to make a thin

cream and stir it into the purée. Return it to a clean pan, bring back to the boil, then lower the heat and simmer the soup for a further 5 minutes.

Allow it to cool slightly, then add the grated orange rind, the lemon and orange juice and a little sugar to taste. Leave to get quite cold before chilling. Float a thin slice of orange on each bowl and serve with thin Almond biscuits (page 164).

Gazpacho

Serves 4
CALORIES PER PORTION: 185 (775 kJ)
PROTEIN CONTENT PER PORTION: 7 grams
PREPARATION & CHILLING TIME: 2½ hours

450 g (1 lb) tomatoes
300 ml (½ pint) cold water
2 cloves of garlic, peeled and finely
*   chopped*
2 tablespoons olive or sunflower oil
2 tablespoons lemon juice
a little iced water (see method)
salt
freshly ground pepper

Accompaniments
100 g (4 oz) finely chopped Spanish
*   onion*
100 g (4 oz) finely chopped red pepper
2 hard-boiled eggs, finely chopped
4 slices of wholemeal bread, crusts
*   removed and cut into slices*

Put the tomatoes into a blender with the cold water, garlic, oil and lemon juice and work until smooth. Pour the soup into a bowl, cover it and chill for 2 hours, or

until required. Put the onion, pepper, chopped eggs and bread cubes each in separate bowls. Make up the chilled soup to 900 ml (1½ pints) with a little iced water just before serving, mix well and season with salt and pepper. Float a few crushed ice cubes on top, if liked, and hand the accompaniments separately, so that each guest can make his own choice.

Gazpacho has been photographed, with its accompaniments, as part of a summer buffet party on page 182.

Chilled apple soup

Serves 6
CALORIES PER PORTION: 160 (670 kJ)
PROTEIN CONTENT PER PORTION: 1 gram
PREPARATION & CHILLING TIME: 3 hours

450 g (1 lb) cooking apples
900 ml (1½ pints) water, plus 1-2
*   tablespoons*
7.5 cm (3 in) strip of lemon rind
100 g (4 oz) granulated sugar
5 cm (2 in) stick of cinnamon
2 tablespoons wholemeal flour

Peel and dice the apples and put them, with their cores, into a pan with the 900 ml (1½ pints) water, the lemon rind, sugar and cinnamon stick and bring to the boil. Lower the heat and allow the soup to simmer for 20-30 minutes, or until the apples have cooked down into a pulp. Rub them through a sieve or Mouli mill and return the purée to the rinsed out pan.

Mix together the flour and the remaining 1-2 tablespoons of water in a bowl to make a thin cream and stir it into the purée. Bring the soup to the boil, lower the heat and let it simmer gently for 5 minutes. Strain the soup through a sieve and let it cool before chilling.

Serve the soup when thoroughly chilled with Almond or Hazelnut biscuits to accompany (page 164).

Chilled pear soup

Serves 4
CALORIES PER PORTION: 65 (272 kJ)
PROTEIN CONTENT PER PORTION: 1 gram
PREPARATION & CHILLING TIME: 3 hours

450 g (1 lb) unripe pears
900 ml (1½ pints) water, plus 2
*   tablespoons*
1 vanilla pod, broken into pieces
2 tablespoons wholemeal flour
a little granulated sugar

Peel and cut the pears into chunks and put them, with their cores, in a pan with the 900 ml (1½ pints) water and the pieces of vanilla pod. Bring to the boil, then lower the heat and simmer the soup for about 30 minutes, or until the pears are tender and pulpy. Remove the pieces of vanilla pod during the cooking if the flavour becomes too pronounced.

Rub the pulp through a sieve or Mouli mill, take out any remaining pieces of

vanilla pod and return the purée to the pan. Bring the soup back to the boil.

In a bowl, stir the flour into the remaining water to make a thin cream, then add a little of the boiling liquid from the pan. Stir well and pour it back into the pear soup, then lower the heat and let the soup simmer for a further 5 minutes. Sweeten with a little sugar to taste, then allow to get cold before chilling. Serve with Almond or Hazelnut biscuits (page 164).

Chilled almond soup

For this soup, you need a blender for crushing the nuts.

Serves 4
CALORIES PER PORTION: 370 (1537 kJ)
PROTEIN CONTENT PER PORTION: 11 grams
PREPARATION & CHILLING TIME: 3 hours

225 g (8 oz) almonds, blanched and
   skinned
900 ml (1½ pints) cold water
225 g (8 oz) potatoes, boiled in their
   skins, then peeled
salt
a few drops of rose water

Put the almonds into a blender with the water and work at high speed until the almonds have turned into a smooth purée. Strain this through a medium-fine sieve, pressing the purée against the sides to extract as much of the milk as possible, then strain it again through a very fine sieve so that the milk is completely smooth and not at all gritty. There should be about 600 ml (1 pint) of almond milk

by this time, so make it up to 900 ml (1½ pints) with extra water. Put the milk into the blender with the still warm potatoes and work until smooth.

Strain the soup again through a very fine sieve and season it lightly with salt. Add a few drops of rose water and serve the soup well chilled with thin Almond or Hazelnut biscuits (page 164).

Lebanese cucumber and yoghurt soup

Serves 4
CALORIES PER PORTION: 70 (295 kJ)
PROTEIN CONTENT PER PORTION: 6 grams
PREPARATION & CHILLING TIME: 3 hours

450 g (1 lb) peeled cucumber, thinly
   sliced
400 ml (¾ pint) natural yoghurt
salt
2 teaspoons finely chopped fresh mint
½ teaspoon grated lemon rind
1-2 tablespoons lemon juice
400 ml (¾ pint) iced water
freshly ground pepper

Spread out the sliced cucumber and sprinkle it with salt. Leave it for 30 minutes to get rid of any bitter juices, then rinse the cucumber slices under running water and pat them dry. Put the cucumber with the mint, lemon rind and juice, yoghurt and water into a blender and work until smooth. Season with salt and pepper and chill for about 2 hours. Serve it with warm wholemeal Pitta bread (page 154) — the contrast between the warm bread and the chilled soup is particularly satisfying.

Note: If you do not have a blender, you can chop the drained, sliced cucumber almost to a pulp before mixing it into the rest of the ingredients. It still makes a good soup.

Potage bonne femme

This soup is equally good served warm.

Serves 4
CALORIES PER PORTION: 270 (1122 kJ)
PROTEIN CONTENT PER PORTION: 6.5 grams
PREPARATION & CHILLING TIME: 2 hours

350 g (12 oz) thinly sliced potatoes
25-50 g (1-2 oz) butter, depending on
   the absorbency of the potatoes
100 g (4 oz) finely chopped onion
100 g (4 oz) halved and sliced leeks
225 g (8 oz) thinly sliced carrots
900 ml (1½ pints) water, or half water
   and half milk
salt and freshly ground pepper

Melt the butter over gentle heat, add the potatoes and onion and cook for 5 minutes, stirring from time to time to prevent them sticking and burning. Add the leeks, half the carrots and the water, or water and milk; bring to the boil, lower the heat and simmer the soup for 20 minutes, stirring occasionally. Meanwhile, simmer the remaining carrots in a little salted water in a separate pan until tender.

When the main vegetables are cooked, put them with their cooking liquid, into a blender and work until smooth, then

rub the purée through a sieve; or rub the vegetables and liquid twice through a sieve.

Thin down the purée with a little extra cold water if the soup is too thick, then season well with salt and pepper and allow to cool before chilling. Pour into individual soup bowls and float the separately cooked, drained carrot slices on the top. Serve with thin slices of wholemeal toast.

Hungarian goulash soup

This is a substantial soup, making enough for 6 large helpings.

CALORIES PER PORTION: 120 (490 kJ)
PROTEIN CONTENT PER PORTION: 4 grams
PREPARATION & COOKING TIME: 1½ hours

225 g (8 oz) finely chopped onions
225 g (8 oz) thinly sliced carrots,
 quartered if large
2 tablespoons olive or sunflower oil
225 g (8 oz) shredded white or green
 cabbage
100 g (4 oz) diced green pepper
2 cloves of garlic, peeled and thinly
 sliced
2-3 tablespoons paprika
1 tablespoon wholemeal flour
900 ml (1½ pints) water
2 teaspoons yeast extract
salt
225 g (8 oz) thickly sliced potatoes
a little sugar (optional)

Heat the oil in a large pan and fry the onions and carrots until the onions are golden brown and the carrots are just beginning to brown, then add the cabbage, pepper and garlic. Sprinkle in the paprika, then add the flour and mix thoroughly before adding the water. Increase the heat and bring the soup to the boil, stirring all the time. Now add the yeast extract and season to taste with salt. Lower the heat and let the soup simmer for about 30 minutes.

Add the potatoes, bring the soup back to the boil and simmer for a further 30 minutes, stirring it from time to time.

Drain the vegetables, reserve the liquid and make it up to 900 ml (1½ pints) with water. Return the vegetables to the pan, add the cooking liquid and a little sugar, if liked, to counteract the bitterness of the paprika. Bring the goulash soup back to the boil once more before serving with thick slices of dark Rye bread (page 151).

Note: If you like, you can omit the potatoes from the soup itself, boil them separately, peel them and add one to each serving. Choose a medium-sized potato for each guest.

Bortsch

This recipe should make enough for 8 servings.

CALORIES PER PORTION: 185 (771 kJ)
PROTEIN CONTENT PER PORTION: 3 grams
PREPARATION & COOKING TIME: 1½ hours

450 g (1 lb) beetroot, peeled and cut in
 thin strips
3 tablespoons olive or sunflower oil
225 g (8 oz) finely chopped onions
100 g (4 oz) diced celery
100 g (4 oz) finely diced carrots
100 g (4 oz) diced parsnips
100 g (4 oz) shredded white cabbage
2 cloves of garlic, peeled and finely
 chopped
1.6 litres (2¾ pints) water
2 tablespoons wine vinegar
salt and freshly ground pepper
225 g (8 oz) finely shredded potatoes
300 ml (½ pint) cultured sour cream

Heat the oil in a pan and fry the onions, celery and carrots until golden brown. Add the rest of the ingredients except the potatoes and sour cream and bring the soup to the boil. Put in the shredded potatoes and simmer for 30-40 minutes until the vegetables are tender and the potatoes have broken down and thickened the soup. Adjust the seasoning, if necessary, before serving the soup with a little sour cream swirled into each portion, accompanied by the traditional Pirozhki.

Pirozhki

Makes 12
TOTAL CALORIES: 2100 (8780 kJ)
TOTAL PROTEIN CONTENT: 69 grams
PREPARATION & COOKING TIME: 3 hours

225 g (8 oz) wholemeal flour
20 g (¾ oz) fresh yeast
½ teaspoon raw brown sugar
3 tablespoons warm milk
2 eggs, well beaten
50 g (2 oz) butter
1 teaspoon salt

The filling
125 g (generous 4 oz) curd or sieved
 cottage cheese
1 tablespoon finely chopped onion
100 g (4 oz) boiled long-grain rice
1 hard-boiled egg, finely chopped
salt
freshly ground pepper
1 egg, well beaten

Put the flour to warm. Mix the yeast with the sugar and milk and keep it in a warm place until it is frothy, then add the beaten eggs. Melt the butter and gently stir it in. Sift the warmed flour with the salt, make a well in the centre and pour in the yeast and egg mixture. Knead it well until a smooth dough is formed, adding a little more flour if the dough is too moist. Leave it in a warm place for 20-30 minutes to rise.

Meanwhile, make the filling. Mix together the curd or cottage cheese, onion, rice and hard-boiled egg to make a paste; season this well with salt and pepper.

When the dough has risen to double its volume, 'knock it back' and turn it out on to a floured board. Roll it out very thinly — to about 5 mm (¼ in) thickness — and cut out twelve circles about 8 cm (3 in) in diameter.

Put a spoonful of the filling in the centre of each one and brush the edges with a little beaten egg. Fold over and gently seal each Pirozhki, stretching the pastry a little, if necessary. Leave them in a warm place for 10 minutes to prove. Set the oven at 180°C (350°F) Gas 4 and bake on a well buttered baking sheet for about 20 minutes. Alternatively, they can be deep fried in oil and drained on absorbent kitchen paper.

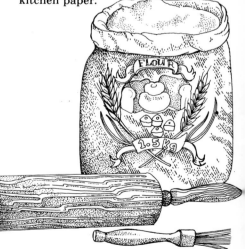

Starters

However much skill, inspiration and effort has gone
into the main course, it is still the starter that creates
for your guests the first impression of the meal to come.
Whether you choose a soup from the preceding chapter,
a simple salad, a soufflé perhaps, or one of the ideas
on the following pages, your starter sets the scene.
It is the prelude or overture to what is in store and
must complement and not overshadow the rest of
the meal.
In my opinion, a starter should be simple. For some
people, a bowl of Ratatouille served hot or cold, a bowl
of black or green olives or juicy small tomatoes, and a
crusty loaf still warm from the oven, would be the
perfect starter . . . If you prefer something a little
more elaborate, serve the Salad platter on page 57.
In this chapter, you will find recipes for cold starters,
followed by hot starters and lastly, a selection of
savoury dips to serve with Crudités.

Stuffed grapefruit

Serves 4
CALORIES PER PORTION: 120 (485 kJ)
PROTEIN CONTENT PER PORTION: 4 grams
PREPARATION & CHILLING TIME: about 1 ½ hours

2 grapefruit
50 g (2 oz) shelled walnuts, preferably freshly picked
2 tablespoons finely diced red pepper
2 tablespoons thinly sliced preserved stem ginger
4 teaspoons Kirsch

Cut each grapefruit in half, and with a grapefruit knife or a similar sharp-pointed knife, carefully cut out the flesh. Remove all the skin and pith from the flesh, divide it into segments and put them into a bowl.

Simmer the walnuts in a little water for 4-5 minutes, take them out of the hot water one at a time with a draining spoon and remove the skins with a sharp-pointed knife. (It is easier to do this while the nuts are still hot). Slice the nuts and mix them with the grapefruit segments, red pepper and stem ginger.

Trim the rim of each grapefruit shell into a zig-zag pattern and fill with the grapefruit mixture. Chill for about 1 hour.

Sprinkle each grapefruit half with a teaspoon of Kirsch before serving.

Melon salad

Serves 4
CALORIES PER PORTION: 265 (1105 kJ)
PROTEIN CONTENT PER PORTION: 9 grams
PREPARATION & CHILLING TIME: 1 ½ hours

450 g (1 lb) honeydew melon, peeled and diced
125 g (4 oz) finely shredded carrot
125 g (4 oz) diced Edam cheese
125 g (4 oz) tomatoes, chopped
50 g (2 oz) finely chopped preserved stem ginger

The dressing
1 tablespoon lemon juice
3 tablespoons olive or sunflower oil
1 tablespoon finely chopped watercress
1 tablespoon finely chopped parsley
1 teaspoon finely chopped mint
salt
freshly ground pepper
a pinch of cayenne

Mix together the melon, carrot, cheese, tomatoes and ginger. Make the dressing by whisking the lemon juice, oil, watercress and herbs together, then season to taste with salt, pepper and cayenne. Pour the dressing over the salad and mix thoroughly. Pile the salad into individual glass bowls and chill for 45 minutes before serving.

Note: this will go well with a Herb loaf (page 132), and makes a good light lunch dish.

Stuffed potatoes

Serves 4
CALORIES PER PORTION: 445 (1860 kJ)
PROTEIN CONTENT PER PORTION: 4 grams
PREPARATION & COOKING TIME: 1 ¼ hours

2 large potatoes, weighing about 225 g (8 oz) each
50 g (2 oz) stoned or stuffed green or black olives, thinly sliced
50 g (2 oz) thinly sliced gherkins
1 teaspoon curry powder
8-9 tablespoons Mayonnaise (page 126)
4 lettuce leaves, to garnish

Wrap each potato in foil and bake in the oven at 200°C (400°F) Gas 6 for about an hour, or until the potato feels soft when pierced with a fork or thin skewer. Unwrap the potatoes and leave them to cool. Cut each one in half and scoop out the middle, leaving only a thin shell about 1 cm (½ in) thick. Roughly chop the cooked potato and mix it with the olives and gherkins, reserving a few olive slices for a garnish.

Mix the curry powder into the Mayonnaise, then combine this with the potato, olive and gherkin mixture. Pile this in the potato skins and garnish with olive slices. Place each potato half on a plate covered with a crisp lettuce leaf for serving.

Vegetables à la grecque

Serves 4
CALORIES PER PORTION: 95 (392 kJ)
PROTEIN CONTENT PER PORTION: 2.5 grams
PREPARATION & COOKING TIME: 45 minutes
CHILLING TIME: 1-2 hours

8 pickling onions, topped and tailed
2 tablespoons olive or sunflower oil
100 g (4 oz) finely chopped onion
450 g (1 lb) skinned tomatoes, roughly chopped
1 clove of garlic, peeled and finely chopped
200 ml (⅓ pint) dry white wine
1 tablespoon lemon juice
salt
freshly ground pepper
225 g (8 oz) cauliflower, broken into small florets
8 button mushrooms

Drop the pickling onions into boiling water and leave them for 5 minutes, then drain, cool and peel.

Heat the oil and fry the chopped onion over moderate heat until transparent. Add the tomatoes, garlic, wine, lemon juice and a little salt and pepper to taste. Lower the heat and cook gently until the tomatoes make a thick sauce, then add the cauliflower and pickling onions. Simmer the vegetables gently in the sauce for about 10 minutes, or until the cauliflower florets are cooked but still firm. Wipe the button mushrooms and add them for the last 5 minutes. Take out all the vegetables and arrange them on a serving dish.

Boil the sauce to reduce it to about 200 ml (⅓ pint), stirring briskly all the time, then adjust the seasoning before pouring it over the vegetables.

Chill well and serve with thinly sliced wholemeal bread or toast spread with a Herb butter (page 198).

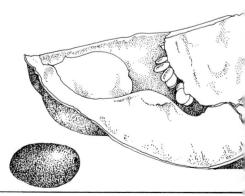

Stuffed avocado

Serves 4
CALORIES PER PORTION: 345 (1400 kJ)
PROTEIN CONTENT PER PORTION: 6 grams
PREPARATION & CHILLING TIME: 1¼ -2 hours

2 medium-sized avocados

The filling
100 g (4 oz) red pepper, cut into thin
* strips*
100 g (4 oz) curd or sieved cottage
* cheese*
grated rind and juice of 1 lemon
salt
freshly ground pepper
1 small clove of garlic, peeled and very
* finely chopped*
1 egg white

To prepare the filling: pour boiling water over the strips of red pepper and leave them for 5 minutes. Drain, then refresh them by plunging into cold water. Mash the curd or cottage cheese in a bowl with the grated lemon rind, salt, pepper and the garlic. Beat the egg white until very stiff, then fold it gently into the curd cheese.

Drain the red pepper strips, dry well on a kitchen cloth or kitchen paper then chop them into small cubes, reserving a few for the garnish. Gently fold them into the cheese mixture. Chill for 1-2 hours. Before using the filling, drain off any clear liquid that has come to the surface.

Just before serving, cut the avocados in half, remove the stones and brush the insides with lemon juice to stop the flesh turning brown. Pile the cheese mixture in them and garnish each with the reserved diced red peppers.

Lebanese avocado salad

Serves 4
CALORIES PER PORTION: 280 (1170 kJ)
PROTEIN CONTENT PER PORTION: 8.5 grams
PREPARATION & CHILLING TIME: 1¼ hours

2 large avocados, peeled and cut into
* chunks*
1-2 cloves of garlic, peeled and crushed
300 ml (½ pint) natural yoghurt
225 g (8 oz) finely diced red peppers

Mix the garlic into the yoghurt and gently fold in the avocado chunks. Pile the mixture into a serving dish, sprinkle the red peppers over the top; cover and chill for 1 hour. Serve with warm Pitta bread (page 154).

Asparagus with tarragon mayonnaise

Serves 4
CALORIES PER PORTION: 1000 (4190 kJ)
PROTEIN CONTENT PER PORTION: 32 grams
PREPARATION & COOKING TIME: 30 minutes
CHILLING TIME: 1 hour

1¼ kg (2 lb) trimmed fresh asparagus
salt
400 ml (¾ pint) Mayonnaise (page 126)
* made with tarragon vinegar*
2 tablespoons finely chopped tarragon

Try this as an alternative to serving asparagus with melted butter, or Hollandaise sauce (page 195).

Tie the asparagus in bundles, stand them upright in a tall, deep pan and cook them in a little boiling salted water — with the asparagus heads in the steam — for 15-20 minutes, or until the shoots are tender (see page 59). Drain, cool, untie the asparagus and chill well. Meanwhile, prepare the mayonnaise, using tarragon vinegar instead of wine vinegar, and mix in the chopped tarragon about an hour before serving. Serve the asparagus with the Mayonnaise handed separately. (You will need finger bowls and napkins).

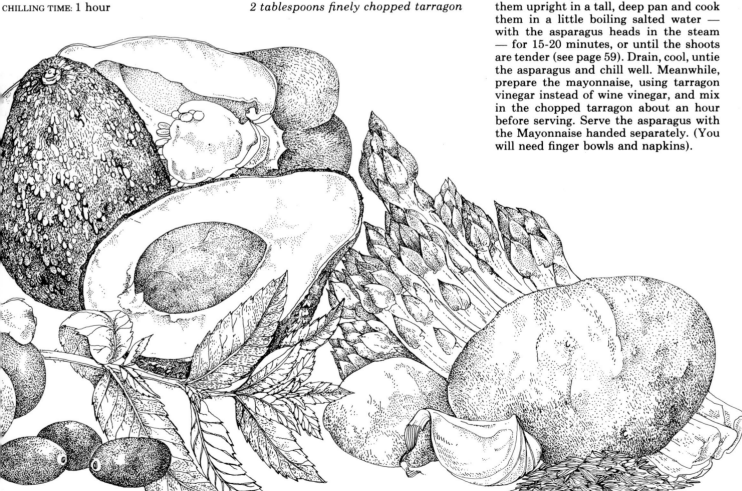

Cauliflower mayonnaise

Serves 4
CALORIES PER PORTION: 970 (4062 kJ)
PROTEIN CONTENT PER PORTION: 4.5 grams
PREPARATION & COOKING TIME: 30 minutes
CHILLING TIME: 20 minutes

450 g (1 lb) cauliflower, broken into
small florets
400 ml (¾ pint) Mayonnaise (page 126)
1-2 tablespoons finely chopped parsley

Cook the cauliflower in a very little boiling salted water until just tender; it should take no more than 10 minutes, as the cauliflower should still be fairly firm. Drain well and allow it to cool.

Dip each floret in the Mayonnaise until well coated, then arrange the florets in a mound on a serving dish. Sprinkle with chopped parsley and chill for 30-45 minutes before serving.

Tomato jelly mould

Serves 4
CALORIES PER PORTION: 105 (427 kJ)
PROTEIN CONTENT PER PORTION: 3 grams
PREPARATION & COOKING TIME: 30 minutes
SETTING TIME: 3 hours

1 kg (2 lb) ripe tomatoes, roughly
chopped
2 tablespoons olive or sunflower oil
100 g (4 oz) finely chopped onion
salt
freshly ground black pepper
1 bay leaf
1 large clove of garlic, peeled and finely
chopped
2 teaspoons agar-agar
2 tablespoons cold water
1 teaspoon wine or cider vinegar
grated rind and juice of ½ lemon
bunch of watercress, to garnish

Heat the oil and cook the onion gently until transparent, taking care the onion does not brown. Add the tomatoes, bay leaf, garlic, salt and pepper and cook to a pulp over gentle heat — about 15 minutes.

Rub the pulp through a nylon sieve or a Mouli mill, return it to a clean pan, bring to the boil and continue boiling briskly, stirring all the time, until it is reduced to a little less than 600 ml (1 pint).

Mix the agar-agar to a smooth cream with the cold water, then slowly pour on the boiling tomato pulp, stirring constantly. Return this to the pan, stir in the vinegar and lemon rind, bring to the boil again and continue boiling for a further 2 minutes. Strain in the lemon juice and

the tomato mixture and pour into a 600 ml (1 pint) capacity ring mould. Allow to cool, then place in the refrigerator and chill for at least 3 hours, or until set.

Turn the jelly out of the mould, fill the centre with watercress and serve with freshly made wholemeal toast.

Note: Cans of Italian plum tomatoes may also be used for this recipe. Drain well before heating the tomatoes.

A selection of cold starters. Left:
Tomato jelly mould, garnished with
watercress. Centre: Eggs, coated with a
tangy Green mayonnaise. Right:
Jellied asparagus – serve this with
helpings of thick Green mayonnaise and
thin slices of wholemeal toast

Jellied asparagus

Serves 4
CALORIES PER PORTION: 80 (345 kJ)
PROTEIN CONTENT PER PORTION: 6 grams
PREPARATION & COOKING TIME: 50 minutes
SETTING TIME: 2 hours

350 g (12 oz) trimmed fresh asparagus
scant 600 ml (1 pint) well-flavoured
*   clear Brown vegetable stock*
2 teaspoons agar-agar
a little green food colouring (optional)

Tie the asparagus in bundles, stand them upright in a tall, deep pan and cook them in a little boiling salted water — with the heads of the asparagus in the steam — for 15-20 minutes, or until tender. Drain off any cooking liquid and make it up to 600 ml (1 pint) with stock. Pour all but 3 tablespoons of this into a pan and bring to the boil. Mix the agar-agar in a bowl to a smooth cream with the reserved cold stock, then gradually pour the boiling stock on to it, stirring briskly as you do so. Return the stock to the pan and cook it for 2 more minutes.

Place 16 of the asparagus spears on the bottom of a 600 ml (1 pint) capacity mould, cutting them to fit as necessary and arranging them to radiate from the centre. Chop the remaining asparagus into pieces about 2 cm (¾ in) long, and add these to the stock with just enough green food colouring (if used) to make it an attractive colour.

Allow the stock to cool slightly, then carefully ladle into the mould just enough liquid to cover the asparagus spears. Put into the refrigerator to set and, when it has, slowly pour the rest of the stock into the mould and leave it to cool.

When it is completely cold, chill the jelly in the refrigerator for 2 hours. Turn it out and serve with a Green mayonnaise (page 126).

Note: Canned asparagus may also be used, in which case use the liquid from the can to make up to 600 ml (1 pint) with stock. Frozen asparagus is also suitable, and should be cooked according to the directions on the packet.

Eggs in tarragon jelly

Serves 4
CALORIES PER PORTION: 200 (845 kJ)
PROTEIN CONTENT PER PORTION: 8 grams
PREPARATION & CHILLING TIME: 2 hours

4 small Oeufs mollets (page 72) or
*   hard-boiled eggs, shelled*
900 ml (1½ pints) clear Brown
*   vegetable stock (page 34)*
1 tablespoon dried tarragon
2 teaspoons agar-agar
salt
freshly ground pepper
4 sprigs of fresh tarragon, to garnish

Prepare the Oeufs mollets, if you are using them, and keep them warm in a pan of hot water. Meanwhile, put the stock and dried tarragon into a pan and boil until the liquid is reduced to 600 ml (1 pint). Sprinkle in the agar-agar, stir well, then simmer for 5 minutes before seasoning to taste with salt and pepper. Place each egg in a ramekin or cocotte dish, fill each one with strained stock and float a sprig of tarragon on top. Leave to cool, then chill well before serving. Serve with slices of lightly buttered, freshly made wholemeal toast.

Eggs with Green (watercress) mayonnaise

Serves 4
CALORIES PER PORTION: 910 (3805 kJ)
PROTEIN CONTENT PER PORTION: 20 grams
PREPARATION & CHILLING TIME: 1 hour

4 hard-boiled eggs, shelled and cut in
*   half lengthways*
4 thin slices of wholemeal bread,
*   halved, crusts removed and lightly*
*   buttered*
300 ml (½ pint) chilled Green
*   mayonnaise (page 126)*
sprigs of watercress, to garnish

Arrange the halved eggs, cut side down, on the slices of bread, spoon the green mayonnaise over the eggs, then chill for no longer than 40 minutes before serving.

Eggs with curry mayonnaise

Serves 4
CALORIES PER PORTION: 910 (3805 kJ)
PROTEIN CONTENT PER PORTION: 20 grams
PREPARATION & CHILLING TIME: 1 hour

Follow the above recipe for Eggs with Green mayonnaise, but substitute 300 ml (½ pint) Curry mayonnaise (page 127) for the Green mayonnaise.

Spinach ramekins

Serves 4
CALORIES PER PORTION: 250 (1047 kJ)
PROTEIN PER PORTION: 6 grams
PREPARATION & COOKING TIME: 45 minutes
CHILLING TIME: about 1 hour

450 g (1 lb) spinach, very carefully
washed
4 tablespoons olive or sunflower oil
6 tablespoons double cream
2-3 tablespoons lemon juice
1 small clove of garlic, peeled and finely
chopped
salt
freshly ground pepper
100 g (4 oz) finely chopped onion

Pour half the oil into a thick-based pan and add the spinach. Cover the pan and cook the spinach over moderate heat for about 7-8 minutes, or until it is almost tender, shaking the pan frequently to stop the spinach from sticking. Remove the lid, lower the heat and continue cooking until any remaining liquid evaporates and the spinach is tender.

Put the spinach in a blender with the cream, lemon juice, garlic, salt and pepper, and work to a smooth purée. Pour this into four ramekins or small individual dishes and chill well.

Fry the onion in the remaining oil until it is crisp and golden brown. Drain well on kitchen paper and allow to cool. Just before serving, garnish each ramekin with a sprinkling of onion and serve with crisp, freshly made wholemeal toast.

Note: If using frozen leaf spinach, cook it according to the directions on the packet, then drain it well before blending with the other ingredients.

Leeks vinaigrette

Serves 4
CALORIES PER PORTION: 250 (1040 kJ)
PROTEIN CONTENT PER PORTION: 2 grams
PREPARATION & COOKING TIME: 20 minutes
CHILLING TIME: about 1 hour

Buy enough leeks to give 450 g (1 lb)
when washed and trimmed

The dressing
1 tablespoon white wine or cider
vinegar
1 tablespoon white wine or lemon juice
6-8 tablespoons olive or sunflower oil
½-1 teaspoon coarsely crushed
coriander seeds
1 small clove of garlic, peeled and finely
chopped
salt
freshly ground pepper

Cut the trimmed leeks in half lengthways and lay them in a shallow pan with the white tops all pointing in the same direction. Add boiling salted water to partly cover and gently simmer the leeks, covered, for 10-15 minutes, or until tender.

Meanwhile, make the vinaigrette dressing. Mix together the vinegar, wine or lemon juice, oil, coriander and garlic and whisk until the dressing is cloudy and well mixed. Season it with salt and pepper. Drain the leeks well, pour the dressing over them and chill. Serve with thin slices of wholemeal bread and butter.

Egg mayonnaise tomatoes

Serves 4
CALORIES PER PORTION: 805 (3367 kJ)
PROTEIN CONTENT PER PORTION: 12 grams
PREPARATION & CHILLING TIME: 1 hour

4 large tomatoes, weighing about 225 g
(8 oz) each, or 8 smaller ones
2 tablespoons finely chopped basil
300 ml (½ pint) thick Mayonnaise
(page 126)
salt
freshly ground pepper
4 hard-boiled eggs, shelled and coarsely
chopped
4 slices of wholemeal bread, crusts
removed and lightly buttered

Cut the tops off the tomatoes at the flower end and scoop out the centres. Turn the tomatoes upside down to drain. Discard the juice and pips and mash the flesh. Mix the basil into the Mayonnaise, then add a little of the tomato flesh, but not enough to make the Mayonnaise too thin.

Sprinkle the inside of each tomato shell with salt and pepper, mix the chopped eggs with half the Mayonnaise and fill the tomato cases. Stand a tomato on each slice of bread and swirl the remaining mayonnaise over the tops. Chill well.

1. Dip each tomato into boiling water for up to 1 minute.

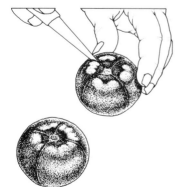

2. Score the tomato skin in quarters, from the top.

3. Peel off all the tomato skin and discard it.

4. Cut open the tomato and remove all juice and seeds.

Tomato sorbet

Serves 4
CALORIES PER PORTION: 100 (417 kJ)
PROTEIN CONTENT PER PORTION: 2.5 grams
PREPARATION & FREEZING TIME: 4½ hours

450 g (1 lb) skinned tomatoes, roughly chopped
25 g (1 oz) finely chopped onion
2 egg yolks
2 tablespoons olive or sunflower oil
salt
1 tablespoon brandy
sprigs of mint or parsley, to garnish

Place all the ingredients, except the parsley, in a blender and work to a smooth purée. Adjust the seasoning, remembering that the flavours will become slightly blander during freezing. Pour the mixture into a suitable china or plastic container, cover tightly and leave in the freezer or freezing compartment of a refrigerator until the edges are set but the centre is still mushy — about 1 hour. Remove from the freezer and stir the mixture well, drawing the sides into the middle, then return it to the freezer and leave it until the edges are set again. Remove and stir the mixture once more, then leave it until frozen hard.

Break the sorbet into small pieces and pile it into individual glasses. Garnish with sprigs of mint or parsley before serving.

Note: If the sorbet has set very hard, remove it from the freezer and leave it in the refrigerator for about 30 minutes to soften before serving.

Egg mayonnaise mousse

Serves 4
CALORIES PER PORTION: 760 (3190 kJ)
PROTEIN CONTENT PER PORTION: 12 grams
PREPARATION & CHILLING TIME: 1 hour

6 hard-boiled eggs, shelled
1 teaspoon agar-agar
4 tablespoons water
300 ml (½ pint) Mayonnaise (page 126)
1 tablespoon onion juice and pulp (see right)
salt
freshly ground pepper

Chill the eggs in the refrigerator while you mix the agar-agar with the water to a thin cream. Bring this to the boil in a small pan, stirring briskly. Pour half the Mayonnaise into a blender, then gradually pour in the dissolved agar-agar as you blend. When the mixture is completely smooth, add it to the rest of the Mayonnaise. Stir in the onion juice and pulp and season with salt and pepper. Gently fold the eggs into the mixture and pour it into a 900 ml (1½ pint) capacity soufflé dish. Chill well before serving, garnished with watercress and thin slices of wholemeal toast.

To make onion juice, cut an onion in half across the rings and rotate the halved onion on a glass lemon or orange squeezer. Do not use a wooden one or the flavour will linger.

Cheese and tomato mousse

Serves 4
CALORIES PER PORTION: 195 (810 kJ)
PROTEIN CONTENT PER PORTION: 11 grams
PREPARATION & COOKING TIME: 30 minutes
CHILLING TIME: 1 hour

450 g (1 lb) skinned tomatoes, cut into eighths
125 g (4 oz) coarsely grated Cheddar cheese
1 teaspoon finely chopped tarragon
1 teaspoon finely chopped basil
125 g (4 oz) very finely chopped onion
salt
freshly ground pepper
300 ml (½ pint) cold Brown vegetable stock (page 34)
1 tablespoon agar-agar
1 tablespoon white wine vinegar
1 teaspoon French-style mustard

Mix together the tomatoes, cheese, herbs and onion and season well with salt and pepper. Stir 6 tablespoons of the stock into the agar-agar to make it into a thin cream, then stir it into the rest of the cold stock. Add the vinegar and mustard and bring it to the boil over a moderate heat, stirring constantly until it thickens. Increase the heat to bring the mixture to the boil, then add the tomato mixture in four helpings, stirring vigorously after each addition to prevent the mousse mixture from setting too soon. When it is thoroughly blended, pour it into a 1 litre (1¾ pint) capacity soufflé dish and stand it in a shallow bowl of iced water for about 1 hour, until it is cold and firmly set.

Loosen the sides with a knife, carefully ease the mousse free. Turn it out and serve with thin slices of freshly made toast.

Note: Served with a potato salad and a large mixed salad, this makes a very good main course. If preferred, the mousse can be served straight from the bowl.

Curried cheese mousse

Serves 4
CALORIES PER PORTION: 335 (1390 kJ)
PROTEIN CONTENT PER PORTION: 2 grams
PREPARATION & COOKING TIME: 40 minutes
CHILLING TIME: 1½-2 hours

225 g (8 oz) curd cheese
1 tablespoon olive or sunflower oil
100 g (4 oz) finely chopped onion
2 level teaspoons agar-agar
300 ml (½ pint) dry white wine
100 ml (4 fl oz) boiling water
½ teaspoon curry powder
1 small clove of garlic, peeled and finely chopped
salt and freshly ground pepper
sprigs of watercress, to garnish

Heat the oil and cook the onion until transparent. Blend the agar-agar to a smooth cream with 2 tablespoons of cold water, then stir in the wine. Pour on to the onion and bring to the boil. Lower the heat, simmer for 2 minutes, pour into a bowl and chill until set.

Place the set mixture in a blender with the curd cheese; add the boiling water, curry powder and garlic and work until smooth. Adjust the seasoning, pour into 4 small dishes, allow to cool then chill well.

Salad platter

The salad platter consists of seven dishes, all with contrasting flavours and textures. Served together, the dishes combine to make an impressive starter to a dinner party for 8 people. Alternatively, you can serve it as a first course at a summer lunch for 4-6 people, depending on appetite.

Stuffed tomatoes

TOTAL CALORIES: 345 (1440 kJ)
TOTAL PROTEIN CONTENT: 16 grams
PREPARATION & CHILLING TIME: 2½ hours

8 large, firm tomatoes, weighing about
  450 g (1 lb)
6 fresh basil leaves, finely chopped
2 tablespoons natural yoghurt
½ teaspoon lemon juice
12 tablespoons fresh wholemeal
  breadcrumbs
salt
freshly ground pepper
fresh basil leaves, to garnish

Cut off the tops of each tomato and scoop out the pulp, discarding the seeds and fibrous cores. Cut a very thin slice from the base of each tomato so that it will stand firmly, taking care not to make a hole through which the filling can run out. Turn the tomatoes upside down to drain.

Mix together the tomato pulp, basil, yoghurt, lemon juice and enough breadcrumbs to make a soft purée. Season this with salt and pepper, then fill the prepared tomato cases. Replace the tops as 'lids' and chill well. Garnish each one with fresh basil leaves just before serving.

Oeufs à l'indienne

TOTAL CALORIES: 1240 (5170 kJ)
TOTAL PROTEIN CONTENT: 34 grams
PREPARATION TIME: 40 minutes

4 hard-boiled eggs, shelled and cut in
  half lengthways
3-4 tablespoons thick Mayonnaise (page
  126)
1 teaspoon finely ground cumin seeds
1 small clove of garlic, peeled and
  crushed
a little lemon juice
75 g (3 oz) long grain rice
1 teaspoon ground turmeric (optional)
sprigs of watercress, to garnish

Remove the yolks from the halved eggs and mash them with enough Mayonnaise, cumin and garlic to make a smooth, fairly firm paste. Add a little lemon juice to taste, but not enough to make the mixture too thin.

Cook the rice in plenty of boiling salted water with the turmeric added, if used. Drain the rice well, rinse under running cold water, then drain it again and leave to cool.

Using a piping bag fitted with a rose nozzle, pipe the yolk mixture into the halved egg whites, or spoon in the mixture with a teaspoon.

Serve the eggs arranged on a bed of rice and garnished with sprigs of watercress.

Marinated mushrooms

TOTAL CALORIES: 1050 (4400 kJ)
TOTAL PROTEIN CONTENT: 2 grams
PREPARATION & CHILLING TIME: 40 minutes

125 g (4 oz) thinly sliced button
  mushrooms
2 tablespoons white wine, or cider,
  vinegar
125 ml (scant ¼ pint) olive or
  sunflower oil

2 teaspoons paprika
¼ - ½ teaspoon chilli powder
1 tablespoon lemon juice
1 tablespoon chopped parsley

Put the mushrooms into a serving bowl and prepare the marinade by mixing together the vinegar, oil, paprika, chilli powder and lemon juice. Pour the marinade over the mushrooms and mix gently until they are well coated, then chill for 30 minutes.

Sprinkle with a little chopped parsley just before serving and spoon a little of the marinade over each helping.

Five dishes from the Salad platter – a
contrast in textures and flavours:
Oeufs à l'Indienne; Stuffed tomatoes;
Shredded celeriac; Stuffed cucumber
rings and tasty Marinated mushrooms

Caviare d'aubergines

TOTAL CALORIES: 615 (2560 kJ)
TOTAL PROTEIN CONTENT: 6 grams
PREPARATION & COOKING TIME: 1½ hours
CHILLING TIME: about 1 hour

450 g (1 lb) aubergines
4 tablespoons olive or sunflower oil
100 g (4 oz) finely chopped onion
50 g (2 oz) finely chopped green pepper
225 g (8 oz) skinned tomatoes, coarsely
    chopped
2 tablespoons dry white wine
1 clove of garlic, peeled and finely
    chopped
salt
freshly ground pepper
1 tablespoon lemon juice
1 tablespoon finely chopped parsley

Set the oven at 180°C (350°F) Gas 4. Prick the aubergines with a stainless steel fork or skewer, then bake them on the top shelf of the pre-heated oven for 1 hour, or until the skins are black and the flesh is soft. Take them out of the oven and set aside to cool.

Heat the oil in a pan and fry the onion and green pepper until the onion is golden brown, then lower the heat, add the tomatoes and continue cooking gently until the tomatoes are reduced to a pulp.

Cut the aubergines in half and scoop out the flesh with a teaspoon. Add this to the tomato mixture in the pan, then add the wine and garlic; season with salt and pepper and cook until the mixture is reduced to a thick purée. Remove the pan from the heat and allow the mixture to cool. Transfer to a serving dish, stir in the lemon juice, adjust the seasoning, sprinkle with parsley and chill well.

Serve with slices of crisp wholemeal toast.

Salt aubergine rings to remove bitter juice. Leave ½ hour, then rinse and dry.

Shredded celeriac

TOTAL CALORIES: 1305 (5470 kJ)
TOTAL PROTEIN CONTENT: 7 grams
PREPARATION TIME: 20 minutes

225 g (8 oz) peeled celeriac
4-8 tablespoons well-flavoured
    Mayonnaise (page 126)
sprigs of parsley or watercress, to
    garnish

Shred the celeriac into matchstick-sized julienne strips and blanch these by cooking in a pan of boiling water for about 2 minutes. Drain, rinse under cold running water, drain again and dry the strips well on kitchen paper. Mix them with just enough Mayonnaise to make a thin, even coating. Pile the celeriac into a serving bowl and garnish with parsley or watercress.

Shredded carrots

TOTAL CALORIES: 560 (2340 kJ)
TOTAL PROTEIN CONTENT: 2 grams
PREPARATION TIME: 15 minutes

225 g (8 oz) shredded carrots
6 thinly sliced spring onions

The dressing
1 tablespoon lemon juice
1 tablespoon dry white wine
4 tablespoons olive or sunflower oil
salt
freshly ground pepper

Mix the carrots with most of the spring onions, reserving a few of the greener onion slices for a garnish. Make the dressing by whisking together the lemon juice, white wine and oil and pour this over the carrot and onion. Season with salt and pepper, then toss the mixture well and pile it into a small serving bowl. Garnish with the reserved green onion slices just before serving.

Stuffed cucumber rings

TOTAL CALORIES: 430 (1810 kJ)
TOTAL PROTEIN CONTENT: 6 grams
PREPARATION TIME: 50 minutes

350 g (12 oz) cucumber, cut into eight
    5 cm (2 in) slices
salt
50 g (2 oz) curd cheese
1 clove of garlic, peeled and crushed
1-2 tablespoons milk
freshly ground pepper
350 g (12 oz) red or green dessert
    apples
8 thin slices of cucumber, to garnish

Carefully remove the flesh from inside the cucumber slices, leaving a thin ring of cucumber skin. Chop the flesh into tiny dice about 5 mm (¼ in) square. Put these into a colander and sprinkle them with a little salt. Leave to stand for about 20 minutes, then rinse under cold running water before draining and drying them well on kitchen paper.

Mix together the curd cheese and garlic, then add just enough milk to make a thick, creamy consistency. Season with salt and pepper.

Peel, core and chop the apples into tiny dice to match the cucumber in size, then mix into the curd cheese.

Arrange the cucumber rings round the edge of a serving plate and fill them with the cucumber and apple mixture. Pile any extra mixture in the centre of the plate. Garnish each one with a cucumber slice, cut into a twist, just before serving.

For cucumber rings, cut into 5cm (2 in) slices, then scoop out all the seeds.

Imam Bayeldi

This dish is also very good served cold, without the cheese topping.

Serves 4

CALORIES PER PORTION: 135 (570 kJ)
PROTEIN CONTENT PER PORTION: 1 gram
PREPARATION & COOKING TIME: 2 hours

*2 aubergines, weighing about 225 g
  (8 oz) each
salt
3-4 tablespoons olive or sunflower oil
¼ teaspoon ground cumin
½ teaspoon ground coriander
a sprinkling of freshly ground pepper
50 g (2 oz) coarsely chopped onion
100 g (4 oz) skinned tomatoes, coarsely
  chopped
25 g (1 oz) sultanas
1 clove of garlic, peeled and finely
  chopped
4 tablespoons tomato paste (optional)
100 g (4 oz) grated Cheddar cheese
  (optional)*

Cut the stems from the aubergines and then slice the aubergines in half lengthways. Using a teaspoon, carefully scoop out the flesh to leave a shell about 5 mm (¼ in) thick. Sprinkle salt over the shells and the flesh and place in a colander to drain for 30 minutes. Rinse and dry well.

Set the oven at 200°C (400°F) Gas 6. Heat the oil, add the cumin, coriander and pepper and cook for about a minute, then add the onion and fry it gently until transparent. Cut the aubergine flesh into small chunks, add these to the onion and fry until they are almost soft. Put in the tomatoes, sultanas and garlic and continue cooking until the tomatoes have almost broken down into a purée. If the mixture seems too dry, add up to 4 tablespoons of tomato paste.

Fill the aubergine shells, sprinkle the grated cheese over the tops, if using, and place them in a baking dish.

Bake the aubergines on the top shelf of the pre-heated oven for about 40 minutes.

Note: Crumpled foil arranged in the baking dish will prevent the aubergines from tilting sideways while they are cooking.

Asparagus au gratin

Serves 4

CALORIES PER PORTION: 190 (795 kJ)
PROTEIN CONTENT PER PORTION: 10 grams
PREPARATION & COOKING TIME: 25-30 minutes

*350 g (12 oz) trimmed fresh asparagus
25 g (1 oz) butter
20 g (¾ oz) wholemeal flour
300 ml (½ pint) milk
50 g (2 oz) grated Cheddar cheese
salt
freshly ground pepper
¼ teaspoon grated lemon rind
about 2 tablespoons finely crumbled
  fresh wholemeal breadcrumbs*

Tie the asparagus in bundles, stand them upright in a tall, deep pan and cook them in a little boiling, salted water, with the asparagus heads in the steam for 15-20 minutes, or until the shoots are tender. While the asparagus is cooking, make the sauce.

Melt the butter in a small pan over moderate heat, stir in the flour and continue stirring until it thickens. Remove the pan from the heat, add the milk gradually, stirring well between each addition. Return the pan to the stove and bring to the boil, stirring continuously until the sauce thickens. Now beat in most of the cheese, season with salt and pepper and add the lemon rind.

Divide the asparagus between four individual flameproof gratin dishes and pour a little of the sauce over each, leaving part of the stems uncoated. Sprinkle with the breadcrumbs and the remaining cheese and place under a hot grill until the top is golden brown and bubbling. Serve immediately.

Note: Frozen or canned asparagus may also be used in this recipe, which also makes a good vegetable dish to follow a main course.

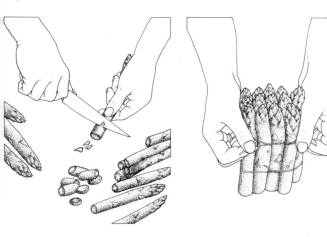

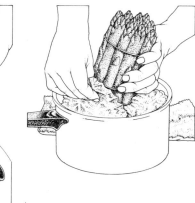

1. Remove any woody stem bases. These cannot be eaten but can be used to flavour stock. Trim the asparagus to a uniform length to fit the pan.

2. Tie the asparagus at top and bottom with thin string. 3. Stand upright in a tall pan, making sure the lid fits comfortably over the heads.

4. If you do not own a suitable tall pan, use foil balls to stand the stems upright, then make a huge foil dome over the whole pan and tie it with string.

Asparagus crêpes

Serves 4
CALORIES PER PORTION: 600 (2525 kJ)
PROTEIN CONTENT PER PORTION: 26 grams
PREPARATION & COOKING TIME: 45 minutes

8 crêpes made from the Basic recipe
  (page 82)
16 fresh or canned asparagus spears
40 g (1½ oz) butter
25 g (1 oz) wholemeal flour
400 ml (¾ pint) milk
175 g (6 oz) grated Cheddar cheese
salt
freshly ground pepper
½ teaspoon English mustard powder

Tie the asparagus in two bundles, stand them upright in a tall, deep pan and cook them in a little boiling salted water with the heads in the steam for 15-20 minutes, or until the shoots are tender. While the asparagus is cooking, make the sauce.

Melt the butter in a pan over moderate heat. Stir in the flour and continue stirring until it thickens. Remove the pan from the heat, gradually add the milk, stirring well between each addition. Return the pan to the stove and bring to the boil, stirring continuously until the sauce thickens. Beat in half the cheese, season well with salt and pepper and add the mustard. Lower the heat and simmer the sauce for 2 minutes, stirring all the time.

Place two drained asparagus spears on each crêpe and pour over 2 tablespoons of the cheese sauce. Roll up the crêpes and arrange them, side by side, in an oven-proof dish. Sprinkle the reserved grated cheese over the top and place under a hot grill until the cheese on the top is golden-brown and bubbling. Serve at once.

Artichokes with rosemary sauce

Serves 4
CALORIES PER PORTION: 285 (1992 kJ)
PROTEIN CONTENT PER PORTION: 4 grams
PREPARATION & COOKING TIME: 1½ hours

4 globe artichokes, well washed
salt
4 cloves of garlic, peeled and coarsely
  chopped
3-4 sprigs of rosemary
300 ml (½ pint) Béarnaise sauce (page
  195), with 2 teaspoons finely chopped
  rosemary added to the onion and
  vinegar at the beginning and ½
  teaspoon at the end, after straining
  the sauce

Break off the stems of the artichokes and trim the points of the leaves. Place the artichokes in a pan just large enough to hold them and add water to come almost halfway up their sides. Add salt, garlic and sprigs of rosemary and bring the water to the boil. (There should be enough rosemary to flavour the water strongly.) Cover the pan, lower the heat and simmer for 30-40 minutes, or until an artichoke leaf will pull out easily. Meanwhile, make the sauce, following the recipe given on page 195.

Turn the artichokes upside-down and leave for 5 minutes to drain. Right them and carefully remove the spiky leaves from the centre, then scoop out and discard the hairy choke (see page 111). Arrange each artichoke on a serving dish and fill the centre with rosemary-flavoured Béarnaise sauce. Hand the rest of the sauce separately.

Favourite hot starters. Back:
Artichoke with rosemary sauce,
adapted from a classic Italian recipe.
Front: Imam Bayeldi, a variation on
the famous Turkish stuffed aubergine
dish. Right: Russian-style Blinis,
served here with egg, onion and cream

Blinis with egg, onion and sour cream

Serves 4
CALORIES PER PORTION: 285 (1185 kJ)
PROTEIN CONTENT PER PORTION: 10.5 grams
PREPARATION & COOKING TIME: 1½ hours

50 g (2 oz) buckwheat flour
50 g (2 oz) unbleached plain white flour
¼ teaspoon salt
10 g (⅓ oz) fresh yeast
150 ml (¼ pint) lukewarm milk and
  water, mixed
1 egg, separated
1 tablespoon melted butter
1 tablespoon oil, or clarified butter

The accompaniments
2 hard-boiled eggs, shelled, chopped
  and chilled well
10-12 spring onions, chopped and
  chilled well
150 ml (¼ pint) cultured sour cream,
  chilled well

Mix the flours together in a bowl and add the salt. Mix the yeast to a cream with a little of the lukewarm milk and water before adding the remainder of the liquid. Stir the yeast liquid into the flours to make a smooth batter and set aside in a warm place for about 30 minutes, or until it has turned frothy and risen to about twice its original volume. (The eggs can be hard boiled and the onions chopped and put to chill while the batter rises.)

When the batter is ready, 'knock down' the dough and lightly whisk in the egg yolk mixed with the melted butter. Beat the egg white until stiff and then fold in.

Heat a griddle or thick-based frying pan over a low-to-moderate heat. Brush the griddle or pan with the oil or clarified butter — if using butter, do not allow it to burn. Spoon the batter on to the hot surface, about 2 tablespoons at a time, to make Blinis of about 10 cm (4 in) in size. When the mixture sets and the surface is covered with broken bubbles, turn over and cook on the other side until lightly browned. Keep the cooked Blinis warm. Serve the chilled chopped eggs, onion and cultured sour cream as accompaniments in separate bowls.

Each guest helps himself to a hot Blini, covers it with egg, onion and sour cream, then places another Blini on top.

Oeufs mollets in artichoke hearts

Serves 4
CALORIES PER PORTION: 380 (1592 kJ)
PROTEIN CONTENT PER PORTION: 17 grams
PREPARATION & COOKING TIME: 65 minutes

4 Oeufs mollets (page 72)
4 globe artichokes, well washed
300 ml (½ pint) thick Cheese sauce
   (page 196)
salt
freshly ground pepper
4 slices of wholemeal bread, crusts
   removed and fried in butter (croûtes)
1 tablespoon finely chopped parsley

Break off stems and put the artichokes in a pan just large enough to hold them, adding water to come almost halfway up their sides. Bring to the boil, add salt, turn down the heat and simmer the artichokes gently for about 30-40 minutes, or until a leaf pulls out easily. Make the Cheese sauce while the artichokes are cooking; cover with buttered greaseproof paper and keep warm in a double boiler.

Meanwhile, prepare the Oeufs mollets, and keep them warm in a bowl of hot water. Drain the artichokes well, then scrape off the soft portion at the base of each leaf and rub this through a sieve. Stir the artichoke purée into the Cheese sauce, season to taste and keep hot.

Discard the hairy chokes from the artichokes and set aside the hearts, making sure they sit level by cutting off any bumps or pieces of stem from the base with a sharp knife.

Put the four bread croûtes on warmed serving plates, place an artichoke heart on each, then pour over a little of the hot sauce. Place an egg on top, then coat it with the remaining sauce. Sprinkle with a little parsley before serving.

Sambusak

Serves 4
CALORIES PER PORTION: 645 (2692 kJ)
PROTEIN CONTENT PER PORTION: 16 grams
PREPARATION & COOKING TIME: 1½ hours

The filling
1 tablespoon olive or sunflower oil
100 g (4 oz) finely chopped onion
1 teaspoon ground cumin, or to taste
350 g (12 oz) cooked fresh or frozen
   peas
salt
freshly ground pepper
oil for deep frying

The pastry
300 g (10 oz) wholemeal or unbleached
   white flour
½ teaspoon salt
150 ml (¼ pint) olive or sunflower oil
150 ml (¼ pint) water
1 egg, lightly beaten

To make the filling, heat the oil and fry the onion and cumin in it until the onion is lightly browned. Add the peas, salt and a very little water. Cook, stirring frequently, until the peas are soft, then mash them into a thick, coarse-textured purée. Adjust seasoning; set aside until cold.

For the pastry, sieve the flour into a bowl and add the salt. Mix the oil with about two-thirds of the water and pour this into the flour. Mix to a firm dough, adding a little more of the water if necessary. Knead lightly and then roll out as thinly as possible.

Using a 75 mm (3 in) diameter pastry cutter, cut into rounds. Put a teaspoon of filling in the centre of each and brush the edges with the beaten egg. Seal the edges together firmly and deep fry in hot oil at 180°C (350°F) until crisp and golden brown. Drain well and serve hot.

Ratatouille

Serves 4
CALORIES PER PORTION: 165 (695 kJ)
PROTEIN CONTENT PER PORTION: 2 grams
PREPARATION & COOKING TIME: 2¼ hours
  (including salting the courgettes and aubergines)

225 g (8 oz) sliced courgettes
225 g (8 oz) aubergines, quartered and sliced
salt
125 g (4 oz) thinly sliced onion
4 tablespoons olive or sunflower oil
350 g (12 oz) skinned tomatoes, coarsely chopped
225 g (8 oz) thinly sliced green peppers
1 large clove of garlic, peeled and finely chopped
freshly ground black pepper

Sprinkle the courgettes and aubergines with salt and leave for about an hour, then rinse and pat dry with a kitchen cloth or kitchen paper. Cook the onion in half the oil until transparent, then add the courgettes and fry them, without browning, for about 10 minutes.

Meanwhile, fry the aubergines in the remaining oil in a separate pan, turning the slices over from time to time until they are just beginning to colour. Add the tomatoes to the onion and courgettes and, when the tomatoes have cooked down to a pulp, add the green peppers, cooked aubergines and the garlic. Season to taste. Simmer gently for about an hour, until the Ratatouille has become a thick, pulpy mass.

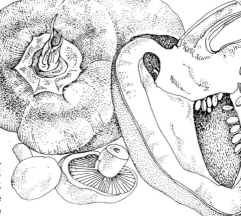

Mushrooms with garlic butter

Serves 4
CALORIES PER PORTION: 255 (1055 kJ)
PROTEIN CONTENT PER PORTION: 2 grams
PREPARATION & COOKING TIME: 30 minutes

350 g (12 oz) coarsely chopped mushrooms
125 g (generous 4 oz) butter, plus 1-2 tablespoons
1-2 cloves of garlic, peeled and finely chopped
2 tablespoons lemon juice
50 g (2 oz) fresh wholemeal breadcrumbs
1 tablespoon chopped parsley

Heat almost all of the butter in a pan and fry the mushrooms over moderate heat until soft and shiny and their juices have almost completely evaporated. Remove from the heat and stir in the garlic and lemon juice. Divide between four small ramekins or individual ovenproof dishes.

Set the oven at 200°C (400°F) Gas 6. Fry the breadcrumbs in the remaining butter, in a thick-based pan until crisp and golden brown. Stir frequently to stop the crumbs from sticking and burning. Add the parsley, mix well and sprinkle the mixture over the mushrooms. Press down lightly with a fork and bake on the top shelf of the pre-heated oven for 10 minutes before serving

Onion croustades

Serves 4
CALORIES PER PORTION: 350 (1465 kJ)
PROTEIN CONTENT PER PORTION: 20 grams
PREPARATION & COOKING TIME: 40 minutes

12 pickling onions
salt
300 ml (½ pint) Béchamel sauce (page 196)
2-3 tablespoons clarified butter (page 198)
4 large thick slices of wholemeal bread, crusts removed
1 teaspoon Meaux, or other French-style mustard
a few drops of Tabasco sauce
freshly ground pepper
225 g (8 oz) cubed Edam or Emmenthal cheese

Peel the pickling onions, drop them into a pan of boiling salted water and cook them for 10-12 minutes, or until soft. Make the Béchamel sauce. Using a 75 mm (3 in) diameter pastry cutter, cut a circle out of the centre of each slice of bread. Heat the clarified butter in a pan and fry the bread circles and the off-cuts until crisp and golden brown. Drain well and keep them hot on a serving dish. Heat up the Béchamel sauce, and add the mustard and Tabasco; season with salt and pepper. Put in the cheese cubes and the cooked onions and mix gently into the sauce.

Spoon some of the mixture into the centre of each of the fried bread slices and top with the fried bread circles. Sprinkle with a little salt and serve immediately.

Stuffed onions with oriental rice

Serves 4
CALORIES PER PORTION: 230 (1222 kJ)
PROTEIN CONTENT PER PORTION: 9 grams
PREPARATION & COOKING TIME: 45 minutes

4 onions, weighing about 100 g (4 oz) each
salt
½ teaspoon ground turmeric
2 teaspoons olive or sunflower oil
15 g (½ oz) butter
2 eggs, well beaten
1 teaspoon lemon juice
200 ml (⅓ pint) natural yoghurt

The rice
4 cardamoms
½-1 teaspoon ground turmeric
½-1 teaspoon ground cumin
1 tablespoon olive or sunflower oil
450 g (1 lb) boiled brown rice — about 225 g (8 oz) uncooked

Cook the peeled onions in boiling salted water for 5 minutes, then drain and cool. Cut each in half across the rings and remove the centres, leaving the two outer layers as a shell. Chop the onion centres finely.

Split the cardamoms, remove the seeds and crush them with the turmeric and cumin, then heat them with the oil for about 1 minute. Add the cooked rice and mix very thoroughly until it is really heated through. Keep it hot until ready to serve.

Heat the turmeric in the 2 teaspoons of oil and the butter and fry the chopped onion in it until it is golden brown. Add the eggs and lemon juice and scramble them quickly. Spoon this spiced egg mixture into the onion shells.

Arrange the rice on a warmed serving dish and place the stuffed onions on top and serve at once with natural yoghurt as a sauce.

Individual cheese custards

Serves 4
CALORIES PER PORTION: 360 (1505 kJ)
PROTEIN CONTENT PER PORTION: 15 grams
PREPARATION & COOKING TIME: 1½ hours

50 g (2 oz) grated strong cheese
1 teaspoon butter
1 teaspoon finely chopped onion
1 teaspoon wholemeal flour
100 ml (4 fl oz) single cream
2 eggs
2 egg yolks
300 ml (½ pint) milk
300 ml (½ pint) Béchamel sauce (page 196)
a sprinkling of paprika
sprigs of parsley, to garnish

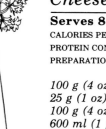

Melt the butter in a small pan over moderate heat and fry the onion until transparent. Sprinkle in the flour and stir until the onion is well coated, then remove the pan from the heat and gradually stir in the cream. Return the pan to the heat and bring the sauce to the boil, stirring until it thickens. Add the cheese and stir until thoroughly melted. Remove the pan from the heat and let the mixture cool slightly.

Beat together the eggs, egg yolks and milk in a bowl. Stir this into the cheese mixture, then pour it all through a sieve into 4 well-buttered ramekins or small ovenproof dishes. Place these in a pan and pour in enough boiling water to come about one-third of the way up the dishes. Cover the pan with a tight-fitting lid and place over moderate heat. Cook the custards for about 15 minutes, or until they are set, then remove the dishes from the pan and allow the custards to cool.

Set the oven at 200°C (400°F) Gas 6, and heat up the Béchamel sauce. Carefully turn the custards out of their dishes on to an ovenproof platter and coat each with hot Béchamel sauce. Bake in the preheated oven for 10-15 minutes until the custards are lightly browned on top and the sauce is sizzling.

Sprinkle with a little paprika, garnish with parsley sprigs and serve.

Cheese beignets

Serves 8
CALORIES PER PORTION: 253 (1058 kJ)
PROTEIN CONTENT PER PORTION: 10 grams
PREPARATION & COOKING TIME: 1¼ hours

100 g (4 oz) grated Cheddar cheese
25 g (1 oz) butter
100 g (4 oz) finely chopped onion
600 ml (1 pint) milk
1 teaspoon salt
1 bay leaf
75 g (3 oz) polenta
1 egg, well beaten
150-300 ml (¼-½ pint) Coating batter (page 194)
oil for deep frying

Melt the butter in a pan over gentle heat, add the onion and fry until golden brown. Add the milk, salt and bay leaf and bring to the boil. Pour in the polenta, lower the heat and let it simmer for 5 minutes, stirring all the time. Remove the pan from the heat and gradually stir in the cheese, then beat in the egg.

Pour the mixture on to an oiled work surface, spreading the paste out to a little over 1 cm (½ in) thick and neatening the edges. Leave until cold.

Cut the paste into 5 cm (2 in) squares and coat each with the batter. Heat the oil to 180°C (350°F), add the squares a few at a time and deep fry until golden brown. Remove them from the pan with a draining spoon and drain well on kitchen paper. Keep them hot while frying the remainder. Serve as soon as possible after cooking.

Eggs soubise

Serves 4
CALORIES PER PORTION: 255 (1072 kJ)
PROTEIN CONTENT PER PORTION: 11 grams
PREPARATION & COOKING TIME: 40-45 minutes

4 Oeufs mollets (page 72)
50 g (2 oz) butter
225 g (8 oz) finely chopped onions
25 g (1 oz) wholemeal flour
300 ml (½ pint) milk
a pinch of freshly grated nutmeg
salt
freshly ground pepper
100 g (4 oz) thinly sliced button mushrooms
4 slices of wholemeal bread, crusts removed and fried in a little extra butter (croûtes)
4 tablespoons grated Cheddar cheese

Melt half of the butter over gentle heat, add the onions and fry until golden brown, stirring frequently so they do not stick. Sprinkle in the flour and cook for 1-2 minutes, stirring all the time. Remove the pan from the heat and gradually pour in the milk, stirring well between each addition. Return the pan to the stove, increase the heat and bring the sauce to the boil, stirring all the time until it thickens.

Pour the sauce into a blender and work at high speed until it is completely smooth. Now return the sauce to the rinsed out pan, add the nutmeg and season well with salt and pepper. Stand the pan in a larger pan almost full of boiling water, or transfer the sauce to a double boiler. Cover the surface of the sauce with a sheet of greaseproof paper to prevent a skin forming and leave to stand for about 20 minutes to allow the sauce to mature.

Meanwhile, prepare the Oeufs mollets and keep them warm in a bowl of very hot water. Make the bread croûtes, if not already prepared. Melt the remaining butter in a small pan over gentle heat. Add the mushrooms and cook them for 1-2 minutes, stirring them frequently. Keep them hot while you place the bread croûtes on a warmed heatproof plate, put a drained egg on each slice and coat with the onion (soubise) sauce.

Sprinkle the cheese on top, then put the plate under a very hot grill to melt the cheese slightly. Garnish with the mushrooms before serving.

Crudités and Savoury dips

Serve a platter of diced or sliced raw vegetables (crudités) as well as the more usual cubes or strips of bread or toast, potato crisps or biscuits, with hot or cold party dips. For 4 servings, choose about 450 g (1 lb) of mixed vegetables; double the amount for 8 people.

As an alternative, these fresh Crudités are delicious served with a bowl of thick Mayonnaise or Aioli (page 126).

Hummus

Serves up to 8
TOTAL CALORIES: 2290 (9570 kJ)
TOTAL PROTEIN CONTENT: 27 grams
PREPARATION TIME: 30 minutes

225 g (8 oz) cooked chick peas
150 ml (¼ pint) tahina paste
150 ml (¼ pint) olive or sunflower oil,
 plus 3 tablespoons
1-2 cloves of garlic, peeled and chopped
6-8 tablespoons lemon juice
1 tablespoon chopped mint or parsley
1 teaspoon paprika

Put the chick peas in a blender with the tahina paste, oil, 150 ml (¼ pint) water, garlic, lemon juice and mint or parsley. Work to a thick purée, adding a little more water by degrees — Hummus should be of a thick coating consistency.

Alternatively, pound the chick peas and garlic to a paste with pestle and mortar before slowly mixing in the other ingredients, lastly adding the water by degrees, to reach the correct consistency.

Spoon the Hummus into a shallow round dish. Mix the paprika into the remaining 3 tablespoons of oil and pour this over the Hummus. Stir the top into a spiral pattern. Serve with Pitta bread.

Horseradish and peanut

Serves up to 8
TOTAL CALORIES: 800 (3355 kJ)
TOTAL PROTEIN CONTENT: 27 grams
PREPARATION TIME: 5-10 minutes

100 g (4 oz) salted peanuts
2 tablespoons grated horseradish, or 2-3
 tablespoons horseradish cream
150 ml (¼ pint) double cream

Place the peanuts in a blender and work until they are finely chopped. Add the horseradish and double cream, and work until you have a thick, fairly smooth dip. Serve with potato crisps and celery sticks.

Avocado

Serves up to 8
TOTAL CALORIES: 930 (3890 kJ)
TOTAL PROTEIN CONTENT: 19 grams
PREPARATION & CHILLING TIME: 1½ hours

2 avocados
2 tablespoons onion juice (see page 55)
3 tablespoons lemon juice
salt and freshly ground pepper
1 tablespoon chopped parsley

Peel and stone the avocados and mash them with a stainless steel fork. Stir in the onion juice, 2 tablespoons of the lemon juice and season to taste. Work the mixture in a blender until very smooth, or rub it through a sieve to a purée.

Pile the dip into a serving bowl. Pour a little extra lemon juice over the top to prevent discoloration and chill well. Garnish with chopped parsley.

Curried cheese

Serves up to 8
TOTAL CALORIES: 270 (1300 kJ)
TOTAL PROTEIN CONTENT: 32 grams
PREPARATION TIME: 10-15 minutes

225 g (8 oz) curd cheese
1-2 teaspoons curry powder, or to taste
2 tablespoons onion juice (see page 55)
1 tablespoon pineapple juice
2 tablespoons crushed pineapple
1 clove of garlic, peeled and crushed
1-2 tablespoons milk
salt and a sprinkling of cayenne

Thoroughly mix all the ingredients, adding just enough milk to make a thick coating consistency. Adjust the seasoning, sprinkle with cayenne, and serve.

Spicy pineapple

Serves 4-6
CALORIES PER PORTION: 100 (417 kJ)
PROTEIN CONTENT PER PORTION: 1 gram
PREPARATION TIME: 20-30 minutes

225 g (8 oz) chopped pineapple
225 g (8 oz) finely chopped onions
2 tablespoons olive or sunflower oil
1 teaspoon ground cinnamon
salt and chilli powder to taste
1 tablespoon wine, or cider, vinegar

Fry the pineapple and onions in the oil until golden brown. Drain off any excess oil and work the pineapple and onion in a blender with the cinnamon, salt, chilli powder and vinegar to a smooth purée.

Masur dhal

Serves 6-8
TOTAL CALORIES: 425 (1785 kJ)
TOTAL PROTEIN CONTENT: 11 grams
PREPARATION & COOKING TIME: 1 hour

125 g (4 oz) cooked red lentils
½ teaspoon salt
1 teaspoon ground cumin
½ teaspoon ground turmeric
½ teaspoon finely ground fenugreek
½ teaspoon mustard seeds
2 tablespoons olive or sunflower oil
225 g (8 oz) finely chopped onions
⅛-¼ teaspoon chilli powder (optional)
2-4 green chillis, finely chopped

Heat the spices in the oil until they give off a strong aroma. Add the onions and fry over moderate heat until they are soft and golden brown. Add the cooked lentils and enough water for a thick sauce.

Adjust the seasoning and, if you want a 'hotter' dhal, stir in a little chilli powder mixed with a little more oil. Serve hot, sprinkled with chopped green chillis.

Note: If you have any left over, reheat it and add a little creamed coconut.

Savoury tomato

Serves 6
CALORIES PER PORTION: 220 (930 kJ)
PROTEIN CONTENT PER PORTION: 11 grams
PREPARATION TIME: 45-60 minutes

1 kg (2¼ lb) ripe tomatoes, coarsely
 chopped
225 g (8 oz) thinly sliced onions
2 cloves of garlic, peeled and finely
 chopped
6 cardamoms
½-1 teaspoon ground cumin
1 bay leaf
salt and freshly ground pepper
1 tablespoon wine vinegar
1 teaspoon raw brown sugar
a few drops Worcestershire sauce
a little chilli powder, to taste

Place the tomatoes and onions in a thick-based pan over gentle heat. Add the garlic, the seeds from the cardamoms, the cumin, bay leaf and salt and pepper to taste. Cook gently for 25-30 minutes until the mixture forms a thick purée, stirring occasionally.

Rub the purée through a sieve into a clean pan and add the vinegar, brown sugar, Worcestershire sauce and chilli powder. Bring the mixture to the boil, adjust the seasoning, reduce the mixture by boiling a little longer; pour into a heated serving bowl.

Eggs and Cheese

From the ubiquitous bread-and-cheese and the simple
breakfast egg to the culinary pinnacle of a superbly
risen cheese soufflé, golden-crusted on the outside,
irresistibly creamy on the inside – each is a part of the
great tradition created by these two basic and protein-
rich foods.

So many of the world's most famous dishes have eggs
and cheese as their starting point.

When you have tried the following recipes – and they
make excellent luncheon dishes, light suppers or, in
the case of a soufflé or quiche, delicious dinner party
starters – follow the example of the Swiss and hold a
winter 'raclette' party. Place a large wedge of cheese,
preferably Gruyère, close to an open fire; as it softens,
cut off slices of melted cheese and serve with hot
potatoes boiled in their skins, accompanied by pickled
cucumbers. A speciality of Valais; a perfect meal . . .

Omelettes

Many people think that some mysterious talent is required to make a good omelette, or that some secret recipe exists which will ensure success every time. This is not true. The basic ingredients for a plain omelette are simply eggs, butter, salt and pepper. There is no mystery or secret recipe, but a few simple rules should be followed.

Always use a thick-based, smooth-surfaced iron pan so that the omelette will cook evenly and will not stick. Do not overbeat the eggs until they are frothy — beat them only enough to break the whites and thoroughly mix them into the yolks. Use plenty of the best unsalted butter to oil the pan before cooking the omelette, but pour away any excess before actually beginning to cook. A perfect omelette should be golden brown and almost crisp on the outside, yet still just liquid on the inside so that it provides its own sauce.

Any evenly diced, cooked vegetables — potatoes, peas, carrots, even nuts — may be added with a sprinkling of herbs as a filling, before folding the omelette over to serve it. It is important to see the vegetables are evenly diced, as it makes such a difference to the finished dish.

Plain omelette

Serves 1
CALORIES: 275 (1150 kJ)
PROTEIN CONTENT: 14 grams
PREPARATION & COOKING TIME: 5 minutes

2 eggs
salt
freshly ground pepper
15 g (½ oz) clarified or unsalted butter

Put the eggs in a bowl, add salt and pepper to taste and beat the eggs lightly just to mix them.

Melt the butter quickly in a 15 cm (6 in) thick-based frying pan over a moderate-to-high heat until it is on the point of turning brown. Pour in the eggs and let them cook for a few moments, then tilt the pan and lift the omelette at one edge with a spatula to allow the uncooked mixture to run underneath. Repeat this two or three more times until most of the uncooked mixture has disappeared.

When the surface of the omelette is beginning to set, but still looks a little liquid, tilt the pan and fold the omelette in half with the spatula. Slide it onto a warmed serving plate and serve immediately. Never keep an omelette waiting!

Note: With practice, and enough utensils, it is possible to make 4 omelettes at the same time. Beat the eggs and salt and pepper in four separate bowls. Heat the pans on the stove, making sure you have equal heat under all 4 pans. Add a little butter to each pan and allow it to melt. Pour the eggs into each pan in the same order as you mixed them, then cook as for individual Plain omelette in turn.

Cheese omelette

Serves 1
CALORIES: 375 (1580 kJ)
PROTEIN CONTENT: 20 grams
PREPARATION & COOKING TIME: 5 minutes

Follow the basic method for Plain omelette, sprinkling on 25 g (1 oz) grated Cheddar cheese just before folding the omelette in half. Serve immediately, or the cheese will go stringy.

A tablespoon of chopped fresh herbs may also be added.

Sweetcorn omelette

Serves 1
CALORIES: 425 (1770 kJ)
PROTEIN CONTENT: 15 grams
PREPARATION & COOKING TIME: 10 minutes

50 g (2 oz) cooked sweetcorn kernels
15 g (½ oz) clarified or unsalted butter

Melt the butter in a pan over gentle heat, add the sweetcorn and cook gently for 4-5 minutes until tender. The buttery flavour of the corn should be perfect on its own, without extra seasoning.

Make a Plain omelette and sprinkle the sweetcorn over just before folding the omelette in half. Serve immediately.

Spring onion omelette

Serves 1
CALORIES: 465 (1940 kJ)
PROTEIN CONTENT: 14 grams
PREPARATION & COOKING TIME: 15 minutes

50 g (2 oz) finely chopped spring onions
15 g (½) butter
1 tablespoon double cream
½ teaspoon finely chopped thyme

Melt the butter over gentle heat, add the spring onions and cook until tender, without letting them colour. Pour on the cream, add the thyme and continue cooking until thick and well blended. Remove the pan from the heat and keep hot.

Make a Plain omelette and spread the spring onion mixture down the centre just before folding the omelette in half.

Pipérade

Serves 4
CALORIES PER PORTION: 365 (1520 kJ)
PROTEIN CONTENT PER PORTION: 11.5 grams
PREPARATION & COOKING TIME: 20 minutes

450 g (1 lb) diced red peppers
4 tablespoons olive or sunflower oil
450 g (1 lb) peeled and quartered
  tomatoes
salt
freshly ground pepper
6 eggs
4 slices of wholemeal bread, crusts
  removed, cut across into triangles and
  fried in a little butter (croûtes)

Gently heat the oil in a pan, add the peppers and fry them for 5 minutes. Add the tomatoes and continue cooking until the juices have almost boiled away and it has cooked down to a purée. Season with salt and pepper.

Put the eggs in a bowl, add salt and pepper to taste and beat them well. Pour this on to the purée and continue cooking, stirring continuously until the eggs have scrambled into the pepper and tomato mixture. Transfer the Pipérade to a warmed serving dish, arrange the fried bread croûtes around the edge and serve immediately.

Omelette paysanne

Serves 4
CALORIES PER PORTION: 360 (1507 kJ)
PROTEIN CONTENT PER PORTION: 16 grams
PREPARATION & COOKING TIME: 30 minutes

450 g (1 lb) finely diced potatoes
50 g (2 oz) clarified or unsalted butter
100 g (4 oz) finely chopped onion
salt
freshly ground pepper
8 eggs

Melt the butter in a 20 cm (8 in) diameter thick-based frying pan over gentle heat, add the potatoes and fry for about 15 minutes until they are nearly cooked through. Cover the pan for the first half of the cooking time, but stir and turn the potatoes occasionally to prevent them sticking. Add the onion and continue cooking for about 5 minutes. By this time the potatoes should be quite tender and the onion transparent. Sprinkle liberally with salt and pepper.

Put the eggs in a bowl with plenty of salt and pepper. Beat them lightly to mix, then pour them over the potatoes. Stir, as though making scrambled eggs, until most of the liquid has set. Place a large, warmed serving plate over the top of the frying pan and carefully turn the pan upside down so that the omelette lands on the plate. Serve at once.

Omelette in tomato sauce

Serves 4
CALORIES PER PORTION: 270 (1135 kJ)
PROTEIN CONTENT PER PORTION: 15.5 grams
PREPARATION & COOKING TIME: 30 minutes

40 g (1½ oz) clarified or unsalted
  butter
100 g (4 oz) finely chopped onion
1 clove of garlic, peeled and crushed
15 g (½ oz) wholemeal flour
salt and freshly ground pepper
450 g (1 lb) coarsely chopped tomatoes
200 ml (⅓ pint) red wine
8 eggs
1 tablespoon finely chopped fennel or
  basil (optional)

Melt 25 g (1 oz) of the butter in a frying pan over gentle heat, add the onion and garlic and cook until transparent but not browned. Add the flour, season with salt and pepper and stir continuously until all the butter has been absorbed. Now add the tomatoes and cook them for 1-2 minutes, stirring to prevent them sticking and burning. Pour in the wine, stir well and bring to the boil, then lower the heat and let the mixture simmer until the sauce thickens. Continue cooking, stirring occasionally, for 15-20 minutes until any taste of uncooked flour has gone.

Meanwhile, make a firm Plain omelette with the rest of the butter and the eggs. Season with salt and pepper. (Cook this in two stages if necessary.)

When the omelette is cooked, cut it into thick slices and place them side by side in a warmed serving dish. Strain on the sauce, turning the omelette slices over so that they are really well coated. Sprinkle with the fennel or basil and serve immediately with cooked brown rice or plainly boiled new potatoes and a salad.

Omelette aux fines herbes

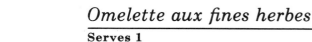

Serves 1
CALORIES: 275 (1150 kJ)
PROTEIN CONTENT: 14 grams
PREPARATION & COOKING TIME: 10 minutes

1 tablespoon finely chopped mixed
  fresh herbs, (parsley, chervil,
  watercress, tarragon)
15 g (½ oz) clarified or unsalted butter
2 eggs

Make a Plain omelette following the basic method, but adding half the herbs to the uncooked egg mixture. Sprinkle the remaining herbs over the cooked omelette just before folding it in half and serving with a pat of Herb butter (page 198).

Basic cheese soufflé

Serves 4
CALORIES PER PORTION: 275 (1162 kJ)
PROTEIN CONTENT PER PORTION: 17.5 grams
PREPARATION & COOKING TIME: 35-40 minutes

100 g (4 oz) grated Cheddar cheese
40 g (1½ oz) butter
25 g (1 oz) wholemeal flour
200 ml (⅓ pint) milk
salt
freshly ground black pepper
a pinch of freshly grated nutmeg
*   (optional)*
4 egg yolks
5 egg whites

Melt about 25 g (1 oz) of the butter in a pan over gentle heat, then sprinkle in the flour. Cook for 1-2 minutes, stirring continuously until it thickens, then remove the pan from the heat and gradually add the milk, stirring well between each addition. Return the pan to the stove, increase the heat and bring it to the boil, stirring all the time until the sauce thickens.

Remove the pan from the stove, beat in the cheese and add salt and pepper to taste, and a pinch of nutmeg, if liked. Leave this to cool slightly before adding the egg yolks and stirring them well into the mixture. Set the oven at 200°C (400°F) Gas 6 and put a 1½ litre (3 pint) capacity soufflé dish to warm.

Whisk the egg whites until they stand in stiff peaks. Pour half the cheese sauce on top of the egg whites, then fold in from the bottom to the top until thoroughly combined. Fold in the remaining cheese sauce in the same way.

Melt the remaining butter and quickly brush the inside of the soufflé dish before pouring in the soufflé mixture. Draw a circle in the top of the mixture about halfway from the edge, using a knife brushed with a little extra melted butter — this will produce the raised 'top hat' effect when the soufflé is cooked.

Bake on the middle shelf of the preheated oven for about 20 minutes if you like the centre of the soufflé to be semi-liquid, or for 25 minutes if a drier soufflé is preferred. Serve immediately.

Spinach soufflé

Serves 4
CALORIES PER PORTION: 470 (1232 kJ)
PROTEIN CONTENT PER PORTION: 20.5 grams
PREPARATION & COOKING TIME: 45 minutes

225 g (8 oz) cooked spinach, chopped
*   and well drained*

Follow the basic recipe for Cheese soufflé, adding the spinach to the sauce just before the cheese.

Note: If a smooth-textured soufflé is preferred, purée the spinach after draining.

Courgette soufflé

Serves 4
CALORIES PER PORTION: 335 (1392 kJ)
PROTEIN CONTENT PER PORTION: 18 grams
PREPARATION & COOKING TIME: 50 minutes

225 g (8 oz) thinly sliced courgettes
25 g (1 oz) butter

Melt the butter in a pan over gentle heat, add the courgettes and cook until they are soft and most of the juices have evaporated. Remove the courgettes from the pan and mash them to a purée.

Follow the basic recipe for Cheese soufflé, adding the mashed courgettes to the sauce just before the cheese.

Sweetcorn soufflé

Serves 4
CALORIES PER PORTION: 320 (1340 kJ)
PROTEIN CONTENT PER PORTION: 19 grams
PREPARATION & COOKING TIME: 35-40 minutes

225 g (8 oz) sweetcorn kernels

Follow the basic recipe for Cheese soufflé, adding the sweetcorn to the 25 g (1 oz) melted butter in the pan before sprinkling in the flour. Cook until the sweetcorn is tender before adding the milk.

Scrambled egg with asparagus

Serves 4
CALORIES PER PORTION: 405 (1695 kJ)
PROTEIN CONTENT PER PORTION: 13 grams
PREPARATION & COOKING TIME: 30 minutes

4 eggs
450 g (1 lb) trimmed fresh asparagus, or
*   the same quantity of frozen or*
*   canned*
225 g (8 oz) onions, cut into rings
2 tablespoons olive or sunflower oil
salt
freshly ground pepper
75 g (3 oz) butter
4 slices of wholemeal bread, toasted
*   with crusts removed*

Fry the onion rings in the oil until crisp; the slower this is done, the better the result — it should take about 20 minutes. Add salt about halfway through, and keep stirring and turning the onions over so that they cook evenly.

Meanwhile, tie the asparagus in bundles and cook in a steamer for 15-25 minutes. (If using frozen or canned asparagus, follow the cooking directions on the packet or can.) Beat up the eggs and season with salt and pepper. Melt two-thirds of the butter in a pan over gentle heat and pour in the beaten eggs. Cook, stirring constantly, until they just thicken; don't stir them too much or the texture will be too smooth; on the other hand, they mustn't

be allowed to burn. When they are ready they should still be moist. Butter the toast and divide the scrambled eggs between the 4 slices. Arrange the asparagus spears on top. Drain the onion rings on kitchen paper, arrange them over the asparagus and serve hot.

Left: Gougère, a choux pastry ring made with eggs and flavoured with cheese, served with a rich Tomato sauce. Right, a superb, light-textured soufflé to melt in the mouth, flavoured with cheese and spinach. Serve it for lunch, or as a dinner party starter

Gougère

Serves 4

CALORIES PER PORTION: 353 (1480 kJ)
PROTEIN CONTENT PER PORTION: 13.5 grams
PREPARATION & COOKING TIME: 1¼ hours

50 g (2 oz) butter
150 ml (¼ pint) water
75 g (3 oz) unbleached white flour
3 eggs
75 g (3 oz) strong hard cheese, cut into
   5 mm (¼ in) cubes
about 300 ml (½ pint) Tomato or
   Piquant sauce for serving (page 196)

Set the oven at 150°C (300°F) Gas 2. Place the butter and water in a medium-sized pan and bring to the boil over moderate heat. Remove the pan from the heat as soon as boiling point is reached and shoot in all the flour at once. Beat vigorously with a wooden spoon until all the flour has been absorbed and the mixture 'follows the spoon' and comes away from the side of the pan to form a firm, smooth ball. Cool very slightly and add the eggs one at a time, beating very thoroughly between each addition so that the mixture becomes smooth and shiny. It may be necessary to use only part of the last egg, as the mixture must be firm enough to hold its shape. Fold in two-thirds of the cheese.

Pipe or spoon the mixture into a 25 cm (10 in) circle on a well-oiled baking sheet. Dot with the remaining cheese cubes and pin a double band of non-stick vegetable parchment round the outside to hold it in shape so that it rises neatly.

Place the Gougère in the middle of the pre-heated oven and increase the heat to 200°C (400°F) Gas 6; choux pastry bakes best on a rising temperature. Bake it for 40 minutes, then turn off the heat, prop the oven door open slightly and leave the Gougère in the oven for 5-10 minutes to cool while you make or heat up your chosen sauce. Transfer the Gougère to a hot serving dish and serve with the sauce.

Spinach roulade

Serves 4
CALORIES PER PORTION: 775 (3245 kJ)
PROTEIN CONTENT PER PORTION: 20 grams
PREPARATION & COOKING TIME: 1 hour

The roulade
225 g (8 oz) fresh cooked spinach, finely
  chopped and well drained
25 g (1 oz) butter
salt
freshly ground pepper
scant 40 g (1½ oz) wholemeal flour
150 ml (½ pint) milk
3 eggs, separated

The filling
3 tablespoons olive or sunflower oil
5 slices wholemeal bread, weighing
  about 100 g (4 oz), crusts removed
  and cut into 1 cm (½ in) cubes
225 g (8 oz) chopped onions
a good pinch of cayenne
225 g (8 oz) curd or sieved cottage
  cheese

Melt the butter in a pan over gentle heat, add the spinach and sauté until any remaining liquid has evaporated. Add salt and pepper to taste, then sprinkle in the flour and cook for 1-2 minutes, stirring continuously. Remove the pan from the heat and gradually add the milk, stirring well between each addition. Return the pan to the stove, increase the heat and bring to the boil, stirring all the time until the sauce thickens.

Remove the pan from the stove and allow the sauce to cool slightly. Set the oven at 200°C (400°F) Gas 6. Beat the egg yolks, then add them to the spinach sauce and stir until thoroughly mixed. Whisk the egg whites until stiff, then fold these into the sauce.

Pour the mixture into a Swiss roll tin lined with oiled vegetable parchment or greaseproof paper and bake on the middle shelf of the pre-heated oven for 30 minutes.

To make the filling: heat 2 tablespoons of the oil in a pan over gentle heat, add the bread cubes and fry until crisp and lightly browned. Remove from the pan with a draining spoon and drain well on kitchen paper. Heat the remaining oil in the pan, add the onions and fry until golden. Remove from the pan with a draining spoon and drain well.

A few minutes before the roulade is cooked, add the fried bread cubes to the onions with a little cayenne pepper and season with salt and pepper. Add the curd or cottage cheese and melt it over gentle heat, taking great care that it does not boil, or it will go stringy. Continue cooking until the cheese is melted and really hot.

Remove the roulade from the oven and take it out of the tin. Spread thickly with the filling. Roll it up by picking up one end of the paper and gently easing the roulade over the filling into a roll. Serve immediately with hot Tomato sauce (page 196) and baked jacket potatoes.

Cheese roulade

Serves 4
CALORIES PER PORTION: 515 (2145 kJ)
PROTEIN CONTENT PER PORTION: 22 grams
PREPARATION & COOKING TIME: 1 hour

125 g (4 oz) Cheddar cheese
25 g (1 oz) wholemeal flour
½ teaspoon finely chopped thyme or
  marjoram
salt
freshly ground pepper
a pinch of cayenne
4 eggs

The filling
450 g (1 lb) finely chopped onions
2-3 tablespoons olive or sunflower oil, or
  melted butter
25 g (1 oz) wholemeal flour
300 ml (½ pint) milk
75 g (3 oz) chopped walnuts
½ teaspoon grated nutmeg
salt
freshly ground pepper
6 tablespoons finely chopped parsley

First make the filling: fry the onions in the oil or melted butter over moderate heat until they are golden brown, stirring occasionally to prevent them sticking. When they are ready — it should take about 30 minutes — drain off any excess oil or butter, sprinkle in the flour and mix it well in before removing the pan from the heat. Gradually pour on the milk, stirring well after each addition. Return the pan to the stove and bring the sauce to the boil, stirring constantly until it thickens.

Add the walnuts and nutmeg and season well with salt and pepper. Cover the top of the sauce with a piece of buttered grease-proof paper and stand the pan in a larger pan half full of boiling water, or transfer the sauce to a double boiler over gentle heat while you make the roulade.

Line a well-buttered Swiss roll tin, 30 × 20 cm (13 × 7 in), with non-stick veg-

etable parchment. Brush this with the rest of the melted butter and set the oven at 200°C (400°F) Gas 6.

Mix together the cheese, flour, thyme or marjoram and season to taste with salt, pepper and a pinch of cayenne, if used. Whisk the eggs until they are thick and mousse-like. Using a knife, fold the dry flour and cheese mixture into the eggs, pour this into the prepared tin and bake in the pre-heated oven for 20 minutes. Remove the roulade from the oven, take it out of the tin and spread about half the filling over the top. Roll it up by picking up one end of the paper and gently easing the roulade over the filling, removing the parchment as you do so. Place the roulade on a warmed serving platter and spread the rest of the sauce over the top. Sprinkle with parsley and serve with a Polonaise sauce (page 196). Serve with Peperonata or Courgettes provençales.

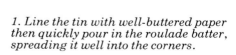

1. *Line the tin with well-buttered paper then quickly pour in the roulade batter, spreading it well into the corners.*

2. *After baking, spread half the filling over, leaving a slight border. Roll up using the paper to help.*

Basic cheese quiche

Serves 4
CALORIES PER PORTION: 365 (1515 kJ)
PROTEIN CONTENT PER PORTION: 12 grams
PREPARATION AND COOKING TIME: 1½ hours

The pastry
100 g (4 oz) unbleached white flour
¼ teaspoon salt
50 g (2 oz) unsalted butter
a little iced water

The filling
25 g (1 oz) butter
50 g (2 oz) finely chopped onion
3 eggs, beaten
300 ml (½ pint) creamy milk
25 g (1 oz) grated Cheddar cheese
salt
freshly ground pepper

Sift the flour and salt into a bowl, then cut the butter into the flour, using a knife or a plain pastry cutter. Crumble the mixture with the fingers until it resembles fine breadcrumbs, then stir in just enough water to mix it to a soft but not sticky dough. Wrap the dough in foil and leave to chill in the refrigerator for 30 minutes.

Roll out the chilled dough very thinly on a lightly floured surface, then use it to line a 20 cm (8 in) diameter flan tin, preferably one with a removable base — flans are easier to serve from these, or you can use a flan ring placed on a baking sheet. Cover the dough with a layer of foil and chill it again while you are making the filling.

Set the oven at 200°C (400°F) Gas 6. Melt the butter in a thick-based pan over gentle heat, add the onion and fry until it is golden brown. Put the eggs in a bowl, add the milk and cheese, season with salt and pepper and beat until well mixed. Remove the onion from the pan with a draining spoon and stir it into the egg mixture.

Remove the foil from the dough case, pour in the filling and bake in the preheated oven for 20 minutes, then lower the heat to 180°C (350°F) Gas 4 and bake for a further 10 minutes. Prop the oven door open and leave the quiche to settle for a few minutes before taking it out. Remove it from the flan dish and serve warm or cold with a salad.

Note: The diced onions can be blanched for a few minutes in a little boiling water instead of frying them, if you prefer.

Cauliflower quiche

Serves 4
CALORIES PER PORTION: 370 (1537 kJ)
PROTEIN CONTENT PER PORTION: 12.5 grams
PREPARATION & COOKING TIME: 1½ hours

225 g (8 oz) cooked cauliflower, puréed
or broken into small florets

Follow the basic recipe for Cheese quiche, adding the cauliflower to the filling with the cheese. Serve, if liked, with a Spiced apricot sauce (page 197).

Spinach quiche

Serves 4
CALORIES PER PORTION: 380 (1857 kJ)
PROTEIN CONTENT PER PORTION: 15 grams
PREPARATION & COOKING TIME: 1½ hours

225 g (8 oz) cooked spinach, puréed

Follow the basic recipe for Cheese quiche, adding the spinach to the filling mixture with the cheese.

Leek and cheese quiche

Serves 4
CALORIES PER PORTION: 410 (1705 kJ)
PROTEIN CONTENT PER PORTION: 13 grams
PREPARATION & COOKING TIME: 1½ hours

225 g (8 oz) very thinly sliced leeks,
simmered in a little butter until
tender, then well drained

Follow the basic recipe for Cheese quiche, adding the leeks to the filling with the cheese.

Curried eggs

Serves 4
CALORIES PER PORTION: 290 (1215 kJ)
PROTEIN CONTENT PER PORTION: 17 grams
PREPARATION & COOKING TIME: 10-15 minutes

4 hard-boiled eggs, shelled and cut in
half lengthwise
2 tablespoons olive or sunflower oil
100 g (4 oz) finely chopped onion
1-2 tablespoons finely chopped root
ginger
1 small clove of garlic, peeled and
crushed
4 teaspoons curry powder, or to taste
½ teaspoon finely grated lemon rind
15 g (½ oz) wholemeal flour
300 ml (½ pint) strong White vegetable
stock (page 34)
1-2 teaspoons lemon juice
225 g (8 oz) boiled basmati rice,
flavoured with turmeric — about
125 g (4 oz) uncooked
1-2 tablespoons shredded coconut

Heat the oil, add the onion and ginger root and fry until golden brown, stirring occasionally to prevent them sticking and burning. Add the curry powder, garlic and lemon rind and stir until well mixed. Sprinkle in the flour and cook for 1-2 minutes, stirring continuously. Remove the pan from the heat and gradually add the stock and lemon juice, stirring well between each addition. Return the pan to the stove, increase the heat and bring the sauce to the boil, stirring constantly until it thickens. Add a little extra stock or water if the sauce is too thick.

Lower the halved eggs carefully into the boiling sauce, then turn down the heat and cook them for at least 5 minutes, while you warm up the rice.

Arrange the eggs on a bed of rice, then coat with some of the curry sauce. Sprinkle over the coconut and serve with the rest of the sauce handed separately.

Welsh rarebit

Serves 4
CALORIES PER PORTION: 230 (957 kJ)
PROTEIN CONTENT PER PORTION: 9 grams
PREPARATION & COOKING TIME: 10 minutes

100 g (4 oz) grated dry Cheddar cheese
25 g (1 oz) butter
25 g (1 oz) wholemeal flour
100 ml (4 fl oz) brown ale or beer
4 slices of warm wholemeal toast

Heat the grill. Melt the butter in a pan over gentle heat, stir in the flour, then the cheese. Cook until the cheese begins to melt, then pour in the beer and stir the mixture well until all the cheese has melted and it is completely smooth. Pour over the slices of toast and put them under the hot grill until the tops bubble and turn golden brown. Serve with slices of pickled cucumber.

Oeufs mollets

Oeufs mollets are, in fact, well-cooked soft-boiled eggs. It should be possible to remove their shells with ease, but the yolks should still be runny. They make very good starters for a dinner party, so I have included one or two in the preceding chapter. They also come in handy for a tasty light lunch or supper dish, as the basic Oeufs mollets can be served in a variety of ways.

To cook them: bring the eggs to room temperature, then lower them into a pan of boiling water, using a frying basket if you are boiling more than one at a time. Do not allow the water to go off the boil for more than a second or two while they are being cooked. Large eggs will take about 6 minutes — allow a little less for smaller eggs — then remove them from the water in the frying basket and plunge straight away into a bowl of cold water to prevent them cooking further. Leave for a minute or two.

To peel them: tap them gently to crack the shells and then, holding the egg in the palm of your hand, carefully lift up part of the shell, taking the underlying membrane with it. Roll the egg in the hand as you peel off the shell, being careful not to let it break in half. Hold the egg under gently running water to remove any stubborn bits of shell, then keep the eggs in a bowl of cold water in the refrigerator until required.

To reheat them: put the eggs in a bowl of hot, but not boiling, water and leave them for 5 minutes.

In addition to the following two recipes, try them on a bed of diced, cooked mushrooms with Madeira sauce; with a mixture of diced, cooked spring vegetables and a rich Béchamel sauce; with lentils and a Catalane sauce, or serve them on a fried bread croûte with a Béarnaise or Maltese sauce (page 127). The other sauces can be found in the chapter of Basic recipes.

Oeufs mollets Crécy

Serves 4
CALORIES PER PORTION: 460 (1917 kJ)
PROTEIN CONTENT PER PORTION: 13 grams
PREPARATION & COOKING TIME: 35 minutes

4 Oeufs mollets
4 tablespoons clarified butter, or olive or sunflower oil
450 g (1 lb) thinly sliced carrots
300 ml (½ pint) thick Béchamel sauce (page 196)
4 slices of wholemeal bread, crusts removed and fried in butter (croûtes)
salt
freshly ground pepper

Heat the butter or oil in a thick-based pan over gentle heat. Add the carrots, cover the pan and cook for 20-30 minutes until the carrots are tender and golden brown, turning them over so they do not burn.

Meanwhile, make the Oeufs mollets, or reheat them in a bowl of hot water for 5 minutes. Gently heat up the sauce, and fry the bread croûtes.

Remove the cooked carrots from the stove, sprinkle with salt and pepper and divide them equally between the slices of fried bread, reserving a few slices of carrot for the garnish.

Place an egg on the bed of carrot in the centre of each croûte and coat with the hot Béchamel sauce. Adjust the seasoning, garnish with the reserved carrots and serve immediately.

Oeufs mollets in potato nests

Serves 4
CALORIES PER PORTION: 435 (1825 kJ)
PROTEIN CONTENT PER PORTION: 22 grams
PREPARATION & COOKING TIME: 1 hour

4 Oeufs mollets
225 g (8 oz) sliced potatoes
2 eggs, well beaten
100 g (4 oz) grated strong Cheddar cheese
salt
freshly ground pepper
300 ml (½ pint) thick Mushroom or Béchamel sauce (page 196)

Cook the potatoes in boiling salted water for 7-10 minutes, or until tender. Drain them, then rub through a sieve. Add the beaten eggs, reserving a little for brushing the potato nests. Add the cheese, season with salt and pepper and beat well. Set the oven at 200°C (400°F) Gas 6.

Put the cheese and potato purée into a piping bag fitted with a large rose nozzle and pipe four circular 'nests' on a well-oiled baking tray. Bake in the pre-heated oven for 5 minutes, then brush with the reserved beaten egg. Return to the oven and bake for a further 15 minutes.

Meanwhile, prepare the Oeufs mollets or reheat them in a bowl of hot water for 5 minutes, if necessary.

Gently heat up the Mushroom or Béchamel sauce.

Transfer the cooked potato nests to a warmed serving plate and pour a little hot sauce into the centre of each. Place the eggs carefully on top, then coat with the remaining sauce. Serve immediately.

Scotch eggs

Serves 4
CALORIES PER PORTION: 395 (1662 kJ)
PROTEIN CONTENT PER PORTION: 25 grams
PREPARATION & COOKING TIME: 1 hour

4 hard-boiled eggs, shelled
450 g (1 lb) cooked soya beans
100 g (4 oz) finely chopped onion
½ teaspoon dried thyme
1 teaspoon dried sage
salt
freshly ground pepper
2 eggs, well beaten
4 tablespoons wholemeal flour
4 tablespoons fine dried wholemeal breadcrumbs
oil for deep frying

Mince the soya beans with the onion and herbs and season well with salt and pepper. Add half the beaten eggs and bind the mixture together thoroughly. Divide it into 4 portions; pat 1 portion out into a round, put a hard-boiled egg in the centre and wrap the soya mixture evenly around it.

Roll each Scotch egg in flour, dip it in the remaining beaten egg, then coat thickly with breadcrumbs.

Heat the oil to 180°C (350°F) in a deep-fat fryer. Lower the Scotch eggs carefully into the oil and deep fry them for 2-3 minutes, or until they are golden brown. Remove them with a draining spoon and drain well on kitchen paper. Leave to cool, then serve cold with a salad.

Pasta

One of the great surprises of Italian cooking, for the uninitiated, is the enormous variety of pasta shapes. It is easy to imagine that, since the basic ingredients are the same, the flavour of each dish must be the same. The shape of the pasta – long, short, hollow, flat or curved – determines how much of the accompanying sauce is taken in with each forkful, and you will be surprised at the difference in taste the shape of the pasta seems to make.

Experiment first with the different types served with the same sauce, then with different sauces and the same pasta shape and you will be amazed at the subtle variations in flavour. Your scope for experimentation is widened by the filled pastas – cannelloni and ravioli – the variations are endless; we have room, alas, for but a few . . . Easy to make, easy to store and very satisfying if you are really hungry, pasta must be the ultimate 'convenience food'. Once you have made your own, using wholemeal flour, you will be reluctant to return to the shop-bought type. Travel in Italy with a notebook, and you will fill it with yet more recipes to savour.

Basic pasta dough

Wholemeal flour produces a coarser pasta dough than white flour and it cannot be rolled out as thinly, but it nevertheless makes delicious pasta.

Serves 4
CALORIES PER PORTION: 410 (1712 kJ)
PROTEIN CONTENT PER PORTION: 19 grams
PREPARATION & COOKING TIME: 1 hour

450 g (1 lb) wholemeal bread flour, or unbleached strong white flour
3 eggs
1 teaspoon salt
1-2 tablespoons water

Put the flour in a large bowl, or in a mound on a work surface, and make a well in the centre. Beat 2 eggs with the salt and work them lightly into the flour with the fingertips until evenly distributed — the mixture should then resemble fresh breadcrumbs. If necessary add part or whole remaining egg to achieve the correct consistency.

Work the mixture to a firm dough on your work surface, adding the water a little at a time until the dough holds together. The exact amount of water used depends on the absorbency of the flour and the size of the eggs. Knead the dough thoroughly for 5-10 minutes until it feels elastic, keeping the hands, dough and work surface well floured. It is now ready

to make into pasta shapes. Here are one or two simple ones.

To make Lasagne verdi

1 Make the pasta dough as directed, adding 75 g (3 oz) cooked spinach purée, thoroughly drained, after the eggs. Stir the spinach into the flour and egg mixture until evenly distributed, then add just enough water to make a firm dough.
2 Proceed as for Tagliatelle, up to and including stage 4.
3 Cut the dough into 75 mm (3 in) squares and put in a single layer on a floured baking tray to dry.

To make Tagliatelle

1 Cut the dough into two equal pieces. Roll one of these into a long 'sausage' with well-floured hands, then sprinkle the work surface, dough and rolling pin lightly with more flour.
2 Starting at one end of the 'sausage', roll a small section of the dough out lengthways, using fairly gentle pressure. Roll from the centre to the left, and from the centre to the right, stretching the dough gently as you roll and trying to keep an even thickness.
3 Continue rolling out the dough in this way a section at a time until the end of the 'sausage' is reached, then work back the other way. Roll and stretch the dough until it is about 45.5 cm (18 in) long and *almost* thin enough to see through, using more flour as necessary. Keep the ends of the dough square and the sides straight by pushing inwards with the rolling pin from time to time as you work.
4 Repeat this rolling and stretching process with the second piece of dough, remembering that the working the dough receives by repeated rolling is part of the process.
5 Roll up each sheet of dough loosely, then cut across the dough at about 5 mm (¼ in) intervals with a sharp, thin bladed knife. Use a sawing action and do not press too hard or the layers will stick together.
6 Unroll the dough ribbons and spread them out onto a clean cloth until required.

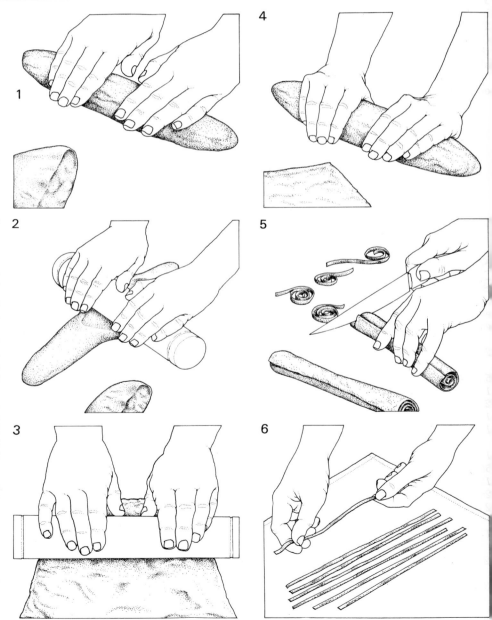

To make Cappelletti

1 Proceed as for Tagliatelle, up to and including stage 4.
2 Cut the dough into 65 mm (2½ in) squares. Put a little of your chosen filling in the centre of each square, then brush the edges with beaten egg.
3 Fold one corner of the dough over the filling to form a triangle, then press the edges firmly to seal. Wind the triangle around your forefinger and pinch the ends together to form the shape of a small 'hat', or 'cappelletto'.

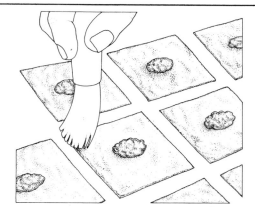

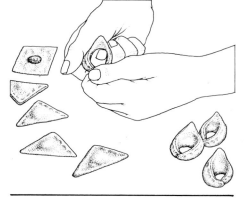

To make Farfalletti

1 Proceed as for Tagliatelle, up to and including stage 4.
2 Cut thin strips of dough about 75 mm (3 in) long and 2 cm (¾ in) wide. Squeeze the centre of each strip to form a bow and allow to dry completely.
  To make frilly bows, use a serrated-edged pastry wheel to cut the dough.

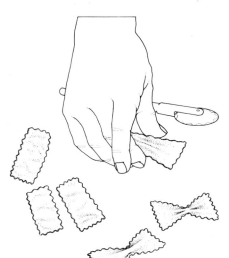

To cook freshly made pasta

Bring 3 litres (generous 5 pints) well-salted water to the boil in a large pan. Add 2 tablespoons of oil to prevent the pasta from sticking to itself while cooking, then boil the pasta for 5-7 minutes until *al dente* (tender, but firm to bite).

  Pour the contents of the pan into a colander and pour a kettle of boiling water through it. Drain the pasta and serve with lashings of butter or a dressing of — preferably — olive oil and finely chopped parsley and garlic. Grated Parmesan cheese can also be served with it, or chopped cooked mushrooms or diced cooked vegetables. In the summer months, when fresh basil is available, serve freshly made pasta with Pesto or Pesto di Formaggio.

Spaghetti or macaroni salad

Serves 4
CALORIES PER PORTION: 1202 (5035 kJ)
PROTEIN CONTENT PER PORTION: 27 grams
PREPARATION & COOKING TIME: 1 hour

225 g (8 oz) wholemeal macaroni or
  spaghetti, broken into small pieces
5 tablespoons olive or sunflower oil
1 teaspoon paprika
2 teaspoons lemon juice
1 tablespoon wine vinegar
175 g (6 oz) thinly sliced button
  mushrooms
1 tablespoon soya sauce
50 g (2 oz) finely chopped spring onions
125 g (4 oz) finely chopped celery
25 g (1 oz) sunflower seeds
2 hard-boiled eggs, shelled and finely
  chopped
175 g (6 oz) coarsely grated Cheddar
  cheese
2 tablespoons finely chopped basil or
  parsley
300 ml (½ pint) garlic-flavoured
  Mayonnaise (page 126)

Cook the pasta in boiling salted water, with 2 tablespoons of the oil added, until *al dente* (tender but firm to bite). Meanwhile mix together the remaining oil, the paprika, lemon juice and vinegar, pour it over the mushrooms and stir until they are evenly coated. When the pasta is cooked, drain it, rinse thoroughly under cold running water and leave until it is quite cold, forking it from time to time so that it does not stick together.

  Mix the cold pasta with the soya sauce, onions, celery, sunflower seeds, eggs, cheese and herbs. Stir in enough Mayonnaise to bind it lightly together, spoon it on to a serving dish and scatter the marinated mushrooms over the top before serving.

Pesto

Serves 4
CALORIES PER PORTION: 405 (1670 kJ)
PROTEIN CONTENT PER PORTION: negligible
PREPARATION TIME: about 10 minutes

50 g (2 oz) fresh basil leaves
3 cloves of garlic, peeled
salt
200 ml (⅓ pint) olive oil

Pound the basil and garlic to a pulp with a little salt. Pound in the oil, drop by drop, until the sauce is the consistency of thin cream. Serve with pasta or Minestrone soup (page 37).

Pesto di formaggio

Serves 4
CALORIES PER PORTION: 665 (2780 kJ)
PROTEIN CONTENT PER PORTION: 12 grams

Pound in 100 g (4 oz) grated Parmesan cheese and 50-100 g (2-4 oz) pine nuts.

Spaghetti with egg and crispy onion rings

Serves 4
CALORIES PER PORTION: 330 (1374 kJ)
PROTEIN CONTENT PER PORTION: 13 grams
PREPARATION & COOKING TIME: 40 minutes

450 g (1 lb) wholemeal spaghetti
salt
1-2 tablespoons oil
oil for deep frying
450 g (1 lb) onions, cut into thin rings
6 eggs, well beaten
1 clove of garlic, peeled and chopped
coarsely ground black pepper

Cook the spaghetti in a large pan of boiling salted water, with 1-2 tablespoons oil added, for 10-15 minutes until *al dente* (tender, but firm to bite).

Meanwhile, heat the oil in the deep fryer to just below 180°C (350°F). Put the onion rings in a frying basket, sprinkle very lightly with salt, then lower the basket into the hot oil. Deep fry the onion rings until golden brown and crisp, stirring from time to time to ensure even cooking. Remove the basket from the pan, drain the onions and keep them hot.

Drain the spaghetti in a colander, pour through a kettleful of boiling water, then drain well and return the spaghetti to the rinsed-out pan. Mix the fried onions and the mushrooms into the spaghetti, then add the beaten eggs and garlic. Cook over gentle heat until the eggs just begin to curdle to a sauce, shaking the pan constantly — try not to let them scramble. Sprinkle with freshly-ground pepper and serve.

Note: Tagliatelle can be used instead of the spaghetti, and the onions can be served on top of the egg and spaghetti, if preferred.

Spaghetti al funghi

Serves 4
CALORIES PER PORTION: 915 (3830 kJ)
PROTEIN CONTENT PER PORTION: 18.5 grams
PREPARATION & COOKING TIME: 35 minutes

450 g (1 lb) wholemeal spaghetti
salt
4-5 tablespoons olive or sunflower oil
450 g (1 lb) finely chopped mushrooms
8 spring onions, sliced in half
*   lengthwise and finely chopped*
freshly ground black pepper
300 ml (½ pint) double cream

Cook the spaghetti in a large pan of boiling salted water, with 1-2 tablespoons of oil added, for 10-15 minutes until *al dente* (tender, but firm to bite). Meanwhile, heat 2 tablespoons of the oil in a pan, add the mushrooms and fry over fairly brisk heat, stirring all the time until they are dark and shiny and most of their juices have evaporated. Remove from the heat and keep hot.

Heat the remaining oil in a small pan, add the spring onions and fry over gentle heat until they are just softened.

Drain the spaghetti in a colander and pour a kettleful of boiling water through it. Drain again, mix it into the mushrooms and season with salt and pepper. Bring the cream to the boil in a separate pan, then pour it over the spaghetti and mushroom mixture. Sprinkle with the onions and serve.

A crisp green salad and a generous sprinkling of Gruyère cheese go well with this dish.

Spaghetti with aubergines

Serves 4
CALORIES PER PORTION: 730 (3057 kJ)
PROTEIN CONTENT PER PORTION: 25 grams
PREPARATION & COOKING TIME: 1¼ hours,
    including salting the aubergines

450 g (1 lb) wholemeal spaghetti
450 g (1 lb) aubergines, cut into thin
*   strips*
100 g (4 oz) thinly sliced onion
salt
6 tablespoons olive or sunflower oil
freshly ground black pepper
2 large cloves of garlic, peeled and very
*   finely chopped (optional)*
300 ml (½ pint) cultured sour cream or
*   yoghurt (optional)*
100 g (4 oz) grated Parmesan cheese

Mix together the aubergines and onion, sprinkle with salt and leave to drain for 30 minutes. Rinse under cold running water and pat dry with kitchen paper. Cook the spaghetti in a large pan of boiling salted water with 2 tablespoons of oil for 10-15 minutes until *al dente* (tender, but firm to bite).

Meanwhile, heat 2 more tablespoons of oil in a pan, add half the aubergines and onions and fry over gentle heat until golden brown and crisp. Keep turning them over frequently to ensure they cook evenly. Press them against the sides of the pan to remove any excess oil, then remove, drain well and keep hot.

Heat the remaining oil, add the rest of the aubergines and onions and fry these over gentle heat until they too, are golden brown and crisp; remove, drain and keep hot.

When the spaghetti is cooked, transfer it to a colander and pour a kettleful of boiling water through it. Drain well, then pile it in a shallow, warmed, ovenproof serving dish. Add the aubergines and onions, sprinkle with salt and pepper and fold them gently into the spaghetti. Sprinkle the top with garlic, if using. Mix in the sour cream, or yoghurt if you need a sauce, and serve with grated Parmesan cheese and a tomato salad.

Top: a dish of succulent wholemeal spaghetti, ready to use in such culinary delights as Spaghetti with aubergines (centre). Try this with sour cream to offset the richness of the vegetables. Front: tasty Brown ravioli squares are filled with a mixture of onion, cheese and parsley, while Gnocchi Romana, made from polenta (right) are sprinkled generously with Parmesan and finished under the grill

Ravioli

It takes practice to make good ravioli; there should be just the right amount of filling for the dough, and the layers of dough should not be too thick. However, it is well worth making your own.

Serves 4
CALORIES PER PORTION: 610 (2555 kJ)
PROTEIN CONTENT PER PORTION: 34 grams
PREPARATION & COOKING TIME: 2 hours

½ quantity of Basic pasta dough
1-2 tablespoons oil
1 small egg, well beaten
300-600 ml (½-1 pint) Tomato sauce
(page 196)
2-3 tablespoons grated Parmesan cheese

The filling
7 g (¼ oz) butter
1 tablespoon finely chopped onion
225 g (8 oz) curd cheese
100 g (4 oz) grated Parmesan cheese
4 tablespoons chopped parsley
a little lemon juice
1 egg, well beaten
salt
freshly ground black pepper

Roll and stretch the dough out on a lightly floured surface until about 50 cm (20 in) square. Keep both sides of the dough well-floured, then cut the dough in half and mark one half into squares measuring a little less than 5 cm (2 in).

To make the filling, heat the butter in a pan and fry the onion until transparent. Put the cooked onion into a bowl with the rest of the filling ingredients and beat well. Place a small teaspoon of filling in the centre of each square of dough. Brush the edges of each marked square with

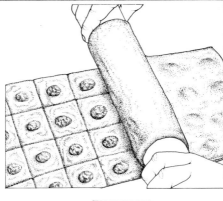
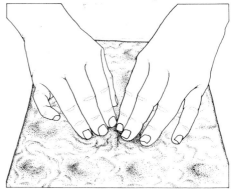
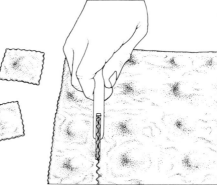
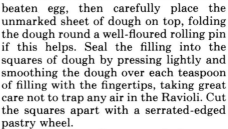

beaten egg, then carefully place the unmarked sheet of dough on top, folding the dough round a well-floured rolling pin if this helps. Seal the filling into the squares of dough by pressing lightly and smoothing the dough over each teaspoon of filling with the fingertips, taking great care not to trap any air in the Ravioli. Cut the squares apart with a serrated-edged pastry wheel.

Place the ravioli in a single layer on floured plates, then cover with a damp-

ened floured cloth and leave for at least 30 minutes, or until required.

Cook the Ravioli in a large pan of boiling salted water, with 1-2 tablespoons of oil for 5-7 minutes until *al dente* (tender, but firm to bite).

Meanwhile, heat the Tomato sauce in a separate pan. Take out the cooked Ravioli with a draining spoon, drain thoroughly and pile into a warmed serving dish. Pour the hot Tomato sauce over and serve with grated Parmesan cheese.

Cannelloni with spinach

This quantity serves 4 as a main course, 8 as a starter.

TOTAL CALORIES: 2330 (9750 kJ)
TOTAL PROTEIN CONTENT: 120 grams
PREPARATION & COOKING TIME: 2 hours

½ quantity of Basic pasta dough
1-2 tablespoons oil
300-600 ml (½-1 pint) Tomato sauce
(page 196)
100 g (4 oz) grated Parmesan cheese

The filling
450 g (1 lb) cooked, fresh or frozen
spinach, thoroughly drained
25 g (1 oz) butter
100 g (4 oz) finely chopped onion
25 g (1 oz) wholemeal flour
100 ml (4 fl oz) milk
1 egg, well beaten
salt and freshly ground black pepper

Roll and stretch the dough on a lightly floured surface, as for tagliatelle, until very thin, then cut out 10 rectangles about 12.5 × 10 cm (5 × 4 in). Cook the pasta in a large pan of boiling salted water, with 1-2 tablespoons of oil added, for 5-7 minutes, or until *al dente* (tender, but firm to bite). Remove from the pan with a draining spoon, then drain well, turn on to a plate (not absorbent kitchen paper or it will stick) and keep it covered.

To make the filling: chop the spinach coarsely, melt the butter over gentle heat, add the onion and fry until golden brown. Sprinkle in the flour and cook for 1-2 minutes, stirring continuously. Remove the pan from the heat, add the milk gradually, stirring well between each addition, then return the pan to the stove. Increase

the heat and bring the sauce to the boil stirring all the time until it thickens.

Add the spinach, stir again, then remove the sauce from the heat and leave it to cool slightly. Add the egg, season with salt and pepper and stir well. Set the oven at 200°C (400°F) Gas 6.

Pour a thin layer of Tomato sauce on the bottom of an ovenproof dish. Divide the spinach filling between the rectangles of Cannelloni, then roll up to enclose the filling. Place the Cannelloni in the dish side by side with the joins underneath, then coat with the remaining Tomato sauce. Sprinkle with half the Parmesan.

Bake in the pre-heated oven for 20-30 minutes until the sauce is bubbling and the cheese is golden brown. Serve hot, and pass the remaining Parmesan.

Lasagne verdi al forno

Serves 6
CALORIES PER PORTION: 650 (2723 kJ)
PROTEIN CONTENT PER PORTION: 25 grams
PREPARATION & COOKING TIME: 2 hours

450 g (1 lb) lasagne verdi, made from
  the basic recipe, cooked and drained

The filling
450 g (1 lb) cooked fresh or frozen
  spinach, thoroughly drained
25 g (1 oz) butter
100 g (4 oz) finely chopped onion
25 g (1 oz) wholemeal flour
100 ml (4 fl oz) milk
1 egg, well beaten
salt
freshly ground pepper

The sauce
2 tablespoons olive or sunflower oil
100 g (4 oz) finely chopped onion
450 g (1 lb) coarsely chopped
  mushrooms
2 cloves of garlic, peeled and finely
  chopped
25 g (1 oz) wholemeal flour
300 ml (½ pint) dry red wine
salt
freshly ground black pepper
600 ml (1 pint) Béchamel sauce (page
  196)
100 g (4 oz) grated Parmesan cheese

Make the filling, following the instructions given in the recipe for Cannelloni.

To make the sauce: heat the oil in a pan, add the onion and fry until golden brown. Add the mushrooms and garlic and continue cooking over fairly brisk heat until the mushrooms are dark and shiny and most of their juice has evaporated. Stir them constantly to prevent them sticking and burning.

Mix in the flour, stir in the wine, increase the heat and bring to the boil. Lower the heat and simmer, stirring briskly, until the sauce thickens. Add salt and pepper, then remove the pan from the heat.

Set the oven at 180°C (350°F) Gas 4. Coat the base of a large, well-buttered ovenproof dish about 7.5 cm (3 in) deep with a little Béchamel sauce, then layer the dish as follows: lasagne, followed by Béchamel, spinach filling and mushroom sauce. Add a sprinkling of grated cheese and continue layering in the same order until all the ingredients are used up finishing with a layer of lasagne and a sprinkling of Parmesan cheese.

Bake on the top shelf of the pre-heated oven for 30 minutes until the top is golden-brown and the sauce bubbling. Serve hot with some extra Parmesan cheese handed separately, if liked.

Tagliatelle with cream sauce

Serves 4
CALORIES PER PORTION: 785 (3285 kJ)
PROTEIN CONTENT PER PORTION: 17.5 grams
PREPARATION & COOKING TIME: 35 minutes

450 g (1 lb) wholemeal tagliatelle, made
  from the basic recipe
1-2 tablespoons olive or sunflower oil
25 g (1 oz) butter
100 g (4 oz) finely chopped onion
225 g (8 oz) curd or sieved cottage
  cheese
a little single cream
50 g (2 oz) grated Parmesan cheese
salt
freshly ground black pepper

Cook the tagliatelle in a large pan of boiling salted water with 1-2 tablespoons of oil, until *al dente* (tender, but firm to bite).

Melt the butter over gentle heat, add the onion and fry until soft and pale gold.

Drain the pasta in a colander, pour through a kettleful of boiling water, then drain again and keep hot. Add the curd or cottage cheese to the onion and stir until melted. (Do not allow the cheese to boil or it will separate and become stringy.) Add the pasta to the cheese mixture, mixing it in well so that each strand of pasta is coated with sauce. Stir in just enough cream to moisten and lighten the texture of the sauce. Stir the grated Parmesan into the pasta, if using. Season with a little salt, plenty of pepper and serve.

Note: if you find 450 g (1 lb) pasta overwhelming for 4, or are serving the dish as a starter, use half to three-quarters of the home-made pasta, but remember that the calorie and protein count will alter accordingly.

Tagliatelle with tomato, celery and almond sauce

Serves 4
CALORIES PER PORTION: 1045 (4375 kJ)
PROTEIN CONTENT PER PORTION: 39 grams
PREPARATION & COOKING TIME: 1 hour

450 g (1 lb) wholemeal tagliatelle, made
  from the basic recipe
225 g (8 oz) finely chopped onions
225 g (8 oz) finely chopped celery
7 tablespoons olive or sunflower oil
25 g (1 oz) wholemeal flour
1 large clove of garlic, peeled and finely
  chopped
450 g (1 lb) skinned tomatoes, coarsely
  chopped
125 g (4 oz) blanched almonds
salt
freshly ground black pepper
175 g (6 oz) grated Parmesan cheese

Cook the pasta in a large pan of boiling salted water, with 1-2 tablespoons of oil added, until *al dente* (tender, but firm to bite). Meanwhile, fry the onions and celery in 4 tablespoons of the oil until they are a pale gold; mix in the flour, add the garlic and tomatoes and continue cooking, stirring constantly, until the tomatoes break down to a pulp and the excess liquid has evaporated.

Fry the almonds in a tablespoon of the oil until they are golden brown, then shred them coarsely. When the tagliatelle is cooked, drain it in a colander, pour through a kettleful of boiling water, then drain again and add it to the sauce. Mix them together gently so that the pasta is thoroughly coated. Season to taste with salt and pepper and pour on to a warmed serving dish. Sprinkle with the cheese and scatter the shredded almonds on top before serving.

Conchiglie with peas

Serves 4
CALORIES PER PORTION: 930 (3895 kJ)
PROTEIN CONTENT PER PORTION: 32 grams
PREPARATION & COOKING TIME: 45 minutes
(longer if fresh peas are used)

450 g (1 lb) conchiglie (pasta shells)
6 tablespoons olive or sunflower oil
225 g (8 oz) fresh or frozen peas
25 g (1 oz) butter
225 g (8 oz) coarsely shredded carrots
225 g (8 oz) finely chopped onions
1-2 cloves garlic, peeled and finely chopped
150 ml (¼ pint) cultured sour cream
25 g (1 oz) dried skimmed milk made into a cream with 4-6 tablespoons cold milk
125 g (4 oz) coarsely grated strong cheese
about 4 tablespoons hot milk
salt
freshly ground pepper

Cook the pasta shells in a large pan of boiling salted water, with 1-2 tablespoons of the oil added, until *al dente* (tender, but firm to bite). Meanwhile, cook the peas gently in the butter, taking care that they do not burn. Fry the carrots and onions in the rest of the oil over moderate heat for 20 minutes, or until they are golden brown.

When the peas are cooked, add them to the carrots and onions, then stir in the garlic, sour cream and the milk solution. Lower the heat and keep the sauce hot, stirring it occasionally. Drain the pasta in a colander and pour a kettleful of boiling water through it. Drain again thoroughly and add it to the sauce.

Sprinkle over the cheese and stir it in, adding a little of the hot milk if the sauce is too thick. Season well with salt and pepper and serve immediately.

Gnocchi Romana

Serves 4
CALORIES PER PORTION: 330 (1377 kJ)
PROTEIN CONTENT PER PORTION: 15 grams
PREPARATION & COOKING TIME: 1 hour

600 ml (1 pint) milk
25 g (1 oz) thinly sliced onion
1 clove of garlic, peeled and finely chopped
1 bay leaf
25 g (1 oz) butter
½-1 teaspoon salt
50 g (2 oz) polenta
1-2 tablespoons melted butter
100 g (4 oz) grated Parmesan cheese
freshly ground black pepper
300 ml (½ pint) Tomato or Mushroom sauce (page 196)

Put the milk, onion, garlic, bay leaf, butter and salt in a pan and bring slowly to the boil, so that the flavours infuse into the milk. Strain the milk into a clean pan, bring back to the boil, then pour in the polenta. Stir until thick, then simmer for 5 minutes, still stirring constantly to prevent it burning and sticking.

Pour the paste out onto a well-oiled marble slab or suitable work surface, then spread it out until about 1 cm (½ in) thick, keeping the edges straight. Leave until cold, then cut into 65 mm (2½ in) rounds. Set the oven at 200°C (400°F) Gas 6. Arrange the rounds overlapping in a well-buttered flameproof dish, brush with melted butter, then sprinkle with a little of the Parmesan cheese and plenty of freshly ground black pepper. Bake on the top shelf of the pre-heated oven for 15-20 minutes until golden. Place the dish under a hot grill for a few minutes to brown the Gnocchi if you like. Serve piping hot with the remaining cheese handed separately, and accompanied by a Tomato or Mushroom sauce.

Spinach gnocchi

Serves 4
CALORIES PER PORTION: 495 (2067 kJ)
PROTEIN CONTENT PER PORTION: 33 grams
PREPARATION AND COOKING TIME: 1½-2 hours

225 g (8 oz) cooked spinach, thoroughly drained
225 g (8 oz) curd or sieved cottage cheese
2 eggs
1 egg white
50 g (2 oz) grated Parmesan cheese
6 tablespoons wholemeal flour
salt
1 tablespoon vinegar
freshly ground pepper

To finish
1-2 tablespoons melted butter
25 g (1 oz) grated Parmesan cheese

Put the spinach in a blender with the curd or cottage cheese, eggs, egg white and half the Parmesan cheese. Blend until fairly smooth, then transfer to a bowl and sprinkle in the remaining Parmesan. Add the flour and mix in thoroughly then leave the dough to stand in a cool place for 30 minutes. Set the oven at 200°C (400°F) Gas 6.

Bring a large pan of boiling salted water to the boil, then add the vinegar. Season the dough well with salt and pepper, then scoop out spoonfuls and, using 2 spoons, shape the dough into balls about the size of golf balls, making the outsides as smooth as possible or the Gnocchi may disintegrate in the pan.

Lower these carefully into the gently simmering water and cook for 2-3 minutes, until they float to the surface, then remove with a draining spoon and drain thoroughly on kitchen paper. Cook the Gnocchi in four batches.

Arrange the cooked Gnocchi in a well-buttered ovenproof dish; pour over a little melted butter and sprinkle with the extra Parmesan cheese. Bake in the pre-heated oven for 10 minutes and serve at once.

Note: A sauce made up of equal quantities of Béchamel and Tomato goes well with Spinach gnocchi.

Main Courses

When planning a dinner party, you should begin by
selecting the main course and building all the other
dishes around this. If you are cooking for non-
vegetarian guests, this is your chance to surprise them
with the variety and excellence of vegetarian cuisine.
Make sure that the complete meal is not only enjoyable,
but also nutritious enough to provide the necessary
protein, vitamins and energy-giving foods. A convenient
division of the day's protein intake would be to allow
one-sixth for breakfast, two-sixths for lunch and
three-sixths for the main meal of the day.
A vegetarian's main sources of protein are the nuts,
pulses, eggs, cheese and milk, and my recipes combine
these with vegetables, herbs and spices to make dishes
that are both delicious and nutritious. Many can be
accompanied by a salad or followed by a simple sorbet
to clear the palate.
I have included recipes from Chinese cuisine – the
Chinese have perhaps the lightest and most delicate
touch with vegetables. Indian recipes also feature in
my selection – remember that there is an infinite variety
to be found in the presentation and cooking of even
the most traditional dishes.

Basic crêpe recipe

Serves 4
CALORIES PER PORTION: 260 (1095 kJ)
PROTEIN CONTENT PER PORTION: 9 grams
PREPARATION & COOKING TIME: 1¼ hours,
   including resting time

2 eggs
½ teaspoon salt
100 g (4 oz) wholemeal flour
300 ml (½ pint) milk
oil or clarified butter for frying

Beat the eggs with the salt, then stir in the flour. Pour on the milk and beat it to a thin smooth cream, adding a little extra milk. if necessary. Set aside to rest for 20 minutes. Put a thick-based frying pan, about 16 cm (7 in) diameter, over a moderate heat and brush it with oil or clarified butter. Pour 2 tablespoons of the batter into the pan and swirl it around so that it spreads evenly over the base of the pan. When the batter has set and the surface has lost its shiny look, turn it over very gently with a spatula and cook on the other side. If the pan is too hot, the batter will set before it has run thinly enough and the crêpes might burn.

Continue until all the mixture is used up, brushing the pan with a little more oil between each one. Place them one on top of another on a large, lightly buttered plate, over a pan of hot water if you intend to use them immediately; otherwise, put them on a cold plate and cover them with foil or transparent wrap and keep them in the refrigerator until needed.

Note: pancakes freeze well, if you put a piece of greaseproof paper or foil between each one before packing and storing.

Crêpes Gruyère

Serves 4
CALORIES PER PORTION: 900 (3757 kJ)
PROTEIN CONTENT PER PORTION: 35 grams
PREPARATION & COOKING TIME: 35 minutes

12 crêpes, made from the Basic recipe
150 g (5 oz) finely diced Gruyère cheese
450 ml (¾ pint) Béchamel sauce, made
   with 50 g (2 oz) butter, 50 g (2 oz)
   wholemeal, or unbleached white, flour
   and 450 ml (¾ pint) milk
1 tablespoon kirsch
4 tablespoons fresh wholemeal
   breadcrumbs
50 g (2 oz) coarsely grated Gruyère
   cheese
2 tablespoons finely chopped parsley

Set the oven at 200°C (400°F) Gas 6. Heat the Béchamel sauce gently and stir in the diced cheese and kirsch. Place a little of the warmed mixture on each crêpe and roll them up. Place them in a hot, well-buttered ovenproof dish and sprinkle with the breadcrumbs and grated cheese.

Bake the crêpes in the pre-heated oven for 10-15 minutes until really hot and golden brown. Sprinkle with the chopped parsley and serve with grilled mushrooms, Pommes Lyonnaise or petits pois.

Leek and yoghurt crêpes

Serves 4
CALORIES PER PORTION: 730 (3045 kJ)
PROTEIN CONTENT PER PORTION: 30 grams
PREPARATION & COOKING TIME: 35 minutes

12 crêpes, made from the Basic recipe
700 g (1½ lb) leeks, washed and cut in
   half, then in 1 cm (½ in) slices
4 tablespoons oil
100 g (4 oz) wholemeal flour
600 ml (1 pint) plain yoghurt
1 teaspoon finely chopped marjoram
salt
freshly ground black pepper
4 tablespoons fresh wholemeal
   breadcrumbs
50 g (2 oz) grated Cheddar cheese

Set the oven at 200°C (400°F) Gas 6. Cook the leeks in the oil until they have lost their pungent taste but are still crunchy and just beginning to colour. Sprinkle with the flour and mix well. Pour on the yoghurt, stir until it is mixed well with the leeks and flour, and bring to the boil, stirring continuously until the mixture thickens. Add the marjoram and season with salt and pepper.

Divide the mixture between the crêpes and roll them up. Place them in a hot, well-buttered ovenproof dish and sprinkle with the breadcrumbs and cheese. Bake them in the pre-heated oven for 10-15 minutes until they are really hot and golden brown. Serve with natural yoghurt as a sauce.

Accompaniments: Fennel with orange sauce, Brussel sprouts with peanuts and herb butter or Carrot loaf.

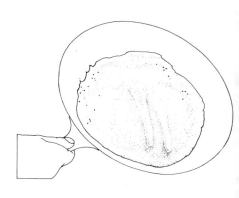

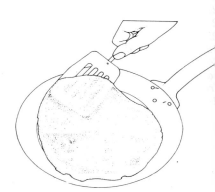

1. Pour a little batter into the pan and quickly tilt the pan to roll the batter evenly round the bottom.

2. When the crêpe is cooked, flip it over with a fish slice and briefly cook the second side before filling and rolling.

Sweetcorn and lemon crêpes

Serves 4
CALORIES PER PORTION: 860 (3595 kJ)
PROTEIN CONTENT PER PORTION: 36 grams
PREPARATION & COOKING TIME: 35 minutes

12 crêpes, made from the Basic recipe
450 g (1 lb) cooked sweetcorn kernels
50 g (2 oz) butter or margarine
225 g (8 oz) finely chopped onions
50 g (2 oz) wholemeal flour
300 ml (½ pint) milk
275 g (10 oz) grated Cheddar cheese
grated rind and juice of 1 lemon
salt
freshly ground pepper
a little freshly grated nutmeg
4 tablespoons fresh wholemeal
   breadcrumbs

Set the oven at 200°C (400°F) Gas 6. Melt the butter or margarine in a saucepan over a moderate heat and cook the onions until soft and just beginning to colour. Add the sweetcorn and cook for a few minutes longer to warm it through. Sprinkle in the flour and mix well. Remove the pan from the heat and gradually stir in the milk. Return to a moderate heat and bring to the boil, stirring continuously until the mixture thickens. Mix in most of the cheese, the lemon rind and juice and stir until the cheese has melted, then season to taste with salt, pepper and nutmeg.

Divide the mixture between the crêpes and roll them up. Place them in a hot, well-buttered ovenproof dish, sprinkle with the breadcrumbs and the remaining cheese and bake in the pre-heated oven for 10-15 minutes until really hot and golden brown.

Serve with Tomato sauce (page 196). Accompaniments: braised celery, green leaf vegetables or a large mixed salad.

Aubergine, onion and tomato crêpes

Serves 4
CALORIES PER PORTION: 570 (2377 kJ)
PROTEIN CONTENT PER PORTION: 18 grams
PREPARATION & COOKING TIME: 1-1¼ hours

12 crêpes, made from the Basic recipe
750 g (1 lb) aubergines
salt
4 tablespoons oil
175 g (6 oz) thinly sliced onions
750 g (1 lb) coarsely chopped tomatoes
175 g (6 oz) grated Cheddar cheese
1-2 tablespoons wholemeal flour
   (optional)
1 teaspoon finely chopped oregano
freshly ground black pepper
4 tablespoons fresh wholemeal
   breadcrumbs

Cut the aubergines into 1 cm (½ in) cubes and place in a colander. Sprinkle with salt and leave to drain for 30 minutes. Rinse under cold running water and dry well. Set the oven at 200°C (400°F) Gas 6. Heat half the oil in a thick-based frying pan and fry the aubergine cubes until golden brown and soft in the centres. Remove them from the pan and keep hot.

Pour the remaining oil into the pan and fry the onions until golden brown. Add the tomatoes and cook gently until reduced to a pulp. Return the aubergines to the pan, add most of the cheese, and stir until the cheese has melted and the aubergines are hot. If the mixture is too moist to hold its shape, thicken it with the flour dissolved in a very little water. Add the oregano and season with salt and pepper.

Divide the mixture between the crêpes and roll them up. Place in a hot, well-buttered ovenproof dish and sprinkle with the breadcrumbs and remaining cheese. Bake in the pre-heated oven until really hot and golden brown.
Accompaniments: Red cabbage with apple, Haricot beans with yoghurt and parsley or Greek salad.

Lentil and mushroom crêpes

Serves 6
CALORIES PER PORTION: 320 (1351 kJ)
PROTEIN CONTENT PER PORTION: 15 grams
PREPARATION & COOKING TIME: 1 hour (not
   including soaking)

12 crêpes, made from the Basic recipe
225 g (8 oz) soaked brown lentils
225 g (8 oz) finely chopped onions
2 tablespoons vegetable oil
225 g (8 oz) sliced mushrooms
125 g (4 oz) coarsely chopped celery
½ teaspoon dried thyme.
salt
freshly ground pepper
1-2 eggs, beaten

Cook the lentils for 30-45 minutes in 300 ml (½ pint) of gently simmering water. Add a little salt when they are nearly cooked — it may be necessary to add a little more water during cooking. Meanwhile, fry the onions in the oil until just beginning to colour. Add the mushrooms and celery and cook the mixture gently for about 10 minutes, taking care that it does not burn and that the mixture stays moist. Add a little water, if necessary. Set the oven at 200°C (400°F) Gas 6.

When the lentils are cooked, drain and add them to the mushroom and onion mixture and season with thyme and salt and pepper. Quickly stir in one of the eggs so that it binds the mixture together. The texture should be that of soft scrambled eggs, but if it is still too crumbly. add the second egg. Divide the mixture between the crêpes and roll them up. Place them in a hot, well-buttered ovenproof dish and bake in the pre-heated oven for 10-15 minutes or until really hot.

Serve with Madeira or Tomato Sauce (page 196).
Accompaniments: Marrow and tomato casserole or Courgettes provençales.

Curd cheese and onion croquettes

Serves 4
CALORIES PER PORTION: 445 (1857 kJ)
PROTEIN CONTENT PER PORTION: 10 grams
PREPARATION & COOKING TIME: 1½ hours

450 g (1 lb) potatoes
1 large bay leaf
100 g (4 oz) soya granules
100 g (4 oz) finely chopped onion
1 tablespoon olive or sunflower oil
1 clove of garlic, peeled and crushed
225 g (8 oz) curd cheese
1 egg, beaten
½ teaspoon finely chopped thyme
½ teaspoon finely chopped marjoram
salt and freshly ground pepper
a little freshly grated nutmeg
wholemeal flour for coating
oil for deep frying

Cook the potatoes with the bay leaf in a little boiling salted water until soft. Drain off and reserve the water, discard the bay leaf, then rub the potatoes through a sieve. Pour the reserved potato water over the soya granules and simmer for 3 minutes. Drain and use the liquid, if wished, to make stock for soup. Fry the onion in the oil until soft and golden brown. Add the garlic, potato purée, soya granules, cheese, egg and herbs, and mix well. Season with the salt, pepper and nutmeg and chill for at least 30 minutes until really firm.

Shape the mixture into 12 large croquettes and coat them well with flour. Deep fry the croquettes in oil at 180°C (350°F) until golden brown and crisp. Drain well on kitchen paper and serve immediately with a Mushroom sauce. Accompaniments: Courgettes with sage and cheese sauce or Haricot beans with yoghurt and parsley or a protein-rich salad.

Note: these croquettes are also good eaten cold.

Cheese and pepper surprise

Makes 40

Serves 4
CALORIES PER PORTION: 450 (1872 kJ)
PROTEIN CONTENT PER PORTION: 22.5 grams
PREPARATION & COOKING TIME: 1¼ -1½ hours

225 g (8 oz) Edam cheese
4 green peppers, weighing about 225 g (8 oz) each
a little prepared French-style mustard
a little wholemeal flour
300 ml (½ pint) Coating batter (page 194)
oil for deep frying

Cut the cheese into 40 strips about 3×1 cm (1½ × ½ in). Remove cores and seeds from the peppers and cut each one lengthwise into 10 strips. Put the pepper strips in a pan, pour over boiling water to cover and simmer until the peppers are limp but not too soft. Drain and plunge them into cold water, then drain again and dry well with kitchen paper.

Spread a little mustard on each piece of cheese then roll a strip of pepper round it and secure with a wooden cocktail stick. Dip in wholemeal flour, shake off the excess and then dip in the batter. Deep fry in hot oil, at 180°C (350°F), until golden brown and crisp. Drain well and serve immediately with Tartare sauce. Accompaniments: cooked lentils, soya beans or peas, or a Tomato salad.

Aubergine and cheese fricadelles

Makes 8

Serves 4
CALORIES PER PORTION: 816 (3415 kJ)
PROTEIN CONTENT PER PORTION: 37 grams
PREPARATION AND COOKING TIME: 1¼ -1½ hours

350 g (12 oz) peeled chopped aubergine
salt
oil for deep or shallow frying
100 g (4 oz) finely chopped red pepper
100 g (4 oz) finely chopped onion
2 tablespoons olive or sunflower oil
100 g (4 oz) soya granules
2 tablespoons water
1 clove of garlic, peeled and finely chopped
225 g (8 oz) fresh wholemeal breadcrumbs
175 g (6 oz) grated Cheddar cheese
1-2 eggs, beaten
freshly ground pepper
600 ml (1 pint) Brown sauce (page 196)

Place the aubergine in a colander, sprinkle with salt and leave to drain for 30 minutes. Rinse under cold running water and dry well. Fry the aubergine in deep or shallow fat until soft and well browned, then drain and allow to cool. Set the oven at 200°C (400°F) Gas 6. Fry the pepper and onion in the 2 tablespoons of oil until soft but not browned. Add the soya granules and water and cook gently for 5 minutes until all the excess liquid has been absorbed. Be ready to add a little more water if necessary, to prevent the mixture from sticking.

Remove from the heat, add the aubergine, garlic, breadcrumbs and cheese and bind with beaten egg. Mix to a firm paste, season with salt and pepper. Shape the mixture into 8 balls, place them in a greased shallow ovenproof dish and flatten them slightly. Bake in the pre-heated oven for 10 minutes, then pour over half of the Brown sauce and bake the fricadelles for a further 10 minutes, basting once. Serve with the remaining sauce. Accompaniments: Lyonnaise potatoes or Savoury brown rice and a salad.

Left: Aubergine and cheese fricadelles – just one of the splendid range of rissoles and croquettes that can be made from a variety of vegetables and pulses. Right: Cornish pasties are perfect for picnics. Try them with your home-made pickles, followed by cheese and fresh fruit

Vegetable rissoles

Serves 4
CALORIES PER PORTION: 305 (1277 kJ)
PROTEIN CONTENT PER PORTION: 14 grams
PREPARATION & COOKING TIME: about 1 hour

*225 g (8 oz) shredded leeks (about 450 g
(1 lb) unprepared weight)*
100 g (4 oz) grated carrot
100 g (4 oz) finely shredded celery
100 g (4 oz) grated turnip
1 tablespoon oil
1 tablespoon cold water
50 g (2 oz) wholemeal flour
100 g (4 oz) wholemeal breadcrumbs
100 g (4 oz) grated Cheddar cheese
1 egg
*1 clove of garlic, peeled and finely
chopped*
½-1 teaspoon finely chopped thyme
½-1 teaspoon finely chopped marjoram
salt and freshly ground pepper
a little oil for brushing

Place all the vegetables in a thick-based pan and add the oil and water. Cover tightly and cook very gently until the vegetables have lost their raw texture, but are still crisp. Shake the pan frequently to prevent the vegetables from sticking and stir the vegetables once or twice. Remove the pan from the heat and allow to cool.

Sprinkle over the flour and mix it well in, then add the remaining rissole ingredients and mix to a fairly firm consistency. Shape into 12 rissoles with well-floured hands and place them on a well-oiled baking sheet. Brush the rissoles with a little oil and cook under a moderately hot grill for 10 minutes on each side, until browned. Serve with Cheese sauce.
Accompaniments: Peas with lettuce and onions, Broccoli surprise or a salad of lentils and tomatoes.

Arancini Siciliani (soya bean and rice croquettes)

Serves 4
CALORIES PER PORTION: 450 (1872 kJ)
PROTEIN CONTENT PER PORTION: 21 grams
PREPARATION & COOKING TIME: 45 minutes

225 g (8 oz) cooked soya beans
*225 g (8 oz) cooked brown short-grain
rice, (100 g (4 oz) when raw)*
50 g (2 oz) grated Parmesan cheese
*1 clove of garlic, peeled and finely
chopped*
½-1 teaspoon finely chopped thyme
1-2 eggs, beaten
salt
freshly ground pepper
*100 g (4 oz) Edam cheese, cut into 8
cubes*
beaten egg
*fresh or dried wholemeal breadcrumbs
for coating*
oil for deep frying
8 sprigs of mint, to garnish

Mix together the soya beans, rice, Parmesan cheese, garlic, thyme and enough beaten egg to bind the mixture. Add salt and pepper to taste.

Divide the mixture into 8 portions and shape each portion into a ball around one cube of cheese. Coat with egg and breadcrumbs, then deep fry in batches in hot oil, heated to 180°C (350°F), until crisp and golden brown. Drain well. and garnish each croquette with a sprig of mint. Serve with Tomato sauce.
Accompaniments: a Watercress and tomato salad, or Chicory, orange and walnut salad, or a Coleslaw.

Walnut and herb rissoles

Makes 12

Serves 4
CALORIES PER PORTION: 590 (2457 kJ)
PROTEIN CONTENT PER PORTION: 17 grams
PREPARATION & COOKING TIME: 1¼ hours

100 g (4 oz) finely ground walnuts
*100 g (4 oz) fresh wholemeal
breadcrumbs*
100 g (4 oz) finely chopped onion
1 clove of garlic, peeled and crushed
½-1 teaspoon finely chopped sage
½-1 teaspoon finely chopped thyme
*6 finely ground allspice berries. or
about ¼ teaspoon ground allspice*
salt and freshly ground pepper
50 g (2 oz) butter
50 g (2 oz) wholemeal flour
scant 300 ml (½ pint) milk
1 teaspoon yeast extract
2 eggs. beaten
*Tomato or Brown sauce (page 196) for
serving*
sprigs of watercress, to garnish

Set the oven at 180°C (350°F) Gas 4. Mix together the nuts, breadcrumbs, onion, garlic, herbs and allspice, then season the mixture with salt and pepper.

Melt the butter over gentle heat, then stir in the flour. Remove the pan from the heat and gradually add the milk, stirring briskly between each addition. Return the pan to the heat and bring to the boil, stirring continuously until the mixture thickens. Allow to cool slightly before stirring in the yeast extract and the eggs, then fold in the nut mixture — the consistency should be firm but moist. Divide into 12 rissoles with well-floured hands, a little extra flour for the mixture, if necessary.

Place on a well-oiled baking sheet and bake in the preheated oven for 20 minutes, until the rissoles are firm and the tops lightly browned. For a darker brown colour, brush the rissoles with a little oil and put them under a hot grill after baking. Arrange them on a serving dish and pour over the Tomato or Brown sauce. Garnish with sprigs of watercress and serve immediately.
Accompaniments: Baked carrot loaf, Beetroot with yoghurt or Courgettes provençales and a Green salad.

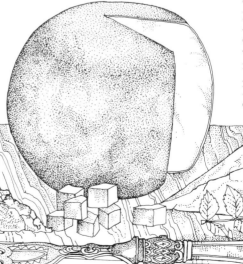

Soya bean and nut burgers

Makes 12 thin or 6 fat ones!

Serves 4-6
CALORIES: 1445 (6040 kJ)
PROTEIN CONTENT: 51 grams
PREPARATION AND COOKING TIME: 1-1¼ hours

225 g (8 oz) cooked soya beans
225 g (8 oz) finely ground walnuts
225 g (8 oz) finely chopped green
*   peppers*
225 g (8 oz) finely chopped onions
2 cloves of garlic, peeled and finely
*   chopped*
12 finely ground allspice berries,
*   or ½ teaspoon ground allspice*
2 eggs, beaten
salt
freshly ground pepper
Wholemeal bread rolls (optional)

Set the oven at 200°C (400°F) Gas 6. Rub the soya beans through a Mouli mill or mincer, or crush in a pestle and mortar, until coarsely ground. Combine all the ingredients, adding the seasoning to the eggs, and mix together very thoroughly. Shape the mixture into 6 or 12 burgers, pressing each one firmly, so that it will not crumble during cooking.

Place the burgers on a well-oiled baking sheet and cook for 15-20 minutes in the pre-heated oven, or until they are golden brown on top. Carefully turn them over and cook for a further 10 minutes. Place each one in a split Wholemeal bread roll and add a slice of cheese for extra protein, or serve with Tomato sauce or tomato ketchup and pickles.

Crocchette di spinaci

Serves 4
CALORIES PER PORTION: 285 (1197 kJ)
PROTEIN CONTENT PER PORTION: 21 grams
PREPARATION & COOKING TIME: 45-60 minutes

450 g (1 lb) cooked spinach
100 g (4 oz) grated Cheddar cheese
100 g (4 oz) fresh wholemeal
*   breadcrumbs*
2 eggs, well beaten
1 tablespoon lemon juice
50 g (2 oz) wholemeal flour
salt
freshly ground pepper
1-2 teaspoons chopped thyme or mint
*   (optional)*
oil for shallow frying

Drain the cooked spinach well; chop it finely. Add the cheese, breadcrumbs, eggs, lemon juice and half of the wholemeal flour and mix thoroughly. Season with salt and pepper and add the chopped herbs, if wished.

Fry about 1 teaspoonful of the mixture in shallow oil to test the consistency; it should hold together. If it doesn't, add a little more flour and keep the croquettes firmly shaped. Don't use too much flour though, or they will be rather heavy.

When the consistency is right, fry large tablespoons in shallow oil until golden brown on both sides. Take care when you turn them over that they do not break in half. Drain well and serve hot with Tomato sauce (page 196).
Accompaniment: Dauphinois potatoes, Paprika beans in sour cream or a Swede soufflé.

Salad nut rissoles

Serves 4
CALORIES PER PORTION: 113 (475 kJ)
PROTEIN CONTENT PER PORTION: 4 grams
PREPARATION TIME: 30-40 minutes

225 g (8oz) finely ground mixed nuts
100 g (4 oz) fresh wholemeal
*   breadcrumbs*
50 g (2 oz) finely chopped spring onion
sprig of mint, finely chopped
½ teaspoon finely chopped marjoram
grated rind of ½ lemon
1 tablespoon lemon juice (optional)
1 egg, beaten
2 tablespoons dry sherry
salt and freshly ground pepper
6-8 tablespoons finely chopped parsley

Combine all the ingredients except the parsley and mix together thoroughly. Shape the mixture into 8 balls and pat into rissoles. Roll each one in chopped parsley until well coated. Chill until required. Serve cold with lemon wedges.
Accompaniments: Elona salad, avocado wedges or a Green salad.

Note: a little melted butter can be included if you find the mixture does not bind together as well as it should.

Cornish pasties

Serves 4
CALORIES PER PORTION: 490 (2050 kJ)
PROTEIN CONTENT PER PORTION: 18 grams
PREPARATON & COOKING TIME: ¾ hour

225 g (8 oz) Wholemeal shortcrust
*   pastry (page 194)*
100 g (4 oz) thinly sliced onion
50 g (2 oz) butter
50 g (2 oz) thinly sliced carrot
50 g (2 oz) diced turnip
100 g (4 oz) diced potato
100 g (4 oz) coarsely chopped
*   mushrooms*
a little wholemeal flour
1 teaspoon yeast extract
100 ml (4 fl oz) milk
1 egg, beaten
100 g (4 oz) grated Cheddar cheese
salt
freshly ground pepper
a little vegetable oil
beaten egg, to glaze

Fry the onion gently in the butter until soft but not browned. Add the carrot, turnip and potato and cook gently for 5 minutes. Add the mushrooms and 2 tablespoons of water; cover the pan and cook over very gentle heat for 10 minutes.

Meanwhile, roll out the dough into a 36 cm (15 in) square and cut into 4. Sprinkle each portion with flour, then cover and put into the refrigerator.

Dissolve the yeast extract in the milk and whisk in the egg. Pour this over the cooked vegetables and stir until the egg cooks and the mixture thickens. Add the cheese, season with salt and pepper and set aside until cold. Set the oven at 200°C (400°F) Gas 6. Pour a little oil onto a baking sheet and spread it evenly. There should be a little excess to make the bottoms of the pasties crisp.

Place the squares of dough on the baking sheet and put a quarter of the filling in the centre of each. Brush the edges of the pastry with water, fold over diagonally and seal the edges together firmly. Bake in the pre-heated oven for 30 minutes. After 20 minutes, brush the tops of the pasties with beaten egg to glaze them.

Serve with a Salad Niçoise or a Coleslaw.

Stuffed aubergines

Serves 6
CALORIES PER PORTION: 485 (2025 kJ)
PROTEIN CONTENT PER PORTION: 19 grams
PREPARATION & COOKING TIME: 1-1¼ hours,
    including draining

3 small aubergines, each weighing about
    100 g (4 oz)
salt
olive or sunflower oil, for brushing
Basic stuffing

Set the oven at 200°C (400°F) Gas 6. Cut the aubergines in half and scoop out the flesh with a teaspoon, leaving a shell about 5 mm (¼ in) thick. Roughly chop the aubergine flesh and place in a colander with the shells. Sprinkle liberally with salt and leave to drain for 30 minutes. Rinse and dry well. Brush the aubergine shells with oil and place them in a shallow, ovenproof dish.

Mix the chopped aubergine with the stuffing and pile into the prepared shells. Brush the tops with oil and bake in the pre-heated oven for 30 minutes. Serve hot with Tomato or Brown sauce (page 196) and a selection of green vegetables.

Stuffed cabbage leaves

Serves 6
CALORIES PER PORTION: 570 (2392 kJ)
PROTEIN CONTENT PER PORTION: 23 grams
PREPARATION & COOKING TIME: 1¼ hours

This recipe can also be used with vine leaves, using smaller portions of stuffing.

12 large green cabbage leaves
Basic stuffing
600 ml (1 pint) Tomato sauce (page
    196)

Set the oven at 200°C (400°F) Gas 6. Trim the thick ends of the of the stalks from the cabbage leaves, then cook the leaves in boiling water for 5 minutes to blanch them. Drain and rinse under cold running water to cool the leaves. Pat dry with kitchen paper.

Place a little of the stuffing at the stalk end of each leaf, fold the sides over the stuffing and then roll up each leaf, completely enclosing the stuffing. Use a wooden cocktail stick, if necessary, to stop the leaf unrolling. Arrange the stuffed leaves in a double layer in a small ovenproof dish and cover with the Tomato sauce. Bake in the pre-heated oven for 45 minutes. Serve hot or cold with rice or lentils.

Basic stuffing

TOTAL CALORIES: 1775 (7420 kJ)
TOTAL PROTEIN CONTENT: 76 grams
PREPARATION TIME: 20-30 minutes

2 eggs
1 teaspoon yeast extract
225 g (8 oz) finely ground mixed nuts
225 g (8 oz) finely chopped onion
100 g (4 oz) finely chopped celery
100 g (4 oz) grated Cheddar cheese
salt
freshly ground black pepper
½ teaspoon finely chopped thyme
½ teaspoon finely chopped marjoram
1 clove of garlic, peeled and crushed

Beat the eggs with the yeast extract. Mix together all the other ingredients and pour in the eggs. Mix well, and use the stuffing as directed in the following recipes.

Nuts, vegetables, cheese and herbs – all are used in this protein-rich Basic stuffing mixture. Right: this filling Vegetable pudding needs only a Tomato salad as a side dish

Stuffed peppers

Serves 6
CALORIES PER PORTION: 505 (2125 kJ)
PROTEIN CONTENT PER PORTION: 21 grams
PREPARATION & COOKING TIME: 45 minutes-
1 hour

6 green or red peppers, weighing about
100 g (4 oz) each
Basic stuffing
olive or sunflower oil, for brushing

Set the oven at 200°C (400°F) Gas 6. Slice the tops off the peppers and remove the core and seeds. Place them in an oven-proof dish. Fill with the stuffing and brush them liberally with oil.

Bake in the pre-heated oven for 30-45 minutes, then serve with Tomato or Brown sauce.

Stuffed marrow

Serves 4
CALORIES PER PORTION: 485 (2022 kJ)
PROTEIN CONTENT PER PORTION: 21 grams
PREPARATION & COOKING TIME: 2½ hours

1 large marrow
salt
Basic stuffing

Set the oven at 200°C (400°F) Gas 6. Cut one end off the marrow and use a long-handled spoon to scoop out the pith and pips. Lightly sprinkle the inside with salt and stand the marrow on its end to drain for 30 minutes. Rinse the inside with cold water and dry well.

Fill the marrow with the stuffing and replace the end, securing it with wooden cocktail sticks or small skewers. Place on its side in a well-buttered ovenproof dish and bake in the pre-heated oven for about 1½ hours, or until tender.

Serve hot with Brown sauce, accompanied by Polish-style cauliflower cheese or broccoli.

Vegetable pudding

Serves 4
CALORIES PER PORTION: 490 (2050 kJ)
PROTEIN CONTENT PER PORTION: 20 grams
PREPARATION & COOKING TIME: 3½ -4 hours

The pudding crust
175 g (6 oz) wholemeal flour
salt
1 teaspoon baking powder
75 g (3 oz) butter
1 egg, well-beaten
a little water

The filling
50 g (2 oz) finely chopped onion
100 g (4 oz) diced parsnips
100 g (4 oz) coarsely chopped
* mushrooms*
100 g (4 oz) fresh or frozen peas
175 g (6 oz) grated Cheddar cheese
2 tablespoons wholemeal flour
½ teaspoon finely chopped marjoram
salt and freshly ground pepper
4 tablespoons water

To make the pudding crust: sieve the flour, salt and baking powder into a bowl and rub in the butter. Add the egg and just enough water to make a fairly firm dough. Divide the dough into one-quarter and three-quarters. Roll out the larger portion and use it to line a 90 ml (1½ pint) capacity pudding basin. Roll out the smaller portion to fit the top.

To make the filling: mix together the vegetables and cheese in a large bowl. Sprinkle with the flour, marjoram, salt and pepper and toss well. Place the filling in the lined bowl, pressing it well down. Pour on the water and cover with the pastry lid. Cover with greaseproof paper or foil and tie securely.

Lower the pudding into a saucepan and add enough boiling water to come halfway up the sides of the basin. Cover the pan with a lid and simmer the pudding for 3 hours, adding more hot water if necessary during the cooking time. Serve with a Tomato salad.

Braised vegetables

Serves 4

CALORIES PER PORTION: 285 (1190 kJ)
PROTEIN CONTENT PER PORTION: 16 grams
PREPARATION & COOKING TIME: 1 hour

4 tablespoons olive or sunflower oil
150 g (5 oz) diced turnips
150 g (5 oz) diced carrots
200 g (7 oz) thinly sliced celery
150 g (5 oz) red and green peppers, in
* equal proportions, de-seeded and*
* sliced*
200 g (7 oz) fresh or frozen peas
200 g (7 oz) fresh or frozen runner beans
2 tablespoons wholemeal flour
600 ml (1 pint) water
1 tablespoon yeast extract
1 clove garlic, peeled and crushed
400 g (14 oz) shredded white cabbage
salt and freshly ground pepper
200 g (7 oz) leaf spinach
50 g (2 oz) coarsely grated cheese

Heat the oil in a thick-based frying pan, add the turnips and carrots and cook, stirring continuously, until golden brown.

Add the celery after about 5 minutes cooking time and add the peppers after another 5 minutes. Cook for 5 minutes longer, about 15-20 minutes altogether. Remove the fried vegetables with a draining spoon and put them into a shallow ovenproof dish about 25 cm (10 in) in diameter.

Add the peas and beans to the oil in the pan and cook them for about 5 minutes — until they are just browning at the edges. Drain and add them to the other vegetables and mix them all together.

Stir the flour into the remaining oil — it may be necessary to add a little more oil at this stage — and stir to make a soft paste. Pour in the water, add the yeast extract and crushed garlic and bring to the boil, stirring until the sauce thickens. Add the cabbage, bring back to the boil and pour this over the other vegetables. Season well.

Set the oven at 220°C (425°F) Gas 7. Wash the spinach leaves well and remove the central stems. Arrange the stems over the dish. Blanch the spinach leaves in plenty of boiling water, removing them and draining them the moment they have gone limp. Cover the mixed vegetables with overlapping leaves and brush with a little olive oil. Sprinkle the grated cheese over the top and bake, on the middle shelf of the pre-heated oven for 20 minutes. Serve with soya beans dressed with finely chopped parsley, butter and lemon juice.

Courgette and tomato casserole with cheese dumplings

Serves 4

CALORIES PER PORTION: 525 (2190 kJ)
PROTEIN CONTENT PER PORTION: 26 grams
PREPARATION & COOKING TIME: 1½ hours

The casserole
450 g (1 lb) courgettes, cut into 5 mm
* (¼ in) slices*
salt
225 g (8 oz) finely sliced onions
2 tablespoons olive or sunflower oil
450 g (1 lb) chopped tomatoes
2 cloves of garlic, peeled and finely
* chopped*
freshly ground black pepper

The dumplings
1 litre (2 pints) milk
1 tablespoon wine vinegar
1 tablespoon water
2 large eggs, lightly beaten
salt and freshly ground black pepper
a sprinkling of cayenne pepper
½-1 teaspoon dried thyme
125 g (4 oz) Cheddar cheese, cut into
* small cubes*
150 g (5 oz) wholemeal breadcrumbs

Sprinkle the sliced courgettes lightly with salt and leave them to drain for 30 minutes while you prepare the dumplings. Bring the milk to the boil, add the vinegar and water, then remove from the stove and stir gently until the curds have more or less separated, leaving an almost clear liquid. Pour through a fine strainer lined with muslin. Return the whey to the saucepan and continue to boil until reduced to 600 ml (1 pint). Leave on one side. Allow the curds to cool slightly, then add them to the eggs and season with salt, pepper, cayenne and thyme. Mix well. Add the cheese to the breadcrumbs. Pour on the egg and curd mixture and mix to a firm dough. Form into 10 round dumplings and put on one side.

Meanwhile, fry the onions in the oil, over a medium-to-low heat, until they are golden brown. Drain well and transfer them to an ovenproof casserole. Rinse the courgettes and dry them with a clean cloth or kitchen paper. Increase the heat and fry the courgettes until the edges just begin to brown. Drain them and add to the casserole. Set the oven at 200°C (400°F) Gas 6.

Fry the tomatoes and garlic until the juices run, season with salt and pepper and continue cooking until they turn to a thick pulp, taking care that they do not burn. Add the whey and bring back to the boil. Pour this mixture over the onions and courgettes in the casserole.

Arrange the dumplings in a single layer in the casserole liquid, taking care to submerge each one, and bake, uncovered, on the middle shelf of the pre-heated oven for 20 minutes. Serve with a Mixed salad and soya beans.

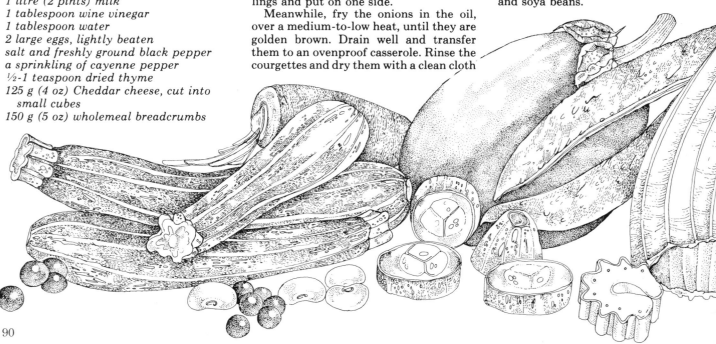

Vegetable moussaka

Serves 4
CALORIES PER PORTION: 435 (1815 kJ)
PROTEIN CONTENT PER PORTION: 21 grams
PREPARATION & COOKING TIME: 1½ hours

450 g (1 lb) sliced aubergines
salt
5 tablespoons olive or sunflower oil
450 g (1 lb) coarsely chopped tomatoes
freshly ground black pepper
1 teaspoon chopped thyme
1 clove of garlic, peeled and finely
*   chopped*
225 g (8 oz) chopped onions
450 g (1 lb) cooked soya beans (about
*   200 g (7 oz) uncooked), coarsely*
*   mashed*
1 egg, beaten
300 ml (½ pint) milk
40 g (1½ oz) dried skimmed milk
*   (optional)*

Sprinkle the aubergine slices with salt and allow them to drain for 30 minutes. Rinse and dry them with a clean cloth or kitchen paper.

Set the oven at 180°C (350°F) Gas 4. **Pour 2 tablespoons of oil into an oven-proof baking dish about 25 cm in diameter, 8 cm deep (10 in by 3 in). Dip the** aubergine slices into the oil and rub them together so that they are evenly coated. Arrange them on a sheet of foil on a baking sheet, not overlapping, and bake them in the pre-heated oven for 20 minutes or until they are browned.

Meanwhile, put the tomatoes into a pan with salt and pepper, the thyme and garlic and cook them gently to a pulp, stirring occasionally to prevent them burning. Set aside. Fry the onions in the remaining 3 tablespoons of oil until golden brown.

Re-set the oven at 200°C (400°F) Gas 6. Line the ovenproof dish, still slightly oiled, with a layer of cooked aubergine, taking care not to break the pieces when removing them from the foil. Mix the beans well with the tomatoes and onions and spoon into the baking dish. Cover with another layer of aubergine, reserving about 6 good-looking slices.

Mix together the egg, milk, dried milk, if using, and season with pepper. Pour this over the top. Garnish with the 6 reserved slices of aubergine and bake near the top of the pre-heated oven for 30 minutes. Serve with a Greek salad.

Vegetable casserole

Serves 4
CALORIES PER PORTION: 510 (2142 kJ)
PROTEIN CONTENT PER PORTION: 21 grams
PREPARATION & COOKING TIME: 1½-2 hours

4 tablespoons vegetable oil
225 g (8 oz) finely chopped onion
225 g (8 oz) thinly sliced celery
225 g (8 oz) thinly sliced carrot
225 g (8 oz) diced turnip
600 ml (1 pint) water
50 g (2 oz) dried skimmed milk
1 teaspoon yeast extract
1 large bay leaf, crumbled
1 teaspoon finely chopped marjoram
salt
freshly ground black pepper
225 g (8 oz) cauliflower florets, thinly
*   sliced*
225 g (8 oz) thinly sliced leeks
225 g (8 oz) unroasted peanuts

Set the oven at 180°C (350°F) Gas 4. Pour the oil into a large, thick-based saucepan and add the onion, celery, carrot and turnip. Place over a moderate heat and cook the vegetables for 20-25 minutes. Shake the pan frequently and stir the vegetables until they begin to colour and soften.

Transfer them to an ovenproof casserole. Blend together the water, dried milk powder, yeast extract, bay leaf and marjoram, season with salt and pepper, and bring to the boil. Pour this stock over the fried vegetables and add the cauliflower, leeks and peanuts.

Bake in the pre-heated oven for 1 hour, then serve the casserole with Cheese dumplings, baked potatoes and a large, Mixed salad.

Nut cassoulet

Serves 6
CALORIES PER PORTION: 755 (3157 kJ)
PROTEIN CONTENT PER PORTION: 32 grams
PREPARATION & COOKING TIME: 2½ hours
    excluding soaking overnight

350 g (12 oz) soaked haricot beans
salt
Basic stuffing (page 88), with garlic
300-450 ml (½-¾ pint) Béchamel sauce
·   (page 196)
2 cloves of garlic, peeled and crushed
grated rind of 1 lemon
2-4 hard-boiled eggs, shelled (optional)
6 tablespoons dried wholemeal
*   breadcrumbs*

Cook the drained haricot beans gently in plenty of simmering water for about 1 hour or until they are soft but not broken. Add ½-1 teaspoon salt to the cooking water when the beans are almost ready. Drain them well.

Set the oven at 200°C (400°F) Gas 6. Shape the stuffing mixture into 12 small rissoles, pressing them firmly so they will keep their shape. Bring the Béchamel sauce to the boil. Add enough of the sauce to the beans to coat them generously — but not excessively. Add the garlic and grated lemon rind, and pour half of the mixture into a fairly shallow ovenproof dish.

Arrange the rissoles with the quartered hard-boiled eggs, if used, on top and cover with the remaining bean mixture. Sprinkle with breadcrumbs and bake in the pre-heated oven for 20-30 minutes, or until the top is well browned and the cassoulet is bubbling.

This is a substantial dish and should be served hot, accompanied only by a crisp salad.

Vegetable goulash with Spetzli

Serves 6

CALORIES PER PORTION: 540 (2266 kJ)
PROTEIN CONTENT PER PORTION: 23 grams
PREPARATION & COOKING TIME: 50 minutes

225 g (8 oz) coarsely chopped onions
225 g (8 oz) chopped turnips
4 tablespoons olive or sunflower oil
225 g (8 oz) coarsely chopped red
  peppers
225 g (8 oz) coarsely chopped white
  cabbage
2 tablespoons paprika
2 tablespoons wholemeal flour
50 g (2 oz) dried skimmed milk
300 ml (½ pint) water (preferably the
  water used to soak the beans)
salt and freshly ground pepper
300 ml (½ pint) brown ale
2 cloves garlic, peeled and crushed
1 tablespoon lemon juice or wine
  vinegar
450 g (1 lb) cooked soya beans (about
  200 g (7 oz) uncooked), very coarsely
  mashed — leaving a good proportion
  whole
50 g (2 oz) sliced gherkins
2 hard-boiled eggs, chopped (optional)
200 ml (⅓ pint) cultured sour cream
  (optional)
2 tablespoons chopped parsley
  (optional)

The Spetzli
225 g (8 oz) wholemeal flour
salt
¼ teaspoon grated nutmeg
2 eggs
2 tablespoons milk
4 tablespoons melted butter

Fry the onions and turnips in the oil in a thick-based pan until golden brown. Add the peppers and cook until any juice has evaporated and the onion has started to brown again. Add the cabbage, then stir in the paprika and wholemeal flour.

Dissolve the milk powder in the water and season with salt and pepper. Pour the brown ale on to the onions, and when the foaming subsides add the dissolved milk, the garlic and lemon juice or wine vinegar. Put in the soya beans, bring back to the boil and simmer, covered, for 10 minutes, stirring occasionally to prevent burning.

Add half the gherkins to the goulash, and mix them well in. Pour it into a heated serving dish and decorate with the chopped eggs, if used and the rest of the gherkins. Swirl in the sour cream and sprinkle with parsley. Serve with Spetzli.

To make the Spetzli: sift the flour, salt and nutmeg together, keeping the bran apart. Lightly beat the eggs with the milk and 1 tablespoon of the melted butter.

Add this to the flour and mix to a soft dough, adding a little extra milk if necessary.

Scoop out small lumps of the dough with a teaspoon or use a forcing bag with a 5 mm (¼ in) plain round nozzle and cut off 1 cm (½ in) lengths. Roll these in the bran, if liked.

Drop the spetzli into a large pan of boiling salted water and boil for about 5 minutes: they should be *al dente* (tender, but firm to bite). Drain and serve with the rest of the melted butter poured over them and a little additional grated nutmeg if desired.

Note: be sure to use fresh paprika. This spice loses its flavour quickly if kept too long and the dish suffers as a result.

Vegetable goulash is served here with a swirl of sour cream to counteract the pungency of paprika. Home-made wholemeal Spetzli, with just a hint of nutmeg, go well with this dish

Leipziger allerlei

Serves 4-6

CALORIES PER PORTION FOR 4: 520 (2182 kJ)
PROTEIN CONTENT PER PORTION FOR 4: 20
  grams
PREPARATION & COOKING TIME: 1 hour

4-6 tablespoons vegetable oil
225 g (8 oz) diced celery
225 g (8 oz) diced carrot
225 g (8 oz) diced parsnip
225 g (8 oz) finely chopped onion
450 ml (¾ pint) Béchamel sauce (page 196)
225 g (8 oz) cooked cauliflower florets
225 g (8 oz) cooked peas
salt
freshly ground pepper
150 g (5 oz) grated Cheddar cheese

Pour the oil into a large thick-based saucepan and add the celery, carrot, parsnip and onion. Place the pan over moderate heat and cook the vegetables for 20-30 minutes, shaking the pan frequently and stirring the vegetables until they colour and soften. Meanwhile, heat up the sauce and cook the cauliflower and peas, if they are not already prepared.

Add about two-thirds of the sauce to the softened vegetables. Pour the mixture into a warmed, shallow flameproof dish, scatter the peas on top and arrange the cauliflower florets down the centre. Season with salt and pepper. Cover with the remaining sauce and sprinkle with the cheese. Place the dish under a hot grill until the cheese melts and turns a crisp, golden brown.

This is a substantial dish and should be served hot with a salad only.

Chili 'sans' carne

Serves 4

CALORIES PER PORTION: 325 (1375 kJ)
PROTEIN CONTENT PER PORTION: 19 grams
PREPARATION & COOKING TIME: about 2½
  hours excluding soaking

225 g (8 oz) red kidney beans, soaked overnight
225 g (8 oz) coarsely chopped onion
2 tablespoons vegetable oil
450 g (1 lb) skinned tomatoes
2 teaspoons finely chopped oregano
1 large clove of garlic, peeled and crushed
1-4 teaspoons chilli powder, to taste
100 g (4 oz) grated Cheddar cheese
salt
freshly ground pepper

Drain the soaked beans, then cook them gently in lightly salted boiling water for about 2 hours, or until they are soft and most of the water has been absorbed. Drain off the excess water and reserve it. Fry the onion in the oil until golden brown, then add the tomatoes and cook them down to a purée. Add the beans with about 4 tablespoons of the reserved water, the oregano, garlic and chilli powder, and mix thoroughly. Sprinkle the cheese over the top and stir until it has melted, then season with salt and pepper.

Serve hot with the traditional Tortillas and a large mixed salad. A lemon-based Rum punch makes a very good 'quencher'.

Tortillas

Serves 8

CALORIES PER PORTION: 170 (705 kJ)
PROTEIN CONTENT PER PORTION: 5.5. grams
PREPARATION & COOKING TIME: 45 minutes

100 g (4 oz) cornmeal
100 g (4 oz) wholemeal flour
½ teaspoon bicarbonate of soda
salt
a little hot water
oil for shallow frying

Mix together the cornmeal, flour, bicarbonate of soda and salt and make into a firm dough with a little hot water. Knead the dough for 3 minutes, then leave it to rest for 30 minutes. Divide it into eight portions, roll each one out into a 'pancake' about 15 cm (6 in) diameter and fry on both sides until golden brown and cooked. Turn the Tortillas over two or three times, taking care that they do not break.

Peanut curry

Serves 4

CALORIES PER PORTION: 455 (1890 kJ)
PROTEIN CONTENT PER PORTION: 13 gram
PREPARATION & COOKING TIME: 45 minutes

225 g (8 oz) unroasted peanuts, coarsely chopped
2 teaspoons ground coriander seeds
1 teaspoon ground turmeric
2 tablespoons vegetable oil
100 g (4 oz) finely chopped onion
1 teaspoon fresh root ginger, peeled and finely chopped
1 clove of garlic, peeled and very finely chopped
salt
25 g (1 oz) thinly sliced green chilli (optional)
225 g (8 oz) skinned tomatoes, coarsely chopped
100 ml (4 fl oz) coconut milk
200 ml (⅓ pint) boiling water
100 g (4 oz) grated fresh coconut
2 tablespoons finely chopped coriander leaves

Heat the coriander and turmeric in the oil for a few moments. Add the onion, ginger and garlic and cook until the onion is soft. Add the peanuts, salt, chilli if used, tomatoes and coconut milk and cook gently until the tomatoes break down to a pulp. Stir in the boiling water and simmer for 20 minutes. Stir in the coconut and 1 tablespoon of the coriander leaves, increase the heat and boil to a thick purée, taking care that it does not stick or burn. Serve in a warmed bowl, sprinkled with the remaining coriander leaves, and with Cucumber raita as an accompaniment.

Cucumber raita

Serves 4

CALORIES PER PORTION: 35 (150 kJ)
PROTEIN CONTENT PER PORTION: 3 grams
PREPARATION & CHILLING TIME: 1½ hours

400 g (14 oz) peeled and diced cucumber
salt
½ teaspoon cumin seeds
200 ml (⅓ pint) natural yoghurt
1 tablespoon finely chopped mint

Sprinkle the cucumber with salt and leave for 20 minutes. Rinse and pat dry. Heat the cumin seeds in a dry saucepan for a few moments until a spicy aroma begins to rise. Crush them with pestle and mortar and mix into the yoghurt. Add the mint and cucumber and mix thoroughly. Chill well before serving.

Layered brown rice pilau

Serves 4
CALORIES PER PORTION: 730 (3057 kJ)
PROTEIN CONTENT PER PORTION: 22 grams
PREPARATION & COOKING TIME: 2-3 hours,
  including soaking

The rice
*225 g (8 oz) brown rice, soaked for 1
  hour*
1 teaspoon finely ground cumin
*2.5 cm (1 in) cinnamon stick, crushed
  into small pieces*
1 teaspoon clove-based garam masala
50 g (2 oz) clarified butter
100 g (4 oz) finely chopped onion
*50 g (2 oz) fresh root ginger, peeled and
  finely chopped*
*3 cloves of garlic, peeled and very finely
  chopped*
500 ml (scant 1 pint) boiling water
salt
4 cardamom seeds, split open
25 g (1 oz) halved pistachio nuts

The filling
1 teaspoon ground turmeric
50 g (2 oz) blanched halved almonds
50 g (2 oz) cashew nuts
½ teaspoon ground cumin
2 tablespoons vegetable oil
100 g (4 oz) thinly sliced onion
*50 g (2 oz) fresh root ginger, peeled and
  finely chopped*
2 cloves of garlic, peeled and crushed
100 g (4 oz) cooked fresh or frozen peas
150 ml (¼ pint) boiling water
*100 g (4 oz) panir (page 200), cut into
  small cubes and fried until golden
  brown*
*25 g (1 oz) red chillis, de-seeded and
  finely chopped (optional)*
4 tablespoons chopped coriander leaves
salt
*2 hard-boiled eggs, shelled and
  quartered*

To prepare the rice: heat together the cumin, cinnamon and garam masala in the butter for a few minutes until a spicy aroma begins to rise. Add the onion, ginger and garlic and cook until the onion is soft. Put in the rice and cook briskly for 2-3 minutes, stirring continuously, then add the boiling water, salt, cardamon seeds and pistachio nuts. Cover the pan tightly and cook the rice over very gentle heat for about 45 minutes, or put into a slow oven 150°C (325°F) Gas 3. If the heat is at the right temperature, the rice will be tender and dry. It may be necessary to add a little more water during the cooking, but do not stir the rice or lift the lid and allow the steam to escape too often. Use a heat-proof glass plate as a cover through which the rice can be clearly seen.

For the filling: heat together the turmeric, nuts and cumin in the vegetable oil until a spicy aroma begins to rise. Add the onion and ginger and continue frying until golden brown. Put in the garlic and cook for a few moments, before stirring in the peas and the boiling water. Simmer for 5 minutes, then add the panir, chilli if used, 3 tablespoons of the chopped coriander and season with salt; cook until thoroughly hot.

Spread half of the rice on a hot serving dish and cover with half of the filling. Spread the remaining rice over the filling and then cover with the remaining filling. Arrange the eggs in the centre. Sprinkle with the remaining coriander and serve.

Curried spinach with red lentils

Serves 4
CALORIES PER PORTION: 215 (900 kJ)
PROTEIN CONTENT PER PORTION: 15 grams
PREPARATION & COOKING TIME: 45-60
  minutes, excluding soaking

*175 g (6 oz) red lentils, washed, then
  soaked for 1 hour*
450 g (1 lb) spinach, well washed
2 tablespoons vegetable oil
1 teaspoon fennel-based garam masala
½ teaspoon finely ground cumin
100 g (4 oz) finely chopped onion
600 ml (1 pint) water
½ teaspoon ground turmeric
*1 clove of garlic, peeled and finely
  chopped*
salt
juice of 1 large lemon

Roughly chop the spinach into 1 cm (½ in) pieces. Pour the oil into a saucepan and heat the garam masala gently with the cumin until a spicy aroma begins to rise. Add the onion and fry gently, stirring until they are soft. Pour on the water, add the drained lentils, turmeric, garlic and salt and cook for 5 minutes. Add the spinach, cover the saucepan and continue cooking for about 20 minutes until nearly all the liquid has been absorbed and the lentils are done. Add a little extra water during the cooking, if necessary. Stir in the lemon juice and serve immediately.

Parsi eggs

Serves 4
CALORIES PER PORTION: 395 (1662 kJ)
PROTEIN CONTENT PER PORTION: 17 grams
PREPARATION & COOKING TIME: 45-50 minutes

8 eggs, well-beaten
450 g (1 lb) potatoes
oil for shallow frying
2 tablespoons vegetable oil
100 g (4 oz) finely chopped onion
*25-50 g (1-2 oz) fresh root ginger,
  peeled and finely chopped*
1 teaspoon ground turmeric
2 green chillis, seeded and thinly sliced
1 clove of garlic, peeled and chopped
*175 g (6 oz) skinned tomatoes, coarsely
  chopped*
salt
a sprinkling of freshly grated nutmeg
1 tablespoon chopped coriander leaves

Boil the potatoes in their skins for 10 minutes. Peel when cool and finely dice. Shallow fry them in hot oil until golden brown and crisp. Keep hot.

Meanwhile, fry the onion and ginger in the oil until soft. Add the turmeric, green chillis, garlic, tomatoes and salt, and cook gently until the tomatoes have broken down to a pulp. Boil vigorously until any excess juice has evaporated, then lower the heat, add the eggs and cook gently until the mixture is of the consistency of scrambled eggs. Pour into the centre of a hot serving dish. Sprinkle the potatoes with salt and a little nutmeg and arrange around eggs. Sprinkle with coriander.

Potato and tomato curry

Serves 4
CALORIES PER PORTION: 275 (1147 kJ)
PROTEIN CONTENT PER PORTION: 4 grams
PREPARATION & COOKING TIME: 45-60 minutes

450 g (1 lb) potatoes
3 tablespoons vegetable oil
1 teaspoon ground turmeric
1 teaspoon coriander-based garam
   masala
½ teaspoon chilli powder (optional)
50 g (2 oz) fresh root ginger, peeled and
   finely chopped
100 g (4 oz) finely chopped onion
1 clove of garlic, peeled and very finely
   chopped
salt
2 thinly sliced green chillis
450 g (1 lb) skinned tomatoes, coarsely
   chopped
2 tablespoons chopped fresh coriander
   leaves or parsley

Boil the potatoes in their skins for 10 minutes. Drain and allow to cool slightly, then peel and slice them thickly. Fry the potatoes in the oil in a thick-based frying pan until they are golden brown on both sides. Remove them from the pan and set aside until required. Heat the turmeric, garam masala and chilli powder for a few moments in the oil in the frying pan, then add the ginger and onion and fry until golden brown. Put in the garlic, salt, chillis and tomatoes, and cook gently until the tomatoes have broken down to a pulp.

Return the potatoes to the pan, cover and cook very gently until they are tender, stirring occasionally to prevent the mixture from sticking and burning. When the potatoes are cooked, increase the heat if necessary and boil away any excess moisture so that the tomato pulp almost becomes a paste. Shake the pan continually to prevent the mixture from sticking. Serve sprinkled with coriander or parsley.

Turkish pilau

Serves 4
CALORIES PER PORTION: 825 (3450 kJ)
PROTEIN CONTENT PER PORTION: 24 grams
PREPARATION & COOKING TIME: 1 hour, not
   including soaking

450 g (1 lb) aubergines
salt
225 g (8 oz) thinly sliced onions
8 tablespoons olive or vegetable oil
125 g (4 oz) sliced mushrooms
225 g (8 oz) long-grain brown rice
600 ml (1 pint) Brown vegetable stock
   (page 34)
225 g (8 oz) skinned tomatoes, chopped
125 g (4 oz) soya grits
125 g (4 oz) unroasted peanuts
1-2 cloves of garlic, peeled and finely
   chopped
½ teaspoon ground cumin
½ teaspoon ground coriander
½ teaspoon ground cinnamon
freshly ground pepper
2 hard-boiled eggs, shelled and finely
   chopped
3 finely chopped spring onions

Cut the aubergines into 1.5 cm (¾ in) cubes and sprinkle them with salt and leave them to drain for 30 minutes. Meanwhile, fry the onions in 4 tablespoons of the oil until they are golden brown. Add the mushrooms and cook them until they are black and shiny. Stir in the rice and continue stirring for 1-2 minutes until it is thoroughly coated with oil.

Pour on the stock and add the tomatoes, soya grits, peanuts, garlic and spices and season with pepper. Cover and simmer for 5 minutes while you rinse the aubergines and dry them. Fry them in the remaining oil in another pan until they are transparent and beginning to brown. Drain them and scatter them over the pilau.

Cover and continue cooking over low heat for 30-40 minutes, or until the rice is tender — it may be necessary to add a little more water during the cooking time; the pilau rice should be moist but not mushy. When the rice is ready, turn the pilau into a warm serving dish and sprinkle the chopped eggs and spring onions over the top. Serve with a Greek salad.

Lentil and rice kedgeree

Serves 4
CALORIES PER PORTION: 635 (2657 kJ)
PROTEIN CONTENT PER PORTION: 22 grams
PREPARATION & COOKING TIME: 1¼ -1½
   hours, not including soaking

225 g (8 oz) green or brown lentils,
   soaked for 2 hours
225 g (8 oz) brown rice
4 tablespoons vegetable oil
1 teaspoon ground turmeric
1 teaspoon finely ground cumin seeds
½ teaspoon clove based garam masala
   (page 200)
½ teaspoon chilli powder (optional)
1-2 chopped green chillis (optional)
50 g (2 oz) fresh root ginger, peeled and
   finely chopped
100 g (4 oz) finely chopped onion
3 cloves of garlic, peeled and finely
   chopped
salt
2 hard-boiled eggs, peeled and halved
2 thickly sliced bananas
50 g (2 oz) halved, blanched almonds
2 tablespoons chopped coriander leaves

Pour the oil into a thick-based frying pan and add the turmeric, cumin, garam masala and chilli powder, if used. Heat gently until a spicy aroma begins to rise then add the green chillis, if used, the ginger and onion and fry until the onion is soft, stirring frequently. Add the garlic, the drained lentils and the rice and fry so that it is evenly coated with oil and spices. Sprinkle with salt and add just enough boiling water to cover.

Cover the pan tightly and simmer very gently for about 45 minutes until the rice and lentils are soft and the water has been completely absorbed. You may have to add a little extra water during cooking — the finished kedgeree should be moist but not mushy. Transfer it to a hot serving dish, garnish with the eggs, banana slices, almonds and coriander and serve immediately.

Vegetarian paella

Serves 4
CALORIES PER PORTION: 555 (2328 kJ)
PROTEIN CONTENT PER PORTION: 23.5 grams
PREPARATION & COOKING TIME: 1 hour

225 g (8 oz) thickly sliced courgettes
salt
225 g (8 oz) coarsely chopped onions
4 tablespoons olive or sunflower oil
225 g (8 oz) brown long-grain rice
600 ml (1 pint) White vegetable stock
    (page 34)
a large pinch of saffron soaked in a
    little water
1 large clove of garlic, peeled and finely
    chopped
125 g (4 oz) thinly sliced red peppers
225 g (8 oz) skinned tomatoes, coarsely
    chopped
freshly ground pepper
75 g (3 oz) coarsely shredded almonds
2 hard-boiled eggs, shelled and finely
    chopped
175 g (6 oz) grated Cheddar cheese
25 g (1 oz) pimiento-stuffed green
    olives, sliced

Sprinkle the sliced courgettes with salt and leave to drain for 30 minutes. Meanwhile, fry the onions in the oil in a thick-based frying pan until they are golden brown. Add the rice and cook over moderate heat for 2 minutes, stirring constantly so that the rice does not stick and is evenly coated with oil. Pour on the stock, add the saffron in its water and the garlic and bring to the boil, stirring constantly. Reduce the heat, cover the pan and simmer for 30 minutes.

Rinse the courgettes, pat them dry with kitchen paper and add them to the pan with the red peppers and tomatoes. Pour on a little more boiling water if the rice is too dry (it should be moist but not mushy). Season with salt and pepper, cover and cook for 10-15 minutes until the rice is soft and the peppers and courgettes are tender.

Turn into a heated flameproof serving dish. Sprinkle over the almonds, chopped eggs and the cheese, garnish with the olive slices and brown under the grill. Serve with a Mixed salad.

Lentil and nut cakes

Serves 4
CALORIES PER PORTION: 345 (1445 kJ)
PROTEIN CONTENT PER PORTION: 11 grams
PREPARATION & COOKING TIME: 35-40 minutes

225 g (8 oz) cooked brown lentils,
    coarsely mashed
2-3 tablespoons vegetable oil
1 teaspoon finely ground cumin
1 teaspoon ground turmeric
1 teaspoon clove-based garam masala
100 g (4 oz) finely chopped onion
25 g (1 oz) fresh root ginger, peeled and
    finely chopped
1 clove of garlic, peeled and chopped
salt
100 g (4 oz) finely ground mixed nuts
2 tablespoons wholemeal flour
1 egg, well-beaten
oil for shallow frying

Heat the spices in the oil for a few moments. Add the onion, ginger, garlic and salt to taste and fry gently until the onion is soft. Stir in the mashed lentils and nuts; sprinkle in the flour, add the egg and mix thoroughly.

Drop large spoonfuls of the lentil mixture on to a well-floured plate and roll them into 8 balls. Flatten slightly and fry on both sides until golden brown. Serve with a bowl of natural yoghurt.

Vegetable couscous

Serves 4-6
CALORIES PER PORTION: 1085 (4540 kJ)
PROTEIN CONTENT PER PORTION: 38 grams
PREPARATION & COOKING TIME: 2¼ hours, not
    including soaking

450 g (1 lb) couscous grains
225 g (8 oz) dried chick peas, soaked
    overnight
3 tablespoons peanut oil
200 g (7 oz) sliced onions
2 large cloves of garlic, peeled and
    crushed
200 g (7 oz) chopped green peppers
200 g (7 oz) carrots
200 g (7 oz) sliced courgettes
3 potatoes, peeled and quartered
225 g (8 oz) pumpkin, cubed (optional)
900 ml (1½ pints) water
100 g (4 oz) sultanas
400 g (14 oz) canned okra, drained
1 teaspoon cayenne pepper
2 teaspoons ground cumin
1 teaspoon paprika
salt and freshly ground black pepper
150 g (5 oz) harissa sauce
40 g (1½ oz) butter
150 g (5 oz) ripe tomatoes, peeled and
    quartered
3 hard-boiled eggs, quartered

First make the couscous. Put the grains into a bowl and pour over about 300 ml (½ pint) of lukewarm salted water. Stir until blended then leave the grains for 30 minutes. Repeat at least once more. Put the chick peas and their soaking liquid into a large saucepan, making sure the peas are well covered. Bring to the boil over high heat, then reduce the heat, cover the pan and simmer for about 1 hour, or until the peas are tender. Drain and set aside.

Heat the oil in a large, deep, thick-based saucepan. Add the onions, garlic, peppers and carrots and fry gently until the onions are soft. Stir in the courgettes, potatoes and pumpkin (if using) and pour on the water. Bring to a boil, reduce the heat, cover the pan and simmer for 20 minutes. Stir in the reserved chick peas, the sultanas, okra, cayenne, cumin, paprika and season with salt and pepper then add about 1 tablespoon of harissa sauce. Bring to the boil again.

Arrange a colander lined with muslin (an open-textured kitchen cloth will do) on top of the pan containing the vegetables, or over a separate pan of simmering water. Seal the space between the colander and pan, if necessary, with a rolled up teacloth. Put the couscous grains into the colander, cover tightly and cook the couscous and vegetable mixture over low heat for 15 minutes.

Remove the colander from the pan and stir the butter gently into the grains. Add the tomatoes and eggs to the vegetable mixture. Return the colander to the pan, re-cover and cook both grains and vegetables for a final 5 minutes.

Arrange the couscous on a large, deep serving dish. Spoon over the vegetable mixture with some of the cooking liquid and hand the rest of the harissa sauce separately (you can thin this a little by stirring in some of the remaining liquid from the pan).

Couscous – served with an exotic and imaginative combination of vegetables; the egg adds protein, too

Vegetable kebabs

Serves 4

CALORIES PER PORTION: 557 (2335 kJ)
PROTEIN CONTENT PER PORTION: 11 grams
PREPARATION & COOKING TIME: 1 hour

225 g (8 oz) courgettes, sliced into 3 cm
(1¼ in) cubes
225 g (8 oz) aubergine, sliced into 3 cm
(1¼ in) cubes
salt
10 tablespoons olive or sunflower oil
½ teaspoon ground cumin
125 g (4 oz) finely chopped onion
2 thin slices of wholemeal bread, cut
into 3 cm (1¼ in) cubes
125 g (4 oz) mushrooms
175 g (6 oz) sliced green peppers
2 halved tomatoes
freshly ground black pepper
125 g (4 oz) grated Cheddar cheese

Sprinkle the courgettes and aubergine with salt and leave to drain for about 30 minutes to remove any bitterness.

Meanwhile, pour 6 tablespoons of the oil into a frying pan and add the cumin and onion and cook over moderate heat until the onion is just beginning to colour. Drain the onion and keep on one side. Fry the bread cubes until they are crisp and golden brown, adding a little more oil if necessary. Remove them from the pan and drain on kitchen paper.

Rinse the courgettes and aubergine and put them into a steamer with the mushrooms and green peppers and cook them for 5 minutes. Remove the vegetables from the steamer, allow them to cool slightly, then arrange them on skewers alternating courgette, aubergine, fried bread, pepper and mushroom. Finish each with a halved tomato and lay the completed kebabs on a lightly oiled baking sheet and pour about a teaspoon of the cumin and onion-flavoured oil over each. Season with salt and pepper and sprinkle with half of the fried onion. Cook them under a hot grill for about 5 minutes, until the vegetables are golden brown. Turn the kebabs, spoon over a little more oil, sprinkle with the rest of the fried onion and cover them with the grated cheese. Return the kebabs to the grill and cook until the cheese has melted. Take care that the heat of the grill is not too fierce or the kebabs will be dry or burnt. Serve with Barbecue sauce (page 197) and plain boiled rice, or boiled rice flavoured with turmeric.

A Tomato salad or Tunisian orange salad both make the ideal accompaniments.

Note: if barbecuing the kebabs, add the tomatoes partway through cooking.

Stir-fried one dish meal (with rice)

Serves 4

CALORIES PER PORTION: 420 (1792 kJ)
PROTEIN CONTENT PER PORTION: 21 grams
PREPARATION & COOKING TIME: 30-40 minutes

4 eggs
a little melted butter
350 g (12 oz) diced bean curd
oil for shallow frying
225 g (8 oz) finely chopped onion
50 g (2 oz) fresh root ginger, peeled and
finely chopped
225 g (8 oz) shredded red pepper
4 tablespoons vegetable oil
225 g (8 oz) mushrooms, sliced parallel
to the stem
225 g (8 oz) bean shoots
225 g (8 oz) coarsely shredded spinach
2 tablespoons miso
2 tablespoons soya sauce
6-8 tablespoons vegetable stock or water
2 tablespoons cream sherry
½ star aniseed pod
salt

Make an omelette with the eggs, following the basic method on page 66, and cut it into thin strips. Keep hot.

Fry the bean curd in shallow oil until it is golden brown and crisp on the outside. Drain and keep hot.

Fry the onion, ginger and pepper in 3 tablespoons of the oil until they are soft. Add the mushrooms and cook them until they are shiny. Add the bean shoots, spinach, miso, soya sauce and stock or water with the sherry and ground aniseed. Stir-fry for a few moments until the bean shoots are hot, adding the remaining tablespoon of oil if necessary. Fold in the omelette strips and fried bean curd and heat through gently. Season to taste with a little salt, if necessary, and serve with plenty of boiled brown rice.

Chinese nut rissoles

Serves 4

CALORIES PER PORTION: 555 (2310 kJ)
PROTEIN CONTENT PER PORTION: 16.5 grams
PREPARATION & COOKING TIME: 1 hour

½ quantity of Basic stuffing (page 88)
Coating batter (page 194)
oil for deep frying

The sweet and sour sauce
225 g (8 oz) thinly sliced onion
225 g (8 oz) shredded red pepper
2 tablespoons vegetable oil
2 tablespoons soya sauce
4 tablespoons wine vinegar
1 finely ground star aniseed pod
2 teaspoons cornflour
300 ml (½ pint) brown stock
3 tablespoons raw brown sugar

Prepare the stuffing mixture and batter.

Fry the onion and pepper in the oil over moderate heat until soft. Stir in the soya sauce, wine vinegar, aniseed, the cornflour mixed with the stock and the sugar. Bring to the boil, stirring continuously until the mixture thickens and then lower the heat and simmer for 5 minutes. Keep hot.

Shape the stuffing mixture into eight balls, dip them in the batter and fry in deep oil until they are golden brown and crisp. Drain well and then put them into the sweet and sour sauce. Bring the sauce back to the boil and serve immediately with plenty of brown rice.

1. Cut all the vegetables into small pieces of a uniform size.

2. Stir-fry, using two forks to lift the vegetables and turn continuously.

Kulebiak

This recipe serves 10-12 and is ideal for a buffet party.

TOTAL CALORIES: 4860 (20,340 kJ)
TOTAL PROTEIN CONTENT: 247 grams
PREPARATION & COOKING TIME: 2½ hours

The yeast dough
25 g (1 oz) fresh yeast (follow the
    manufacturer's instructions for dried
    yeast)
2 teaspoons soft brown sugar
300 ml (½ pint) lukewarm milk
450 g (1 lb) wholemeal flour
1 teaspoon salt
225 g (8 oz) finely grated Cheddar
    cheese
2 eggs, beaten

The filling
1 kg (2 lb) finely shredded white
    cabbage
2 teaspoons salt
150 ml (¼ pint) cold water
225 g (8 oz) finely chopped onions
75 g (3 oz) butter
225 g (8 oz) coarsely chopped
    mushrooms
50 g (2 oz) wholemeal flour
200 ml (⅓ pint) milk
225 g (8 oz) grated Cheddar cheese
salt
freshly ground pepper
1 tablespoon finely ground coriander
    (optional)
3 hard-boiled eggs, shelled and chopped
beaten egg, to glaze

To make the yeast dough; mix the yeast with the sugar, add the lukewarm milk and leave in a warm place for about 10 minutes until it is frothy. Put the flour and salt into a bowl. Sprinkle in the cheese and mix lightly. Make a well in the centre, pour the yeast mixture into the flour, add the beaten eggs and mix to a soft but not sticky dough. Add a little more warm milk if necessary. Turn out on to a floured board and knead until completely smooth. Put it into a lightly oiled bowl, cover and set aside in a warm place until the dough has doubled in size.

Meanwhile, make the filling. Put the cabbage in a thick-based saucepan with the salt and water. Bring to the boil and simmer for about 10 minutes until the cabbage has reduced in bulk and is just tender then continue cooking the cabbage for a further 2-3 minutes until all the water has evaporated. Take care that the cabbage does not burn. Remove from the heat and allow to cool.

Fry the onions in the butter until soft and golden brown. Add the mushrooms and fry until dark and shiny, then remove the pan from the heat and stir in the flour. Add the milk gradually, mixing well between each addition. Return the pan to the heat and bring to the boil, stirring continuously, until the mixture thickens. Remove from the heat, add the cheese and stir until melted. Mix the onion and-mushroom mixture into the cabbage and season well with salt, pepper and coriander, if liked. Set aside until completely cold.

To finish the pie, 'knock back' the risen dough and divide it into 2 portions. Knead each portion well and roll into a rectangle about 25 cm×38 cm (10×15 in). Place one portion on a well-oiled baking sheet and cover with the filling, leaving a border of about 5 cm (2 in) around the edge. Sprinkle the chopped eggs over, brush the edges with water and cover with the second portion of dough. Seal and crimp the edges and make 2 or 3 slits in the top for steam to escape. Leave in a warm place to rise for about 30 minutes. Set the oven at 200°C (400°F) Gas 6, then bake the Kulebiak in the pre-heated oven for 20 minutes.

Brush the top with beaten egg to glaze and bake for a further 10-15 minutes until it is golden brown.

Mixed vegetable pie

Serves 4

CALORIES PER PORTION: 555 (2332 kJ)
PROTEIN CONTENT PER PORTION: 18 grams
PREPARATION & COOKING TIME: 1-1¼ hours

350 g (12 oz) Wholemeal shortcrust
    pastry (page 194)
100 g (4 oz) finely chopped onion
25 g (1 oz) butter
100 g (4 oz) cooked soya beans
100 g (4 oz) cooked peas
100 g (4 oz) coarsely chopped
    mushrooms
50 g (2 oz) dried skimmed milk
200 ml (⅓ pint) milk
2 tablespoons wholemeal flour
salt
freshly ground pepper
½-1 teaspoon finely chopped marjoram
1 bay leaf, crumbled
1 small clove of garlic, peeled and finely
    chopped

Keep the dough, well wrapped, in the refrigerator until required. Set the oven at 200°C (400°F) Gas 6. Fry the onion gently in the butter until it is golden brown. Add the beans, peas, mushrooms and a tablespoon of water, and cook over a gentle heat until the mushrooms are dark and shiny. Remove from the heat and leave until cold. If necessary, place the pan in a bowl of cold water to speed up the cooling process.

Stir the dried milk into the fresh milk and then blend in the flour. Stir into the cold vegetables, season with salt and pepper and add the marjoram, bay leaf and garlic.

Roll out half of the dough and line a well-oiled 20 cm (8 in) flan tin, or flan ring on a baking sheet. Fill with the prepared vegetable mixture. Roll out the remaining dough and cover the pie. Seal the two dough layers together and flute the edge. Decorate with dough trimmings and make a hole in the centre for steam to escape. Bake in the pre-heated oven for 30 minutes.

Accompaniments: Polish-style cauli-flower, courgettes or broccoli.

Raised vegetable pie

Serves 6
CALORIES PER PORTION: 744 (3113 kJ)
PROTEIN CONTENT PER PORTION: 24 grams
PREPARATION & COOKING TIME: 2-2½ hours

The pastry
350 g (12 oz) wholemeal flour
1 teaspoon salt
175 g (6 oz) butter
1 egg, well beaten

The filling
175 g (6 oz) finely chopped onion
225 g (8 oz) red pepper, de-seeded and
    cut into 2 cm (1 in) slices
100 g (4 oz) coarsely chopped celery
225 g (8 oz) diced turnip
100 g (4 oz) diced carrot
4 tablespoons olive or sunflower oil
225 g (8 oz) cabbage, cut into 1 cm
    (½ in) squares
1 clove of garlic, peeled and finely
    chopped
salt
freshly ground pepper
½-1 teaspoon finely chopped marjoram
1 bay leaf, crumbled
4 hard-boiled eggs, shelled

The binding sauce
2 tablespoons vegetable oil
25 g (1 oz) wholemeal flour
2 teaspoons agar-agar
300 ml (½ pint) milk
150 g (5 oz) grated Cheddar cheese
salt
freshly ground pepper

To make the pastry; put the flour and salt into a bowl and rub in the butter. Add the beaten egg and mix to a firm dough, adding a little cold water if necessary, wrap well and keep in a refrigerator until required.

To make the filling; place all the prepared vegetables, except the cabbage, in a large thick-based saucepan. Add the oil and place over a moderate heat. Cook the vegetables, shaking the pan frequently to turn them, until they are just beginning to colour and are almost tender. This will take about 20 minutes. Add the cabbage, garlic, seasonings and herbs, and cook quickly for about 5 minutes, shaking the pan continuously. Remove from the heat and leave to cool.

Meanwhile, make the binding sauce. Heat the oil in a small saucepan until just beginning to sizzle. Stir in the flour and mix well. Take the pan off the heat. Blend the agar-agar with a little of the milk to make a creamy mixture. Stir in the remaining milk then add this gradually to the flour mixture in the pan, mixing well between each addition. Return to the heat, bring to the boil and stir until the sauce thickens. Add the cheese, continue stirring until it has melted and then season well with salt and pepper. Add the sauce to the cooked vegetables and mix very thoroughly.

Set the oven at 180°C (350°F) Gas 4. Roll out three-quarters of the dough and line a well-greased 1 litre (2 pint) hinged raised pie tin. Alternatively, use a 1 kg (2 lb) loaf tin. Put in half the vegetable filling and arrange the eggs on top. Cover with the remaining filling. Roll out the remaining dough to fit the top of the pie, brush the edges with water and seal the two dough layers firmly together. Trim off any surplus and use it to decorate the top of the pie. Make a hole in the centre to allow steam to escape, and decorate with dough trimmings. Bake in the pre-heated oven for 1 hour. Allow the pie to cool completely before removing from the tin.

Serve cold with Mayonnaise or Rémoulade sauce and a choice of salads.

Cashew loaf

Serves 6
TOTAL CALORIES: 1180 (7580 kJ)
TOTAL PROTEIN CONTENT: 63 grams
PREPARATION & COOKING TIME: 1½ hours

The loaf
225 g (8 oz) ground cashew nuts
100 g (4 oz) fresh wholemeal
    breadcrumbs
100 g (4 oz) finely chopped onion
25 g (1 oz) butter
1 clove of garlic, peeled and finely
    chopped
2 eggs, beaten
150 ml (¼ pint) milk
grated rind of 1 lemon
½ teaspoon finely chopped marjoram
salt
freshly ground black pepper

The filling
100 g (4 oz) finely chopped onion
225 g (8 oz) shredded red pepper
25 g (1 oz) butter
freshly ground black pepper
salt
100 g (4 oz) coarsely grated Edam or
    Cheddar cheese
1 egg, beaten

Set the oven at 200°C (400°F) Gas 6. Mix together the nuts and breadcrumbs in a bowl. Fry the onion in the butter until soft and golden brown. Add the garlic and fry gently for a few moments longer without allowing it to colour. Take out of the pan and add to the mixed nuts and crumbs.

Beat the eggs with the milk, lemon rind, marjoram, salt and pepper. Pour into the nut and crumb mixture and mix thoroughly.

To make the filling; fry the onion and red pepper in the butter until almost soft but not browned. Season liberally with black pepper and a little salt, then remove from the heat and add the cheese and enough beaten egg to bind the mixture.

Line a 1 litre (2 pint) capacity hinged loaf tin with greaseproof paper or non-stick vegetable parchment and press half the nut mixture into the bottom of the tin. Spread the filling mixture on top, then cover with the remaining nut mixture. Bake in the pre-heated oven for 30-40 minutes, or until firm. Serve hot with Béarnaise sauce (page 195), accompanied by cauliflower or broccoli.

Note: This loaf is also good served cold with salads.

Soya bean loaf

Serves 6
TOTAL CALORIES: 1040 (4350 kJ)
TOTAL PROTEIN CONTENT: 58 grams
PREPARATION & COOKING TIME: 1-1¼ hours

400 g (14 oz) cooked soya beans
100 g (4 oz) finely chopped onion
100 g (4 oz) finely chopped celery
2 tablespoons olive or sunflower oil
2 eggs
200 ml (⅓ pint) milk
1 clove of garlic, peeled and finely
    chopped
½-1 teaspoon finely chopped winter or
    summer savory
salt and finely ground black pepper

Set the oven at 200°C (400°F) Gas 6. Thoroughly mash the soya beans. Line a 450 g (1 lb) capacity hinged loaf tin with non-stick vegetable parchment or greaseproof paper.

Fry the onion and celery in the oil until soft but not browned. Add to the soya beans and mix well. Beat the eggs with the milk, garlic, savory, salt and pepper, and stir into the soya bean mixture.

Place the mixture in the prepared tin and bake in the pre-heated oven for 30 minutes. Allow to cool for a few moments before removing from the tin. Serve with Tomato or Mushroom sauce and a green vegetable or a salad.

Curried peanut loaf

Serves 6
TOTAL CALORIES: 2185 (9140 kJ)
TOTAL PROTEIN CONTENT: 110 grams
PREPARATION & COOKING TIME: 1¼ -1½ hours

The loaf
225 g (8 oz) ground peanuts
225 g (8 oz) fresh wholemeal breadcrumbs
225 g (8 oz) finely chopped onions
100 g (4 oz) finely chopped celery
1 teaspoon ground cumin
1 teaspoon ground coriander
½ teaspoon caraway seeds
1 teaspoon salt, or to taste
1 teaspoon ground turmeric
1 large clove of garlic, peeled and chopped
4 cm (1½ in) piece of root ginger, peeled and finely chopped
3 eggs, well beaten

The topping
200 ml (⅓ pint) milk
2 eggs
¼ teaspoon salt
1 teaspoon curry powder

Set the oven at 200°C (400°F) Gas 6. To make the loaf, place all the dry ingredients in a bowl and mix very thoroughly. Add the eggs and bind the mixture well. Press it into a 450 g (1 lb) capacity hinged loaf tin, lined with non-stick vegetable parchment or greaseproof paper, or an oven-proof dish if you are serving the cooked loaf straight from its dish — this way the custard topping will not break. Bake in the pre-heated oven for 15 minutes.

To make the topping; mix together all the ingredients and pour on to the loaf, then continue baking for 30-35 minutes. At the end of the baking time, when the loaf should be firm and golden brown, allow to cool a little before removing the loaf from the tin, taking care not to break it, or the custard on top.

Serve hot with Tomato sauce, subtly flavoured with curry powder, and a Mixed salad, or Tomato salad. Alternatively, serve cold.

Pizza

Serves 4
CALORIES PER PORTION: 620 (2600 kJ)
PROTEIN CONTENT PER PORTION: 29 grams
PREPARATION & COOKING TIME: 2 hours

400 g (14 oz) wholemeal flour
2 teaspoons salt
25 g (1 oz) fresh yeast (follow manufacturer's instructions for dried yeast)
1 teaspoon soft brown sugar
200 ml (⅓ pint) lukewarm milk
350 g (12 oz) red pepper, deseeded and cut into 1 cm (½ in) strips
olive or sunflower oil
400 g (14 oz) skinned tomatoes, cored and cut into 8 segments
225 g (8 oz) thinly sliced Mozzarella cheese
salt
freshly ground black pepper
a sprinkling of fresh or dried oregano
24 black olives, stoned and cut in half

Sieve the flour and salt into a bowl and make a well in the centre. Mix the yeast with the sugar and 2 tablespoons warm water. Put in a warm place for about 5 minutes until it is frothy. Add to the warm milk and pour it into the flour. Mix well, adding a little more warm milk if necessary to make a soft but not sticky dough. Knead on a well-floured board until it is completely smooth. Place in a lightly oiled bowl, cover and leave to rise in a warm place until it has doubled in size.

'Knock back' the dough and divide it into four portions. Shape each portion into a 20 cm (8 in) diameter circle and place on well-oiled baking trays. Set the oven at 200°C (400°F) Gas 6.

Meanwhile, cook the peppers in a little oil (preferably olive) and water until they are soft. Arrange strips of pepper, chunks of tomato and slices of cheese on each round of dough. Sprinkle a little oil over them and season generously with salt, pepper and oregano. Garnish with the black olives. Leave the Pizzas in a warm place for 20 minutes, until they are just beginning to rise. Bake in the pre-heated oven for 30 minutes, and serve with a Mixed or Green salad and a robust red wine or cider.

Top: Curried peanut loaf is served straight from the dish to show the delicate custard topping. Right: savoury Cashew loaf has a middle layer of cheese and red peppers; the loaf itself is flavoured with marjoram and garlic. Below: ever-popular Pizzas, topped with Mozzarella cheese, olives, tomatoes and – for the authentic Italian touch – oregano

Pea, sweetcorn and spring onion flan

Serves 6
CALORIES PER PORTION: 480 (3012 kJ)
PROTEIN CONTENT PER PORTION: 27 grams
PREPARATION & COOKING TIME: 1 hour

prebaked 22 cm (9 in) flan case, made
  with Wholemeal shortcrust pastry
  (page 194)
100 g (4 oz) soya granules
225 g (9 oz) cooked peas
225 g (8 oz) cooked sweetcorn kernels
25 g (1 oz) butter
25 g (1 oz) wholemeal flour
300 ml (½ pint) milk
100 g (4 oz) grated Cheddar cheese
6 large spring onions, coarsely chopped
2 eggs, beaten
salt
freshly ground pepper

Set the oven at 200°C (400°F) Gas 6. Simmer the soya granules in a little water for 5-8 minutes, adding as much water as necessary to keep the mixture moist — but there should be no excess liquid. Add the peas and sweetcorn and leave to cool.

Melt the butter in another pan over gentle heat, then stir in the flour. Remove the pan from the heat and gradually add the milk, stirring well between each addition. Return the pan to the stove and bring to the boil, stirring continuously until the mixture thickens. Add the cheese

and stir until it melts, then stir in the spring onions and the soya mixture. Allow to cool slightly, then mix in the eggs and season well with salt and pepper.

Pour the mixture into the prepared flan case and bake in the pre-heated oven for about 30 minutes or until the filling is set and the top golden brown. Serve hot or cold with a spiced Apricot or Cherry sauce (page 197) and a salad.

Potato, cheese and onion flan

Serves 4
CALORIES PER PORTION: 645 (2707 kJ)
PROTEIN CONTENT PER PORTION: 22 grams
PREPARATION AND COOKING TIME: 1 hour

pre-baked 20 cm (8 in) flan case, made
  with Wholemeal shortcrust pastry
  (page 194)
350 g (12 oz) thinly sliced potatoes
100 g (4 oz) coarsely chopped onion
175 g 6 oz) grated Cheddar cheese
2 tablespoons finely chopped parsley
1 egg, beaten
200 ml (⅓ pint) milk
1 clove of garlic, peeled and finely
  chopped
salt
freshly ground pepper

Cook the potatoes in a little boiling salted water until just soft, then drain. Set the oven at 200°C (400°F) Gas 6. Put the onion in a pan with just enough water to cover and bring to the boil. Drain the onion and leave to cool. Sprinkle one-third of the cheese over the bottom of the prepared flan case, cover with half the drained potato slices and sprinkle with half the parsley. Add half the onion, then repeat the layers of potato, cheese, parsley and onion.

Mix the egg with the milk and add the garlic, salt and pepper. Pour this over the layers of filling in the flan case. Sprinkle with the remaining cheese and bake in the pre-heated oven for 30-40 minutes, or until the filling is set and the top is golden brown. Serve with a green vegetable or Green or Mixed salad.
Variation: the onion can be fried in 25 g (1 oz) butter intead of being blanched, if preferred.

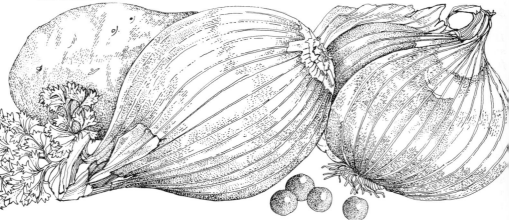

Savoury soya bean flan

If a smooth-textured filling is required, the soya beans can be worked in a blender before being added to the rest of the ingredients.

Serves 4
CALORIES PER PORTION: 600 (2517 kJ)
PROTEIN CONTENT PER PORTION: 21 grams
PREPARATION & COOKING TIME: 1 hour

pre-baked 20 cm (8 in) flan case, made
  with Wholemeal shortcrust pastry
  (page 194)
350 g (12 oz) cooked soya beans
100 g (4 oz) finely chopped onion
25 g (1 oz) butter
100 ml (4 fl oz) milk
1 clove of garlic, peeled and finely
  chopped
1 egg, beaten
¼ teaspoon chopped thyme
50 g (2 oz) grated Cheddar cheese
salt
freshly ground pepper

Set the oven at 200°C (400°F) Gas 6. Fry the onion in the butter until soft and golden brown. Mix the soya beans with the rest of the ingredients, using half the cheese. Season with salt and pepper. Pour into the prepared flan case, sprinkle with the remaining cheese and bake in the pre-heated oven for 30-40 minutes, or until the filling is set and the top is golden brown.

Serve with Okra créole, Beetroot or Leeks in yoghurt sauce.

Cauliflower vol-au-vent

Serves 4
CALORIES PER PORTION: 1290 (5865 kJ)
PROTEIN CONTENT PER PORTION: 22 grams
PREPARATION & COOKING TIME: 35-40 minutes

1 large 20 cm (8 in) diameter vol-au-vent case made from Puff pastry (page 194)
350 g (12 oz) cauliflower, in florets
1 tablespoon dried rosemary
225 g (8 oz) sliced mushrooms
25 g :1 oz) butter
25 g (1 oz) wholemeal flour
50 g (2 oz) dried skimmed milk
300 ml (½ pint) milk
salt and freshly ground pepper

Set the oven at 200°C (400°F) Gas 6 and roll out the pastry on a lightly-floured surface. Cut 2 circles 20 cm (8 in). Cut a 16 cm (6½ in) diameter lid from the centre of one. Brush the edge of the whole circle with beaten egg. Position the ring on top and brush the ring and lid with egg. Bake base and lid, without touching, on a dampened baking sheet for 25 minutes.

Put rosemary into a pan with 600 ml (1 pint) water and bring to the boil. Place the cauliflower florets in a steamer over the flavoured water and cook for about 10 minutes, or until just tender.

Fry the mushrooms in the butter for 3-4 minutes then stir in the flour and remove the pan from the heat. Dissolve skimmed milk in the fresh milk and pour this gradually into the pan, stirring well between each addition. Add the cauliflower, return the pan to the stove and cook over a very gentle heat, stirring frequently until the mixture thickens. Season with salt and pepper, spoon into the hot vol-au-vent case and serve immediately.

Note: individual vol-au-vents can be made in the same way; bake for 20 minutes. Keep the florets small. A sprinkling of cheese also adds flavour.

Courgette vol-au-vent

Serves 4
CALORIES PER PORTION: 1550 (6490 kJ)
PROTEIN CONTENT PER PORTION: 25 grams
PREPARATION & COOKING TIME: 1 hour

1 large 20 cm (8 in) diameter vol-au-vent case made from Puff pastry (page 194), made as above
450 g (1 lb) thinly sliced courgettes
125 g (4 oz) finely chopped onions
25 g (1 oz) butter or vegetable oil
225 g (8 oz) thinly sliced button mushrooms
1-2 cloves of garlic, peeled and finely chopped
3-4 tablespoons water
300 ml (½ pint) Béchamel sauce (page 196)
125 g (4 oz) grated Cheddar cheese
salt
freshly ground black pepper

Put the vol-au-vent case to heat through in a moderate oven, set at 180°C (350°F) Gas 4. Sprinkle the courgettes with salt and leave to drain for 30 minutes to remove any bitterness. Fry the onions in the butter or oil until they are pale golden. Rinse the courgettes, pay them dry on kitchen paper and add them to the pan with the mushrooms and garlic and continue cooking for a few moments until the juices start to run. Add the water, cover the pan and cook over low heat for about 5 minutes, or until the courgettes are cooked but still fairly firm. Check that they do not stick and burn.

Heat the Béchamel sauce and stir in the cheese; add the vegetables, season to taste with salt and pepper and mix thoroughly. Pour the filling into the heated vol-au-vent case and serve immediately.

Note: If you are making individual vol-au-vent cases, this mixture should fill about 6-8, depending on size.

Nut and lentil pâté

Serves 6-8
TOTAL CALORIES: 1720 (7208 kJ)
TOTAL PROTEIN CONTENT: 56 grams
PREPARATION & COOKING TIME: 2½ hours, excluding cooling

350 g (12 oz) ground mixed nuts
350 g (12 oz) cooked brown lentils
150 :5 oz) finely chopped celery
225 g (8 oz) finely chopped onion
2 cloves of garlic, peeled and finely chopped
400 g (14 oz) coarsely chopped tomatoes
100 g (4 oz) butter
3 eggs, well beaten
½-1 teaspoon finely chopped thyme
1-2 teaspoons finely chopped oregano
salt
freshly ground pepper

Set the oven at 200°C (400°F) Gas 6. Mix together the nuts, lentils, celery, onion and garlic. Cook the tomatoes very gently until reduced to a pulp, then rub this through a sieve. There should be about 200 ml (⅓ pint) of tomato purée; if there is more, reduce it by boiling; if less, add a little water. Melt the butter in the tomato purée and allow to cool slightly before adding the eggs, herbs, and salt and pepper

Pour this mixture into the ingredients in the bowl and mix thoroughly. Press into a well-oiled 1 litre (2 pint) capacity hinged loaf tin and bake in the pre-heated oven for 1½-2 hours, or until set. Allow to cool completely before removing the pâté from the tin. Serve chilled with slices of wholemeal toast.

Mushroom and nut loaf

Serves 6
TOTAL CALORIES: 410 (1715 kJ)
TOTAL PROTEIN CONTENT: 12 grams
PREPARATION & COOKING TIME: 2-2½ hours

100 g (4 oz) sliced mushrooms
225 g (8 oz) chestnuts
225 g (8 oz) finely chopped onion
2 tablespoons vegetable oil
1 clove of garlic, peeled and finely chopped
225 g (8 oz) ground walnuts
100 g (4 oz) fresh breadcrumbs
50 g (2 oz) wholemeal flour
½-1 teaspoon finely chopped sage
½-1 teaspoon finely chopped thyme
salt and freshly ground black pepper
1 teaspoon yeast extract
150 ml (¼ pint) warm milk
2 eggs, beaten

Slit the chestnuts and cook in boiling water for about 30 minutes, or until soft. Drain, and while still warm, remove the outer shell and the inner skin. Break the nuts into quarters and place in a bowl.

Set the oven at 200°C (400°F) Gas 6. Line a 1 litre (2 pint) capacity hinged loaf tin with non-stick vegetable parchment or greaseproof paper. Fry the onion in the oil until soft and golden brown. Add the mushrooms and garlic, and fry gently for 3-4 minutes. Add to the chestnuts together with the walnuts, breadcrumbs, flour and herbs and season well.

Dissolve the yeast extract in the milk, whisk in the eggs and pour into the chestnut mixture, mixing very thoroughly. Spoon it into the prepared loaf tin and bake in the pre-heated oven for 30-40 minutes or until firm and golden brown.

Serve hot with Tomato or a Brown sauce, accompanied by Peas with lettuce and onions, Pommes Lyonnaise, fried spinach, or cold with salads.

Sformato di piselli

Serves 4-6
TOTAL CALORIES: 1275 (5340 kJ)
TOTAL PROTEIN CONTENT: 60 grams
PREPARATION & COOKING TIME: 2-2½ hours

400 g (14 oz) cooked peas
100 g (4 oz) finely chopped onion
50 g (2 oz) butter
25 g (1 oz) wholemeal flour
200 ml (⅓ pint) milk
100 g (4 oz) grated Cheddar cheese
3 eggs, separated
salt and freshly ground black pepper

Fry the onion in the butter until soft but not browned. Add the peas and fry for 1-2 minutes. Sprinkle in the flour and stir well. Take the pan off the heat and gradually add the milk and cheese, stirring well between each addition. Return the pan to a moderate heat and bring to the boil. Continue stirring until the mixture thickens.

Work it in a blender to a smooth purée or pass through a Mouli mill. Transfer the purée to a bowl, add the egg yolks and mix thoroughly and season.

Whisk the egg whites until stiff enough to stand in peaks and fold them gently into the purée. Pour it into a well-buttered 18 cm (7 in) soufflé dish and cover with a well-buttered paper. Place in a pan and pour in enough hot water to come half way up the sides of the dish and simmer gently for 1-1½ hours, or until set.

When cooked, either serve from the soufflé dish, or if the mixture is really firm, cool slightly and then turn out on to a serving dish. This can be tricky, as the amount of moisture in the peas can affect the 'set'. Serve with Tomato or Mushroom sauce, accompanied by baked potatoes.

Savoury nut roast

Serves 4
CALORIES PER PORTION: 580 (2430 kJ)
PROTEIN CONTENT PER PORTION: 22 grams
PREPARATION AND COOKING TIME: 1¼ -1½ hours

225 g (8 oz) ground mixed nuts
225 g (8 oz) fresh wholemeal breadcrumbs
100 g (4 oz) finely chopped onion
2 tablespoons olive or sunflower oil
2 eggs, beaten
salt and freshly ground black pepper
1-2 large cloves of garlic, peeled and finely chopped
1-2 teaspoons yeast extract
½-1 teaspoon finely chopped thyme
½-1 teaspoon finely chopped parsley
100 g (4 oz) grated Edam or Cheddar cheese

Set the oven at 180°C (350°F) Gas 4. Mix the nuts and breadcrumbs together in a bowl. Fry the onion in the oil until soft but not browned, then add it to the nuts and breadcrumbs. Beat up the eggs again with the remaining ingredients, pour into the nut mixture and knead thoroughly together. Leave the mixture to stand for 15 minutes, then shape it into a roll about 15 cm (6 in) long and place on a well-oiled baking sheet. Bake in the pre-heated oven for 30-45 minutes until it is firm and golden brown. Serve with a Brown sauce or Mushroom sauce and a choice of vegetables.

Vegetable scallops au gratin

Serves 4
CALORIES PER PORTION: 730 (3060 kJ)
PROTEIN CONTENT PER PORTION: 31 grams
PREPARATION AND COOKING TIME: 1 hour

500 g (generous 1 lb) potatoes
175 g (6 oz) grated Cheddar cheese
1 egg, beaten
a little milk
225 g (8 oz) finely chopped onions
225 g (8 oz) finely chopped green peppers
100 g (4 oz) finely chopped celery
50 g (2 oz) butter
225 g (8 oz) unroasted peanuts
1 tablespoon chopped parsley
2 tablespoons wholemeal flour
25 g (1 oz) dried skimmed milk
150 ml (¼ pint) milk
salt
freshly ground pepper
a pinch of cayenne (optional)

Boil the potatoes in their skins until tender. Drain and rinse under cold running water until they are cool enough to handle, then peel and mash them with two-thirds of the cheese, the beaten egg and enough milk to make a fairly soft consistency, suitable for piping. Using a piping bag fitted with a large rose nozzle, pipe a border around four small ovenproof plates or gratin dishes about 13 cm (5 in) diameter, and set aside until required.

Set the oven at 200°C (400°F) Gas 6. Fry the onions, peppers and celery in the butter until they are beginning to brown. Add the peanuts, parsley and flour and mix well. Remove from the heat and allow to cool slightly. Dissolve the dried milk in the fresh milk and pour it on to the vegetables, stirring vigorously. Return the pan to a gentle heat and stir until the mixture thickens.

Season with salt and pepper and divide the filling between the potato rings. Sprinkle with the remaining cheese and dust with cayenne, if used. Bake in the pre-heated oven for 30 minutes and serve hot.

Croûtes

Serves 4
CALORIES PER PORTION: 239 (990 kJ)
PROTEIN PER PORTION: 2 grams
COOKING TIME: 7 minutes

4 slices of wholemeal bread, crusts removed and quartered diagonally
125 g (generous 4 oz) butter, preferably clarified, or oil
a little salt, or grated Parmesan cheese

Melt the butter in a thick-based frying pan over gentle heat. Put in the slices of bread and fry on both sides until crisp. Drain on kitchen paper and sprinkle with salt, or Parmesan cheese.

Vegetable Accompaniments

It seems to me a pity that the Anglo-Saxon habit of serving all vegetables together with the main course – often on the same plate – has become so widespread. As a result, many people have ceased to appreciate and enjoy a dish of vegetables in its own right, as a separate course after the main dish. This is where I would place the vegetable accompaniment in my menu. There is a preparation chart on page 202. Follow this, resist the temptation to overcook your vegetables or smother them in sauces – and you, too, will come to love them for themselves again.

Vegetables: preparation and cooking

Most vegetables can be eaten raw; cooking destroys vitamin C and much of the vitamin B complex; vitamin C and the B complex are water-soluble. These three facts provide us with a guide for cooking vegetables. Cook them for the minimum possible time in the minimum amount of water, and serve as soon after cooking as possible. Keeping vegetables warm for any length of time spoils their flavour and completes the vitamin destruction.

Prepare vegetables just before cooking by discarding any discoloured, bruised or damaged portions and then washing them thoroughly to remove any sand or insects. Root vegetables should be scrubbed with a brush. Leaf vegetables such as spinach, kale and most greens should be washed, leaf by leaf, under a running tap. Root vegetables will go brown if they are left in the air after peeling; as the most nutritious part of the root lies just below the skin, it is really much better to cook them unpeeled after thoroughly scrubbing them and removing any blemishes. Old root vegetables with tough skins which need to be peeled should have only the thinnest layer removed and should then be immersed in water. Keep the peelings for use in vegetable stock.

Root and leaf vegetables can often be cooked and served whole, halved or quartered. But for stir-frying or quick cooking they need to be torn, sliced, diced or shredded. This should be done immediately before cooking to minimise vitamin loss. Try, too, not to leave prepared vegetables soaking in water for any length of time.

Tearing

Hold the leaf between the index finger and the thumb of one hand and tear off pieces approximately 5 cm (2 in) square. The advance of tearing and not cutting is that the leaf is not bruised; when time is short, arrange the leaves one on top of another, cut into slices and then shred the slices into squares.

Slicing

Cut the vegetable in half lengthways, then holding it down firmly on a chopping board, with the index finger and thumb, use a 12 cm (5 in) paring knife to cut it down to the board into 2-5 mm (⅛-¼ in) slices. Alternatively, one can use a longer knife, 25 cm (10 in), with a stiff blade, as the Chinese do; do not cut the vegetable in half, make the first cut at 30° and roll the vegetable through 180° and cut again at 30° and so on. This produces a rather decorative, wedge-shaped slices. One can achieve considerable speed with practice!

Dicing

Cut the slices into strips of the same thickness — 1 cm (½ in)in). Keeping the slices together and flat, cut across into small cubes.

Shredding

Use a coarse grater, preferably made of stainless steel, and rub the vegetable up and down against it, taking care to keep your fingers well out of the way; it might be a good idea to hold whatever is being grated in a thick linen cloth.

There are various gadgets, hand-operated or electric, for shredding and grating, which are well worth the investment as salad making and vegetable preparation become almost instananeous.

One can also shred leaf vegetables by first quartering them, if they are firm like cabbage, and then, holding the wedge firmly on a board and cutting very thin slices. Or pile the individual leaves of loose-leaved vegetables such as spinach one on top of the other and then cut them into very thin strips.

Vegetables can be baked, braised, roasted, boiled, steamed, fried and stir-fried. Each method gives a distinctive quality and flavour to the finished dish, and gives tempting variations to everyday meals. Compare the effect of adding fresh herbs or salt before and after cooking. Serve vegetables with a knob of butter and a vinaigrette dressing made with olive or walnut oil and a herb, wine, or cider, vinegar.

Cooked vegetables should never be mushy; test them with a sharp skewer — it should penetrate but there should be a slight resistance. Root vegetables should still be firm.

Baking

The basis of baking is that the food is cooked in a dry atmosphere. Root vegetables and vegetable fruits generally have thick enough skins to prevent them from drying out. Try inserting a sliver of garlic into a potato or aubergine before baking it. Other vegetables have to be wrapped in aluminium foil or greaseproof paper to prevent too much water loss; a few drops of oil, melted butter, wine or stock can be added to increase moisture. Do not forget to prick the skins to prevent bursting.

Spinach, young cabbage leaves or any

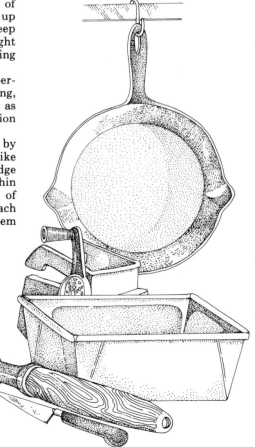

other tender young greens can be sprinkled with herbs — basil, oregano or summer savory are all good — a little salt and pepper and a dash of oil and melted butter inside, then rolled up into sausages and tied with string. Brush the outsides with oil and bake on a baking sheet in a hot oven for 20-30 minutes. The outside leaves become crisp and the inner ones are succulent and delicious.

Braising

Here, the food is cooked in a moist atmosphere surrounded by heat; in earlier days, braising pans had specially shaped lids so that coals and hot ashes could be piled up on top and the pot then stood on the side of the cooking range. Today braising is generally understood to mean pre-browning the food in oil or butter and then continuing the cooking in the oven, in a close covered pot with a little added liquid. Celery and onions are particularly good when braised.

Roasting

Roasting completes the basic oven methods. The food is cooked at a high temperature in oil or butter. It is really a form of frying; its main advantage is that the food cooks and browns evenly and, as many of the aromatics — spices and herbs — are soluble in oil, the food can be subtly flavoured by adding them to the oil in which the food is being roasted. Try cinnamon with roast carrots or mace or nutmeg with parsnips.

Boiling

Use as small a saucepan as possible for boiling green vegetables and ensure that it has a well-fitting lid. A well-proportioned saucepan should have its height equal to two-thirds of its diameter.

Measure the quantity of water to cover the bottom of the pan to a depth of 5-10 mm (¼ - ½ in) and bring it to the boil in a kettle or another saucepan. Preheat the vegetable pan, then add the prepared vegetables and pour on the boiling water; add salt, cover with the lid and cook for the required time. Experience will show the setting of the heat; ideally there should only be a tablespoon or so of liquid remaining to pour over the vegetables as it is, or slightly thickened with kneaded butter (beurre manié — see the recipe for Cream of leek soup on page 41).

When boiling root vegetables, use enough boiling salted water to cover the prepared vegetables, and cook for the required time. Use the water in which they were cooked to make stock.

Steaming

One can buy specially designed equipment to steam vegetables, ranging from the very attractive Chinese bamboo baskets which stand one on top of another over a saucepan of boiling water, to metal constructions which would not seem out of place in a science fiction film.

One can easily improvise; the aim is to surround the food with steam at a temperature of 100°C (212°F). Try standing a shallow heatproof dish on a trivet in a saucepan containing 2 cm (1 in) of boiling water and piling the food loosely on it, or packing the food very lightly into a colander and standing it over a saucepan of boiling water, keeping it closely covered.

If using the Chinese baskets, ensure they fit snugly one into another and that there is a close fit between the lowest basket and the saucepan. The food requiring the longest cooking is put into the lowest basket; if there is a chance of juices running out of the food, as it does from some fungi, place the food on a small dish or plate but be sure to leave enough space between the plate and the side of the basket for the steam to circulate. Try experimenting; all herbs and spices have volatile oils, so by adding them to the water, one cooks with flavoured steam: try squeezing lemon juice, or sprinkling a little soya sauce or wine over first.

Frying

The term frying describes two different methods of cooking in very hot oil (180° or 350°F is the safest) or melted clarified butter, or unclarified butter. Though I use butter a great deal, it does burn at a lower temperature than oil so take care; you can use a mixture of the two.

Unless seasoning is specifically included in a recipe, it is better to season the food after frying.

Shallow frying

The food is cooked in a thick-based frying pan with the pre-heated oil or fat coming just over half-way up the food; whole, par-boiled potatoes can be fried in about 1 cm (½ in) of oil if they are turned over and over until they are evenly cooked. Fry the food on one side until crisp and golden brown and then turn it over with a spatula and a guiding fork and fry the other side. The temperature should be controlled to prevent it rising too high and burning or to prevent it falling and make the food greasy. The food should be completely cooked when both sides are crisp and flecked with brown. Remove from the pan with a perforated spoon or slice and drain on kitchen paper on a plate in an open hot oven. Serve immediately on hot plates.

Deep-frying

The food is cooked in a frying basket immersed in a saucepan of hot oil (180°C or 350°F). The saucepan should be only just over half full. A cooking thermometer is almost essential for good deep-frying. A good test of whether the oil has reached frying temperature is to drop in a cube of day-old bread. It should turn golden-brown in 60 seconds. Deep-frying, however, is the ideal method for cooking croquettes, rissoles and food coated in batter and crumbs. Take care not to leave any water drops on the vegetables as it will cause the hot oil to spatter dangerously.

Do not put too much food in at a time as, if the temperature of the oil drops, the food will not be sealed instantly and will absorb oil or disintegrate. There is also the danger that the oil will froth over on to the hot stove and catch fire.

When the food is done, remove it from the basket and drain and keep hot as for shallow frying. Allow the oil to regain full frying temperature before putting in the next batch. Remove particles constantly with a small strainer, otherwise they will burn and flavour the food.

Allow the oil to cool down completely before straining it through fine muslin and returning it to the bottle.

If the oil catches fire, do not bring water near it! Turn off the heat, cover the pan with the lid, then gently move the pan off the heat. Cover it with a damp tea cloth to quench the flames.

Stir-frying

This is the ideal way of cooking vegetables. With a little practice, four pans can easily be used at the same time. The vegetables are sliced, diced or shredded, then a little oil or butter is put into a thick-based pan; the Chinese wok is ideal as it was designed for this style of cooking (see page 98). The vegetables are added and stirred over and over with a wooden spoon — the most tender and quickest-cooking ingredients being put in last. Then a little stock, water, wine or soya sauce is added and the food continues cooking. If the vegetables are prepared correctly and cut thinly enough the whole process takes only 5-10 minutes.

Salting

As a rough guide, allow ½ teaspoon of salt to 450 g (1 lb) of green vegetables and 1 teaspoon to the same quantity of root vegetables; in addition add ½ teaspoon salt to 300 ml (½ pint) of water. It is easier to add salt than to remove it! Never add bicarbonate of soda; it totally destroys the vitamin C content.

Brussels sprouts with peanuts and herb butter

Serves 4
CALORIES PER PORTION: 14 (597 kJ)
PROTEIN CONTENT PER PORTION: 7 grams
PREPARATION & COOKING TIME: 30 minutes

350 g (12 oz) Brussels sprouts
50 g (2 oz) finely chopped onion
50 g (2 oz) peanuts
12 large leaves of marjoram, chopped
25 g (1 oz) butter
2 tablespoons lemon juice

Cook the sprouts in a very little boiling salted water for 10-15 minutes, or until just tender. (If using frozen sprouts, follow the instructions on the packet, but under-cook them slightly. They will finish cooking in the lemon juice and onion.) Meanwhile, put the onion into another pan of boiling water and cook for 1 minute, then drain. Pour the peanuts into a blender or nut mill and grind them for a few seconds, or chop them with a sharp-bladed knife; they should be fine but not so fine that they bind together. Brush away the red skins. Work the marjoram into the butter, divide it into four pats and chill.

When the sprouts are done, drain them, reserving the water for making stock, and add the onion and lemon juice. Replace the pan of sprouts over the heat and stir them gently, sprinkling the peanuts over as you do so. Turn out into a heated dish and put a pat of herb butter on each helping.

Broccoli surprise

Serves 4
CALORIES PER PORTION: 275 (1242 kJ)
PROTEIN CONTENT PER PORTION: 14 grams
PREPARATION & COOKING TIME: 30 minutes

225 g (8 ox) broccoli spears
2 tablespoons olive or sunflower oil
2 tablespoons wholemeal flour
150 ml (¼ pint) milk
salt
50 g (2 oz) grated Cheddar cheese
4 eggs, separated

Cook the broccoli spears in boiling, salted water for 10 minutes, keeping them on the firm side. Drain and keep warm. Set the oven at 180°C (350°F) Gas 4. Mix together the oil and flour in a small pan over moderate heat, then draw the pan off the heat and stir in the milk and season with salt. Return to the stove and cook, stirring, until the sauce boils and thickens. Remove the pan from the stove and stir in the grated cheese. Allow to cool slightly, then add the egg yolks and mix well. Butter four small ovenproof soufflé dishes or ramekins and put them into the pre-heated oven to warm through for 5 minutes.

Meanwhile, whisk the egg whites until they hold stiff peaks, then fold in the cheese sauce. Put a large spoonful of the soufflé into each dish and carefully arrange a portion of broccoli on top. Then divide the rest of the soufflé mixture between the four dishes and bake for 10 minutes. The soufflé should not be completely set, but just make a light sauce for the broccoli.

Red cabbage with apple

Serves 4
CALORIES PER PORTION: 80 (365 kJ)
PROTEIN CONTENT PER PORTION: 3 grams
PREPARATION & COOKING TIME: : Version 1:
    30-40 minutes, Version 2: 1½ hours

450 g (1 lb) shredded red cabbage
225 g (8 oz) cooking apple
1 tablespoon olive or sunflower oil
50 g (2 oz) chopped onion
1 teaspoon yeast extract
200 ml (⅓ pint) warm water
1 tablespoon wine, or cider, vinegar
¼ teaspoon ground cinnamon
    (optional)
2 teaspoons wholemeal flour
1 tablespoon cold water
salt

Heat the oil in a large pan and fry the onion until golden brown. Peel and dice the apple. Dissolve the yeast extract in the warm water. Add the cabbage, apple and yeast extract solution with the vinegar and cinnamon to the onion and stir so that the apple is evenly mixed with the cabbage. Either continue cooking in a cov-ered pan over low heat until the cabbage is tender but still crisp, or, for a more traditional Middle European flavour, set the oven at 180°C (350°F) Gas 4 and transfer the cabbage to an ovenproof cas-serole to continue cooking in the oven for 1-1½ hours. Whichever method is used, the liquid which remains at the end of the cooking time should be thickened as fol-lows: mix the flour to a cream with the cold water in a small pan. Pour on the cooking juices, stirring well, and bring to the boil. Cool until the juices thicken, adjust the seasoning if necessary and pour them on to the cabbage; stir well.

Vegetable accompaniments can make a meal in themselves. Top left: Carrots with apple and crispy onion rings. Front: a savoury Spinach crumble and Right: Courgettes Provençales. Combine a selection of dishes like these for supper

Spinach crumble

Serves 4
CALORIES PER PORTION: 235 (985 kJ)
PROTEIN CONTENT PER PORTION: 8 grams
PREPARATION & COOKING TIME: 30 minutes

*450 g (1 lb) leaf spinach, very
  thoroughly washed*
50 g (2 oz) finely chopped onion
2 tablespoons olive or sunflower oil
25 g (1 oz) wholemeal flour
100 ml (4 fl oz) dry white wine
salt
*50 g (2 oz) fresh wholemeal
  breadcrumbs*

Cut out the thick stems from the spinach and use for stock. Fry the onion in about half the oil in a thick-based pan. Coarsely chop the spinach and, when the onion is transparent, add it to the pan. Lower the heat and cook gently for 10 minutes or until the spinach is just tender. Meanwhile, mix the flour with 1 tablespoon of oil, when the spinach is done, drain the cooking juices on to the oil and flour mixture and stir well. Return it to the spinach in the pan and stir until it thickens. Pour in the wine, add the salt and mix well. Remove the pan from the heat.

Set the oven at 180°C (350°F) Gas 4. Heat the remaining oil in a separate pan and fry the breadcrumbs until crisp and browned. Pour the cooked spinach into a shallow ovenproof dish, sprinkle the crumbs over the top and bake on the top shelf of the pre-heated oven for 10-15 minutes.

Note: This also makes a good light lunch or supper dish. For a more substantial meal, make four hollows in the mixture after adding the crumbs, break an egg into each hollow and sprinkle with cheese.

Cauliflower beignets

Serves 4
CALORIES PER PORTION: 500 (2087 kJ)
PROTEIN CONTENT PER PORTION: 20.5 grams
PREPARATION & COOKING TIME: 45 minutes

450 g (1 lb) cauliflower florets
Coating batter (page 194)
oil for deep frying
125 g (4 oz) grated Parmesan cheese
a sprinkling of cayenne

The spiced apple sauce
125 g (4 oz) finely chopped onion
*2 tablespoons melted butter or
  vegetable oil*
*350 g (12 oz) cooking apples, peeled
  and chopped*
4 finely ground cloves
½ teaspoon ground cinnamon
1 tablespoon raw brown sugar
150 ml (¼ pint) white wine

Put the cauliflower florets into a pan with a little salted water and bring to the boil. Cover and simmer for 5 minutes. Remove the cauliflower florets from the pan and dry them carefully; allow to cool, then dip them in the batter and fry in batches in deep oil heated to 180° (350°F) until they are golden brown and crisp. Drain them on kitchen paper and keep each batch warm while you cook the rest.

Make the sauce by frying the onion in the butter or oil until golden brown, add the apples, spices and sugar and cook for a further 2 minutes, then pour in the wine and the same quantity of water and continue cooking until the apples have broken down to a pulp. Rub the sauce through a sieve and reheat it.

Arrange the cauliflower on a warm serving dish and sprinkle over the cheese and cayenne. Hand the sauce separately.

Cauliflower Polish-style

Serves 4
CALORIES PER PORTION: 130 (550 kJ)
PROTEIN CONTENT PER PORTION: 7 grams
PREPARATION & COOKING TIME: 35 minutes

450 g (1 lb) cauliflower, broken into
*   florets*
salt
2 eggs
50 g (2 oz) finely chopped onion
25 g (1 oz) butter
50 g (2 oz) fresh wholemeal
*   breadcrumbs*
4 tablespoons chopped parsley
freshly ground pepper

Cook the cauliflower florets in boiling salted water to cover for 10-15 minutes, or until they are just done — the stems should still be firm. Hard-boil the eggs, shell them and keep them warm in a pan of hot water. Fry the onion in the butter until golden brown, then add the breadcrumbs and continue frying over moderate heat until slightly crisp. Add the chopped parsley and mix well. Drain the cauli-flower and arrange about half the flore on a heated serving dish. Sprinkle a gen erous half of the crumb mixture betwee them, season with salt and pepper an arrange the rest of the cauliflower ove the crumbs. Sprinkle the rest of th crumbs between the cauliflower florets o the top layer. Roughly chop the eggs, pi them in the centre of the dish and serv immediately.

Buttered cabbage with caraway

Serves 4
CALORIES PER PORTION: 187 (785 kJ)
PROTEIN CONTENT PER PORTION: 6.5 grams
PREPARATION & COOKING TIME: 15 minutes

350 g (12 oz) white cabbage, cut in 1 cm
*   (½ in) strips*
salt
50 g (2 oz) butter
freshly ground black pepper
½ teaspoon caraway seeds
75 g (3 oz) grated Cheddar cheese
a sprinkling of paprika

Cut the cabbage strips into squares and place them in a saucepan. Bring 1 litre (2 pints) of water to the boil and pour it over the cabbage; add salt and bring back to the boil. Strain off the water immedi-ately and add the butter, pepper and car-away seeds and continue cooking very gently for 10 minutes, keeping the pan covered.

Stir in the cheese, turning the cabbage over until all the cheese has melted and coated the cabbage. Turn into a warm dish and sprinkle the top with paprika.

1. Cut the cabbage into quarters.

2. Shred very finely cutting downward.

Colcannon

Serves 4
CALORIES PER PORTION: 300 (1260 kJ)
PROTEIN CONTENT PER PORTION: 4 grams
PREPARATION & COOKING TIME: 30 minutes

450 g (1 lb) sliced potatoes
salt
225 g (8 oz) shredded cabbage
125 g (4 oz) thinly sliced onion
3 tablespoons olive and sunflower oil
freshly ground pepper
50 g (2 oz) butter, or 3 tablespoons
*   extra oil*

Cook the potatoes in boiling salted wate for 5-10 minutes, or until they can just b pierced with a fork. Put the cabbage in pan with just enough water to cover, brin it to the boil and then drain. Fry the onio in the oil until it is golden brown and jus beginning to crisp. Add the drained cat bage and continue frying until it is als beginning to brown; sprinkle with salt an pepper and keep hot. Fry the parboile potatoes in the butter or extra oil unt they are brown and crisp. Add them t the cabbage and serve at once.

Braised celery

Serves 4
CALORIES PER PORTION: 160 (660 kJ)
PROTEIN CONTENT PER PORTION: 3 grams
PREPARATION & COOKING TIME: 1 hour

450 g (1 lb) celery, broken into 5 cm
*   (2 in) lengths*
4 tablespoons olive or sunflower oil
50 g (2 oz) coarsely chopped onion
2 tablespoons wholemeal flour
300 ml (½ pint) Brown vegetable stock
*   (page 34)*
1 teaspoon yeast extract
salt and freshly ground pepper

Heat the oil and fry the celery until it is just beginning to brown. Remove the pie-ces as they do and drain well on kitchen paper. When the celery is cooked, add the onion to oil in the pan and fry until well browned. Pour off any excess oil and sprinkle in the wholemeal flour. Stir until it is smoothly mixed with the onion, then gradually pour on the stock, stirring to prevent lumps and add the yeast extract.

Bring to the boil, stirring all the tim then lower the heat a little and cook unt the sauce is thick and smooth. Meanwhil set the oven at 180°C (350°F) Gas Check the seasoning and add salt an pepper if necessary.

Put the celery in an ovenproof dish an pour over the sauce. Cover and bake i the pre-heated oven for 30-45 minute allow extra time if the dish is thick.

Celery with tomato

Serves 4
CALORIES PER PORTION: 65 (267 kJ)
PROTEIN CONTENT PER PORTION: 2 grams
PREPARATION & COOKING TIME: 45 minutes

450 g (1 lb) celery, broken into 1 cm
  (½ in) lengths
40 g (1½ oz) butter
100 g (4 oz) finely chopped onion
350 g (12 oz) skinned tomatoes,
  chopped and seeded
salt
freshly ground pepper

Melt the butter over gentle heat and cook the onion for 5 minutes, or until transparent. Add the celery and cook for 5 minutes, taking care that it does not brown. Add the tomatoes and a little salt and pepper and stir over a moderate heat until the tomatoes break down into a pulp. Continue simmering gently for 10 minues with the pan covered, then remove the lid and increase the heat so the tomato sauce boils and reduces rapidly to a purée. Remove the pan from the heat and serve.

Stuffed artichoke hearts

Serves 4
CALORIES PER PORTION: 230 (960 kJ)
PROTEIN CONTENT PER PORTION: 7 grams
PREPARATION & COOKING TIME: 1½ hours,
  including chilling

4 medium-sized globe artichokes,
  soaked and trimmed
salt
25 g (1 oz) butter
2 tablespoons wholemeal flour
freshly ground pepper
150 ml (¼ pint) milk
1 egg white
300 ml (½ pint) Béchamel sauce (page
  196)
2 tablespoons chopped parsley

Cook the artichokes in boiling salted water for 30-45 minutes, or until a leaf will pull out easily. Remove all the leaves, discard the chokes and reserve the hearts. Scrape off the soft lower portion of each leaf with the back of a knife blade, removing any fibres as you go. Melt two-thirds of the butter in a small pan, add the flour, season with salt and pepper and stir together until smooth. Take the pan off the heat and gradually pour on the milk, stirring between each addition. Return the pan to the heat and bring the sauce to the boil, stirring until it thickens. Place over a pan of simmering water and leave for 30 minutes to mature, or transfer the sauce to a double boiler. Beat in the remaining butter.

Meanwhile, rub the artichoke purée from the leaves through a sieve and keep on one side. When the sauce is ready, add the purée first, then the egg white; mix thoroughly and adjust the seasoning. Chill for about 30 minutes.

Twenty minutes before serving, pile the purée on to the artichoke hearts. Put them into a steamer and steam at full boil for 20 minutes. Heat up the Béchamel sauce towards the end of the cooking time. Carefully remove the hearts from the steamer and arrange them on a shallow heated serving dish. Mask them with Béchamel sauce and sprinkle with a little parsley.

Do not be tempted to grate cheese over the dish too, as the flavour of the artichoke is much too delicate.

Italian stuffed artichokes

Serves 4
CALORIES PER PORTION: 210 (882 kJ)
PROTEIN CONTENT PER PORTION: 7 grams
PREPARATION & COOKING TIME: 1¼ hours

4 medium sized globe artichokes,
  soaked and trimmed

The stuffing
125 g (4 oz) very finely chopped onion
2 tablespoons olive or sunflower oil
125 g (4 oz) chopped mushrooms
20 leaves of fresh rosemary, finely
  chopped
salt
8 tablespoons fresh wholemeal
  breadcrumbs
1 egg, well beaten
freshly ground pepper (optional)
300 ml (½ pint) Tomato sauce (page
  196)

Cook the artichokes in boiling salted water for 30-45 minutes, or until a leaf will pull out easily. Turn them upside down to drain and let them cool slightly. Meanwhile, make the stuffing. Fry the onion in the oil until just transparent, add the mushrooms and continue cooking until the mushrooms are soft and shiny. Remove the pan from the heat, add the rosemary, salt and breadcrumbs and mix well. (If fresh rosemary is not available, use ½ teaspoon dried). Allow to cool, then pour in the egg and mix thoroughly. Add pepper, if using.

Set the oven at 180°C (350°F) Gas 4. Open the artichokes and remove the small central leaves and the choke. Fill the centre cavities with the stuffing, dividing it equally between the 4 artichokes. Close up the leaves and put the artichokes into a large ovenproof casserole.

Pour the Tomato sauce over the artichokes, cover the casserole and bake in the pre-heated oven for 30 minutes.

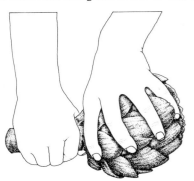

1. Remove the coarse artichoke stalk, cutting as close as you can to the bottom of the leaves.

2. Trim the tips from all the leaves to midpoint with the scissors. This makes access to the middle easier.

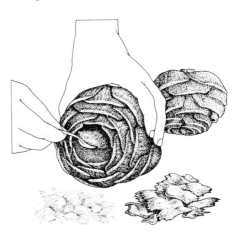

3. Pull away the soft middle leaves in one go. Then use a spoon to scrape the bristly choke off the base. Rinse out.

Braised chicory with cheese sauce

Serves 4
CALORIES PER PORTION: 160 (665 kJ)
PROTEIN CONTENT PER PORTION: 3 grams
PREPARATION & COOKING TIME: 1 hour

1-2 heads of chicory per person
2 tablespoons olive or sunflower oil
1 tablespoon lemon juice
150 ml (¼ pint) vegetable stock
salt
freshly ground pepper
150 ml (¼ pint) Cheese sauce (page 196)

Set the oven at 200°C (400°F) Gas 6. Cut off the base of each chicory head and discard any bruised or discoloured outside leaves. Pour the oil into a flameproof dish and tilt it so that the oil runs over the bottom. Put in the chicory heads and turn them over so that each head is evenly coated with oil. Mix the lemon juice into the stock and pour this over the chicory. Season liberally with salt and pepper, cover the dish with aluminium foil or oiled greaseproof paper and bake in the pre-heated over for 45 minutes to 1 hour, or until the chicory is tender.

Heat up the Cheese sauce towards the end of the cooking time and, when the chicory is cooked, pour off any cooking liquid into a pan, reduce it to about a tablespoonful and add it to the hot sauce. Pour this over the chicory and serve.

Left: Sweetcorn fritters with fried bananas. Right: Haricot beans with yoghurt and parsley. Front: Florence fennel coated with orange sauce

Fennel with orange sauce

Serves 4
CALORIES PER PORTION: 115 (475 kJ)
PROTEIN CONTENT PER PORTION: 4 grams
PREPARATION & COOKING TIME: 20 minutes

2-4 heads of fennel, together weighing about 450 g (1 lb)
salt
20 g (¾ oz) butter
2 teaspoons wholemeal flour
100 ml (4 fl oz) orange juice
grated rind of 2 oranges
1-2 tablespoons chopped parsley

Trim and cut large heads of fennel into quarters, or if using smaller ones, cut them in half. Cook in boiling, salted water until just tender, about 10-15 minutes. Meanwhile, melt the butter in a separate pan, sprinkle in the flour and stir until thick. Pour on the orange juice and stir over gentle heat until the sauce boils and thickens. Remove the pan from the stove and add the orange rind and most of the parsley. Keep warm.

Drain the fennel and arrange the pieces, cut sides uppermost, on a heated serving dish. Spoon over the sauce, opening the leaves of the fennel to allow the sauce to penetrate. Sprinkle with the remaining parsley and serve.

Green beans with yoghurt and almonds

Serves 4
CALORIES PER PORTION: 160 (657 kJ)
PROTEIN CONTENT PER PORTION: 4 grams
PREPARATION & COOKING TIME: 10-20 minutes

450 g (1 lb) fresh or frozen green beans, trimmed
50 g (2 oz) split blanched almonds
1-2 teaspoons olive or sunflower oil
coarse salt
25 g (1 oz) butter
½ teaspoon wholemeal flour
100 ml (4 fl oz) natural yoghurt

Cook fresh beans in a little boiling salted water for 10-15 minutes, or until they are just tender. (Cook frozen beans according to the instructions on the packet.) Put the almonds in a pan with a very little oil and cook them over gentle heat until they are brown. There should be just enough oil to coat the bottom of the pan, with a little to spare. Take out the almonds and sprinkle them with a little coarse salt.

Melt the butter in a separate pan, sprinkle in the flour and cook gently until the mixture is golden brown and smooth. Add the yoghurt and bring to the boil very slowly, stirring all the time. (Middle Eastern cooks say that you should only stir yoghurt in one direction as this prevents it curdling.) Continue cooking until the sauce is reduced by about half, then add the beans and turn them until they are evenly coated.

Pile them into a heated dish for serving and either sprinkle the almonds over the top, or hand them separately.

Paprika beans in cream

Serves 4
CALORIES PER PORTION: 115 (487 kJ)
PROTEIN CONTENT PER PORTION: 2 grams
PREPARATION & COOKING TIME: 20 minutes

450 g (1 lb) green beans, trimmed
50 g (2 oz) thinly sliced onion
200 ml (⅓ pint) cultured sour cream
2 tablespoons paprika

Cook fresh beans in a little boiling salted water for 10-15 minutes, or until they are just tender. (Cook frozen beans according to the instructions on the packet.) Add the onion slices halfway through the cooking time. Bring the cream to the boil in a small pan, stirring all the time to prevent it burning. When the beans are tender pour off any remaining water, sprinkle over the paprika and turn the beans until they are evenly coated. Pile them in the centre of a heated shallow bowl and pour the cream round them. Serve at once, spooning a little cream over each serving.

Sweet and sour beans

Serves 4
CALORIES PER PORTION: 65 (262 kJ)
PROTEIN CONTENT PER PORTION: 1 **gram**
PREPARATION & COOKING TIME: 15-20 minutes

450 g (1 lb) fresh or frozen green beans,
  trimmed
salt
20 g (¾ oz) butter
50 g (2 oz) finely chopped onion
4 tablespoons wine or cider vinegar
1 tablespoon raw brown sugar
6 large mint leaves, chopped almost to
  a pulp

Cook fresh beans in a very little boiling
salted water for 10-15 minutes, or until
they are just tender. (If using frozen
beans, cook them according to the instructions on the packet.) Meanwhile, melt the
butter in a pan over gentle heat, add the
onion and the vinegar and cook for 5
minutes.

When the beans are tender, there
should be little or no water left (drain
frozen beans if necessary). Add the sugar,
stir until the beans are evenly coated, then
add the onion. Stir in the mint and continue stirring gently until the onion and
mint are thoroughly mixed into the beans.
Turn into a heated dish for serving.

Succotash

Serves 4
CALORIES PER PORTION: 230 (752 kJ)
PROTEIN CONTENT PER PORTION: 4 **grams**
PREPARATION & COOKING TIME: 40 minutes

225g (8 oz) shelled broad beans
1 large or 2 medium-sized corns on the
  cob or 225 g (8 oz) canned or frozen
  sweetcorn kernels
4 tablespoons water
25 g (1 oz) unsalted butter
100 ml (4 fl oz) double cream
2 teaspoons finely chopped parsley
salt

Cook the beans in boiling salted water for
7-10 minutes, or until they are just tender.
Strip the corn off the cobs, if using, and
simmer the kernels in the water and butter
in a small covered pan for 10 minutes
without salt, as this will make them tough.
(If using canned or frozen corn, drain it
well before heating through in a pan with
the water and butter for 4-5 minutes.)
When cooked, drain the corn thoroughly,
pour on the cream, stir in the parsley and
keep hot. Remove the skins from the
beans, add with salt. Stir the mixture
gently until it is all mixed together and
sprinkle over a little extra parsley.

Sweetcorn fritters with fried bananas

Serves 4
CALORIES PER PORTION: 470 (1960 kJ)
PROTEIN CONTENT PER PORTION: 11 grams
PREPARATION & COOKING TIME: 50 minutes

1 large or 2 medium-sized corns on the
  cob, or 225 g (8 oz) canned or frozen
  sweetcorn kernels
oil for shallow frying
4 bananas
a pinch of ground cinnamon or grated
  ginger root

The batter
100 g (4 oz) wholemeal flour
½ teaspoon salt
a little freshly ground pepper
1 large egg, beaten
50 g (2 oz) grated Cheddar cheese
200 ml (⅓ pint) milk

Cook the corn cobs, if using, in boiling
unsalted water for 5-10 minutes, or until
they are tender, then rinse under cold
running water before scraping off the kernels with a sharp knife. (Cook canned or
frozen corn according to the instructions
on the can or the packet.) Meanwhile,
make the batter.

Sift together the flour, salt and pepper,
make a well in the centre, add the egg
then stir in the cheese and gradually mix
in the milk until the batter is smooth.
Leave it to stand until the corn is cooked.

Drain the corn well and mix it thoroughly into the batter. Heat 1 cm (½ in)
oil in a thick-based frying pan and fry
large spoonful of the mixture on both sides
until golden brown; drain the fritters on
kitchen paper, keeping them hot until the
bananas are ready.

Peel the bananas, cut them in half
lengthwise, then cut each half into 8 pieces. Dust with cinnamon or ginger, reheat
the oil and fry the bananas to a golden
brown. Pile the fritters in the middle of
a warm plate, arrange the banana around
the rim and serve while hot.

Puréed peas with cheese croûtes

Serves 4
CALORIES PER PORTION: 250 (1040 kJ)
PROTEIN CONTENT PER PORTION: 10 grams
PREPARATION & COOKING TIME: 25 minutes

350 g (12 oz) shelled fresh or frozen
    peas
salt
4 slices of wholemeal bread, crusts
    removed
50 g (2 oz) butter
25 g (1 oz) grated strong cheese
a sprinkling of cayenne
a little milk
freshly ground pepper
1-2 tablespoons double cream
2 large mint leaves, finely chopped

If using fresh peas, cook them in a little boiling salted water until they are tender — about 10-15 minutes. (If using frozen peas, follow the instructions on the packet.) Cut each slice of bread into 4 triangles and fry in the butter, turning once, until they begin to crisp and turn brown; drain them on kitchen paper. Sprinkle with the cheese and dust with cayenne. Put the slices under a hot grill until the cheese melts and begins to brown.

Meanwhile, pour the peas and the tablespoon or so of remaining water into a blender and work until smooth — it may be necessary to add a few drops of milk from time to time for the purée to have the right consistency.

Return the purée to the pan and stir over a moderate heat until thoroughly hot. Season with salt and pepper, turn it into a heated serving dish and pour the cream over. Sprinkle with the finely chopped mint and arrange the cheese croûtes round the edge of the dish.

Peas with lettuce and onions

Serves 4
CALORIES PER PORTION: 175 (725 kJ)
PROTEIN CONTENT PER PORTION: 6 grams
PREPARATION & COOKING TIME: 20 minutes

350 g (12 oz) shelled fresh or frozen
    peas
100 g (4 oz) coarsely torn lettuce
65 g (2½ oz) butter
50 g (2 oz) finely chopped onion
1 tablespoon wholemeal flour
½ teaspoon salt
freshly ground pepper

Melt 50 g (2 oz) of the butter in a pan and cook the onion until transparent. Add the lettuce before the onion colours and cook until the juice runs. Bring to the boil, add the peas, bring back to the boil and continue cooking for 5-10 minutes if fresh peas are used (less time is needed for frozen ones). Add a little extra water if necessary. Combine the flour and salt with the rest of the butter in a bowl, then pour on the liquid from the pan and stir well. Return to the pan, season with salt and pepper and boil until the sauce thickens before serving.

Okra créole

Serves 4
CALORIES PER PORTION: 165 (682 kJ)
PROTEIN CONTENT PER PORTION: 3 grams
PREPARATION & COOKING TIME: 30 minutes

225 g (8 oz) okra cut into 2 cm (1 in)
    chunks
4 tablespoons olive or sunflower oil
225 g (8 oz) finely chopped onions
100 g (4 oz) chopped celery
225 g (8 oz) diced red peppers
salt
200 ml (⅓ pint) water

Heat the oil in a pan, add the onions and cook until they just begin to take colour, then add the celery. Cook very gently for 5 minutes before adding the peppers and okra. Season with salt, add the measured water, cover the pan and simmer for 15-20 minutes, or until the okra is tender. Drain before turning into a heated dish for serving.

Note: 4 quartered tomatoes may be added and the sauce thickened with a little flour.

Mattar Panir

Serves 4
CALORIES PER PORTION: 335 (1395 kJ)
PROTEIN CONTENT PER PORTION: 18 grams
PREPARATION & COOKING TIME: 20 minutes

400 g (14 oz) cooked fresh or frozen
    peas
6 tablespoons ghee or clarified butter
225 g (8 oz) panir (page 200)
1 teaspoon ground turmeric
1 teaspoon red chilli powder
2 tablespoons chopped fresh coriander
salt
pinch of sugar (optional)

Heat the ghee in a thick-based frying pan, add the peas, turmeric, and chilli powder and stir together for 3-4 minutes over medium heat.

Add the panir, mix well and cook gently for 2 minutes. Stir in the chopped coriander, season with salt and cook at just below simmering point for about 10 minutes, or until the peas are tender. Add a little sugar if the panir tastes too sour.

Okra in batter

Serves 4
CALORIES PER PORTION: 300 (1255 kJ)
PROTEIN CONTENT PER PORTION: 10 grams
PREPARATION & COOKING TIME: 30 minutes

225 g (8 oz) trimmed okra
salt
oil for deep frying
Coating batter (page 194) with ½
    teaspoon ground cumin and ½
    teaspoon ground cinnamon added to
    the sifted flour

Cook the okra in boiling salted water for 5-10 minutes, or until they are tender but not soft. Drain off the water and refresh them by rinsing in cold water immediately, then drain again and dry.

Make the batter, and mix it thoroughly until smooth, then dip the okra into the batter and deep-fry in batches in heated oil, 180°C (350°F), until golden brown and crisp. Drain on kitchen paper and serve hot with a Piquant tomato or Tartare sauce (page 196 and 127).

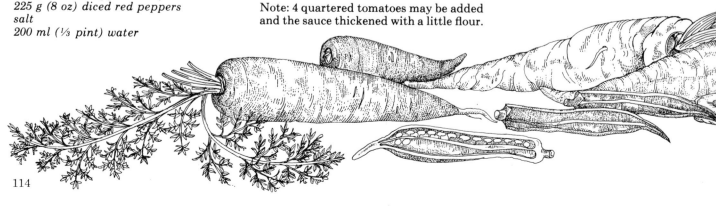

German-style carrots with apple

Serves 4

CALORIES PER PORTION: 175 (726 kJ)
PROTEIN CONTENT PER PORTION: 1.5 grams
PREPARATION & COOKING TIME: 40-50 minutes

350 g (12 oz) scraped young carrots
salt
175 g (6 oz) peeled and cored cooking
   apples
a little wholemeal flour
4 tablespoons olive or sunflower oil
100 g (4 oz) onion, cut into rings
freshly ground pepper

Cut the carrots lengthwise into thin strips
and cook them in very little boiling salted
water in a large pan for 10-15 minutes, or
until just tender; a stainless steel sauté
pan with a lid is ideal — a cast iron one
can discolour the carrots. There should
only be very little water left in the pan by
the time the carrots are cooked.

Meanwhile, cut the apples into segments about 1 cm (½ in) thick. Dip them
in the flour and fry in about 3 tablespoons
of the oil, turning them over so that they
brown on both sides; take care that they
do not become mushy though — the trick
is to have the oil hot enough so a crisp
skin forms on the outside of the apples.
Drain them on kitchen paper and keep
hot while you fry the onion rings in the
rest of the oil. Drain the onions when they
are crisp and golden. Arrange the carrots
interleaved with apple slices, and with
crisp onion rings scattered over the top.
Season with salt and pepper before
serving.

Swede soufflé

Serves 4

CALORIES PER PORTION: 165 (688 (688 kJ)
   with cream; 85 (355 kJ) without
PROTEIN CONTENT PER PORTION: 7 grams with
   cream, 6 grams without
PREPARATION & COOKING TIME: 50 minutes

450 g (1 lb) chopped swedes
salt
2 tablespoons onion juice (see page 55)
¼ teaspoon ground cinnamon
freshly ground black pepper
1 tablespoon wine or cider vinegar
3 eggs, separated
cultured sour cream (optional)

Cook the swedes in boiling salted water
for about 20 minutes; they should be soft
but not mushy. Put them into a blender
and work them to a purée, or use a Mouli
mill — or rub them through a sieve. Add
the onion pulp, cinnamon, pepper, vinegar
and a little salt and mix well. Beat in the
egg yolks, one at a time. Set the oven at
180°C (350°F) Gas 4.

Whisk the egg whites until they stand
in peaks, then fold them into the purée.
Spoon into a hot, buttered soufflé dish
holding about 1 litre (2 pints) and bake
in the pre-heated oven for 25 minutes.
Serve with a little cultured sour cream.

Baked carrot loaf

Serves 4

CALORIES PER PORTION: 83 (349 kJ)
PROTEIN CONTENT PER PORTION: 6 grams
PREPARATION & COOKING TIME: 1 hour

350 g (12 oz) scraped young carrots
2 eggs
150 ml (¼ pint) natural yoghurt
salt and freshly ground pepper
¼ teaspoon finely chopped thyme
50 g (2 oz) finely chopped onion
juice and grated rind of ½ lemon

Cook the carrots in a very little boiling
salted water for 10-15 minutes, or until
they are tender; ideally there should be
almost no water left in the pan when they
are done. Set the oven at 200°F (400°F)
Gas 5. Put the carrots into a blender with
the rest of the ingredients and blend until
smooth. If you do not have a blender, rub
the carrots through a sieve or Mouli mill
and then mix the other ingredients thoroughly into the purée. Pour into a well-
buttered cake tin, 18 cm (7 in) in diameter
and 6 cm (2½ in) deep, and bake in the
pre-heated oven for about 30 minutes.

Remove loaf from the oven and allow
it to cool for a few minutes before turning
out on to a warm, shallow serving dish.
Serve with boiled peas or broad beans.

Parsnip rissoles

Serves 4

CALORIES PER PORTION: 170 (701 kJ)
PROTEIN CONTENT PER PORTION: 3.5 grams
PREPARATION & COOKING TIME: 40 minutes

450 g (1 lb) chopped parsnips
salt and little freshly ground pepper
50 g (2 oz) finely chopped onion
1 tablespoon olive or sunflower oil
1 small egg
a sprinkling of freshly grated nutmeg
oil for deep frying

Cook the parsnips in boiling salted water
for 20-30 minutes, or until they are tender
but not mushy. Fry the onion in a little
oil until transparent. Rub the parsnips
through a sieve or Mouli mill, or purée
them in a blender and put on one side to
cool completely. Beat up the egg with ½
teaspoon salt, pepper and nutmeg; add it,
with the fried onion, to the parsnip purée
and mix well.

Heat the oil to 180°C (350°F) and put
a frying basket into the pan. Scoop up
tablespoonfuls of the purée mixture, each
about the size of 2 walnuts, trim off any
untidy bits and gently drop the rissoles
into the oil. Fry them, 3 or 4 at a time,
until golden brown and crisp. Drain them
on kitchen paper, keep hot and serve.

Glazed carrots with cinnamon

Serves 4
CALORIES PER PORTION: 100 (415 kJ)
PROTEIN CONTENT PER PORTION: 1 gram
PREPARATION & COOKING TIME: 40 minutes

450 g (1 lb) scraped carrots
salt
50 g (2 oz) finely chopped onion
2 tablespoons olive or sunflower oil
2 teaspoons raw brown sugar
1 teaspoon ground cinnamon

Cut four equally spaced shallow furrows lengthwise around each carrot; slice the carrots into 2 mm (⅛ in) slices and cook them in a little boiling salted water in a covered pan for about 5 minutes, or until they are just tender.

When the carrots are nearly done, remove the lid, increase the heat and boil until almost dry. Meanwhile, fry the onion in the oil until golden brown, add the sugar and cinnamon and stir until the onion is well coated. Add the carrots and continue stirring until they, too, are well coated with the glaze. Serve at once.

Beetroot in yoghurt

Serves 4
CALORIES PER PORTION: 115 (485 kJ)
PROTEIN CONTENT PER PORTION: 5 grams
PREPARATION & COOKING TIME: 15 minutes

450 g (1 lb) cooked diced beetroot
(preferably baked)
1 tablespoon chopped onion
1 tablespoon olive or sunflower oil
1 tablespoon wholemeal flour
½ teaspoon ground cumin
3 tablespoons chopped parsley
salt
freshly ground pepper
200 ml (⅓ pint) yoghurt

Fry the onion in the oil until transparent, add the beetroot and stir gently until it is thoroughly heated and beginning to fry. Sprinkle over the flour, cumin and ⅔ of the parsley and season with salt and pepper. Mix well, then pour on the yoghurt and stir over moderate heat until the mixture thickens, then reduce the heat and simmer for a few moments longer before serving with a little extra parsley sprinkled over.

Louisiana sweet potatoes

Serves 4
CALORIES PER PORTION: 190 (807 kJ)
PROTEIN CONTENT PER PORTION: 2 grams
PREPARATION & COOKING TIME: 1 hour 20 minutes

700 g (1½ lb) sweet potatoes
salt
15 g (½ oz) butter
25 g (1 oz) finely chopped onion
½ tablespoon wholemeal flour
100 ml (4 fl oz) vegetable stock
2 tablespoons chopped parsley
1 tablespoon lemon juice

Wash the sweet potatoes and leave them in their skins. Cook them in a pan of boiling salted water for at least 40 minutes, until a skewer can go through them easily, though they should still be fairly firm. Allow to cool slightly, then peel them and, with a melon baller, scoop out balls about the size of small walnuts.

Melt the butter in a frying pan and cook the onion over gentle heat until transparent. Sprinkle in the flour and stir until the onion is well coated, then pour on the stock and stir until it boils and thickens. Add half the parsley and the lemon juice, then put in the potato balls, adding a little more stock, if necessary. Heat through quickly, stirring until they are well coated with the sauce and parsley, then turn into a heated serving dish and sprinkle over the rest of the parsley.

Note: For a stronger lemon flavour, add the grated rind of half a lemon.

Heaven and Earth (potatoes and apple)

Serves 4
CALORIES PER PORTION: 245 (1016 kJ)
PROTEIN CONTENT PER PORTION: 2.5 grams
PREPARATION & COOKING TIME: 30 minutes

350 g (12 oz) diced potatoes
salt
450 g (1 lb) cooking apples
225 g (8 oz) thinly sliced onions
½ teaspoon ground cinnamon
4 tablespoons olive or sunflower oil

Cook the potatoes in well-salted boiling water for about 10 minutes; they should still be firm. Meanwhile, peel and dice the apples and add them to the potatoes after 7 minutes — the apples should cook until they are tender but not squashy. Fry the onions in a thick-based frying pan with the cinnamon in half the oil until they are golden brown. Remove the onions and keep them hot. Wipe out the pan, return it to the heat and add the rest of the oil.

Drain the potatoes and apple, pat dry with kitchen cloth or paper and put them into the hot oil. Fry until they are just beginning to brown, turning them over gently. Ideally, the potatoes and apple should finish their cooking during the frying. Turn them on to a hot serving dish and sprinkle the fried onions on top.

Lyonnaise potatoes

Serves 4
CALORIES PER PORTION: 205 (850 kJ)
PROTEIN CONTENT PER PORTION: 3 grams
PREPARATION & COOKING TIME: 30 minutes

450 g (1 lb) thinly sliced potatoes
salt
50 g (2 oz) butter
225 g (8 oz) onions, cut into thin rings

Lower the potato slices carefully into a pan of boiling, salted water and cook them for 10-15 minutes — the potatoes should still be slightly firm. Meanwhile, melt the butter in a thick-based frying pan, add the onion rings and cook gently until transparent, turning them from time to time and taking care they do not burn. Remove the onions from the pan and keep them hot. Strain the butter into a dish to remove any onion specks which would otherwise burn and spoil the flavour of the dish. Wipe out the pan with kitchen paper and pour back the butter.

Drain the cooked potatoes well, pat them dry with a kitchen cloth or paper then fry them in the onion-flavoured butter on both sides, in 2 or 3 batches, until crisp and golden. Arrange the potato and onion in alternate layers on a hot serving dish and sprinkle with a little salt.

Dauphinois potatoes

Serves 4
CALORIES PER PORTION: 275 (1150 kJ)
PROTEIN CONTENT PER PORTION: 7 grams
PREPARATION & COOKING TIME: 1 hour

550 g (1¼ lb) thinly sliced potatoes
40 g (1½ oz) butter
500 ml (scant 1 pint) milk
1 teaspoon salt
freshly ground black pepper
1 bay leaf (optional)
1 clove of garlic, peeled (optional)

Set the oven at 200°C (400°F) Gas 6. Butter an ovenproof dish about 23 cm (9 in) in diameter with about a third of the butter. Gently heat the milk in a pan, add the rest of the butter, the salt and pepper, and crumble in the bay leaf, if used. Rub the inside of your baking dish with a cut clove of garlic, if liked.

Arrange the potatoes in overlapping layers in the dish, and pour over the milk. Bake in the pre-heated oven for 45 minutes, until the potatoes are cooked and well browned on top and the milk has become a creamy sauce.

Left: Dauphinois potatoes, the classic French dish, spiked with garlic and cooked in a creamy sauce. Right: crisp and buttery Swiss Rösti turns potatoes into a gourmet's treat

Swiss rösti

Serves 4
CALORIES PER PORTION: 145 (602 kJ)
PROTEIN CONTENT PER PORTION: 2 grams
PREPARATION & COOKING TIME: 35 minutes

450 g (1 lb) thickly sliced large potatoes
25 g (1 oz) unsalted butter
salt
freshly ground black pepper

Carefully lower the sliced potatoes into a pan of boiling water and cook them for about 10 minutes. Drain well and allow the potatoes to cool.

Melt the butter over gentle heat in a thick-based frying pan and shred the potato slices into the butter, using a coarse grater, sprinkling with salt and pepper as you go.

Using two forks, neaten the edges of the potato nest and flatten the top lightly to form a cake measuring about 18 cm (7 in) in diameter and 1 cm (½ in) thick. Cover the pan and fry over moderate-to-low heat for about 10 minutes, then remove the lid and gently turn the cake over to cook on the other side for a further 10 minutes. Serve immediately.

Jerusalem artichokes provençale

Serves 4
CALORIES PER PORTION: 90 (383 kJ)
PROTEIN CONTENT PER PORTION: 2.5 grams
PREPARATION & COOKING TIME: 30 minutes

450 g (1 lb) thinly sliced Jerusalem
* artichokes*
50 g (2 oz) finely chopped onion
2 tablespoon olive or sunflower oil
225 g (8 oz) skinned tomatoes, coarsely
* chopped*
1 large clove of garlic, peeled and finely
* chopped*
salt
freshly ground black pepper
1 tablespoon finely chopped parsley

Fry the onion in the oil until transparent; add the artichoke slices and continue cooking over a moderate heat for a few minutes, or until the artichokes are just beginning to brown. Add the tomatoes, garlic, salt and pepper and increase the heat. Bring to the boil and cook until the tomatoes have broken down into a pulp and most of the extra liquid has evaporated, leaving the artichoke slices coated with quite a thick purée. Take care that they do not overcook, or stick to the bottom of the pan and burn. Pour into a heated shallow dish, sprinkle with parsley and serve.

Roast winter vegetables

Serves 4
CALORIES PER PORTION: 375 (1576 kJ)
PROTEIN CONTENT PER PORTION: 8 grams
PREPARATION & COOKING TIME: 1 hour 20
  minutes

4 medium-sized potatoes
4 parsnips
4 medium-sized onions
450 g (1 lb) pumpkin
a little olive or sunflower oil
salt
freshly ground pepper
a little ground cinnamon

Wash and peel all the vegetables. Cut the potatoes in half, halve the parsnips lengthwise and slice the pumpkin into 8 pieces. Put all the vegetables into a pan, cover with hot water and bring it to the boil. Set the oven at 200°C (400°F) Gas 6. Drain the vegetables immediately, arrange them in a roasting pan with 5 mm (¼ in) oil in it and brush with more oil. Sprinkle liberally with salt and pepper and sprinkle cinnamon over the parsnips and pumpkin. Roast in the pre-heated oven for 45 minutes to 1 hour, turning the vegetables over 3 times during the cooking.

Leeks in red wine

Serves 4
CALORIES PER PORTION: 95 (400 kJ)
PROTEIN CONTENT PER PORTION: 2 grams
PREPARATION & COOKING TIME: 30 minutes

Buy enough young leeks to give 450 g
* (1 lb) when trimmed, then cut to*
* equal lengths and split lengthways*
2 tablespoons olive or sunflower oil
1 teaspoon crushed coriander
200 ml (⅓ pint) red wine

Heat the oil in a thick-based pan, place the leeks in it, keeping them all lying in the same direction, and sprinkle with the crushed coriander. Cook over gentle heat for about 5 minutes, or until the leeks just begin to brown. Turn them over carefully and cook on the other side, for the same length of time, then pour on the wine and simmer, covered, for 10 minutes before serving. Served cold, this makes a very good starter.

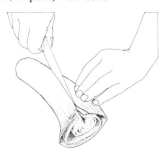

1. Slit the leek along its length and almost to the base.

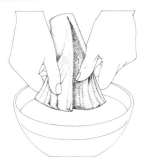

2. Fan it out, upside down, under water to release any trapped dirt.

Baked spiced onions

Serves 4
CALORIES PER PORTION: 125 (535 kJ)
PROTEIN CONTENT PER PORTION: 3 grams
PREPARATION & COOKING TIME: 35 minutes

4 medium-sized onions, each weighing
* approximately 100 g (4 oz)*
2 tablespoons olive or sunflower oil
½ teaspoon ground cumin
½ teaspoon ground coriander
salt
freshly ground black pepper
8 heaped tablespoons fresh wholemeal
* breadcrumbs*

Remove the brown outer skin from th onions and cut each one in half horizon tally. Cook in boiling water for 10 minutes then drain and remove the centres, leavin only two outer layers as a shell. Coarsel chop the onion centres. Set the oven a 180°C (350°F) Gas 4.

Heat the oil in a small pan and fry th spices with the salt and pepper for abou 10 seconds, then add the chopped onio and cook until just golden. Add the bread crumbs and mix thoroughly. Pile th stuffing into the 8 onion shells and arrang them in a well-oiled ovenproof dish. Bak in the pre-heated oven for 15-30 minutes or until tender. Cover the tops with fo if the onions are browning too quickly.

Spring onions in butter

Serves 4
CALORIES PER PORTION: 146 (612 kJ)
PROTEIN CONTENT PER PORTION: 2 grams
PREPARATION & COOKING TIME: 15 minutes

450 g (1 lb) spring onions, trimmed to
* equal length, leaving about 10 cm*
* (4 in) of the green top*
40 g (1½ oz) butter
a few drops of lemon juice
4-8 tablespoons fresh wholemeal
* breadcrumbs*
salt
freshly ground paper

Melt the butter in a thick-based pan an cook the onions over gentle heat for 5-1 minutes, until the leaves are just gon limp and the onions have lost their pep pery, hot flavour. If you keep all the onion lying in the same direction as you coo them, it makes all the difference to th appearance of the finished dish.

Squeeze a few drops of lemon juice ove the onions to offset the oiliness of th butter. Sprinkle with enough bread crumbs to soak up the rest of the butte season with a little salt and pepper an serve — a simple dish with an air luxury.

Peperonata

Peperonata also makes a splendid dish served cold.

Serves 4
CALORIES PER PORTION: 110 (473 kJ)
PROTEIN CONTENT PER PORTION: 2.5 grams
PREPARATION & COOKING TIME: 45 minutes

350 g (12 oz) ripe tomatoes, quartered
200 ml (⅓ pint) red wine
2 bay leaves
2 cloves of garlic, peeled and chopped
225 g (8 oz) thinly sliced onions
2 tablespoons olive or sunflower oil
350 g (12 oz) sliced red peppers
salt

Put the tomatoes with the wine, bay leaves and garlic into a pan and bring to the boil. Turn down the heat and simmer gently until the tomatoes begin to break down. Fry the onions in the oil until they are just beginning to brown. Add the red peppers and continue frying over a moderate heat for 10 minutes, stirring so that they do not burn. Strain the tomatoes and rub the pulp through a sieve; return it to the pan and, if necessary, boil to reduce to 450 ml (¾ pint).

Add this sauce to the peppers and onions and simmer in a covered pan for 20 minutes, stirring occasionally to prevent the sauce from sticking and burning. Serve with plenty of plainly boiled Italian long-grain rice to soak up the sauce.

Courgettes with sage and cheese sauce

Serves 4
CALORIES PER PORTION: 180 (758 kJ)
PROTEIN CONTENT PER PORTION: 7 grams
PREPARATION & COOKING TIME: 45 minutes
    (including salting courgettes)

450 g (1 lb) courgettes, quartered
    lengthways
salt

The sauce
25 g (1 oz) butter
25 g (1 oz) finely chopped onion
20 g (¾ oz) wholemeal flour
300 ml (½ pint) milk
50 g (2 oz) grated Cheddar cheese
½-1 teaspoon finely chopped sage
salt
freshly ground pepper
100 ml (4 fl oz) dry white wine

Sprinkle the courgettes with salt and leave to drain for 30-45 minutes. Meanwhile, make the sauce; melt the butter in a small pan and cook the onion until it just begins to colour. Stir in the flour and mix well, then draw the pan off the heat and pour on the milk, stirring well between each addition. Return the pan to the heat and bring the sauce to the boil, stirring all the time until it thickens. Add the grated cheese, the chopped sage, or ½ teaspoon dried sage, and season with salt and pepper. Cover the top of the sauce with a piece of buttered greaseproof paper and place the pan in another larger pan containing boiling water, or transfer to a double boiler; keep it cooking very gently for about 30 minutes for the sauce to mature.

Rinse the courgettes, pat them dry and cook them in a very little boiling water, salted if necessary, for 10-15 minutes. Five minutes before serving, add the white wine to the sauce, take the top saucepan out of the larger pan or double boiler and bring to the boil. Adjust the seasoning, if necessary; drain the courgettes, pour over the sauce and serve.

Baby squash with eggs

Serves 4
CALORIES PER PORTION: 130 (537 kJ)
PROTEIN CONTENT PER PORTION: 7 grams
PREPARATION & COOKING TIME: 20-25 minutes

2 squash, weighing about 225 g (8 oz)
    each
salt
4 teaspoons butter
freshly ground pepper
4 small eggs, separated

Cook the squash in boiling salted water until tender — between 10-20 minutes. Drain and cut each in half. Using a teaspoon, scoop out a little of each centre and put a teaspoon of butter in each half; when it has melted, sprinkle with a little salt and pepper and prick with a fork to help the butter soak into the flesh. Put an egg yolk into each buttered hollow, taking care not to break it, and then cut the whites with two knives, held parallel to each other, until they are liquid and flow easily. Pour in enough egg white just to fill up the cavities and steam the squash for 3-4 minutes or until the eggs are just 'veiled', the whites set and the yolks still runny.

Courgettes provençales

Serves 4
CALORIES PER PORTION: 100 (405 kJ)
PROTEIN CONTENT PER PORTION: 2 grams
PREPARATION & COOKING TIME: 1½ hours
    (including salting)

450 g (1 lb) sliced courgettes
salt
100 g (4 oz) thinly sliced onion
2 tablespoons olive oil
350 g (12 oz) skinned tomatoes,
    quartered
1-2 cloves of garlic, peeled and chopped
1 tablespoon chopped parsley

Sprinkle the courgette slices with salt and leave them for 30-45 minutes. Rinse and pat dry with a kitchen cloth or kitchen paper. Cook the onion in the oil until golden brown, then remove it with a draining spoon, taking care not to leave any bits behind to burn and spoil the flavour of the dish. Put the courgettes into the frying pan, turn up the heat a little to brown them slightly without burning — do not let them stew in their juices. Once they have browned, lower the heat and allow some juice to collect; add the tomatoes and garlic, season with salt and continue cooking until the courgettes are tender and only a little of the sauce remains. Add the onions, pour into a heated serving dish and sprinkle with parsley. This recipe works well with okra.

Aubergines au gratin

Serves 4
CALORIES PER PORTION: 170 (721 kJ)
PROTEIN CONTENT PER PORTION: 12 grams
PREPARATION & COOKING TIME: 1½ hours

600 g (1¼ lb) aubergines
scant 200 ml (⅓ pint) milk or single
    cream
2 eggs
salt
1 clove of garlic, peeled and chopped
50 g (2 oz) fresh wholemeal
    breadcrumbs
50 g (2 oz) grated Cheddar cheese

Wipe the aubergines, prick the skins and wrap them in foil. Bake in a moderate oven, 180°C (350°F) Gas 4, for 45 minutes, or until they are soft. Allow them to cool slightly and then scrape the pulp out of the skins. Work it in a blender with the milk, eggs, salt and garlic until smooth, or purée by rubbing it through a sieve then adding the other ingredients.

Pour the purée into a shallow ovenproof dish 30 cm (12 in) long. Sprinkle the top first with the crumbs, then the cheese and bake for 20-30 minutes in the pre-heated oven before serving.

Baked savoury pumpkin

Serves 4
CALORIES PER PORTION: 125 (510 kJ)
PROTEIN CONTENT PER PORTION: 4 grams
PREPARATION & COOKING TIME: 45 minutes

450 g (1 lb) peeled pumpkin, cut in
  chunks 1 cm (½ in) thick
1 little olive or sunflower oil
25 g (1 oz) finely chopped onion
15 g (½ oz) butter or 1 tablespoon oil
salt
freshly ground pepper
1 egg
200 ml (⅓ pint) milk
1 tablespoon chopped parsley

Set the oven at 200°C (400°F) Gas 6.
Brush the pumpkin with a little oil and
place the chunks in a single layer in a
well-oiled baking dish, preferably a metal
one. Put it into the pre-heated oven and
bake for 30 minutes. Fry the chopped
onion in the butter or oil until it just
begins to colour.

When the pumpkin is tender, sprinkle
it liberally with salt and pepper. Beat the
egg with the milk, add the parsley, onion
and season with salt. Pour the mixture
over the pumpkin, return it to the oven
and bake for another 10 minutes before
serving.

Mushroom and leek stir-fried with bean curd

Serves 4
CALORIES PER PORTION: 120 (507 kJ)
PROTEIN CONTENT PER PORTION: 7 grams
PREPARATION & COOKING TIME: 20 minutes

225 g (8 oz) prepared leeks, cut in 4 cm
  (1½ in) lengths
2 tablespoons vegetable oil
225 g (8 oz) sliced button mushrooms
1 tablespoon soya sauce
225 g (8 oz) thinly sliced bean curd

Cook the leeks in half of the oil in a frying
pan or wok over moderate heat for a couple of minutes, until they are just beginning to soften. Add the mushrooms and
soya sauce, and continue stir frying until
they are cooked. Remove from the pan
and keep hot while you fry the bean curd
in the remaining oil until crisp and golden
brown on both sides. Take care when
frying as the curd may spatter when put
into oil. Put the leeks and mushrooms on
to a warm serving dish and arrange the
bean curd on top. Alternatively, the vegetables can be returned to the pan with
the bean curd and stir fried together for
a few moments before serving.

Creamed mushroom with yoghurt

Serves 4
CALORIES PER PORTION: 120 (502 kJ)
PROTEIN CONTENT PER PORTION: 6 grams
PREPARATION & COOKING TIME: 20 minutes

450 g (1 lb) mushrooms, wiped or peeled
300 ml (½ pint) natural yoghurt
100 g (4 oz) finely chopped onion
2 tablespoons olive oil
salt

Fry the onion in the oil until golden brown.
Add half the mushrooms broken into pieces about 2 cm (¾ in) square. Press with
a wooden spoon until the juices begin to
run and, when the first batch has reduced
add the rest. Cook them until they are
dark and shiny, then drain off some of the
juice, add the yoghurt and salt. (I use
yoghurt which has been left to stand for

2 days as the culture is then fairly strong.
Commercial yoghurt tends to be too solid
and bland.) Continue cooking until all the
liquid has evaporated and just a paste is
left coating the mushrooms. Turn in to a
warm serving dish.

This also makes a good filling for vol-
au-vent cases.

Stuffed mushrooms

Serves 4
CALORIES PER PORTION: 265 (1108 kJ)
PROTEIN CONTENT PER PORTION: 17 grams
PREPARATION & COOKING TIME: 40 minutes

450 g (1 lb) large field mushrooms
100 g (4 oz) finely chopped onion
75 g (3 oz) butter
350 g (12 oz) cooked lentils — 150 g
  (5 oz) uncooked
1 clove of garlic, peeled and chopped
2 tablespoons chopped parsley
1 tablespoon lemon juice
salt and freshly ground pepper

Fry the onion in half the butter until
golden brown, peel the mushrooms and
remove the stalks; coarsely chop the stalks
and add them to the onions and cook for
about 2-3 minutes. Liberally butter a shallow ovenproof dish and cover the bottom
with about half of the mushrooms, gills
uppermost.

Set the oven at 200°C (400°F) Gas 6.
Add the lentils, garlic and parsley to the
cooked onions; mix well and continue
cooking until the lentils are really hot.
Add a little water to prevent them from
burning, if necessary. Put a spoonful or

two of the lentil stuffing into each mushroom and sprinkle with lemon juice. Season with salt and pepper, cover the filled
mushrooms with the rest of the mushrooms, gills downwards, then melt the rest
of the butter and brush this over the tops.
Bake for 30 minutes.

*More vegetable accompaniments for the
discriminating palate. Top: Baked
savoury pumpkin. Centre: Chinese-
style Mushroom and leek stir-fried with
bean curd. Bottom: Large field mushrooms, stuffed with lentils and onion*

Mushroom pudding

Serves 4
CALORIES PER PORTION: 365 (1534 kJ)
PROTEIN CONTENT PER PORTION: 11 grams
PREPARATION & COOKING TIME: 1 hour 20
  minutes

450 g (1 lb) coarsely chopped
  mushrooms
50 g (2 oz) finely chopped onion
2 tablespoons olive or sunflower oil
salt
freshly ground black pepper
50 g (2 oz) fresh wholemeal
  breadcrumbs
2 eggs, well beaten
150 ml (¼ pint) cultured sour cream
300 ml (½ pint) Brown sauce for
  serving (page 196)

Brown the onion in the oil, season with
salt and pepper and add the mushrooms.
Continue cooking until most of the juices
have evaporated, then remove the pan
from the heat and allow the mixture to
cool slightly before adding the crumbs,
eggs and cream. Mix well and pour into
a well-buttered ½ litre (1 pint) capacity
pudding basin; cover the top with a layer
of greaseproof paper and tie it on firmly.
Steam in a pan of boiling water for about
an hour, adding more water, if necessary.
Turn out and serve with a rich Brown
sauce.

German bread and tomato pudding

Serves 4
CALORIES PER PORTION: 210 (872 kJ)
PROTEIN CONTENT PER PORTION: 9 grams
PREPARATION & COOKING TIME: 40 minutes

about 8 wafer thin slices of wholemeal bread
175 g (6 oz) finely chopped onion
25 g (1 oz) butter
2-3 tablespoons fresh wholemeal breadcrumbs
450 g (1 lb) sliced tomatoes
¼ teaspoon grated nutmeg
1 egg
150 ml (¼ pint) milk
salt
1-2 tablespoons grated Cheddar cheese

Set the oven at 200°C (400°F) Gas 6. Fry the onion in the butter until it is golden brown. Liberally butter a shallow oven-proof dish about 23 cm (9 in) in diameter and cover the bottom with slices of the bread, reserving 3 or 4. Fill the spaces between the slices with the crumbs. When the onion is cooked, pour the butter from the pan over the bread and sprinkle with half the onion and the nutmeg. Arrange a layer of tomatoes, sprinkle it with the rest of the onion and cover the dish with the rest of the sliced bread. (This time, do not fill the spaces with crumbs.)

Beat the egg with the milk and a pinch of salt and pour it over the pudding. Sprinkle the top with the cheese and bake in the pre-heated oven for 30 minutes.

This is a fairly substantial dish and makes a good light lunch or supper if served with a salad.

Red-cooked bean curd with bean shoots

Serves 4
CALORIES PER PORTION: 235 (992 kJ)
PROTEIN CONTENT PER PORTION: 9 grams
PREPARATION & COOKING TIME: 30 minutes

225 g (8 oz) bean curd, cut into 1 cm (½ in) slices
4 tablespoons vegetable oil
4 tablespoons soya sauce
100 g (4 oz) finely chopped onion
100 g (4 oz) cucumber, quartered lengthways, then sliced
100 g (4 oz) bean shoots
1 clove of garlic, peeled and very finely chopped
2 tablespoons cream sherry
2 teaspoons vinegar
4 tablespoons water
1 teaspoon cornflour
2 hard-boiled eggs, coarsely chopped

Fry the bean curd in half the oil until the outside is golden brown. Sprinkle with 3 tablespoons of the soya sauce, remove from the heat and leave to marinate, turning it over from time to time.

Fry the onion in the remaining oil until soft. Add the cucumber and the bean shoots, and stir fry for 1½ minutes before adding the garlic, the remaining tablespoon of soya sauce, the sherry, vinegar and the water blended with the cornflour. Continue cooking until the sauce has thickened. Add the drained bean curd and cook until hot. Transfer to a warm shallow plate, sprinkle the chopped eggs into the centre and trickle over a little of the soya sauce remaining from the marinade. Serve immediately.

Spring rolls

Makes 4
CALORIES PER PORTION: 1155 (4415 kJ)
PROTEIN CONTENT PER PORTION: 13 grams
PREPARATION & COOKING TIME: 1 hour

3 large spring onions, finely chopped
50 g (2 oz) finely chopped mushrooms
2 tablespoons vegetable oil
100 g (4 oz) bean sprouts
50 g (2 oz) finely shredded Chinese cabbage
100 g (4 oz) diced bean curd
1 tablespoon soya sauce
1 teaspoon cornflour
350 g (12 oz) Basic puff pastry (page 194)

Set the oven at 200°C (400°F) Gas 6. Stir fry the spring onions and mushrooms in the oil over moderate heat until they soften and the juices evaporate. Add the bean sprouts, cabbage and bean curd, and cook for 2 minutes. Add the soya sauce, sprinkle the cornflour over the vegetables then stir together until the mixture has thickened. Allow to cool.

Roll out the dough to a thin rectangle, 30 × 40 cm (12 × 16 in) and cut it into four equally-sized rectangles. When the filling is quite cold, divide it between the four dough pieces. Fold in the sides and roll up. Place on an oiled baking sheet with the dough join underneath and bake in the pre-heated oven for about 20 minutes, or until crisp and brown. Serve hot.

Sweet and sour cabbage

Serves 4
CALORIES PER PORTION: 115 (490 kJ)
PROTEIN CONTENT PER PORTION: 2 grams
PREPARATION & COOKING TIME: 30 minutes

225 g (8 oz) shredded white cabbage
1 tablespoon olive or sunflower oil
50 g (2 oz) finely chopped onion
8 finely ground cloves
1-2 pinches of finely ground caraway or aniseed
1-2 tablespoons honey
½ teaspoon fresh root ginger, peeled and finely chopped
2-3 tablespoons of cider or wine vinegar
25 g (1 oz) halved blanched almonds
50 g (2 oz) coarsely shredded carrot
small piece of preserved ginger, finely chopped (optional)

Heat the oil in a wok or frying pan and fry the onion until soft but not browned. Add the finely ground spices and the cabbage and stir fry until the cabbage begins to reduce in bulk and turn moist. Add the honey and root ginger, and when the honey has melted add the vinegar. Continue cooking until the cabbage is limp but still crunchy; this should take about 10 minutes altogether.

Mix in the almonds, carrot and preserved ginger, if used, and serve immediately.

Stir-fried bean sprouts

Serves 4
CALORIES PER PORTION: 250 (1047 kJ)
PROTEIN CONTENT PER PORTION: 4 grams
PREPARATION & COOKING TIME: 15 minutes

400 g (14 oz) bean sprouts
50 g (2 oz) finely chopped onion
25 g (1 oz) finely chopped fresh root ginger
1 clove of garlic, peeled and very finely chopped
3 tablespoons vegetable oil
6 sliced water chestnuts
100 g (4 oz) coarsely chopped watercress
1 teaspoon salt
2 tablespoons cream sherry
1 tablespoon soya sauce
½ teaspoon monosodium glutamate (optional)
½ tablespoon sesame oil

Fry the onion, ginger and garlic in the oil until soft but not browned. Add the bean sprouts, water chestnuts, watercress and salt, and cook for 2-3 minutes, turning frequently. Add the sherry, soya sauce, monosodium glutamate (if using) and sesame oil and cook for another 2-3 minutes. Serve on a hot shallow plate.

Fried rice dish

Serves 6
CALORIES PER PORTION: 385 (1607 kJ)
PROTEIN CONTENT PER PORTION: 13 grams
PREPARATION & COOKING TIME: 30 minutes

400 g (14 oz) dry cooked rice
100 g (4 oz) finely chopped onion
4 tablespoons vegetable oil
4 eggs
salt
100 g (4 oz) cooked peas
100 g (4 oz) cooked sweetcorn kernels
100 g (4 oz) shredded leeks
100 g (4 oz) finely chopped mushrooms
2 tablespoons soya sauce
freshly ground pepper
1-2 tablespoons chopped parsley

Fry the onion in 1 tablespoon of the oil until golden brown. Beat the eggs with ½ teaspoon of salt, pour them into the pan with the onion and scramble them lightly. Remove from the pan and keep hot. Pour another tablespoon of oil into the pan and fry the peas and sweetcorn for 2 minutes. Add the leeks and fry for a further 1½ minutes stirring all the time. Finally, add the mushrooms and fry until their juices have almost evaporated. Remove from the pan and keep hot.

Pour the remaining oil into the pan and fry the rice over a gentle heat until hot, turning it over continually with a spatula to prevent it sticking and burning. When it is thoroughly hot, add the vegetables, eggs and soya sauce. Mix together lightly, add salt and pepper, if necessary, and serve sprinkled with chopped parsley.

Washing, soaking and cooking pulses and cereals

Washing
Spread the dry pulses or cereals onto a clean flat surface and pick out any stones or foreign bodies, then put the pulses or cereals into a bowl of water; throw out any that float, and any bits of wood or leaf.

Soaking
Rinse two or three times in fresh water and then leave to soak for 1-2 hours for lentils and peas and overnight for beans and chick peas. Rice, wheat and polenta do not need preliminary soaking.

An alternative method for beans, which also removes some of their flatulent affect, is to cover them with plenty of cold water, bring it to the boil and simmer for 5 minutes before removing from the stove and allowing it to cool. Discard the water, replace it with fresh and then boil them until they are cooked.

Cooking
The age and method of drying affects the cooking time of pulses and cereals so use the following times as a guide only.

Beans, peas and lentils should be cooked in about two to three times their volume of water. Bring the soaked beans, peas or lentils to the boil and simmer, partially covered, until they are soft, adding salt towards the end of the cooking time and extra water if necessary. Use any water left over for stock.

Most beans take 1-2 hours to cook, as do chick peas, but soya beans take 3-5 hours. Brown and green lentils take 30 minutes to 1 hour. Yellow or red split lentils and yellow or green split peas take 30-45 minutes.

Add brown or polished white rice to 2½ times their volume of lightly salted boiling water and simmer in a covered pan over gentle heat. Brown rice will take 35-45 minutes and polished white rice will take 12-15 minutes. Transfer the cooked rice to a colander and pour a jug of boiling water through it to wash away any starch, then drain thoroughly. Put it into a warm serving dish and lightly separate the grains with a fork. The rice should be dry, not mushy, and the grains separate.

If you use a pressure cooker, the cooking times can be reduced by between a half and a third. Cook the food in a bowl inside the pressure cooker, with the liquid, and pour the recommended quantity of water to make the steam, stand the bowl on the trivet. Take care not to release the pressure suddenly or the food may froth out of the bowl.

Cook whole, cracked or crushed wheat and barley as for brown rice; they will take about the same time. Burghul cooks in 15-45 minutes. Genuine burghul needs only to be soaked before it is used in salads. See page 124 for polenta.

Savoury brown rice

Serves 4
CALORIES PER PORTION: 240 (997 kJ)
PROTEIN CONTENT PER PORTION: 4.5 grams
PREPARATION & COOKING TIME: 1 hour

225 g (8 oz) well washed brown rice
750 ml (1¼ pints) water
½ teaspoon salt
100 g (4 oz) finely chopped onion
1 tablespoon olive or sunflower oil
a little grated nutmeg
1 tablespoon finely chopped parsley
½ teaspoon very finely chopped thyme

Bring the water to the boil, add the salt then the rice. Bring the water back to the boil, cover the pan, turn down the heat and cook gently for 35-45 minutes. Test a few grains after 30 minutes. Meanwhile, fry the onion in the oil until golden brown.

When the rice is cooked, drain it well if necessary. Sprinkle the nutmeg over the onion and mix well before adding the parsley and thyme; the latter should be chopped almost to a powder. Mix a little of the cooked rice into the onion and herbs, then add the rest of the rice and mix well so that it is evenly distributed. Spoon into a heated serving dish, cover and keep warm for 15 minutes before serving.

Haricot beans with yoghurt and parsley

Serves 4
CALORIES PER PORTION: 170 (720 kJ)
PROTEIN CONTENT PER PORTION: 14 grams
PREPARATION AND COOKING TIME: 2-3 hours,
    excluding soaking

225 g (8 oz) dried haricot beans, washed
    and soaked overnight
150 ml (¼ pint) natural yoghurt
5 tablespoons finely chopped parsley

Drain the beans and replace with fresh water to cover. Bring to the boil, lower the heat, cover the pan and simmer the beans, until they are soft. Add more water if necessary, but by the end of the cooking time most of the liquid should have absorbed. Drain off any excess.

Pour on the yoghurt, sprinkle with tablespoons of the parsley and gently mi together. Heat up the beans withou allowing them to boil or the yoghurt wil separate and spoil the appearance of the dish. Pour out into a heated serving dish and sprinkle with the remaining parsley.

Red kidney beans with onions and coriander

Serves 4
CALORIES PER PORTION: 225 (947 kJ)
PROTEIN CONTENT PER PORTION: 13 grams
PREPARATION AND COOKING TIME: 2-2½
    hours, excluding soaking

225 g (8 oz) red kidney beans, washed
    and soaked
225 g (8 oz) onions, cut into rings
2 tablespoons olive or sunflower oil
2 cloves of garlic, peeled and finely
    chopped
1 teaspoon ground coriander
1 tablespoon chopped parsley
1 tablespoon wine vinegar

Drain the soaking water from the beans and cook them in water to cover in a covered pan for 1½-2 hours or until tender, adding extra water if necessary. Drain the cooked beans and reserve a little of the cooking liquid.

Fry the onion rings in the oil over moderate heat until they are transparent, then add the rest of the ingredients and mix well. Pour in the beans and 1-2 tablespoons of the reserved cooking liquid. Turn the beans over and over with a spatula until they are evenly mixed with the onions. This dish makes a good cold salad.

Polenta

Serves 4
CALORIES PER PORTION: 177 (745 kJ)
PROTEIN CONTENT PER PORTION: 4.5 grams
PREPARATION AND COOKING TIME: 35 minutes

225 g (8 oz) polenta (coarsely ground
    cornmeal)
700 ml (1¼ pints) cold water
salt

Pour the water into a double boiler or into a saucepan which will fit into another Add salt and bring the water to the boil Stir in the polenta and continue stirring over gentle heat until it is thick and smooth. Place over the double boiler, or a pan of boiling water and keep it simmering for 30 minutes. Serve the polenta hot with a rich Tomato sauce (page 196) Alternatively, cut cold polenta into slices and fry in hot oil until crisp and golden brown.

Soya falafel

Serves 4
CALORIES PER PORTION: 87 (330 kJ)
PROTEIN CONTENT PER PORTION:
PREPARATION AND COOKING TIME: 1 hour,
    excluding soaking

225 g (8 oz) dried soya beans, washed
    and soaked
100 g (4 oz) chopped onion
1 teaspoon ground cumin
1 teaspoon ground coriander
salt
a generous pinch of cayenne
2 cloves of garlic, peeled and sliced
4 tablespoons finely chopped parsley

Drain the beans with the onion. Sprinkle with spices, salt and the cayenne, then add the garlic and parsley and put the mixture through the mincer. Transfer it to a heavy-based saucepan, or a mortar, and pound with the end of a rolling pin to a fairly smooth paste.

Form tablespoonfuls of the mixture into small balls, cover with a cloth and leave for 15 minutes before deep frying in hot oil, 180°C (350°F) until a good brown. Drain well, keep hot and serve as soon as the last one is cooked.

This makes a good accompaniment to a vegetable casserole or, if made smaller, a perfect cocktail snack.

Whole wheat pilau

Serves 4
CALORIES PER PORTION: 282 (1187 kJ)
PROTEIN PER PORTION: 7 grams
PREPARATION AND COOKING TIME: 1-1½ hours

225 g (8 oz) whole wheat, cooked as for
    brown rice
225 g (8 oz) sliced aubergine
salt
2 tablespoons olive or sunflower oil
100 g (4 oz) very finely chopped onion
½ teaspoon ground cumin
½ teaspoon ground coriander
1 clove of garlic, peeled and finely
    chopped
freshly ground black pepper
50 g (2 oz) sultanas
2 tablespoons orange juice
8 orange segments

Place the sliced aubergine in a colander, sprinkle with salt and leave to drain for 30 minutes. Rinse and pat dry with kitchen paper. Fry the aubergine slices gently in the oil until they look oily and are just beginning to brown. Add the onion and continue cooking until the onion is transparent.

Add the spices, garlic and pepper, then the cooked wheat, with the sultanas. Gently mix into the vegetables and spices, then sprinkle with orange juice. Turn into a shallow dish, arrange the orange segments around it and serve hot.

Purée of chick peas

Serves 4
CALORIES PER PORTION: 260 (1082 kJ)
PROTEIN CONTENT PER PORTION: 13 grams
PREPARATION AND COOKING TIME: 5½ hours,
    excluding soaking

225 g (8 oz) dried chick peas, washed and
    soaked
200 ml (⅓ pint) milk
25 g (1 oz) butter
salt
freshly ground pepper
2 tablespoons finely chopped parsley

Drain the water from the soaked chickpeas and replace with enough fresh water to completely cover. Bring to the boil then lower the heat, cover the pan and simmer for 3-5 hours, or until the peas are very soft.

When the peas are cooked, drain and work a few at a time to a purée in a blender with a little milk. Alternatively, put the chick peas twice through a fine-bladed mincer, or rub through a sieve before stirring in the milk. Melt the butter add the chick pea purée and reheat and serve sprinkled with chopped parsley.

Salads and Salad Dressings

Salads play a particularly important role in the vegetarian's diet. Not only can they be a valuable source of additional protein and vitamins, but they are extremely versatile and the choice of texture, flavour and colour is immense. They can be served as a light meal on their own, as a first course or as an exciting contrast to the main course. They can also be used as 'punctuation' during a meal to clear the palate between courses.

It is said that the secret of a successful salad dressing is similar to successful diplomacy – 'to know just how much oil to put with the vinegar'. The vital point to remember is that the flavour should be a simple harmony. I don't find it a good idea to mix up a large quantity of dressing and store it in the refrigerator; if it is not all used up fairly quickly, the results are very much less than appetising . . . For greater variety, try using lemon juice instead of vinegar, walnut oil instead of olive oil and add herbs, horse-radish, grated orange or lemon rind instead of the now almost obligatory garlic. The salad recipes that follow use fruits and vegetables, pulses and nuts; try making one meal of the day entirely of salad and see how much better you feel!

Making salads

When making a salad choose your ingredients for their contrasting flavours, textures and colours. As a guide, choose something from each of the following:

The lettuces — crisp-hearted; soft round ones, or long, crisp-leaved types.

The other leaves — white or red cabbage, young spinach, beet and mustard greens, Chinese cabbage or dandelion.

The curly leaves — endive, escarole, corn or lamb's lettuce, celtuce or celery leaves.

The crunchy ones — chicory, celery, crisp dessert apples or cucumber.

The tangy ones — watercress, nasturtium leaves, geranium leaves, red and green peppers, radishes, spring onions, Spanish onions, tomatoes and the beautiful red leaves of the Italian radicche.

The herbs — parsley, of course, and basil, tarragon, fennel, thyme, chervil and mint; but also try fresh coriander leaves, bergamot leaves and flower petals, nasturtium leaves or flowers, apple mint or lemon thyme and balm or lovage.

The other ingredients — can be any fruit, cooked vegetable, pulse or grain, nut, seed or dairy product that blends or contrasts harmoniously with the rest of the salad.

Having chosen a combination of leaves and herbs, wash them carefully, paying particular attention to the curly leaved ones — grit is not a texture one wants in a salad. Discard any damaged or discoloured leaves, cut off the roots and root plates of the plants and remove any fibrous cores, stems, strings or membranes from fruits, shoots or leaves.

Dry the leaves thoroughly; there is nothing worse than a watery salad, where the dressing is diluted and runs off the leaves, and all the flavour is lost. Use either a salad basket or centrifugal spinner; failing these, shake the salad gently in a clean kitchen cloth or towel. To ensure that the salad is really crisp, put it in a covered bowl and chill it for an hour or so.

When using tomatoes in a mixed salad, remove the seeds and juice otherwise they will make it too wet. Also remove all the pith and pips from red and green peppers as these are very bitter.

The final consideration is the dressing. Bear in mind what you want the dressing to do — provide piquancy, soften otherwise too-strong flavours, add a flavour that is missing in the rest of the ingredients or is it to be a cream in which all can blend? Choose from the following:

Mayonnaise

Makes about ½ pint. For 4 servings.

CALORIES PER PORTION: 640 (2667 kJ)
PROTEIN CONTENT PER PORTION: 1 gram
PREPARATION TIME: 20 minutes by hand; 5 minutes in a blender

2 egg yolks
300 ml (½ pint) olive or sunflower oil
1-2 tablespoons wine vinegar
salt
freshly ground pepper

By hand
If you have never made Mayonnaise by hand before, follow this method exactly. Once you have gained experience you can speed up. The main thing to understand is that when you make Mayonnaise, you are making an emulsion: very small globules of oil coated with a layer of egg to prevent them from joining up again. When you add the vinegar at the end to thin the mayonnaise down and give it sharpness, you make the layer of egg more liquid. As you stir the oil into the egg yolks, the movement of the spoon breaks it up into small drops separated by layers of yolk.

Use a bowl that is just large enough to hold the final quantity, about 300 ml (½ pint). Put the 2 eggs into it and stir until they are mixed together, then add 1 tea-spoon of oil and stir 20 times. Repeat with another teaspoon of oil and continue in this way until the Mayonnaise begins to thicken. Then add the oil 2 teaspoons at a time. When all the oil has been used, the mixture will resemble a thick, buttery mass. Stir in 1 tablespoon of vinegar and mix well. Add more to give the consistency and piquancy you require, and season.

When you have made Mayonnaise several times, you will find you are able to add more oil to the yolks than the amount given above. If the Mayonnaise begins to look dry and granular, add no more oil.

In a blender or food mixer
Put the egg yolks into the blender or a bowl if using a food mixer, and with the whisk attachments, whisk — or blend — at full speed. Gradually trickle in the oil from a small jug, increasing the flow as the Mayonnaise thickens, add the vinegar at the end.

If the Mayonnaise curdles or separates, pour it into a jug, clean the bowl and put another lightly beaten egg yolk into it. Follow the above procedure, using the curdled Mayonnaise in place of the oil.

Mayonnaise forms the basis of a number of cold sauces; these can be made by adding the following ingredients to the basic recipe:

Green mayonnaise

CALORIES AND PROTEIN CONTENT PER PORTION: as for Mayonnaise

Put the egg and oil mixture into a blende and add 1-2 tablespoons chopped water cress leaves. Blend until uniformly green add a little vinegar or lemon juice to ge the correct consistency and sharpness The leaves make quite a lot of liquid s be careful not to make the Mayonnais too runny. Blanched spinach is tradition ally used, but watercress makes a mor piquant sauce.

Aioli

CALORIES AND PROTEIN CONTENT PER PORTION: as for Mayonnaise

Add 2-4 cloves of garlic, chopped to pulp, to the Mayonnaise and mi thoroughly.

Tartare sauce

CALORIES PER PORTION: 1000 (4197 kJ)
PROTEIN CONTENT PER PORTION: 5.5 grams

Mash 4-5 hard-boiled egg yolks with salt and pepper, then gradually work in 300

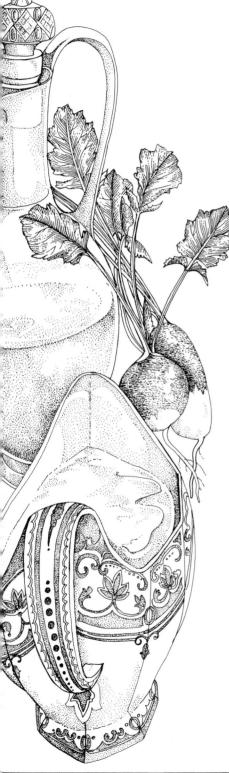

ml (½ pint) olive oil. Add 1 teaspoon vinegar, 2 tablespoons Mayonnaise and mix in 1 tablespoon finely chopped chives.

Roquefort dressing

CALORIES PER PORTION: 680 (2852 kJ)
PROTEIN CONTENT PER PORTION: 4.5 grams

Add 50 g (2 oz) crumbled Roquefort cheese to a little of the Mayonnaise and mash until it is completely smooth. Stir it into the rest of the Mayonnaise and sharpen with a little lemon juice. Alternatively, add the same quantity of Roquefort cheese to 300 ml (½ pint) of Vinaigrette dressing.

Curry mayonnaise

CALORIES AND PROTEIN CONTENT PER PORTION:
as for Mayonnaise

Add a teaspoon or two of curry powder to the Mayonnaise and mix thoroughly. A hotter sauce can be made by adding a pinch of chilli powder or a dash of chilli sauce to the curry powder.

Curd cheese dressing

CALORIES PER PORTION: 140 (595 kJ)
PROTEIN CONTENT PER PORTION: 1 gram
PREPARATION TIME: 10 minutes

125 g (4 oz) curd cheese
1 tablespoon lemon juice
1 tablespoon finely chopped chives
1-2 tablespoons milk
salt
freshly ground pepper

Mash the curd cheese with the lemon juice and the chives. Pour a little milk into the bowl and continue stirring until the mixture becomes a thick cream, then continue adding milk until the cheese dressing has the consistency of thin cream. Season with salt and pepper and pour over the salad.

Thousand Island dressing

CALORIES PER PORTION: 689 (2872 kJ)
PROTEIN CONTENT PER PORTION: 4.5 grams

Add 2 tablespoons chopped olives, 2 finely chopped hard-boiled eggs, 1 teaspoon paprika and a dash or two of chilli sauce to taste. Season with salt and pepper.

Sour cream dressing

CALORIES PER PORTION: 400 (1667 kJ)
PROTEIN CONTENT PER PORTION: 2 grams

Add 150 ml (¼ pint) cultured sour cream to an equal quantity of Mayonnaise and mix together. Alternatively, add the cultured sour cream to an equal quantity of Vinaigrette dressing.

Maltese sauce

CALORIES PER PORTION: 647.5 (2733 kJ)
PROTEIN CONTENT PER PORTION: 1 gram

Add the grated rind and 2 tablespoons of juice from a blood orange, with 1 tablespoon fresh tomato purée and 1 tablespoon vinegar to a firm Mayonnaise.

French or Vinaigrette dressing

This should be enough for a plain green salad for 4 people.

CALORIES PER PORTION: 210 (890 kJ)
PROTEIN CONTENT PER PORTION: nil
PREPARATION TIME: 5 minutes

2 tablespoons wine or cider vinegar
salt
freshly ground pepper
6-8 tablespoons olive or sunflower oil
1-2 tablespoons chopped fresh herbs
  (optional)

Add the salt and pepper to the vinegar and mix well. Stir in the oil and whisk again until the sauce is smooth textured and creamy; put these ingredients with the herbs, if using, in a screw-topped glass jar and shake vigorously until well mixed, or blend together. Alternatively replace one tablespoon of vinegar with a tablespoon of lemon juice or dry white wine, or use a mixture of all three. Lemon juice and white wine whisked with the oil makes a very good dressing for young lettuce. For a change, use walnut oil instead of olive oil — excellent with chicory!

Classic green salad

In my opinion, a green salad should contain green or blanched leaves, fresh herbs, a simple dressing of olive or walnut oil, lemon juice, white wine and wine or cider vinegar. Add a suggestion of garlic, a little salt and freshly ground pepper — and that is all.

Serves 4
CALORIES PER PORTION: 300 (1255 kJ)
PROTEIN CONTENT PER PORTION: 1.5 grams
PREPARATION TIME: 25 minutes

*350-450 g (12 oz-1 lb) green leaves —
    choose from lettuce, endive, mustard
    and cress, watercress, corn salad,
    celtuce, young dandelion or spinach
    leaves, or chicory, but let the main
    ingredient be the lettuce, preferably a
    crisp-hearted cabbage type, or a well-
    grown Cos*
*1-2 tablespoons chopped fresh herbs
    (optional)*

The dressing
1 tablespoon wine or cider vinegar
*1 tablespoon white wine or 2 teaspoons
    lemon juice*
*1 teaspoon chopped herbs — chervil,
    tarragon, basil, or a mixture of these*
8 tablespoons olive or walnut oil
salt
freshly ground pepper
1 clove of garlic, cut in half
*1 small slice of very dry wholemeal
    bread or toast, rubbed with garlic and
    soaked in olive oil — a chapon
    (optional)*

Carefully wash the chosen salad greens, discarding any discoloured or bruised leaves. The French rightly claim that a salad should be eaten with a fork only, so tear all the leaves into bite-sized pieces; do not cut them as this will bruise them. Cut chicory into 2 cm (¾ in) slices.

Make the dressing by whisking together the vinegar, wine or lemon juice and fresh herbs, then whisk in the oil. Season with salt and pepper. If you have a blender you can pour all the liquids into the bowl and blend for a few moments; or put all the ingredients in a screw-topped glass jar and shake it vigorously — with the lid on! Rub the inside of the salad bowl with the cut clove of garlic or place the *chapon* at the bottom. Pour the dressing into the bowl, but do not dress the salad itself until just before serving, or the leaves — especially the lettuce — will go limp.

Toss the salad by turning it over and over in the bowl until it is evenly coated with dressing. Remove the *chapon*, which should have been tossed with the salad, or keep it on one side while the salad is being tossed; it can then be divided among the garlic-lovers.

*Left: thinly-sliced cucumber and
strawberries combine to make a cool
Elona salad. Right: Javanese salad has
onion, celery, red pepper and banana
piled on slices of fresh pineapple – a rare
combination, and a feast in itself*

Mixed salad

The appeal of a mixed salad should be the subtle change of flavour from one mouthful to the next. This is why the sizes of the prepared ingredients should be as equal as possible.

Serves 4
CALORIES PER PORTION: 270 (1120 kJ)
PROTEIN CONTENT PER PORTION: 1.5 grams
PREPARATION & CHILLING TIME: 30-40
    minutes
*225 g (8 oz) lettuce or a mixture of
    salad leaves, torn into small pieces*
50 g (2 oz) finely diced red pepper
*125 g (4 oz) cucumber, quartered
    lengthwise, then cut into chunks*
*125 g (4 oz) skinned tomato, seeded and
    roughly chopped*
25 g (1 oz) finely chopped onion
50 g (2 oz) chopped celery
50 g (2 oz) thinly sliced chicory
6-12 thinly sliced radishes (optional)

The dressing
8 tablespoons olive or sunflower oil
1 tablespoon lemon juice
1 tablespoon wine or cider vinegar
salt
freshly ground pepper
1 tablespoon finely chopped fresh herbs

Mix all the salad ingredients together in a bowl and chill well. Whisk together the oil, lemon juice and vinegar and season with salt and pepper. Add the herbs to the dressing, then pour it over the salad ingredients and thoroughly toss it just before serving.

Elona salad

Serves 4
CALORIES PER PORTION: 36 (150 kJ)
PROTEIN CONTENT PER PORTION: 1 gram
PREPARATION & CHILLING TIME: 45 minutes

*450 g (1 lb) peeled cucumber, very
    thinly sliced*
*225 g (8 oz) sliced strawberries (about
    16)*
1 tablespoon lemon juice
4 tablespoons dry white wine
salt

Mix the lemon juice with the wine, season with salt and pour over the cucumber. Leave for 30 minutes, then drain. Arrange a ring of cucumber slices round the outside edge of a large plate then, working from the outside, continue with rings of alternating slices of cucumber and strawberries. Reserve a few choice strawberry slices for a garnish. Arrange these in the centre with 'leaves' cut from the cucumber skin if liked. Chill and serve.

Hawaiian salad

Serves 4
CALORIES PER PORTION: 465 (1940 kJ)
PROTEIN CONTENT PER PORTION: 3.5 grams
PREPARATION & CHILLING TIME: 50 minutes

225 g (8 oz) Cos lettuce, torn into small
* pieces*
125 g (4 oz) finely diced red peppers
225 g (8 oz) roughly chopped tomatoes,
* de-seeded*
125 g (4 oz) shredded or grated coconut
225 g (8 oz) fresh or canned pineapple,
* cubed*
1 tablespoon lemon juice
4 tablespoons dark rum
1 tablespoon wine or cider vinegar
6 tablespoons olive or sunflower oil
salt
freshly ground pepper
1 clove of garlic, peeled and finely
* chopped*
grated rind of 1 small lemon (optional)

Mix together the lettuce, peppers and
tomatoes. Sprinkle the coconut over the
pineapple cubes, reserving a little, and
pour on the lemon juice and rum. Make
the dressing by whisking together the
vinegar, oil, salt and pepper, garlic and
lemon rind, if used, and pour this over the
lettuce, peppers and tomatoes. Pile the
salad in a shallow dish and arrange the
pineapple on top. Sprinkle with the
reserved coconut and serve slightly
chilled.

Creole salad

Serves 8
CALORIES PER PORTION: 210 (887 kJ)
PROTEIN CONTENT PER PORTION: 3 grams
PREPARATION TIME: 30 minutes

225 g (8 oz) peeled avocados, cut into
* chunks and dipped in 2 tablespoons*
* lemon juice*
225 g (8 oz) fresh or canned pineapple,
* cubed*
125 g (4 oz) diced red peppers
125 g (4 oz) diced celery
salt
freshly ground pepper
225 g (8 oz) boiled brown rice
1 tablespoon lemon juice
1 tablespoon wine or cider vinegar
6 tablespoons olive or sunflower oil

Drain the avocado chunks and mix with
the pineapple, peppers and celery; season
with salt and pepper.

Gently mix in the rice, taking care not
to break the avocado up too much. Whisk
together the lemon juice, vinegar and olive
oil. Season well with salt and pepper and
pour this dressing over the salad.

Javanese salad

Serves 4
CALORIES PER PORTION: 575 (2417 kJ)
PROTEIN CONTENT PER PORTION: 9 grams
PREPARATION & COOKING TIME: 50 minutes

125 g (4 oz) finely chopped onion
1 tablespoon olive or sunflower oil
¼ teaspoon ground cinnamon
½ teaspoon ground cumin
125 g (4 oz) peanuts
pinch of chilli powder
1 tablespoon wine or cider vinegar
50 g (2 oz) finely chopped celery
1 large banana, sliced
salt
freshly ground pepper
150 ml (¼ pint) Mayonnaise (page 126)
4 slices of fresh or canned pineapple
2 tablespoons chopped red pepper

Fry the onion in the oil until it is golden
brown; add the cinnamon and cumin and
fry for a few minutes longer. Add the
peanuts, chilli powder and vinegar. Stir
well, then remove from the stove and
leave, covered, to cool. When it is cold,
add the celery and banana and season
with salt and pepper. Pour the Mayonnaise over the salad and stir until thoroughly mixed.

Pile the mixture on the pineapple slices,
sprinkle the red peppers over the top and
serve.

Roquefort pear salad

This dish can make a very good last course to a meal — something between a savoury and a salad.

Serves 4
CALORIES PER PORTION: 805 (3370 kJ)
PROTEIN CONTENT PER PORTION: 10 grams
PREPARATION & CHILLING TIME: 1 hour

4 firm, peeled, ripe pears
100 g (4 oz) crumbled Roquefort cheese
4 finely chopped spring onions
scant 300 ml (½ pint) Green
*   mayonnaise (page 126)*
4 sprigs of watercress to garnish

Cut a small slice off the base of each pear so that it stands upright. Cut each one in half and scoop out the core, leaving a hollow for the filling. Mash the cheese, mix it with the onions and bind with about 6 tablespoons of mayonnaise to make a firm paste. Fill the pears with this and re-shape them. If you do not have a blender finely chop the watercress leaves before adding them to the mayonnaise. It may be advisable to do this in two stages a the final mayonnaise must be thick enough to hold its shape.

Coat the pears thinly and evenly with Green mayonnaise, using a knife to spread the mayonnaise evenly as though icing a cake. Finally, insert a spray of watercress in each to resemble pear leaves.

Arrange the pears on a plate, taking care that they stay upright and do no split, and chill well before serving.

Florida salad

Serves 6
CALORIES PER PORTION: 440 (1841 kJ)
PROTEIN CONTENT PER PORTION: 3 grams
PREPARATION TIME: 45 minutes

450 g (1 lb) fresh, firm pears, peeled,
*   cored, cut into 2 cm (¾ in) cubes,*
*   well coated with lemon juice*
4 tablespoons olive or sunflower oil
4 slices of wholemeal bread, crusts
*   removed, cut in 1 cm (½ in) cubes*
125 g (4 oz) finely diced red peppers
225 g (8 oz) curd cheese
225 g (8 oz) crisp lettuce, preferably
*   Cos, torn into small pieces*
225 g (8 oz) thinly sliced cucumber

The dressing
1 tablespoon lemon juice
1 tablespoon wine or cider vinegar
6-8 tablespoons olive oil
salt
freshly ground pepper
a little grated lemon rind
1 tablespoon finely chopped parsley

Heat the oil in a pan and fry the bread cubes until they are crisp. Drain them on absorbent kitchen paper and leave to get completely cold.

To make the dressing, whisk together the lemon juice, vinegar and oil and season with salt and pepper. Add a little grated lemon rind and sprinkle in the parsley.

Mix the peppers with the curd cheese and marinated pears, but reserve about 12 dice. Arrange the lettuce on a large round plate and pour over the dressing. Make a ring of cucumber slices around the centre and pile the curd cheese and pear mixture in the middle of this ring. Decorate with the reserved diced pepper and scatter the croûtons round the edge of the salad. Mix it all together at the table just before serving.

Tunisian orange salad

Serves 4
CALORIES PER PORTION: 50 (220 kJ)
PROTEIN CONTENT PER PORTION: 1 gram
PREPARATION & CHILLING TIME: 35 minutes

4 large oranges, peeled and thinly
*   sliced 'across the equator'*
2 tablespoons rose water
a little ground cinnamon

Remove every bit of pith from the orange slices and arrange them on a plate in overlapping circles. Pour over the rose water, sprinkle with a little cinnamon and chill.

Just before serving, tilt the plate, carefully pour off the juice into a bowl and pour it again over the orange slices.

Chicory salad

Serves 4
CALORIES PER PORTION: 180 (765 kJ)
PROTEIN CONTENT PER PORTION: 3 grams
PREPARATION TIME: 30 minutes

225 g (8 oz) chicory, cut into 1 cm
*   (½ in) slices*
2-3 peeled oranges
1 egg yolk
salt and freshly ground pepper
1 teaspoon white wine vinegar
2 tablespoons olive or sunflower oil
orange juice (see method)
50 g (2 oz) shelled walnuts, shredded

Divide each orange into segments, cutting between the flesh and membranes of each segment with a sharp knife to remove all the pith. Cut each segment in half and discard any pips. Make the dressing by beating the egg yolk with the salt, pepper and vinegar, then whisk in the oil and any juice from the orange. Mix together the orange segments and the chicory and pour the dressing over them. Pile the salad in a shallow bowl and scatter the walnuts on top before serving.

Orange and apple salad

Serves 4
CALORIES PER PORTION: 345 (1445 kJ)
PROTEIN CONTENT PER PORTION: 3 grams
PREPARATION & CHILLING TIME: 45 minutes

4 peeled oranges, segmented (see
*   previous recipe)*
4 large dessert apples, cored, diced and
*   sprinkled with lemon juice*
25 g (1 oz) chopped dates
50 g (2 oz) finely chopped red pepper
25 g (1 oz) pine nuts

The dressing
1 tablespoon vinegar
1 tablespoon lemon juice
½ teaspoon ground cumin
salt and freshly ground pepper
6 tablespoons olive or sunflower oil

Whisk together the vinegar, lemon juice cumin, salt and pepper with the oil. Stir in the apple chunks, halve each orange segment and mix these well with the apples. Add the dates and red peppers and pile the salad on a shallow dish. Scatter with pine nuts and serve well chilled.

Tomato salad

Serves 4
CALORIES PER PORTION: 140 (582 kJ)
PROTEIN CONTENT PER PORTION: 1 gram
PREPARATION TIME: 20 minutes

450 g (1 lb) thinly sliced tomatoes
2 tablespoons very finely chopped basil
2 tablespoons very finely chopped onion
4 tablespoons olive or sunflower oil
1 tablespoon wine or cider vinegar
1 tablespoon lemon juice
salt
freshly ground pepper

Arrange the slices of tomato in overlapping layers on a large flat plate. Sprinkle the chopped basil over half the tomatoes and the onion over the other half. Whisk together the oil, vinegar and lemon juice and pour it over the salad, then sprinkle with salt. Grind a little pepper over the onions, not the basil as it may detract from the flavour. Keep the two portions separate when serving.

Tomato, celery and apple salad

Serves 4
CALORIES PER PORTION: 170 (717 kJ)
PROTEIN CONTENT PER PORTION: 4.5 grams
PREPARATION TIME: 20 minutes

350 g (12 oz) chopped tomatoes, seeded
125 g (4 oz) thinly sliced celery
125 g (4 oz) peeled and diced dessert apple
2 tablespoons lemon juice
50 g (2 oz) finely diced Cheddar cheese
3 tablespoons olive or sunflower oil
salt
freshly ground pepper

Toss the celery and apple with the lemon juice, making sure that the apples are well coated, otherwise they will turn brown. Add the tomatoes and the cheese, and mix all the ingredients together. Pour on the oil and continue turning the salad, seasoning with salt and pepper as you do so.

Salade Niçoise

This salad should be chunky in texture, and the recipe makes enough for 8.

CALORIES PER PORTION: 184 (771 kJ)
PROTEIN CONTENT PER PORTION: 3 grams
PREPARATION TIME: 30 minutes

225 g (8 oz) lettuce, torn into small pieces
225 g (8 oz) quartered tomatoes, seeded
225 g (8 oz) cooked potatoes, cut into chunks
125 g (4 oz) thinly sliced celery
125 g (4 oz) thinly sliced red or green peppers
2 hard-boiled eggs, shelled and cut into quarters
12 stoned black olives
6 thinly sliced radishes (optional)

The dressing
1 tablespoon lemon juice
2 tablespoons wine or cider vinegar
8 tablespoons olive oil
1 clove of garlic, peeled and chopped or pounded to a pulp
salt and freshly ground pepper

Mix together the salad ingredients, then make the dressing. Whisk together the lemon juice, vinegar, oil and garlic and season with salt and pepper. Mix this dressing carefully into the salad and garnish with the quartered eggs, olives and radishes before serving.

Tomato and cress salad

Serves 4
CALORIES PER PORTION: 336 (1407 kJ)
PROTEIN CONTENT PER PORTION: 2 grams
PREPARATION TIME: 30 minutes

1 good bunch watercress, shredded
(scissors are best for this task)
450 g (1 lb) halved tomatoes, plus 4
tablespoons of their juice

The Mayonnaise
1 egg yolk
150 ml (¼ pint) olive or sunflower oil
salt
freshly ground pepper

Remove the cores and seeds from the tomatoes and strain off and reserve 4 tablespoons of their juice. Cut them into thin strips and arrange them on a plate. Sprinkle the watercress over.

Make a Mayonnaise with the egg yolk and the oil, following the basic recipe on page 126. Take a little more care when adding the oil as it is more difficult to make a Mayonnaise with only one egg yolk. When it has thickened, mix in the tomato juice. Sprinkle the salad with salt and pepper and serve the tomato-flavoured Mayonnaise separately.

Avocado salad

This salad and the Lebanese avocado salad (page 51) both contain garlic, but surprisingly it does not overpower the delicate flavour of the avocado. It is one of a number of unexpected combinations of flavours which complement or develop each other.

Serves 4
CALORIES PER PORTION: 290 (1212 kJ)
PROTEIN CONTENT PER PORTION: 3 grams
PREPARATION & CHILLING TIME: 45 minutes

2 large ripe but firm avocados, peeled
and thickly sliced
several small lettuce leaves
1 clove of garlic, peeled
2 tablespoons lemon juice
salt
freshly ground pepper
4 tablespoons olive or sunflower oil

Arrange the lettuce leaves on a plate to form four small cups. Make the dressing by crushing the clove of garlic with the lemon juice, salt and pepper. Mix thoroughly and pour on the oil as you whisk. Strain the dressing over the avocado slices, making sure they are completely coated otherwise they will discolour. Pile them in the lettuce cups and chill before serving.

Herb loaf

CALORIES: 1895 (7930 kJ)
PROTEIN CONTENT: 40 grams
PREPARATION & HEATING: 40 minutes

Thickly slice a French or wholemeal loaf, but stop cutting each slice just before you get to the bottom. Beat about 125 g (4 oz) of butter or margarine with 2 tablespoons finely chopped fresh herbs (preferably thyme, sage, tarragon or fennel) until softened and spread each slice with the herb butter. Reshape the loaf, wrap it in foil and warm it in a moderate oven 180°C (350°F) Gas 4 for about 30 minutes.

Garlic loaf

CALORIES: 1895 (7930 kJ)
PROTEIN CONTENT: 40 grams
PREPARATION & HEATING: 40 minutes

Thickly slice a French or wholemeal loaf, but stop cutting each slice just before you get to the bottom. Soften about 125 g (4 oz) of butter or margarine and beat in 2 peeled and finely chopped cloves of garlic. Spread this on the cut slices of the loaf, wrap and bake as for Herb bread.

Mixed bean salad

This salad seems to have an almost universal appeal, as well as being highly nutritious. The three kinds of dried beans should be separately blanched for 5 minutes (page 123), then soaked, preferably overnight, before being cooked in separate pans. This recipe makes enough for 6.

CALORIES PER PORTION: 230 (968 kJ)
PROTEIN CONTENT PER PORTION: 5 grams
PREPARATION & CHILLING TIME: 1 hour

125 g (4 oz) cooked soya beans
125 g (4 oz) cooked red kidney beans
125 g (4 oz) cooked butter beans
salt
freshly ground pepper
grated rind of 1 lemon
1 clove of garlic, peeled and finely
*   chopped*
50 g (2 oz) finely chopped onion
2 teaspoons paprika
1 tablespoon lemon juice
1 tablespoon wine vinegar
8 tablespoons olive or sunflower oil

Mix the cooked beans together in a bowl, season with salt and pepper and sprinkle with the lemon rind and garlic. Pound the onion almost to a pulp with the paprika, then mix in the lemon juice and vinegar. Gradually stir in the oil and pour the finished dressing over the beans and mix it in thoroughly. Chill the salad well before serving.

Left: chunks of avocado piled on crisp lettuce leaves, dressed with lemon juice Front: a protein-rich salad of soya, red kidney and butter beans, tossed in a well-flavoured Vinaigrette. Right: Tomato and cress salad is served with a tomato-flavoured Mayonnaise and accompanied by hot Herb loaf

Chick pea salad

Serves 4
CALORIES PER PORTION: 255 (1070 kJ)
PROTEIN CONTENT PER PORTION: 9 grams
PREPARATION TIME: 20 minutes

450 g (1 lb) cooked chick peas — 225 g
*   (8 oz) uncooked*
12 large capers
2 tablespoons finely chopped parsley
3 tablespoons olive or sunflower oil
1 tablespoon lemon juice

Pound the capers with the parsley to a smooth paste. Mix this with the oil and lemon juice and pour over the cooked peas. Serve at room temperature, not chilled, as chilling deadens the flavour.

Rice and lentil salad

Serves 4
CALORIES PER PORTION: 255 (1070 kJ)
PROTEIN CONTENT PER PORTION: 6 grams
PREPARATION TIME: 15 minutes

250 g (9 oz) boiled rice — 100 g (4 oz)
*   uncooked*
250 g (9 oz) cooked lentils — scant
*   100 g (4 oz) uncooked*
25 g (1 oz) finely chopped onion
1 tablespoon wine or cider vinegar
4 tablespoons olive or sunflower oil
salt
freshly ground pepper
250 g (9 oz) chopped tomatoes, seeded

Mix together the rice, lentils and onion. Whisk together the vinegar and the oil, season well and pour the dressing over the lentils and rice. Scatter the tomatoes on top. Turn the salad over a couple of times to mix the ingredients thoroughly and coat them with dressing, and serve.

Tabbouleh

This is traditionally made with burghul, but if you find this difficult to obtain, substitute whole, or cracked, wheat. It's a favourite buffet party dish of mine.

Serves 4
CALORIES PER PORTION: 300 (1262 kJ)
PROTEIN CONTENT PER PORTION: 5.5 grams
PREPARATION & COOKING TIME: 1-2 hours

350 g (12 oz) burghul, soaked in cold
*   water for 45 minutes, or cold cooked*
*   wheat*
125 g (4 oz) chopped parsley
2 tablespoons chopped mint
2 tablespoons finely chopped spring
*   onions*

The dressing
2 tablespoons lemon juice
4-6 tablespoons olive or sunflower oil
salt
freshly ground pepper
2 chopped tomatoes, to garnish

Mix together the drained burghul, or cooked wheat, with the chopped parsley, mint and spring onions. Make a dressing by whisking together the lemon juice and the oil and seasoning it with salt and pepper. Pour this over the burghul or wheat and cover the bowl with a plate. Holding them both together firmly, shake them up and down and round and round so that the dressing is thoroughly mixed into the salad. Pile the Tabbouleh on a shallow dish, garnish with the chopped tomatoes and serve after 15 minutes.

Egg and lettuce salad

Serves 4
CALORIES PER PORTION: 225
PROTEIN CONTENT PER PORTION: 7 grams
PREPARATION & COOKING TIME: 1 hour

4 hard-boiled eggs, shelled
4-5 tablespoons olive or sunflower oil
1 tablespoon wine or cider vinegar
salt
freshly ground pepper
225 g (8 oz) cabbage lettuce
6 spring onions, cut in half lengthways,
   then finely sliced
1-2 teaspoons finely chopped capers
   (optional)

Cut the eggs into 5 mm (¼ in) slices. Carefully remove the yolks and rub them through a sieve into a small bowl, or mash them thoroughly with fork, keeping the white rings on one side. Slowly stir the oil into the mashed yolks using a wooden spoon, then add the vinegar and continue stirring until thoroughly blended. Season with salt and pepper.

Mix together the lettuce and spring onions and arrange them in a shallow bowl, reserving a few of the greenest onion slices. Finely chop the 'solid' pieces of egg white from each end of the egg and add them to the egg yolk dressing.

Pour this into the centre of the salad, arrange the egg white rings around this and sprinkle on the green spring onion slices. Toss just before serving.

I find this salad is pleasantly bland; however if you would like a more piquant flavour, add 1-2 teaspoons finely chopped capers to the egg yolks.

Potato and walnut salad

Serves 4
CALORIES PER PORTION: 396 (1650 kJ)
PROTEIN CONTENT PER PORTION: 5 grams
PREPARATION & COOKING TIME: 1½ hours,
   including cooking the potatoes

450-600 g (1-1¼ lb) potatoes — the
   firmest available, boiled in their
   jackets
50 g (2 oz) shelled walnuts, preferably
   fresh
4-8 tablespoons olive or sunflower oil
1-2 tablespoons vinegar
salt
freshly ground pepper
125 g (4 oz) onion, cut into rings

Whisk together the oil and vinegar — the exact quantity depends on how much the potatoes absorb — and season with salt and pepper. Peel and thickly slice the potatoes and put them in a shallow dish. Pour boiling water — the water in which you cooked the potatoes will do — over the onion rings and leave them to stand for a few minutes. Drain and rinse them in cold water, then mix them with the potatoes. Shred the walnuts in a nut mill or blender and scatter them over the salad. Stir the dressing again and pour it over the salad. Allow to cool before serving, though this salad loses flavour if it is served chilled.

Corn and red pepper salad

Serves 4
CALORIES PER PORTION: 405 (1705 kJ)
PROTEIN CONTENT PER PORTION: 3 grams
PREPARATION & CHILLING TIME: 1 hour

225 g (8 oz) cooked sweetcorn kernels
125 g (4 oz) finely chopped red peppers
225 g (8 oz) fresh or canned pineapple,
   cubed

The Mayonnaise
1 egg yolk
2 tablespoons lemon juice
150 ml (¼ pint) olive or sunflower oil
salt

Mix together the sweetcorn, peppers and pineapple. Make a Mayonnaise with the egg yolk, lemon juice and oil, following the basic method given on page 126. Stir this into the salad and adjust the seasoning.

Pile the salad on a plate and chill well before serving.

Note: a French or Vinaigrette dressing also goes well with this salad.

Arabian bread salad

Serves 4
CALORIES PER PORTION: 170 (727 kJ)
PROTEIN CONTENT PER PORTION: 3 grams
PREPARATION & CHILLING TIME: 45 minutes

4 slices of white or wholemeal toast,
   about 1 cm (½ in) thick, crusts
   removed
3 tablespoons lemon juice
4 tablespoons finely chopped parsley
2 tablespoons finely chopped mint
1 tablespoon chopped coriander leaves
3-4 tablespoons olive or sunflower oil
1 clove of garlic, peeled and very finely
   chopped
225 g (8 oz) peeled cucumber, quartered
   and cut into 1 cm (½ in) slices
225 g (8 oz) chopped tomatoes, seeded
salt
freshly ground pepper

Cut the slices of toast into small cubes and leave them to cool on a wire rack. Mix together the lemon juice, parsley, mint, coriander, oil and garlic and pour this over the cucumber slices in a bowl. Pat the tomatoes dry, or you will find that the toast absorbs their juice and this spoils the flavour of the oil and lemon juice. Add the tomatoes to the salad bowl and mix well, then add the cubes of toast. Mix these in, season the salad with salt and pepper and serve it well chilled.

Red bean salad

Serves 4
CALORIES PER PORTION: 205 (855 kJ)
PROTEIN CONTENT PER PORTION: 15 grams
PREPARATION TIME: 15 minutes

350 g (12 oz) cooked red beans — 125 g
   (4 oz) uncooked
50 g (2 oz) chopped celery
2 pickled cucumbers, thinly sliced
125 g (4 oz) roughly chopped tomatoes,
   de-seeded
150 ml (¼ pint) cultured sour cream or
   Mayonnaise (page 126)
salt and freshly ground pepper
50 g (2 oz) finely chopped onion
2 tablespoons finely chopped parsley

Combine all the vegetables with the Mayonnaise or sour cream, and adjust the seasoning. Pile the mixture on a shallow plate and sprinkle with the parsley

Note: Use dill-flavoured pickled cucumbers for preference.

Italian green bean salad

Serves 4
CALORIES PER PORTION: 265 (1107 kJ)
PROTEIN CONTENT PER PORTION: 4.5 grams
PREPARATION TIME: 15 minutes

450 g (1 lb) cooked green beans
50 g (2 oz) onion (preferably Spanish),
  cut into rings
2 hard-boiled eggs, finely chopped

The dressing
1 tablespoon wine or cider vinegar
1 tablespoon lemon juice
6-8 tablespoons olive or sunflower oil
salt
freshly ground pepper
1 clove of garlic, peeled and finely
  chopped
½-1 teaspoon finely chopped fresh
  oregano or winter savory

Mix together the vinegar, lemon juice, oil, salt, pepper, garlic and herbs. Gently mix the onion rings with the beans, pouring over the dressing at the same time. Pile the mixture in a shallow dish and sprinkle the chopped eggs on top.

Note: If you like a milder onion flavour, or Spanish onions are not available, blanch the onion slices lightly by pouring boiling water over them and leaving them to stand for 5 minutes. Drain and refresh them by rinsing them in cold water and patting dry before adding to the salad, or follow the method given in the recipe for Onion ring salad (below).

Onion ring salad

Blanched onion rings also make a very good addition to other salads.

Serves 4
CALORIES PER PORTION: 115 (490 kJ)
PROTEIN CONTENT PER PORTION: 1 gram
PREPARATION & COOKING TIME: 15 minutes

450 g (1 lb) mild-flavoured onions,
  preferably Spanish, cut in rings
½ teaspoon wine vinegar
3 tablespoons olive or sunflower oil
salt
freshly ground pepper
1 tablespoon chopped parsley

Bring a large pan of water to the boil. Fill a bowl with plenty of ice cubes or iced water. Put the onion rings into a frying basket and lower it into the boiling water. Use a draining spoon to keep the onion rings below the surface, and the moment the water comes back to the boil, remove the basket and plunge it into the iced water. Shake the basket a little so that all the onions cool immediately, then drain them well on absorbent kitchen paper. If you have a centrifugal salad shaker, use this. Arrange them in a shallow dish.

Whisk together the vinegar and oil and pour it over the onions. Season with salt and pepper and sprinkle with parsley.

Note: After blanching the onions and refreshing them straight away they should be milder-flavoured, but still crisp.

Greek salad

Serves 4
CALORIES PER PORTION: 315 (1330 kJ)
PROTEIN CONTENT PER PORTION: 7 grams
PREPARATION TIME: 20 minutes

225 g (8 oz) crisp lettuce, preferably
  Cos, torn into small pieces
12 small stoned black olives, sliced
100 g (4 oz) finely chopped tomatoes
6 spring onions, thinly sliced
100g (4 oz) diced green and red peppers
6-8 tablespoons olive or sunflower oil
1 tablespoon wine or cider vinegar
1 tablespoon lemon juice
a little grated lemon rind
1 clove of garlic, peeled and finely
  chopped
1 tablespoon chopped coriander leaves
  or parsley
salt
freshly ground pepper
100 g (4 oz) Feta cheese, cut in 1 cm
  (½ in) cubes

Mix together the lettuce, olives, tomatoes, spring onions and peppers in a wide, shallow bowl. Whisk together the oil, vinegar, lemon juice and rind, garlic and coriander or parsley, and season with salt and pepper. Pour the dressing over the salad and turn over until the whole salad is evenly coated and glistening. Scatter the cheese over the top and serve.

Caesar salad

Serves 4
CALORIES PER PORTION: 380 (1600 kJ)
PROTEIN CONTENT PER PORTION: 9 grams
PREPARATION & COOKING TIME: 45 minutes

450 g (1 lb) crisp lettuce, preferably
  Cos, torn into small pieces
4 tablespoons olive or sunflower oil
4 slices wholemeal bread, crusts
  removed and cut into 1 cm (½ in)
  cubes
50 g (2 oz) freshly grated Parmesan
  cheese

The dressing
1 egg
4 tablespoons olive or sunflower oil
1 teaspoon wine vinegar
salt
freshly ground pepper
1 small clove of garlic, peeled and finely
  chopped
1 teaspoon lemon juice

Heat the oil in a pan and fry the bread-cubes over moderate heat until they are crisp; drain them on kitchen paper and allow to get completely cold.

Meanwhile, make the dressing by whisking together the egg, the oil, vinegar, salt and pepper, garlic and lemon juice until well blended, or put in a blender and work until smooth. Put the lettuce into a salad bowl and strain the dressing over; toss it well. Arrange the croûtons of bread in the centre and sprinkle the Parmesan round them. Mix them all together at the table.

The vegetarian chef's salad

This popular salad must have been invented by a chef in a hurry, who had to produce something for late arrivals in a restaurant, using only the ingredients to hand. It makes a very good light lunch or supper dish with a bowl of soup beforehand and some fresh fruit to follow.

Serves 4

CALORIES PER PORTION: 920 (3855 kJ)
PROTEIN CONTENT PER PORTION: 19.5 grams
PREPARATION & COOKING TIME: 30 minutes

4 eggs
1 tablespoon olive or sunflower oil
salt
freshly ground pepper
350 g (12 oz) cabbage lettuce, torn into small pieces
225 g (8 oz) thinly sliced celery
50 g (2 oz) finely chopped spring onions
125 g (4 oz) watercress leaves
225 g (8 oz) thinly sliced chicory
125 g (4 oz) cheese, preferably Emmenthal, cut in thin strips
300 ml (½ pint) Mayonnaise (page 126)
a little single cream

Make an omelette with the eggs and oil (page 66), season with salt and pepper and leave it to get cold. You can speed up this process by putting it on a cold plate over some ice-cubes. Meanwhile, mix the salad greens, celery and chicory in a bowl with the cheese.

Cut the cooled omelette into strips about 1 cm (½ in) x 7.5 cm (3 in), and add these to the salad, mixing them in well but taking care not to break up the cheese sticks or the omelette more than you can help.

Pour in the mayonnaise, thinned with a little cream, and continue turning the salad, checking the seasoning as you do so. Pile it on a flat plate to serve.

Cole slaw 1

Serves 4

CALORIES PER PORTION: 540 (2275 kJ)
PROTEIN CONTENT PER PORTION: 17 grams
PREPARATION TIME: 20 minutes

350 g (12 oz) white cabbage, shredded into small pieces
8 tablespoons olive or sunflower oil
2 tablespoons wine or cider vinegar
salt
freshly ground pepper
125 g (4 oz) coarsely grated Cheddar cheese
125 g (4 oz) peeled and shredded dessert apple, sprinkled with 2 tablespoons lemon juice
100 g (4 oz) sunflower seeds

Put the cabbage into a bowl. Whisk together the oil, vinegar, salt and pepper. Sprinkle the cheese over the cabbage with some of the dressing, mixing it in gradually, otherwise the cheese will stick together in lumps. Add the apple, lemon juice and sunflower seeds, then pour in the remainder of the dressing and mix thoroughly. Turn out into a shallow bowl for serving.

Cole slaw 2

Serves 4

CALORIES PER PORTION: 492 (2062 kJ)
PROTEIN CONTENT PER PORTION: 12 grams
PREPARATION TIME: 20 minutes

350 g (12 oz) white cabbage, shredded into small pieces
125 g (4 oz) peeled and shredded dessert apple, sprinkled with 2 tablespoons of lemon juice
8 tablespoons olive or sunflower oil
1 tablespoon wine or cider vinegar
1 tablespoon clear honey
salt
freshly ground pepper
1 egg, lightly beaten
50 g (2 oz) finely chopped onion
125 g (4 oz) unroasted peanuts

Put the cabbage in a bowl. Whisk together the oil, vinegar, honey, salt, pepper and the egg. Strain this dressing over the cabbage and add the apple, lemon juice and onion. Work the peanuts in a blender for a few seconds, or put them through a nut mill — or crush them coarsely with pestle and mortar. Add them to the salad and mix thoroughly; turn into a shallow bowl.

Cole slaw 3

Serves 4

CALORIES PER PORTION: 455 (1872 kJ)
PROTEIN CONTENT PER PORTION: 8 grams
PREPARATION TIME: 20 minutes

225 g (8 oz) shredded white cabbage
225 g (8 oz) cooked brown lentils — about 100 g (4 oz) uncooked
125 g (4 oz) peeled and shredded dessert apple, sprinkled with 2 tablespoons lemon juice
8 tablespoons olive or sunflower oil
1 tablespoon wine or cider vinegar
1 tablespoon thick or clear honey
1 teaspoon curry powder
1 small clove garlic, peeled and very finely chopped
salt and freshly ground pepper
1 egg, lightly beaten
125 g (4 oz) curd cheese

Put the cabbage in a bowl with the lentils, apple and lemon juice. Whisk together the oil, vinegar, honey, curry powder, garlic, salt and pepper and the egg. Stir this slowly into the curd cheese to make a smooth cream. Pour this dressing over the cabbage, lentils and apple and mix well.

More salad suggestions

Try the following salad mixtures, served with Mayonnaise or a French or Vinaigrette dressing:

Cold cooked macaroni with chopped unroasted peanuts, sliced tomatoes and blanched and chopped onions.
Grated raw carrot, diced red pepper and pineapple cubes.
Thinly sliced cooked courgettes, cooked diced potatoes and thinly sliced or whole radishes.
Large continental tomatoes stuffed with julienne strips of cheese, cooked potatoes and spring onions.

Thin slices of cheese interleaved with layers of blanched or raw onion rings and sliced tomatoes.
Curd cheese with chopped raw or pickled cucumber piled up on a plain coleslaw with a little grated strong cheese and a pinch of cayenne sprinkled over the top.
Grated raw carrot, finely chopped celery, peanuts and a little finely chopped onion on slices of dark rye bread.
Cooked soya beans with chopped onion and grated cheese and covered with sliced raw mushrooms marinated in lemon juice.

Fresh peaches, halved and filled with finely chopped celery and red peppers on a bed of torn lettuce leaves; dress the lettuce with a Vinaigrette dressing and the peaches with Mayonnaise.
Shredded celeriac with diced apples, cucumber and watercress.
Thinly sliced Jerusalem artichokes with sliced tomatoes, celery and chopped parsley.
Diced cooked beetroot in whipped cream flavoured with caraway seeds and lemon juice and rind.

Puddings

However successful your dinner party so far, and however well-received the main course, it is the dessert which really gives you the chance to shine. It is the crowning point of the meal and even if your guests affect not to like puddings or rich, cream-filled gateaux, you will be surprised at how many change their mind once your pièce de résistance is on the table.

This is the course where your favourite flavours can come into their own, where fruits can shine, softly whipped syllabubs, luscious filled crepes and heart-warming sponge puddings can rule the day. Choose a dessert that will complement the main course and remember that a cold pudding can be very refreshing after a hot, spicy main course, even in winter. Whether you serve your cheeseboard before the pudding in the French style, or to round off the meal in the English manner, try to have at least one representative of each of the main cheese 'families'.

A well-balanced cheeseboard should include one of the soft, creamy cheeses – a Bel Paese, Port Salut, a Camembert or Brie; then a blue-veined Dolcelatte, a Roquefort or Stilton, and a hard cheese such as a mature Cheddar, a Gruyere, an Edam or Gouda.

Apricot soufflé

Serves 4
CALORIES PER PORTION: 200 (845 kJ)
PROTEIN CONTENT PER PORTION: 9 grams
PREPARATION & COOKING TIME: 1 hour,
    excluding soaking

225 g (8 oz) dried apricots, soaked
    overnight in cold water to cover
1 vanilla pod
25-50 g (1-2 oz) raw brown sugar,
    according to taste
3 tablespoons double cream
3 egg yolks
5 egg whites
a little melted butter

Drain the apricots, then put them in a pan with the vanilla pod, sugar and enough water just to cover. Bring to the boil, cover the pan, then lower the heat and simmer for 15-20 minutes, until the apricots are soft but not falling apart.

Meanwhile, prepare a 15 cm (6 in) diameter soufflé dish; cut a strip of doubled greaseproof paper long enough to go around the outside of the dish overlapping by 2-5 cm (1-2 in); and standing 5-8 cm (2-3 in) higher than the rim. Tie the paper securely around the outside of the dish.

When the apricots are soft enough to purée, remove the vanilla pod and work the apricots in a blender until smooth, or rub them through a sieve. Stir in the cream and egg yolks and mix well. Set the oven at 180°C (350°F) Gas 4 and put in the prepared soufflé dish to warm while you beat the egg whites until stiff enough to stand in peaks.

Remove the soufflé dish from the oven and brush the inside and the inside of the paper collar with melted butter. Fold the beaten egg whites into the apricot purée and pour it into the prepared soufflé dish. Bake in the pre-heated oven for about 20 minutes until it is well-risen, but still slightly soft in the centre. Carefully remove the paper collar, then serve immediately with single cream.

Baked orange soufflé

Serves 4
CALORIES PER PORTION: 300 (1257 kJ)
PROTEIN CONTENT PER PORTION: 10 grams
PREPARATION & COOKING TIME: 35 minutes

20 g (¾ oz) butter
20 g (¾ oz) flour
300 ml (½ pint) milk
100 g (4 oz) sugar
grated rind of 3 oranges
4 eggs, separated
a little melted butter

Melt the butter in a pan over gentle heat and add the flour. Stir until thick, then allow to cook for 1 minute. Take the pan off the heat and gradually stir in the milk. Return the pan to the heat, add the sugar and continue stirring until the sauce thickens. Remove the pan from the heat.

Add the grated orange rind to the sauce and stir well, then allow to cool.

Add the egg yolks to the sauce. Set the oven at 190°C (375°F) Gas 5. Tie a paper collar round the outside of a 15 cm (6 in) diameter soufflé dish to overlap by 2-5 cm (1-2 in) and stand 5-8 cm (2-3 in) higher than the rim. Place the dish in the oven to warm for 10 minutes. Just before the end of the 10 minutes, beat the egg whites until stiff enough to stand in peaks and fold them into the sauce.

Liberally brush the inside of the hot soufflé dish and collar with melted butter. Immediately pour in the soufflé mixture. Bake for 20 minutes, until well risen, and serve immediately.

Chocolate soufflé

Serves 4
CALORIES PER PORTION: 250 (1080 kJ)
PROTEIN CONTENT PER PORTION: 9 grams
PREPARATION & COOKING TIME: 30 minutes

125 g (4 oz) plain cooking chocolate,
    broken into small pieces
2 tablespoons brandy
25 g (1 oz) raw brown sugar
4 egg yolks, well beaten
6 egg whites
a little melted chocolate

Set the oven at 180°C (350°F) Gas 4. Put the chocolate pieces in a small heatproof bowl with the brandy and sugar. Stand the bowl over a pan of boiling water until the chocolate has melted, stirring occasionally with a warm spoon — if you do not warm the spoon, the chocolate will set round it. Make a collar of double greaseproof paper long enough to go around the outside of a 15 cm (6 in) diameter soufflé dish, overlap by 2-5 cm (1-2 in) and stand 5-8 cm (2-3 in) higher than the rim. Tie the paper securely in place round the outside of the dish and put the dish in the oven to heat through. Remove the bowl from the pan and leave the chocolate to cool slightly, then add the egg yolks a little at a time, stirring well after each addition. Remove the soufflé dish from the oven and brush the inside and the inside of the paper collar with melted butter. Beat the egg whites until stiff enough to stand in peaks, then fold them into the chocolate mixture. Pour in the soufflé mixture, then bake in the pre-heated oven for 15-20 minutes until it is well risen. Carefully remove the paper collar and serve with single cream and Almond biscuits (page 164).

Lemon amber

Serves 4

CALORIES PER PORTION: 185 (780 kJ)
PROTEIN CONTENT PER PORTION: 5 grams
PREPARATION & COOKING TIME: 1 hour (longer if whisking by hand)

finely grated rind and juice of 1 large lemon
2 eggs, separated
125 g (4 oz) caster sugar
a little melted butter
25 g (1 oz) plain white flour
150 ml (¼ pint) milk

Put the lemon rind and juice, egg yolks and sugar in a bowl. Place the bowl over a pan of hot water if you are using a hand whisk. Whisk together until the mixture leaves a ribbon trail across the top when the whisk is lifted.

Set the oven at 180°C (350°F) Gas 4. Butter a 20 cm (8 in) sandwich tin and set aside. Put the flour in a bowl with a little of the milk and mix well, then gradually stir in the remaining milk.

Beat the egg whites until stiff enough to stand in peaks. Stir the milk mixture into the lemon and egg yolks, then fold in the egg whites. Pour the mixture into the prepared tin, stand the tin in a roasting tin and pour in just enough boiling water to come halfway up the sides of the sandwich tin. Bake in the pre-heated oven for 45 minutes and serve hot with single cream or a fruit purée.

Almond surprise

This is a very rich pudding, but 4 people will finish it without much effort.

CALORIES PER PORTION: 655 (2950 kJ)
PROTEIN CONTENT PER PORTION: 12 grams
PREPARATION & COOKING TIME: 1 hour (longer if whisking by hand)

125 g (4 oz) ground almonds
4 eggs, separated
125 g (4 oz) caster sugar
300 ml (½ pint) double cream
finely grated rind of 1 orange
good pinch of freshly grated nutmeg
a little melted butter

Prepare a 15 cm (6 in) diameter soufflé dish: cut a strip of doubled greaseproof paper long enough to go round the outside of the dish, overlap by 2-5 cm (1-2 in) and stand 5-8 cm (2-3 in) higher than the rim. Tie the paper securely around the outside of the dish.

Whisk together the egg yolks and sugar with an electric whisk until the mixture leaves a ribbon trail across the top when the whisk is lifted. (Stand the bowl over a pan of hot water, if using a hand whisk).

Add the cream and continue whisking until thick, then stir in the almonds, orange rind and nutmeg.

Beat the egg whites until stiff enough to stand in peaks, then fold them into the almond mixture. Pour into the well-buttered soufflé dish, stand the dish in a large pan and pour in enough boiling water to come halfway up the side of the dish. Cover and simmer for 45 minutes; remove the paper collar, and serve hot, with Caramel sauce (page 198).

Crêpes pralinés

Serves 4

CALORIES PER PORTION: 625 (2615 kJ)
PROTEIN CONTENT PER PORTION: 14 grams
PREPARATION & COOKING TIME: 50 minutes

100 g (4 oz) unblanched almonds
50 g (2 oz) granulated sugar
12 thin crêpes made from the Basic mixture (page 82)
75 g (3 oz) unsalted butter
2 tablespoons dark rum, or to taste

To make the praline: cook the almonds with the sugar in a thick-based pan over moderate heat until the sugar melts and coats the almonds. Stir constantly to prevent it burning. Remove the pan from the heat and pour the praline onto a lightly oiled plate, or a sheet of non-stick vegetable parchment. Leave until cold and set, then crush finely with a rolling pin, or work to a powder in a blender.

Warm the crêpes between two heatproof plates over a pan of boiling water. Cream the butter in a bowl with a wooden spoon until soft, add the praline and work it in well. Add the rum a few drops at a time, beating well after each addition, until the mixture is light and fluffy. Spread a little of the praline mixture on each crêpe, then fold it over to enclose the filling. Arrange the crêpes on a warm serving dish and serve with cream and an apple purée flavoured with cinnamon.

Crêpes with curd cheese and raisins

Serves 4
CALORIES PER PORTION: 775 (3255 kJ)
PROTEIN CONTENT PER PORTION: 13 grams
PREPARATION & COOKING TIME: 45 minutes

*12 thin crêpes made from the Basic
  mixture (page 82)*
225 g (8 oz) curd cheese
1 teaspoon grated lemon rind
4-8 tablespoons raw brown sugar
2 tablespoons lemon juice
50 g (2 oz) raisins
2 tablespoons melted unsalted butter

Set the oven at 200°C (400°F) Gas 6. Beat the curd cheese well, then add the lemon rind and 2-4 tablespoons of the sugar, half the lemon juice and the raisins and mix thoroughly. Divide the mixture between the crêpes, roll them up and arrange the filled crêpes side by side on a well-buttered baking sheet.

Brush each one with melted butter, sprinkle with the remaining lemon juice and sugar and place in the pre-heated oven for 10 minutes, until they are really hot and sizzling. Serve with wedges of lemon and a bowl of brown sugar.

As a variation, flavour the sugar with a little ground cinnamon.

Crêpes aux cerises

Serves 4
CALORIES PER PORTION: 715 (2997 kJ)
PROTEIN CONTENT PER PORTION: 14 grams
PREPARATION & COOKING TIME: 45 minutes

*12 thin crêpes made from the Basic
  mixture (page 82) with a few drops of
  almond essence added*
*225 g (8 oz) stoned black cherries,
  cooked and coarsely chopped*
50 g (2 oz) raw brown sugar
4 tablespoons water
4 tablespoons Kirsch
300 ml (½ pint) whipping cream
25 g (1 oz) shredded blanched almonds

Keep the crêpes warm between 2 heat-proof plates over a pan of boiling water. Put the cherries, sugar and water in a pan and heat gently until the sugar has dissolved. Remove the pan from the heat and stir in the Kirsch.

Set the oven at 200°C (400°F) Gas 6. Put a spoonful of the cherry mixture on each crêpe, then roll them up and arrange side by side in an ovenproof dish. Pour over any remaining cherry juice and half the cream, if liked, then sprinkle with the almonds. Bake in the pre-heated oven for 10 minutes. Serve hot with cream — or the remaining cream — lightly whipped and handed separately.

Note: cook stoned fresh cherries by simmering them in a little water with sugar to taste — until they are just soft, but not squashy. Canned cherries can also be used.

Lemon meringue pie

Serves 6
CALORIES PER PORTION: 1150 (4815 kJ)
PROTEIN CONTENT PER PORTION: 26 grams
PREPARATION & COOKING TIME: 45 minutes

finely grated rind of 2 lemons
200 ml (⅓ pint) lemon juice
*pre-baked 22 cm (9 in) flan case, made
  with Wholemeal shortcrust pastry
  (page 194)*
*2 tablespoons apricot jam, heated and
  sieved*
4 eggs, separated
*two 300 ml (½ pint) cans full cream
  sweetened condensed milk*
225 g (8 oz) caster sugar

Set the oven at 150°C (300°F) Gas 2. Brush the inside of the flan case with the warm apricot jam. Put the lemon rind and juice in a bowl with the egg yolks and condensed milk and mix well. Pour this filling into the flan case.

Beat the egg whites until stiff enough to stand in peaks, then fold in the sugar. Spread this meringue mixture over the top of the lemon filling, making sure that the filling is completely covered. Swirl the meringue mixture into a pattern with a fork.

Bake in the pre-heated oven for 20-30 minutes or until the meringue is crisp and browned. Allow to cool slightly before serving.

Apricot meringue pie

Serves 4
CALORIES PER PORTION: 500 (2095 kJ)
PROTEIN CONTENT PER PORTION: 9 grams
PREPARATION & COOKING TIME: 1 hour,
  excluding soaking time

*225 g (8 oz) dried apricots, soaked
  overnight in cold water to cover*
*about 50 g (2 oz) raw brown sugar, or to
  taste*
1 vanilla pod
200 ml (⅓ pint) water
2 egg whites
50 g (2 oz) caster sugar
*pre-baked 20 cm (8 in) flan case, made
  with Wholemeal shortcrust pastry
  (page 194)*
*2 tablespoons apricot jam, heated and
  sieved*

Drain the apricots, then put them in a pan with the brown sugar, vanilla pod and water. Bring to the boil, cover the pan then lower the heat and simmer for 15-20 minutes, until the apricots are soft but not falling apart. Remove the apricots from the heat, drain off any excess liquid, remove the vanilla pod and leave them to cool slightly. Taste for sweetness and add more brown sugar if necessary.

Set the oven at 150°C (300°F) Gas 2. Lightly brush the inside of the flan case — still in its tin — with the warm apricot jam. Arrange the drained apricots in the flan case. Beat the egg whites until they are stiff enough to stand in peaks, then fold in the caster sugar. Spread the meringue mixture over the top so that it covers the apricots completely and swirl it into a pattern with a fork.

Bake in the pre-heated oven for about 30 minutes, or until the meringue is crisp and browned. Allow to cool slightly before serving with rum-flavoured whipped cream or Chantilly cream (page 198).

A luscious selection of hot puddings and desserts. Top left: Apricot meringue pie with its crispy topping. Top right: steamed Lemon pudding with Raspberry sauce. Below left: thin crêpes filled with black cherries and sprinkled with almonds. Below right: Chinese sugar apples in sesame-flavoured syrup

Cheesecake

Serves 4
CALORIES PER PORTION: 695 (2910 kJ)
PROTEIN CONTENT PER PORTION: 14 grams
PREPARATION & COOKING TIME: about 1 hour

175 g (6 oz) Wholemeal shortcrust
* pastry (page 194)*
2 tablespoons apricot jam, warmed and
* sieved*
75 g (3 oz) raw brown sugar
2 eggs, separated
225 g (8 oz) curd cheese
25 g (1 oz) sultanas
finely grated rind and juice of 1 lemon

Roll out the dough and line an 18 cm (7 in) diameter flan tin or ring on a baking sheet. Brush the bottom with warm apricot jam. Put the sugar and egg yolks in a bowl, then cream together until light. Add the cheese, sultanas, lemon rind and juice and beat until well mixed.

Set the oven at 180°C (350°F) Gas 4. Beat the egg whites until stiff and standing in peaks, then fold these into the cheese mixture. Pour into the flan case, then bake in the pre-heated oven for 45 minutes until set. Leave to cool slightly before serving.

Alsatian apple flan

Serves 6
CALORIES PER PORTION: 630 (2620 kJ)
PROTEIN CONTENT PER PORTION: 12 grams
PREPARATION & COOKING TIME: 1 hour

1 kg (2 lb) cooking apples, preferably
* Bramleys*
pre-baked 25 cm (10 in) flan case, made
* with Wholemeal shortcrust pastry*
* (page 194)*
2 tablespoons apricot jam, heated and
* sieved*
125 g (4 oz) caster sugar
½ teaspoon ground cinnamon
scant 120 ml (4 fl oz) top-of-the-milk
½ teaspoon vanilla essence
2 eggs well beaten
1 tablespoon raw brown sugar

Set the oven at 200°C (400°F) Gas 6. Peel and core the apples, then cut them into segments about 1 cm (½ in) thick. Put these in a pan with boiling water to cover, simmer for 2 minutes, then drain and rinse under cold running water, and pat them dry.

Lightly brush the inside of the flan case with the warm apricot jam. Arrange the blanched apple segments in overlapping layers in the flan case, then mix the sugar with the cinnamon and sprinkle this over the apple layers. Bake in the pre-heated oven for 15-20 minutes, or until the apples are soft when pierced with a skewer.

Mix together the milk, vanilla essence, eggs and brown sugar and pour this over the apples. Return the flan to the oven and bake for a further 15 minutes until the custard has set. Serve with single cream or Custard sauce (page 198).

Chinese sugar apples

These apple fritters are a speciality of Peking cuisine. They can be dipped in syrup at the table, then 'set' in iced water.

Serves 4
CALORIES PER PORTION: 540 (2265 kJ)
PROTEIN CONTENT PER PORTION: 7.5 grams
PREPARATION AND COOKING TIME: 1 hour

350 g (12 oz) cooking apples, preferably
* Bramleys*
Coating batter (page 194)
oil for deep frying
150 g (5 oz) granulated sugar
4 tablespoons sesame oil
2 tablespoons sesame seeds

Peel and core the apples, then cut them into chunks. Put them in a bowl with the batter and stir them to make sure they are well coated.

Heat the oil in a deep-fat fryer to 180°C (350°F). Put 6-8 apple chunks into the frying basket and deep fry in the hot oil for 1-2 minutes until golden. Remove from the oil, drain on absorbent kitchen paper and keep hot while frying the remainder.

Melt the sugar in a thick-based pan without letting it brown. Pour in the sesame oil and heat for a moment or two longer. Prepare a bowl of iced water.

Put the apple fritters into the pan a few at a time and turn them over to coat them well in the sugar and oil. Transfer to an oiled plate, keeping each fritter separate or they will stick together. Sprinkle with the sesame seeds and then dip immediately into iced water, using oiled spoons. Serve at once.

Spiced beignets

Serves 4
CALORIES PER PORTION: 385 (1615 kJ)
PROTEIN CONTENT PER PORTION: 9 grams
PREPARATION & COOKING TIME: 1 hour

200 ml (⅓ pint) milk
75 g (3 oz) unsalted butter
100 g (4 oz) unbleached white flour
¼ teaspoon ground cinnamon
pinch of salt
1 teaspoon raw brown sugar
2-3 eggs
oil for deep frying
a little icing sugar

Bring the milk to the boil in a pan with the butter. Sift together the flour, cinnamon and salt and stir in the sugar.

When the milk comes to the boil, take the pan off the heat and pour in the flour mixture all at once. Beat vigorously and return the pan to the heat. Continue beating until the mixture comes away from the sides of the pan, then remove the pan from the heat again and leave the mixture to cool slightly before beating in the eggs one at a time until the mixture is firm, smooth and glossy. If the eggs are large it may not be necessary to add the whole of the third egg.

Heat the oil in a deep-fat fryer to 180°C (350°F). Drop teaspoonfuls of the mixture into the hot oil and deep fry for 1-2 minutes until golden brown. Remove the beignets from the pan with a draining spoon and drain on kitchen paper. Keep each batch hot while frying the remainder. If there is any moisture in the oven or warming drawer, they will lose their crispness.

Pile the beignets on a warmed serving plate, sprinkle lightly with icing sugar and serve hot with Honey and orange sauce.

Honey and orange sauce

CALORIES PER PORTION: 115 (490 kJ)
PROTEIN CONTENT PER PORTION: 0.25 grams
PREPARATION & COOKING TIME: 10 minutes

150 g (5 oz) thick honey
200 ml (⅓ pint) hot water
2 teaspoons cornflour
finely grated rind of 2 oranges

Heat together the honey and water in a pan, stirring constantly until the honey has dissolved. Mix the cornflour to a paste with a little cold water, then stir in a little of the hot honey mixture and return it to the pan. Bring the sauce to the boil, then simmer until the sauce thickens, stirring constantly. Add the orange rind, pour the sauce into a warmed jug and serve hot.

Note: omit the cornflour to make a thin sauce.

Curd cheese with strawberries and Kirsch

Serves 4
CALORIES PER PORTION: 320 (1345 kJ)
PROTEIN CONTENT PER PORTION: 4 grams
PREPARATION & CHILLING TIME: 2½ hours

25 g (8 oz) mild curd cheese
egg whites
50 g (12 oz) hulled strawberries (or
raspberries)
teaspoons Kirsch or lemon juice
bowl of caster sugar, for serving

Work the cheese in a bowl with the back of a wooden spoon until smooth. Beat the egg whites until stiff enough to stand in peaks, then fold these into the cheese. (If the cheese is too firm, stir in a little egg white.) Put the mixture into a fine sieve, stand it over a bowl, then leave to drain in the refrigerator for 2 hours.

Turn the cheese out on to a serving plate, arrange the strawberries around it and sprinkle with the Kirsch or lemon juice. Hand the sugar separately.

Compote of dried fruit

Serves 4
CALORIES PER PORTION: 275 (1160 kJ)
PROTEIN CONTENT PER PORTION: 3.5 grams
PREPARATION & COOKING TIME: 3 hours
SOAKING TIME: overnight

25 g (4 oz) dried apricots
25 g (4 oz) prunes
25 g (4 oz) dried apple rings
00 ml (1 pint) water
vanilla pod
5 g (1 oz) halved blanched almonds
5 g (1 oz) currants
sprig of mint
5 g (3 oz) raw brown sugar
5 g (1 oz) finely sliced preserved
ginger, in syrup
teaspoon rose water
-2 tablespoons Kirsch

Wash the apricots, prunes and apple rings carefully and put them into separate bowls with a third of the water in each, and leave to soak overnight. The following morning, transfer the fruit and water to separate pans, adding a little more water if necessary; the fruit should just be covered. Put the vanilla pod and almonds with the apricots, the currants with the prunes and the mint with the apples.

Divide the sugar between the fruit and bring each to the boil. Simmer, covered, until the fruit is tender, stirring occasionally. The apricots and prunes should take about 30 minutes and the apple rings about 10 minutes. Add a little more water, if necessary but the fruit should not be swimming in syrup.

Allow to cool and then mix the fruits and their syrups together. Stir in the ginger, rose water and kirsch and chill for an hour. Serve with lightly whipped cream.

Jamaican bananas

Serves 4
CALORIES PER PORTION: 720 (2997 kJ)
PROTEIN CONTENT PER PORTION: 1 gram
PREPARATION & COOKING TIME: 10 minutes

ripe but firm bananas
5 g (1 oz) butter
5 g (1 oz) soft brown sugar
good pinches of freshly grated nutmeg
00 ml (generous ⅛ pint) rum
00 ml (½ pint) cranberry sauce

Peel the bananas and cut them in half lengthways. Fry them gently in the butter in a chafing dish (or frying pan which can be taken to the table) until golden brown. Sprinkle on the brown sugar and grated nutmeg and, by gently shaking the pan from side to side and with a spatula, cover the bananas with the sugar and nutmeg. Pour over the rum and set it alight. Serve, while still flaming, with a little Cranberry sauce between the two halves and with lightly whipped cream and crisp Almond or Hazelnut biscuits.

Fruit fool

Serves 4
CALORIES PER PORTION: 410 (1717 kJ)
PROTEIN CONTENT PER PORTION: 11 grams
PREPARATION & CHILLING TIME: 2½ hours
(not including preparing the fruit)

225 g (8 oz) cooked fresh or dried fruit
— apples, apricots, gooseberries,
peaches, plums, prunes
300 ml (½ pint) thick Custard sauce
(page 198)
150 ml (¼ pint) double cream
(optional)

Put the fruit in a blender and work to a smooth purée, or rub through a Mouli mill or sieve. Mix the purée thoroughly into the Custard sauce. Whip the cream until thick, if using, then fold into the purée. Chill in the refrigerator for about 2 hours, then serve with Langue de chat biscuits

Orange sherry syllabub

Serves 4
CALORIES PER PORTION: 775 (3238 kJ)
PROTEIN CONTENT PER PORTION: 6 grams
PREPARATION & CHILLING TIME: 1½ hours

grated rind of 2 oranges
100 ml (4 fl oz) cream sherry
600 ml (1 pint) double cream
1-2 tablespoons honey
2 eggs, separated
2 tablespoons lemon juice

Whip the cream with the orange rind and honey until it holds its shape. Whisk the egg yolks until light and foamy, then add the lemon juice and sherry and mix them into the cream. Whisk the egg whites until they form soft peaks and fold into the cream. Pour the posset into eight tall glasses and serve chilled. Sweet Almond biscuits (page 164) go well with this pudding.

Coffee Marquise

Serves 4
CALORIES PER PORTION: 575 (2400 kJ)
PROTEIN CONTENT PER PORTION: 10 grams
PREPARATION & CHILLING TIME: 3-4 hours

2 teaspoons instant coffee powder
2½-3 teaspoons agar-agar
450 ml (¾ pint) milk
50 g (2 oz) raw brown sugar
2 egg yolks, well beaten
8 sponge finger biscuits
2 tablespoons cream sherry

To finish
300 ml (½ pint) whipping cream,
whipped
50 g (2 oz) coarsely grated plain
chocolate

Sprinkle the agar-agar over the milk in a pan, leave for 5 minutes then stir well. Add the coffee powder and sugar, then bring to the boil over moderate heat, stirring constantly to prevent sticking. Lower the heat and simmer for 2 minutes, then remove from the heat and cool slightly.

Whisk a little of the hot liquid into the egg yolks, then gradually whisk in the remaining liquid. Pour the mixture into a shallow 20 cm (8 in) diameter round cake tin, then dip the sponge fingers into the sherry and press them in a layer on top of the mixture, radiating from the centre like the spokes of a wheel.

Leave to cool, then chill in the refrigerator for 2-3 hours, or until set. Invert a serving plate over the tin, then turn the Marquise out onto the plate. Spread the cream over the Marquise to mask it completely, then sprinkle with the chocolate. Serve chilled.

143

Summer pudding

Serves 6
CALORIES PER PORTION: 350 (1472 kJ)
PROTEIN CONTENT PER PORTION: 11 grams
PREPARATION & CHILLING TIME: at least 8
  hours, preferably overnight

500 g (1¼ lb) mixed summer fruit —
  raspberries, hulled strawberries,
  stoned red or black cherries, red or
  black currants — washed
100 g (4 oz) honey
8-10 slices of freshly made, but cold,
  wholemeal bread, about 1 cm (½ in)
  thick, crusts removed

Caramel oranges

Serves 4
CALORIES PER PORTION: 210 (885 kJ)
PROTEIN CONTENT PER PORTION: 1 gram
PREPARATION & CHILLING TIME: about 4 hours

4 large oranges, preferably seedless
175 g (6 oz) granulated sugar
200 ml (⅓ pint) warm water

Carefully remove the outer skin (zest) of
2 oranges with a sharp knife, then cut this
into matchstick strips. Put the strips in
a small pan, cover with water and bring
to the boil. Boil for 10 minutes to remove
any bitterness, then drain and rinse under
cold running water.

Remove the peel and pith from all 4
oranges, together with the outer skin from
the segments. Discard the pips, if any.
Slice the orange flesh thinly into rounds,
then arrange in overlapping circles in a
shallow serving bowl.

Put the sugar in a heavy pan and heat
very gently until the sugar has melted,
stirring constantly and breaking up any
lumps with the back of the spoon. Continue cooking until the syrup turns golden
brown, stirring all the time.

Pour in about a quarter of the water
and stir vigorously, taking care to cover
your hands as the caramel will spatter.
Add the remaining water in four helpings,
stirring constantly, then add the strips of
orange rind and simmer until transparent.

Remove the orange strips from the
syrup with a draining spoon and sprinkle
them over the orange slices in the serving
bowl. Pour over the syrup and leave to
cool. Chill well, then serve on their own,
or with single cream.

Left: The best of summer's fruits in an
irresistible Summer pudding. Right:
Caramel oranges – serve them on their
own or with thin, single cream. Front
and back: Lemon and orange possets are
a variation on the old-fashioned
syllabub

Put the washed fruit into a saucepan with
the honey and bring it gently to the boil;
poach just until the fruit begins to break
up and the juice starts to run.

Cut eight pieces of bread, shaping them
into triangles to cover the bottom of a 15
cm (6 in) diameter soufflé dish. Cut more
bread into rectangles and completely line
the sides of the dish, spreading over a
little of the fruit to hold the bread in
place. Then pour in the rest of the fruit,
keeping about 100 ml (⅛ pint) of the juice
to one side. Cover the top of the dish with
the remaining bread, cut into triangles.

Put either a plate or the rust-proof loose
base of a round cake tin which fits inside
the soufflé dish on top of the bread and
press it down with a heavy weight. Chill
overnight or for at least 8 hours. Keep the
reserved juice in the refrigerator.

Remove the plate or cake tin base and
gently turn out the pudding, taking care
that it does not distintegrate. If the slices
of bread have been arranged without any
gaps between them there should be no
problem. Pour the reserved juice over any
dry areas. Serve with a light Custard sauce
(page 198) or lightly whipped cream.

Scottish posset

Serves 4
CALORIES PER PORTION: 848 (3550 kJ)
PROTEIN CONTENT PER PORTION: 7.5 grams
PREPARATION & CHILLING TIME: 1 hour

eggs, separated
grated rind and juice of 1 lemon
tablespoons honey
tablespoons whisky
00 ml (1 pint) double cream
tablespoons oatmeal

Beat together the egg yolks, lemon rind and juice, honey and whisky. Whip the cream until it holds its shape, and whisk the egg whites until they are stiff enough to stand in peaks.

Combine the egg yolk mixture with the cream, then fold in the beaten egg whites. Pour into four tall glasses.

Toast the oatmeal in a clean saucepan, shaking it from side to side continuously over a medium heat until it is a good nut-brown colour. Allow it to cool, then sprinkle a tablespoon over each glass. Serve chilled.

Lemon and orange posset

The eggs and cream should be well chilled for making this dessert.

Serves 4
CALORIES PER PORTION: 750 (3142 kJ)
PROTEIN CONTENT PER PORTION: 5 grams
PREPARATION & CHILLING TIME: 1 hour

finely grated rind and juice of 2 large
  lemons
150 ml (¼ pint) dry white wine
2-3 tablespoons raw brown sugar
finely grated rind of ½ orange
600 ml (1 pint) double cream, chilled
3 egg whites, chilled

Put the lemon juice, half the wine and the sugar in a pan and heat gently until the sugar has dissolved, stirring occasionally. Remove from the heat, stir in the lemon and orange rind and remaining wine, then leave until cold.

Whip the cream until thick, then stir in the wine mixture until evenly distributed. Beat the egg whites until stiff enough to stand in peaks, then fold these into the cream mixture.

Divide the mixture equally between four serving glasses, then chill in the refrigerator for about 45 minutes before serving with Langue de chat biscuits (page 164).

Zabaglione

If possible, use a hand-held electric whisk to make this dessert. The Italians use a balloon whisk, but this requires practice and experience and you will probably have more success with the electric whisk at first.

Serves 4
CALORIES PER PORTION: 142 (597 kJ)
PROTEIN CONTENT PER PORTION: 3 grams
PREPARATION & COOKING TIME: 15 minutes

4 egg yolks
4 tablespoons light brown sugar
4 tablespoons Marsala wine

Put all the ingredients in a heatproof bowl, then stand the bowl in a shallow pan of gently simmering water. Whisk for about 5 minutes until the mixture is thick and foamy, taking care not to allow the mixture to get too hot or it will cook (it should feel hot to the touch, but not hot enough to scald).

Remove the bowl from the pan and continue whisking until the mixture cools slightly so that the surface does not set. Serve immediately with sponge fingers or Langue de chat biscuits (page 164).

Steamed lemon pudding

Raw brown sugar should not be used in this recipe as it will spoil the colour of the finished pudding.

Serves 6
CALORIES PER PORTION: 375 (1571 kJ)
PROTEIN CONTENT PER PORTION: 7.5 grams
PREPARATION & COOKING TIME: 2-2½ hours

finely grated rind and juice of 1 large lemon
125 g (4 oz) plain white flour
2 teaspoons baking powder
¼ teaspoon salt
225 g (8 oz) fresh white breadcrumbs
125 g (4 oz) butter or margarine
125 g (4 oz) granulated sugar
2 eggs, beaten
approx 125 ml (4 fl oz) milk

Sift the flour, baking powder and salt into a bowl, then add the breadcrumbs and mix well.

Cream the butter or margarine with the sugar in a separate bowl until light and fluffy. Add the eggs a little at a time, beating well after each addition, then stir in the lemon rind and juice.

Stir the dry mixture gradually into the creamed mixture, adding enough milk to give a soft dropping consistency. Butter the inside of a 1 litre (2 pint) capacity pudding basin, then pour in the mixture. Cover with a piece of well-buttered grease-proof paper or foil, making a pleat in the centre to allow the pudding to rise. Tie securely with string.

Put the basin in a steamer, or pan with enough boiling water to come halfway up the sides of the basin, and steam or boil for 1½-2 hours, topping up with more boiling water as necessary during steaming. Take the basin carefully out of the pan then untie and remove the grease-proof paper or foil. Turn the pudding out on to a warmed serving plate and serve hot with plain or Tipsy custard, or a Raspberry sauce (page 199).

Pineapple upside-down pudding

Serves 6
CALORIES PER PORTION: 650 (2723 kJ)
PROTEIN CONTENT PER PORTION: 7.5 grams
PREPARATION & COOKING TIME: 1 hour 10 minutes

The filling
350-400 g (12-14 oz) canned pineapple, drained and cut into chunks
100 g (4 oz) raw brown sugar
100 ml (4 fl oz) water
50 g (2 oz) butter or margarine
1 teaspoon ground cinnamon
2 teaspoons cornflour
finely grated rind and juice of 1 lemon

The topping
100 g (4 oz) wholemeal flour
2 teaspoons baking powder
1 teaspoon ground cinnamon
100 g (4 oz) butter or margarine
100 g (4 oz) raw brown sugar
2 large eggs, well beaten
2-4 tablespoons milk

To make the filling: put the pineapple in a pan with the sugar, water, butter or margarine and cinnamon. Bring to the boil, stirring until the sugar has dissolved, then lower the heat. Mix the cornflour to a paste with a little cold water then pour on some of the syrup, stirring constantly, add the lemon rind and juice and return to pan. Simmer until it thickens, stirring all the time, then remove from the heat and keep warm.

To make the topping: mix together the flour, baking powder and cinnamon in a bowl. Cream together the butter or margarine and sugar in a separate bowl until light and fluffy. Add the eggs a little at a time, beating well after each addition. Stir the dry mixture gradually into the creamed mixture, adding just enough milk to give a soft, dropping consistency. Set the oven at 200°C (400°F) Gas 6. Butter a 23 cm (9 in) diameter sandwich tin, then drain and arrange the pineapple in a single layer in the bottom of the tin. Pour over enough of the sauce to come halfway up the pineapple, then spread the cake mixture over the top.

Bake in the pre-heated oven for 30 minutes, then turn out the pudding carefully on to a warmed serving plate. Warm through the remaining sauce and pour it over the pudding. Serve hot with Custard sauce.

Almond castles

Serves 6
CALORIES PER PORTION: 250 (1046 kJ)
PROTEIN CONTENT PER PORTION: 6 grams
PREPARATION & COOKING TIME: 1 hour 10 minutes

125 g (4 oz) ground almonds
50 g (2 oz) wholemeal flour
1 teaspoon baking powder
a pinch of salt
50 g (2 oz) butter or margarine
50 g (2 oz) raw brown sugar
2 eggs, well beaten
1 tablespoon milk
1 tablespoon brandy
6 dates, finely chopped (optional)

Mix the almonds, flour, baking powder and salt in a bowl and set aside.

Cream the butter or margarine with the sugar in a separate bowl until light and fluffy. Add the eggs a little at a time, beating well after each addition.

Stir the dry ingredients gradually into the creamed mixture, adding the milk and brandy to give a soft, dropping consistency. Add the dates, if using.

Butter the insides of six dariole moulds, then divide the mixture equally between them, filling them not more than three-quarters full. Cover each mould with a piece of greaseproof paper or foil, making a pleat in the centre to allow the pudding to rise. Tie the paper securely with string. Put the moulds in a steamer, or pan with enough boiling water to come halfway up the sides of the moulds, and steam for 35 minutes, topping up with more boiling water as necessary during steaming.

Take the moulds carefully out of the pan, then untie and remove the grease-proof paper, or take off the foil. Turn the puddings out on to warmed served plates and serve hot with a Caramel or Custard sauce (page 198).

Bread and butter pudding with rum

This is a sophisticated version of the nursery pudding. Use day-old white bread, preferably home-made from unbleached flour.

Serves 4

CALORIES PER PORTION: 307 (1287 kJ)
PROTEIN CONTENT PER PORTION: 8 grams
PREPARATION & COOKING TIME: 1 hour 10 minutes

8 slices of white bread, crusts removed and quartered
a little melted butter
30 g (generous 1 oz) unsalted butter
50 g (2 oz) sultanas
300 ml (½ pint) milk
1 vanilla pod or ½ teaspoon vanilla essence
25-50 g (1-2 oz) raw brown sugar
finely grated rind of 2 oranges
2 eggs, well beaten with 1 tablespoon dark rum

Brush the inside of a shallow ovenproof dish with a little melted butter. Spread the slices of bread with the unsalted butter and arrange in the dish in overlapping circles, sprinkling the sultanas in between the slices.

Set the oven at 180°C (350°F) Gas 4. Heat the milk gently in a pan with the vanilla pod, if using, then set aside for a few minutes for the flavour to infuse. Remove the vanilla pod, return the pan to the heat, then stir in half the sugar and the orange rind. Continue stirring until all the sugar has dissolved.

Stir in the eggs and rum, and the vanilla essence if using this instead of the vanilla pod, then pour over the bread in the dish. Sprinkle the remaining sugar over the top and bake the pudding in the pre-heated oven for 40 minutes, or until the custard is set and the top is well browned. Serve hot.

Chocolate nut pudding

Serves 4

CALORIES PER PORTION: 510 (2125 kJ)
PROTEIN CONTENT PER PORTION: 11.5 grams
PREPARATION & COOKING TIME: 2 hours

100 g (4 oz) plain cooking chocolate
100 g (4 oz) fresh white breadcrumbs
50 g (2 oz) wholemeal flour
50 g (2 oz) finely ground mixed nuts
1 teaspoon baking powder
¼ teaspoon salt
50 g (2 oz) butter or margarine
50 g (2 oz) raw brown sugar
2 eggs, beaten
150 ml (¼ pint) milk

Put the breadcrumbs, flour, nuts, baking powder and salt in a bowl, then grate in the chocolate. Mix well and set aside.

Cream together the butter or margarine and sugar in a separate bowl until light and fluffy. Add the eggs a little at a time, beating well after each addition.

Stir the dry mixture gradually into the creamed mixture, adding just enough milk to give a soft, dropping consistency. Butter the inside of a 1 litre (2 pint) capacity pudding basin then pour in the mixture. Cover with a piece of well-buttered greaseproof paper or foil, making a pleat in the centre. Tie paper securely with string.

Put the basin in a steamer, or pan half filled with enough boiling water to come halfway up the sides of the basin, and steam for 1½ hours, topping up with more boiling water as necessary. Take the basin out of the pan, remove the greaseproof paper or foil and turn out on to a warmed serving plate and serve hot with Chocolate Sauce (page 199).

College pudding

Serves 6

CALORIES PER PORTION: 500 (2087 kJ)
PROTEIN CONTENT PER PORTION: 9 grams
PREPARATION & COOKING TIME: 1¾ hours

50 g (2 oz) wholemeal flour
125 g (4 oz) fresh wholemeal breadcrumbs
1 teaspoon baking powder
50 g (2 oz) each of currants and sultanas
pinch each of ground cloves, allspice, freshly grated nutmeg, cinnamon
125 g (4 oz) butter or margarine
50 g (2 oz) raw brown sugar
2 eggs, well beaten
3-4 tablespoons milk

Mix together the flour, breadcrumbs, baking powder, fruit and spices in a bowl. Cream together the butter or margarine and sugar in a separate bowl until light and fluffy. Add the eggs a little at a time, beating well after each addition.

Stir the dry mixture gradually into the creamed mixture, adding just enough milk to give a soft, dropping consistency. Butter the inside of a 1 litre (2 pint) capacity pudding basin, then pour in the mixture. Cover with a piece of well-buttered greaseproof paper or foil, making a pleat in the centre. Tie securely.

Put the basin in a steamer or pan with enough boiling water to come halfway up the sides of the basin and steam for about 1½ hours, topping up with more boiling water as necessary during steaming. Take the basin carefully out of the pan, then untie and remove the greaseproof paper or foil. Turn the pudding out.

Christmas pudding

This recipe makes two 1 litre (2 pint) puddings.

TOTAL CALORIES: 3480 (14,560 kJ)
TOTAL PROTEIN CONTENT: 69 grams
PREPARATION & COOKING TIME: 10-11 hours

125 g (4 oz) wholemeal flour
1½ teaspoons baking powder
125 g (4 oz) fresh wholemeal breadcrumbs
25 g (1 oz) ground almonds
½ teaspoon salt
¼ teaspoon freshly grated nutmeg
¼ teaspoon ground allspice
¼ teaspoon ground cinnamon
100 g (scant 4 oz) currants
100 g (scant 4 oz) sultanas
100 g (scant 4 oz) seedless raisins, chopped if large
100 g (scant 4 oz) coarsely chopped glacé cherries
50 g (2 oz) halved blanched almonds
125 g (4 oz) unsalted butter
50 g (2 oz) raw brown sugar
3 eggs, beaten
finely grated rind and juice of 2 oranges
6 tablespoons brandy
225 ml (8 fl oz) milk

Put all the dry ingredients in a large bowl and mix well. Add the fruit and nuts and stir until evenly distributed; set aside.

Cream together the butter and sugar in a separate bowl until light and fluffy. Add the eggs a little at a time, beating well after each addition. Stir in the orange rind and juice and 4 tablespoons of the brandy.

Stir the dry mixture gradually into the creamed mixture, adding enough milk to give a soft, dropping consistency. Liberally butter the insides of two 1 litre (2 pint) capacity pudding basins, then divide the mixture equally between them, pressing it down well. Cover each basin with a piece of well-buttered greaseproof paper or foil, making a pleat in the centre to allow the pudding to rise. Tie securely.

Put each basin in a steamer or pan half filled with boiling water and steam for 6 hours, topping up with more boiling water as necessary during steaming.

Take the basins carefully out of the pans and immediately remove the greaseproof paper or foil. Pour 1 tablespoon of brandy over the top of each pudding, leave until cold, then cover with clean greaseproof paper or foil, pleated as before. Tie securely with string, then store in a cool, dry place until required.

Before serving either of the Christmas puddings, steam for 4 more hours. Remove the basin carefully from the pan, then untie and discard the greaseproof paper or foil. Turn the pudding out on to a warmed serving plate.

Bavarois with brown sugar meringues

Serves 4
CALORIES PER PORTION: 380 (1602 kJ)
PROTEIN CONTENT PER PORTION: 9 grams
PREPARATION & CHILLING TIME: 3½ hours

2 teaspoons agar-agar
2 tablespoons cold water
450 ml (¾ pint) milk
1 tablespoon honey
grated rind of 2-3 oranges
3 egg yolks, well beaten
150 ml (¼ pint) whipping cream

The meringues
2 egg whites
100 g (4 oz) soft brown sugar
2 oranges, peeled and sliced (optional)

Mix together the agar-agar and water. Bring the milk, honey and orange rind to the boil and pour this onto the agar-agar and stir well.

Return to the saucepan and boil for 2 minutes. Add the hot milk mixture to the egg yolks, stirring continuously to prevent curdling. Return to the saucepan and heat gently, stirring all the time, until it has formed a thin custard. Strain off the orange rind at this point if you want a very smooth cream. Pour into a 600 ml (1 pint) mould and leave to cool, then refrigerate for 2 hours.

To make the meringues: set the oven at 110°C (225°F) Gas ¼. Beat the egg whites until they are stiff enough to stand in peaks. Add the sugar gradually while beating and continue to beat until all the sugar is mixed in and the mixture holds its shape. Using a teaspoon, dot walnut-sized pieces of meringue on to a well-buttered baking sheet, or one lined with a non-stick vegetable parchment. Bake in the cool oven for about 2 hours. To test when they are done, remove one from the oven and allow it to cool, then break it in half. Meringues are soggy until they are cold.

Whip the cream, turn out the Bavarois and spread thinly with the whipping cream. Dot meringues over the cream just before serving, and serve with slices of fresh orange, and the extra meringues. Or sandwich the extra meringues together with orange-flavoured whipped cream and serve for tea.

Make Brown sugar meringues to accompany the Bavarois, or sandwich them with orange-flavoured whipped cream and hand round as a teatime treat

Mont blanc

Serves 4
CALORIES PER PORTION: 435 (1825 kJ)
PROTEIN CONTENT PER PORTION: 3 grams
PREPARATION & CHILLING TIME: 2 hours

450 g (1 lb) chestnuts
300 ml (½ pint) whipping cream
1-2 tablespoons caster sugar, according
   to taste

Put the chestnuts in a pan, cover with water and boil for 30 minutes. Drain, then remove the peel and inner brown skin. Mash the chestnuts, then work in a blender or rub through a sieve. Leave to cool.

Put the chestnut purée in a bowl with half the cream, then beat until thick and light. Beat in sugar to taste. Turn the mixture out onto a serving plate and fork into a pyramid shape. Whip the remaining cream until just thick, then swirl it over the chestnut pyramid. Chill in the refrigerator for 1 hour, then serve with Almond biscuits (page 164).

Breads, Cakes and Pastries

*How wonderful to be grown up and no longer subject
to the sensible nursery law of 'bread and butter before
cakes and biscuits'. Even so, there could be something
of a dilemma . . .*

*If the bread is freshly home-baked, filling the kitchen
with the glorious aroma of loaves straight from the
oven, and there is a dish of pale, creamy farmhouse
butter waiting to be spread over each still-warm slice –
who could possibly leave room for cakes and biscuits?*

*And if the bread and butter were spread with a
delicious, home-made preserve (see the next chapter),
then the cakes may go back into their tins for another
day.*

*If bread is the staff of life, cakes and pastries must be
the rose in the buttonhole. And you can enjoy them at
any time of day – a slice of Madeira or rich fruit cake
with a glass of sherry (or Madeira, of course) – instead
of morning coffee or afternoon tea; sweet wholemeal
biscuits with your cheeseboard; tiny cream-filled
éclairs or palmiers for your teatime guests – my
recipes will suit all tastes. This is an indulgent
selection, with as many of my favourite recipes as we
had room to include. Choose the ones you will enjoy . . .*

Making bread, cakes and pastries

Read the recipe right through before you start; set the oven to the required temperature and allow enough time for it to reach it before you need to use it. Weigh and measure out all the ingredients and arrange them at the back of your work surface in order of use. If you follow this routine you will work much more efficiently and you won't have to go searching for some missing ingredient with your hands covered in dough.

Flour: Most of my recipes specify wholemeal flour; if you like a smooth-textured result, some of the bran can be removed by putting it through a coarse sieve, or by mixing it with a proportion of unbleached white flour, strong or soft as required. If the bran is sifted out, don't forget to weigh it and make up the quantity with extra sifted flour to the quantity originally specified. Strong flour (a flour with a high gluten content) should be used for making breads and Puff pastry; soft flour (with a low gluten content) is used when a lighter texture is required — in cakes and pastries, French bread and rolls.

Butter: If butter is to be creamed, bring it to room temperature first and, if it is still too hard, cut it into small pieces and stand it in a bowl in a barely warm oven for a few minutes to soften. Take care that it does not melt or turn oily. Butter for rubbing-in should be cold and hard so that it will not melt with the heat of your hands. If you are inclined to have warm hands, use a scone hoop or two knives and cut it with these.

Sugar: I have used raw brown sugar in most of the recipes because I like its flavour and value its mineral content. If you do not favour brown sugar, or feel it masks the flavour of any other ingredient, use white granulated or caster sugar instead. The texture of the finished cake or biscuit will be different, though.

Dried fruit: Choose good-quality dried fruit. If it is unwashed, put it into a bowl of clean cold water and leave it for five minutes, then immerse the hands in the water and rub the fruit gently between the fingers. Transfer the fruit into a colander or sieve and hold it under cold running water. Do not pour the bowl of water directly into the colander or you will also pour any sand or grit with it.

Drain the fruit thoroughly and dry between two clean kitchen towels. Spread out thinly on a baking sheet and place in a warm oven 100°C (225°F) Gas ¼ until any water on the surface has evaporated. This technique can also be used if the fruit is over-dry. Make sure that it is completely dry before you use it, or it can make your cake heavy.

Tins: When greasing tins, I use clarified butter. I also line the tins with non-stick vegetable parchment to prevent any chance of the cake sticking; it also helps prevents the cake burning if your oven is inclined to be 'hot'.

Yeast: Yeast is a living vegetable organism which requires moisture, sugar or carbohydrate to grow. The temperature of the milk or water in which it is mixed should be close to blood heat; any hotter and the yeast will be killed. Ensure that the liquid is no hotter than 38°C (100°F). If due attention is paid to these requirements, yeast cookery is as easy as any other form of cooking. If you are using dried yeast, follow the manufacturer's instructions to obtain the equivalent of fresh yeast. Otherwise, I would suggest adding it to the warm liquid with ½ teaspoon of sugar per 300 ml (½ pint) of water and leaving it in a warm place until frothy. This process take 20 minutes.

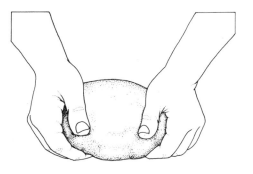

1. Roll the bread dough into a ball in the bowl and turn out onto a lightly-floured surface.

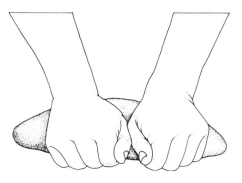

2. Working away from you, and always in the same direction, flatten the dough with the palms of your hands.

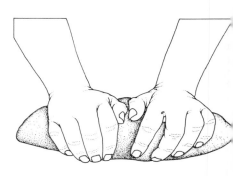

3. Using the 'heels' of your hands, push out the dough to form a long sausage shape.

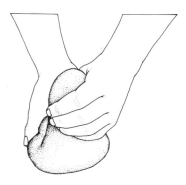

4. Roll up the dough, overlapping it in three layers, to make a ball again. Turn the dough ball sidewards.

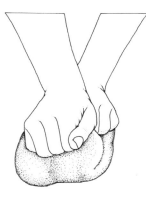

5. Flatten the ball and push it out again in front of you. This will stretch the dough again in a different direction.

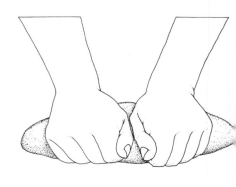

6. Continue pushing out, folding and turning, with a rhythmic rocking action, until the dough is elastic.

Basic quick bread

Makes two 450 g (1 lb) loaves

CALORIES PER LOAF: 1762 (7375 kJ)
PROTEIN CONTENT PER LOAF: 78 grams
PREPARATION & COOKING TIME: 1½-2 hours,
    including rising

1 tablespoon soft brown sugar
50 g (2 oz) fresh yeast (follow
    manufacturer's instructions for dried
    yeast)
600 ml (1 pint) lukewarm water
1 kg (2¼ lb) stone-ground wholemeal
    flour, or half wholemeal and half
    strong, unbleached white flour
2 teaspoons salt
50 g (2 oz) dried skimmed milk
    (optional)
1 tablespoon honey (optional)

Add the brown sugar and dried yeast to the warm water and mix well; fresh yeast should be first mixed into a paste with the brown sugar and a little of the water and then added to the rest of the warm water. Stand in a warm place for about 15 minutes until the liquid is frothy. Sift the flour and salt together into a bowl, keeping the bran for dusting the baking tins and the tops of the loaves. Add the dried skimmed milk and honey (if used) to the yeast liquid and stir until dissolved. (The honey helps to keep the bread moist.)

Pour the liquid into the flour and mix well with a spoon to a fairly firm dough, adding extra water if necessary.

Turn the dough out on to a floured board and knead with floured hands for 3-5 minutes, or until the dough becomes elastic. Divide the dough in half and place each half in a 450 g (1 lb) loaf tin. The tins should be well-buttered and dusted with some of the bran from the flour. Press the dough well down into the corners — it should come about halfway up the tin. Brush the top of the dough with a little milk and sprinkle over the remaining bran.

Cover the tins with a sheet of foil or greaseproof paper and leave in a warm place until the dough has doubled in size. The time this takes will vary, depending on the temperature of the room and the quality of the yeast.

Set the oven at 200°C (400°F) Gas 6. Place the loaves on the middle shelf of the pre-heated oven, and bake for 10 minutes, then reduce the temperature to 180°C (350°F) Gas 4 and continue baking for 20-30 minutes, or until the loaves sound hollow when taken out of their tins and tapped. The loaves can be turned upside down for the last few minutes if the undersides are not quite done. Allow to cool on a wire rack.

Rye bread

CALORIES PER LOAF: 1715 (7165 kJ)
PROTEIN CONTENT PER LOAF: 66 grams
PREPARATION & COOKING TIME: 2 hours,
    including rising

Use 650 g (22 oz) stone-ground wholemeal flour, or strong, unbleached white flour and 350 g (12 oz) finely ground rye flour; if coarsely-ground rye flour is used it may be necessary to reduce the liquid or add more flour to get a firm dough. Add ¼ teaspoon caraway seeds if liked. Rye flour needs longer kneading and should be put into the oven when it reaches the top of the tins, i.e. a little before it has doubled in size. Otherwise, follow the recipe for Basic quick bread.

Soya and wholemeal bread

CALORIES PER LOAF: 1750 (7320 kJ)
PROTEIN CONTENT PER LOAF: 98 grams
PREPARATION & COOKING TIME: 1½-2 hours,
    including rising

Use 225 g (8 oz) soya meal (preferably fully cooked) and 775 g (27 oz) wholemeal flour; a little more liquid might also be required. Otherwise, follow the recipe for Basic quick bread.

Soda bread

Makes one 450 g (1 lb) loaf

CALORIES: 1795 (7500 kJ)
PROTEIN: 69 grams
PREPARATION & COOKING TIME: 40 minutes

450 g (1 lb) wholemeal flour
2 teaspoons bicarbonate of soda
2 teaspoons cream of tartar
1 teaspoon salt
25 g (1 oz) butter
1 tablespoon honey
300 ml (½ pint) buttermilk

Sift the flour, bicarbonate of soda, cream of tartar and salt together, keeping the bran left in the sieve to one side. Melt the butter and honey in a pan over gentle heat, then remove the pan from the stove and stir in the cold buttermilk. Pour this into the flour and mix to a soft dough, adding a little extra water if necessary. Set the oven at 200°C (400°F) Gas 6.

Turn the dough on to a floured board and shape into a round 25 cm (9 in) in diameter. Mark the loaf into four triangular sections with the back of a knife and sprinkle the bran over the top. Place on a well-floured baking sheet and bake in the centre of the pre-heated oven for 30 minutes. Serve warm or cold.

Sourdough rye bread

CALORIES PER LOAF: 1715 (7165 kJ)
PROTEIN CONTENT PER LOAF: 66 grams
PREPARATION & COOKING TIME: overnight plus
    1 hour

650 g (22 oz) stone-ground wholemeal
    flour, or strong unbleached white
    flour
350 g (12 oz) finely ground rye flour
600 ml (1 pint) lukewarm water
50 g (2 oz) fresh yeast (follow the
    manufacturer's instructions for dried
    yeast)
1 tablespoon soft brown sugar
50 g (2 oz) dried skimmed milk
1 tablespoon honey (optional)
2 teaspoons salt

Mix the flours in a bowl, divide in half and set aside one half. Mix the other into a soft dough with a little more than half the water and cover the bowl. Leave in a warm place overnight, or up to 24 hours if a more sour dough is wanted.

Cream the yeast with the sugar, stir in the rest of the water and leave until it is frothy, about 15-20 minutes. Add the dried skimmed milk and honey, if used, and stir until dissolved. Add the salt to the remaining flour and pour in the yeast solution; stir until the liquid has been absorbed and then add the sour dough. Turn out onto a lightly floured board, and knead the two doughs together with well-floured hands, mixing them thoroughly until they are smooth and elastic. Then follow the recipe for Basic quick bread.

Croissants

Makes 12 croissants

CALORIES: 2875 (12030 kJ)
PROTEIN CONTENT: 61 grams
PREPARATION & COOKING TIME: 4 hours,
  including rising and resting

25 g (1 oz) fresh yeast (follow
  manufacturer's instructions for dried
  yeast)
1 teaspoon soft brown sugar
250 ml (scant ½ pint) lukewarm water
450 g (1 lb) strong, unbleached white
  flour
2 teaspoons salt
150 g (5 oz) butter
2 eggs, lightly beaten
1 tablespoon water

Add the yeast and sugar to the warm water and leave in a warm place until frothy; this will take 15-20 minutes. Sift the flour and salt into a bowl and, using a scone hoop or 2 knives, cut 25 g (1 oz) of the butter into the flour so that the mixture resembles coarse breadcrumbs.

Add one lightly beaten egg to the yeast liquid and pour it into the flour. Stir with a wooden spoon until most of the flour is mixed in.

Turn out on to a well-floured board and knead for about 5 minutes, or until the dough is completely smooth and elastic. Add a little more water or flour if necessary to make a firm dough. Roll out to a rectangle 40 cm by 25 cm (16 in by 10 in). Dust with flour and fold into three; wrap in greaseproof paper or foil and put into the freezing compartment of the refrigerator for 10 minutes.

Dust the remaining butter with flour and cut it into three equal pieces; *dust again with flour and cut the first butter into 16 even-sized cubes. Take the dough out of the freezer and unfold it — if necessary pressing it out to its original size — and place the cubes of butter, evenly spaced, over two-thirds of the rectangle, leaving 1 cm (½ in) border round the edges without butter.

Fold the unbuttered section over one-third of the length of the dough, then fold the double sections over the remaining buttered portion and seal the open edges with a slight pressure of the rolling pin. Turn the dough through 90° and flatten it out with the hands or by making a series of presses with the rolling pin. Then roll out to the original measurements.** Repeat from * to ** with the two remaining slabs of butter.

Fold the dough in three and wrap in greaseproof paper or foil and return to the freezer or freezing compartment for 30 minutes. Remove from the freezer or freezing compartment, remove the paper or foil and roll the dough to the same rectangular shape as before. Then turn the dough through 90° again and roll out to a rectangle 45 cm by 30 cm (18 in by 12 in). Dust with flour, fold in three, wrap in greaseproof paper and return to the freezer for a further 30 minutes. (This makes a total of five rollings.)

Remove the dough from the refrigerator, unfold it and mark it into six equal squares, each 15 cm (6 in) square. Cut each one into two triangles and brush lightly with some of the remaining eggs, well beaten with the tablespoon of water.

Roll each triangle up, starting from the base, and place on a baking sheet with the apex of the triangle underneath. Gently ease the dough into crescents, leaving plenty of room between them to allow for rising. Leave them at room temperature for 45 minutes to rise, then brush with a little more beaten egg. Bake in a pre-heated oven (middle shelf) at 220°C (425°F) Gas 7 for 15-20 minutes. Serve warm.

Corn bread rolls

Makes 12 rolls

CALORIES: 835 (3490 kJ)
PROTEIN CONTENT: 30 grams
PREPARATION & COOKING TIME: 30 minutes

175 g (6 oz) corn meal
1 teaspoon baking powder
½ teaspoon bicarbonate of soda
½ teaspoon salt
200 ml (⅓ pint) milk
1 egg, well beaten

Set the oven at 200°C (400°F) Gas 6. Mix the dry ingredients together and pour in the milk. Add the egg, mix thoroughly, and pour into 12 patty tins brushed with melted butter or margarine. Bake in the pre-heated oven for 15-20 minutes until well risen and golden brown.

Serve immediately. They make a very good accompaniment to fried eggs and grilled tomatoes for a special weekend breakfast.

In the basket: a fine selection of stone-ground wholemeal loaves and rolls. Left: brown Poppy seed plait. Right: this Fruit and honey loaf is delicious toasted and Front: wholemeal flour can also be used for making Croissants

Poppy seed plait

Makes 1 loaf

CALORIES: 2230 (9330 kJ)
PROTEIN CONTENT: 76 grams
PREPARATION & COOKING TIME: 2 hours

15 g (½ oz) fresh yeast
1 teaspoon raw brown sugar
300 ml (½ pint) lukewarm milk
½ teaspoon salt
450 g (1 lb) wholemeal flour
50 g (2 oz) softened butter
2 tablespoons raw brown sugar
1 tablespoon milk
1 tablespoon poppy seeds

Cream the yeast with the sugar and pour on half the milk. Leave to stand for 15-20 minutes until frothy. Sift the salt with the flour and pour in the yeast mixture. Add enough milk to make a soft dough, then add the softened butter. Knead until the dough is smooth and elastic. Place in a bowl lightly brushed with melted butter, cover and leave in a warm place until the dough has doubled in size. Take it out and knead it for a few moments, then divide it into three. Roll each portion into a 'sausage' about 30 cm (12 in) long and plait them together. Carefully place on a baking sheet brushed with melted butter and the ends tucked underneath, and leave in a warm place to rise (about 1 hour).

Meanwhile, make the sugar glaze by dissolving the sugar in the milk over moderate heat. Set the oven at 200°C (400°F) Gas 6. When the loaf is ready for baking, lightly brush the top with glaze and sprinkle with poppy seeds. Bake in the pre-heated oven for 20-30 minutes, or until it is well risen and sounds hollow when the base is tapped with the knuckles.

French bread and rolls

Makes 1 loaf or 18 rolls

CALORIES: 1995 (8340 kJ)
PROTEIN CONTENT: 52 grams
PREPARATION & COOKING TIME: 4½ hours, including rising and resting

150 ml (¼ pint) lukewarm milk
150 ml (¼ pint) lukewarm water
1 teaspoon soft brown sugar
20 g (¾ oz) fresh yeast (follow manufacturer's instructions for dried yeast)
450 g (1 lb) unbleached soft white flour
1 teaspoon salt
3 tablespoons melted butter

Mix together the milk, water, sugar and yeast and leave in a warm place for about 15 minutes, or until frothy. Add this to the sifted flour and salt and stir until most of the flour is mixed in. Turn out on to a floured board and knead, with floured hands, for 10 minutes to a soft dough.

Pour a tablespoon of melted butter into a warm bowl and put the dough into it, turning it over to coat it all with the butter. Cover and leave in a warm place for 1 hour or until it has doubled in size.

Turn the dough out of the bowl and knead on a floured board for another 3 minutes. Pour another tablespoon of melted butter into the bowl and leave the dough in it, after turning it over, for a further hour or until it has once again doubled in bulk. Knead again for 3 minutes.

Shape the dough into a long sausage and, unless you have a special French loaf tin, place it on a well-buttered baking sheet and leave in a warm place until well risen (about 2 hours). Bake for 20 minutes at 220°C (425°F) Gas 7 in the centre of a pre-heated oven. I make a foil trough with a flat base and walls of rolled-up foil, brush it liberally with melted butter and put the sausage-shaped dough in it; this gives the final loaf a better shape. Glaze the top with the remaining butter during the last 5 minutes of cooking; it may also be necessary to increase the temperature in order to get an attractive brown top.

Alternatively, shape the dough into 18 rolls. Put them on a well-buttered baking sheet and leave them to rise in a warm place for 1½-2 hours, or until they have doubled in size. Bake in the centre of a pre-heated oven at 220°C (425°F) Gas 7 for 15-20 minutes.

Cheese and herb bread and rolls

CALORIES: 2300 (9600 kJ)
PROTEIN CONTENT: 72 grams
PREPARATION & COOKING TIME: 4½ hours, including rising and resting

Add 75 g (3 oz) finely grated dry cheese and ½ teaspoon dried mixed herbs to the flour and salt and follow the recipe above.

Pitta

Makes 8 small or 4 large pitta

CALORIES: 850 (3560 kJ)
PROTEIN CONTENT: 31 grams
PREPARATION & COOKING TIME: 2-2½ hours

225 g (8 oz) wholemeal flour
½ teaspoon salt
8 g (¼ oz) fresh yeast (see manufacturer's instructions for dried yeast)
½ teaspoon raw brown sugar
150 ml (¼ pint) warm water
1 tablespoon olive oil

Sift the flour and salt into a bowl. Cream the yeast with the sugar, pour on the water and leave in a warm place for about 20 minutes until frothy. When the yeast mixture is ready, add to the flour and mix to a soft dough. Turn on to a lightly floured surface and knead until the dough is elastic and completely smooth. Pour the olive oil into a warm bowl and turn the dough in it until it is coated all over, cover and leave in a warm place for about 40 minutes or until it has doubled in size. 'Knock back' the dough on a lightly floured surface and knead until the oil is mixed in.

Set the oven at 200°C (400°F) Gas 6.

Divide into eight equal portions for small pitta or four for large ones and roll each portion into an oval shape about 7 mm (¼ in) thick. Place on greased baking sheets and bake in the pre-heated oven for 7-10 minutes until they are well risen and just about to colour. Remove them from the baking sheet and cool on a wire rack.

Serve warm as an accompaniment to Lebanese avocado salad, Greek salad or Vegetable kebabs, or slit them open at one end, cut through the dough to make a sort of pouch and fill with a vegetable curry.

Wholemeal scones

Makes about 6 scones

CALORIES: 1305 (5460 kJ)
PROTEIN CONTENT: 45 grams
PREPARATION & COOKING TIME: 30 minutes

225 g (8 oz) wholemeal flour
½ teaspoon salt
1 teaspoon baking powder
50 g (2 oz) butter
1 egg, well beaten
150 ml (¼ pint) milk
beaten egg for glazing (optional)

Sift the flour, salt and baking powder into a bowl and rub in the butter until the mixture resembles fine breadcrumbs. Add the egg and two-thirds of the milk and mix to a soft dough, adding more milk if necessary.

Set the oven at 200°C (400°F) Gas 6. Turn out on to a lightly floured surface and knead very lightly until smooth. Roll out to about 2 cm (1 in) thick and cut into rounds or triangles. Place on a floured baking sheet and bake in the pre-heated oven for about 10-15 minutes until well risen and browned. Glaze the tops if desired with a little beaten egg before putting the scones into the oven.

Fruit scones: Mix 1 tablespoon of raw brown sugar with the flour and add 50 g (2 oz) currants, sultanas, raisins or chopped dates after the butter has been rubbed in.

Cheese scones: Add 2 or 3 tablespoons of dry grated Cheddar cheese to the rubbed-in mixture and pinch of cayenne, if desired.

Fruit and honey loaf

CALORIES: 2190 (9160 kJ)
PROTEIN CONTENT: 62 grams
PREPARATION & COOKING TIME: 2 hours

15 g (½ oz) fresh yeast (follow
    manufacturer's instructions for dried
    yeast)
25 g (1 oz) raw brown sugar
150 ml (¼ pint) lukewarm milk
350 g (12 oz) wholemeal flour
½ teaspoon salt
50 g (2 oz) butter
2 tablespoons honey
1 egg, well beaten
50 g (2 oz) currants, washed and dried
50 g (2 oz) sultanas, washed and dried

Cream the yeast with 1 teaspoon of the sugar, stir in the milk and leave in a warm place for about 20 minutes until frothy. Meanwhile, sift the flour and salt into a bowl and rub in the butter. When the yeast mixture is ready, stir in the honey, the egg and the remaining sugar. Pour into the flour and mix thoroughly.

Turn out on to a lightly floured board and knead with well-floured hands until the dough is smooth: it should be fairly soft and almost sticky. Place in a bowl, lightly covered, and leave in a warm place until the dough has doubled in size.

Take it out and knead it for a few moments, adding the fruit as you do so.

Put the dough into a greased 1 kg (2 lb) loaf tin and leave to rise in a warm place for about 45 minutes, or until it has doubled in bulk. Set the oven at 200°C (400°F) Gas 6.

Bake the loaf in the pre-heated oven for 15 minutes, then reduce the heat to 180°C (350°F) Gas 4 and continue baking for a further 20 minutes. Allow to cool slightly in the tin, then turn out and place the loaf on a wire rack to continue cooling.

Fruit and honey loaf is particularly good toasted.

Bagels

Makes about 8 bagels

CALORIES: 1225 (5130 kJ)
PROTEIN CONTENT: 42 grams
PREPARATION & COOKING TIME: 2½ hours

225 g (8 oz) wholemeal flour
½ teaspoon salt
15 g (½ oz) fresh yeast (follow
    manufacturer's instructions for dried
    yeast)
15 g (½ oz) raw brown sugar
100 ml (4 fl oz) lukewarm milk
1 egg, well beaten
40 g (1½ oz) melted butter

Sift the flour and salt into a bowl. Cream the yeast with the sugar, add three-quarters of the milk and leave in a warm place for about 20 minutes until frothy. When the yeast solution is ready, add the beaten egg and melted butter. Pour this into the flour and mix to a fairly soft dough, adding the rest of the milk, if necessary.

Turn the dough on to a lightly floured surface and knead until smooth. Put it into a warm, buttered bowl and leave in a warm place until the dough has doubled its size. 'Knock back' the dough and knead it for a few minutes.

Take pieces of dough about the size of a golf ball and form into thin rolls about 13 cm (5 in) long by 1 cm (½ in) in diameter, form them into circles and pinch the ends together. Lay them on a well-floured baking sheet or board, cover with a floured cloth and leave in a warm place for 30 minutes until they have risen a little. Set the oven at 200°C (400°F) Gas 6. Lift gently and drop them one at a time into gently simmering water and cook until they float to the surface.

Remove from the pan with a draining spoon and lay on a well-oiled baking sheet. Bake in the pre-heated oven for 20-30 minutes until they are golden brown and crisp.

Popovers

Makes 4 or 6

CALORIES: 1490 (6230 kJ)
PROTEIN CONTENT: 70 grams
PREPARATION & COOKING TIME: 45 minutes

225 g (8 oz) wholemeal flour
½ teaspoon salt
4 eggs, well beaten
400 ml (¾ pint) milk
25 g (1 oz) melted butter

Set the oven at 200°C (400°F) Gas 6. Sift the flour and salt into a bowl. Mix the eggs with the milk and melted butter, pour into the flour and beat until the mixture is thick, creamy and completely smooth. Half-fill well-oiled patty tins with the mixture and bake in the pre-heated oven for 20-30 minutes, or until they are well risen and golden brown.

When cooked, the centres will be hollow. They are delicious filled with a vegetable ragôut or lightly cooked chopped vegetables in a cheese sauce and served hot.

Madeira cake

CALORIES: 2750 (11510 kJ)
PROTEIN CONTENT: 54 grams
PREPARATION & COOKING TIME: 1 ½ hours

150 g (5 oz) butter or margarine
150 g (5 oz) raw brown sugar
1 teaspoon finely grated lemon rind
3 eggs
250 g (generous 8 oz) wholemeal flour
½ teaspoon salt
1 ½ teaspoon baking powder
a little milk
5 cm (2 in) piece of candied peel, cut
    into thin slices

Line a 1 kg (2 lb) loaf tin with grease-proof paper or non-stick vegetable parchment. Brush this with a little melted butter or margarine. Cream the butter or margarine with the sugar and lemon rind until light and fluffy. Add the eggs one at a time, beating the mixture well after each addition.

Set the oven at 180°C (350°F) Gas 4. Sift the flour with the salt and baking powder, using a sieve which only removes the coarser bran. Fold the sifted flour into the creamed mixture, adding a little milk, if necessary, to make a soft dropping con-sistency. Transfer the mixture to the pre-pared tin and bake in the pre-heated oven for 20 minutes. Take out the tin, lay the slices of peel down the centre to decorate and continue cooking for a further 40 minutes, until the cake is well-risen, golden brown and firm. Test it by insert-ing a skewer into the centre; it should be clean when it is removed.

Remove the tin from the oven, allow to cool for 5 minutes then turn the cake out onto a wire rack. Carefully remove the paper and leave the cake to cool completely.

Wholemeal sandwich cake

TOTAL CALORIES: 2890 (12100 kJ)
TOTAL PROTEIN CONTENT: 45 grams
PREPARATION & COOKING TIME: 55 minutes

175 g (6 oz) wholemeal flour
1 ½ teaspoons baking powder
½ teaspoon salt
175 g (6 oz) butter or margarine
125 g (4 oz) raw brown sugar
3 eggs, well beaten
½ teaspoon vanilla essence
a little milk
3-4 tablespoons home-made jam, or
    Brown sugar butter cream (page 199)
a little icing sugar

Brush the insides of two 20 cm (8 in) diameter sandwich tins with melted butter or margarine. Mix together the flour, baking powder and salt. Cream together the butter or margarine and sugar until light and fluffy, then gradually add the eggs, beating well after each addition.

Set the oven at 180°C (350°F) Gas 4. Add the vanilla essence to the creamed mixture, then fold in the sifted ingredients, adding a little milk, if necessary, to make a soft, dropping consistency. Divide the mixture equally between the two prepared tins and level the surfaces.

Bake the cakes in the pre-heated oven for 25-30 minutes until they are well risen and just beginning to shrink away from the edges. Turn out on to a wire rack to cool. Sandwich the two cakes together with jam or Brown sugar butter cream and sprinkle the tops with icing sugar, or fill with flavoured Butter cream and top with glacé icing.

Variations: for a coffee-flavoured cake, use light brown sugar and sift instant coffee powder into the dry ingredients, then follow the method for Wholemeal sandwich cake. Fill with coffee or chocolate-flavoured butter cream and spread the top with chocolate glacé icing.

For a chocolate version, use light brown sugar and sift cocoa powder into the dry ingredients. Sandwich with Raspberry jam and top with Peanut butter icing (page 199).

Cherry cake

CALORIES: 3115 (13020 kJ)
PROTEIN CONTENT: 55 grams
PREPARATION & COOKING TIME: 1 ½ hours

Follow the basic recipe for Madeira cake but replace the lemon rind with ½ tea-spoon vanilla essence and omit the candied peel.

Dust 175 g (6 oz) glacé cherries with some of the flour mixture, stir them in with the rest of the flour and bake as for the Madeira cake.

Cut-and-come-again cake

CALORIES: 2690 (11260 kJ)
PROTEIN CONTENT: 59 grams
PREPARATION AND COOKING TIME: 2¼ hours

225 g (generous 8 oz) wholemeal flour
2 teaspoons baking powder
1 teaspoon ground allspice
1 teaspoon salt
125 g (4 oz) butter or margarine
50 g (2 oz) ground almonds
50 g (2 oz) currants, washed and dried
50 g (2 oz) sultanas, washed and dried
2 tablespoons honey
150 ml (¼ pint) milk
2 eggs, well beaten

Set the oven at 170°C (325°F) Gas 3. Brush a 15 cm (6 in) round deep cake tin with a little melted butter or margarine and cut a round of greaseproof paper or non-stick vegetable parchment to line the base. Brush this, too, with a little melted butter or margarine.

Mix together the flour, baking powder, allspice and salt in a bowl and rub in the butter or margarine until the mixture looks like fine breadcrumbs. Stir in the ground almonds and dried fruit. Warm the honey over gentle heat until melted, remove the pan from the stove and stir in the milk and eggs. Pour this into the dry

ingredients in the bowl and mix thoroughly.

Spoon the mixture into the prepared cake tin and bake in the pre-heated oven for about 1¾ hours until well risen and firm — a skewer inserted into the centre should come out clean. Leave the cake in the tin for about 10 minutes, then turn out on to a wire rack to cool.

Slice in half when cool and sandwich the two halves together with Almond paste (page 199). For a special occasion, the top can be covered with an icing, or frosting.

Genoese sponge cake

CALORIES: 1150 (4810 kJ)
PROTEIN CONTENT: 31 grams
PREPARATION & COOKING TIME: 50-60 minutes
for basic sponge

3 large eggs
50 g (2 oz) butter or margarine, plus a
little extra for brushing tins
75 g (3 oz) raw brown sugar
½ teaspoon vanilla essence
75 g (3 oz) wholemeal flour

Set the oven at 180°C (350°F) Gas 4. Melt the butter or margarine in a small pan over gentle heat, then allow to cool. Lightly brush the inside of an 18 cm (7 in) square deep cake tin with melted butter or margarine. Line the bottom with a circle of greaseproof paper or non-stick vegetable parchment and lightly brush this, too, with butter or margarine.

Whisk the eggs and sugar in a bowl until

thick and mousse-like and the whisk leaves a trail on top of the mixture when lifted. If you are using a hand whisk, it helps to speed up the process if you place the bowl over a pan of hot water while whisking. When the egg and sugar mixture is ready, check that the melted butter or margarine is ready, add the vanilla essence to it and pour it on to the eggs while still whisking. Mix the flour in and fold it in gently.

Pour into the prepared cake tin and bake in the pre-heated oven for 30 minutes, or until the cake is firm when lightly pressed with the fingertips. Carefully turn the cake on to a wire rack, peel off the paper and leave to cool. Dust with icing sugar before serving.

Variations: make double the quantity, bake in two 18 cm (7 in) diameter sandwich tins and sandwich the cooled cakes together with jam and whipped cream. Cover the tops and sides with Brown sugar frosting (page 199) or plain or flavoured glacé icing.

For Coffee Genoese cake, flavour the basic mixture by adding instant coffee powder to the eggs and sugar while whisking, and cover the finished cake with coffee flavoured Brown sugar frosting or glacé icing. Use light brown sugar if you find the darkest raw brown sugar masks the coffee flavour.

Try making double quantity of the Genoese cake, adding cocoa powder to the eggs and sugar, and sandwiching the finished cakes with chocolate butter cream and topping with chocolate icing.

Behind left: a rich-tasting, fruit-filled Cut-and-come-again cake, sandwiched with Almond paste. Behind right: this Cherry cake will soon become a family favourite. Right: crisp, satisfying wholemeal pastry makes a special Apple pie and Front: home-made Black cherry jam fills this Wholemeal sponge

Old-fashioned sponge ring

CALORIES: 1795 (7520 kJ)
PROTEIN CONTENT: 61 grams
PREPARATION AND COOKING TIME: 1½ hours

6 eggs, separated
200 g (7 oz) raw brown sugar
150 g (5 oz) wholemeal flour
1 teaspoon baking powder
½ teaspoon salt
100 ml (4 fl oz) boiling water
a little icing sugar

Whisk the egg yolks with the sugar, either with an electric whisk, or with a hand whisk over a pan of hot water, until the mixture is thick and mousse-like and will leave a trail when the whisk is lifted. Remove from the pan and continue whisking until cool.

Set the oven at 170°C (325°F) Gas 3. Sift the flour with the baking powder and salt using a sieve which only removes the coarser bran, then whisk the egg whites until they stand in peaks. Fold the flour into the whisked egg yolks, adding a little of the boiling water after each addition. Lastly, fold in the egg whites and pour the mixture into an unbuttered 25 cm (10 in) diameter deep ring mould with a remove-able base (you can butter just the base).

Bake in the pre-heated oven for about 65 minutes, or until the mixture is firm to the touch. To prevent the cake from sinking, turn the tin upside down and stand it over the neck of a milk bottle. When the cake is quite cold, remove the milk bottle and turn the cake out of the mould — you may have to use a sharp knife to cut between cake and mould for the best results. Dust the top with icing sugar.

Alternatively, slice the cake into two layers and sandwich them together with jam and whipped cream. Ice the top and sides with Brown sugar frosting (page 199) or plain or flavoured glacé icing.

Swiss roll

CALORIES: 1580 (6610 kJ)
PROTEIN CONTENT: 45 grams
PREPARATION & COOKING TIME: 1 hour, excluding cooling

3 eggs, weighed in their shells
the weight of the eggs in raw brown sugar and sifted wholemeal flour

Set the oven at 180°C (350°F) Gas 4. Line a 35 cm (14 in) by 24 cm (9½ in) shallow baking tin or Swiss roll tin with grease-proof paper or non-stick vegetable parchment. Brush with a little melted butter.

Put the eggs and sugar into a bowl and whisk with an electric whisk, or place the bowl over a pan of hot water and whisk with a hand whisk until light and foamy, and the whisk, when lifted, leaves a thick trail or ribbon on the surface. (It is very much easier if you use an electric whisk.) Fold in the flour, turn the mixture into the prepared tin and bake for 20-30 minutes, or until the sponge is just firm when pressed lightly with the finger tips.

Remove from the oven and turn out on to a piece of greaseproof paper or non-stick vegetable parchment. Peel off the lining paper and immediately roll up the sponge. Leave to get quite cold and then carefully unroll and spread with jam, or fresh fruit such as sliced pears or peaches and whipped cream, or Brown sugar butter cream (page 199). Sprinkle a little icing sugar over the top.

Sour cream lemon cake

CALORIES: 1950 (8150 kJ)
PROTEIN CONTENT: 51 grams
PREPARATION & COOKING TIME: 1½ hours

175 g (6 oz) wholemeal flour
1 teaspoon baking powder
½ teaspoon bicarbonate of soda
½ teaspoon salt
225 ml (generous 8 fl oz) sour cream
2-3 eggs
175 g (6 oz) raw brown sugar
1 teaspoon grated lemon rind
1 tablespoon icing sugar

Set the oven at 180°C (350°F) Gas 4. Brush the inside of an 18 cm (7 in) square deep cake tin with melted butter or margarine. Sift the flour into a bowl with the baking powder, bicarbonate of soda and salt.

Whisk the eggs with the sugar until very frothy — this should take about 5 minutes with an electric mixer at high speed, longer with a hand whisk. To speed up the process, if you are using a hand whisk, place the bowl over a pan of very hot water and continue whisking. When the eggs and sugar are thick enough to leave a trail when the whisk is lifted, stir in the cream and lemon rind. Fold in the flour and pour into the prepared cake tin.

Bake in the pre-heated oven for 35-45 minutes until the cake is risen, golden brown and just firm when pressed lightly with the finger tips. Leave the cake in the tin for 5 minutes, then turn on to a wire rack to cool. Dust the top with icing sugar.

Boston molasses cake

CALORIES: 3140 (13140 kJ)
PROTEIN CONTENT: 47 grams
PREPARATION & COOKING TIME: 1¾ hours

125 g (4 oz) butter or margarine
125 g (4 oz) golden syrup
125 g (4 oz) molasses
75 g (3 oz) raw brown sugar
225 g (generous 8 oz) wholemeal flour
½ teaspoon salt
1 teaspoon ground allspice
2 teaspoons baking powder
2 eggs, well beaten
125 g (4 oz) raisins, washed and dried

Set the oven at 170°C (325°F) Gas 3. Line an 18 cm (7 in) square deep cake tin with greaseproof paper, or non-stick vegetable parchment and brush with a little melted butter or margarine.

Put the butter or margarine, syrup, molasses and sugar into a pan over gentle heat until the butter has melted, stirring occasionally to prevent the sugar from sticking. Remove the pan from the heat. Sift together the flour, salt, allspice and baking powder, then stir the eggs into the melted mixture, followed by the sifted ingredients and, lastly, the raisins. Mix thoroughly and pour into the cake tin.

Bake in the pre-heated oven for 1¼-1½ hours, or until the cake is just beginning to shrink away from the edges of the tin. Turn out to cool on a wire rack.

Honey spice cake

CALORIES: 2770 (11560 kJ)
PROTEIN CONTENT: 45 grams
PREPARATION AND COOKING TIME: 1¾ hours

Follow the recipe for Boston molasses cake, but replace syrup and molasses with 225 g (8 oz) honey and omit the raisins.

Spiced apple cake

CALORIES: 4120 (17240 kJ)
PROTEIN CONTENT: 68 grams
PREPARATION & COOKING TIME: 1 hour

450 g (1 lb) peeled and cored cooking
    apples (about 800 g/1¾ lb whole)
200 ml (⅓ pint) hot water
300 g (11 oz) raw brown sugar
125 g (4 oz) soft butter or margarine
3 eggs, well beaten
½ teaspoon finely grated orange rind
350 g (12 oz) wholemeal flour

½ teaspoon baking powder
1½ teaspoons bicarbonate of soda
1½ teaspoons salt
½ teaspoon each of ground cinnamon,
    ground cloves and allspice
50 g (2 oz) walnut pieces
125 g (4 oz) raisins

Set the oven at 180°C (350°F) Gas 4 and line two 23 cm (9 in) diameter sandwich tins with greaseproof paper or non-stick vegetable parchment. Brush the insides of the tins with a little melted butter or margarine.

Cook the apples in half the water until they are soft; rub them through a sieve and mix in the sugar, butter or margarine,

the eggs, orange rind and remaining water. Sift together all the dry ingredients and stir them into the apple mixture. Beat the mixture thoroughly, then stir in the nuts and raisins.

Pour the mixture into the two prepared sandwich tins and bake in the pre-heated oven for 35-40 minutes, or until the cakes are well risen, golden brown and firm. Turn them out onto a lightly greased wire rack, carefully remove the greaseproof paper or parchment and leave the cakes to get quite cold.

Sandwich them together with Brown sugar butter cream (page 199), using one third as a filling and the rest for covering the top and sides.

Apple strudel

Serves 6
CALORIES PER PORTION: 740 (3107 kJ)
PROTEIN CONTENT PER PORTION: 9.5 grams
PREPARATION & COOKING TIME: 2 hours

The pastry
225 g (8 oz) unbleached white flour
150 g (5 oz) unsalted butter
150 ml (¼ pint) warm water
a little icing sugar

The filling
100 g (4 oz) wholemeal breadcrumbs
    fried in 50 g (2 oz) unsalted butter
    until just beginning to crisp
450 g (1 lb) cooking apples, peeled,
    cored, chopped and soaked in the
    juice of 2 lemons
50 g (2 oz) raw brown sugar
25 g (1 oz) slivered blanched almonds
50 g (2 oz) sultanas
¼ teaspoon freshly grated nutmeg
¼ teaspoon ground cinnamon

1. Put your hands under the dough on
the cloth and lift, moving outwards.
2. Roll up the pastry with the filling and
crumbs, using the cloth to help.

Put the flour into a warmed bowl. Melt 50 g (2 oz) of the butter in the water and pour it, little by little, into the flour, stirring all the time. Knead until you have a smooth dough. Take it out of the bowl and knead it for 10 minutes — the dough should be soft and pliable so add a little more warm water if it feels dry. Return to the warmed bowl and cover and leave it for 30 minutes.

Lay a clean cloth about 1 m (3 ft) square on a table where you can walk around. Sprinkle the cloth with flour and place the rested dough in the centre. Gently roll it out to a square and then place the hands under the dough and carefully stretch it outwards. Melt the remaining butter and brush a little of it over the dough if it looks as though it is getting dry. Continue stretching until the dough is so thin you can almost read through it. Try to keep it the same thickness all over with slightly thicker edges to work on.

When all the dough is of a uniform thickness, brush it lightly all over with most of the melted butter and cut off the thick outer edges. Set the oven at 180°C (350°F) Gas 4. Neaten the shape and sprinkle the breadcrumbs along one side,

followed by the apples, the sugar, the almonds, the sultanas and the spices, keeping the filling neatly along one end of the strudel. Then, by lifting up the cloth, gently roll the strudel up so that the filling is trapped between layers of very thin buttery pastry. Form the roll into a horseshoe and gently ease it on to a well-buttered baking sheet. Brush the top liberally with the remaining melted butter and bake in the centre of the pre-heated oven for 30-40 minutes, or until the pastry is golden brown and crisp.

Remove from the baking sheet, sprinkle the top with icing sugar and serve hot or cold with lightly whipped cream.

While this recipe seems rather a performance, it is not nearly as difficult as it might appear at first sight. Practise the first time with half quantities; if holes appear in the dough, repair them by making a patch with a piece from the edge, otherwise the hole will grow. Some cooks work section by section; I work from the centre outwards, and in Austria it is generally done by four people working around a square table. When you have mastered it, you will realise why the Strudel is one of the most popular sweets in Europe.

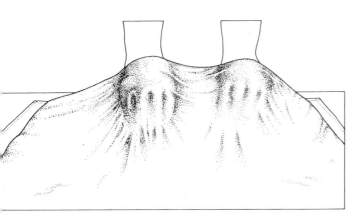
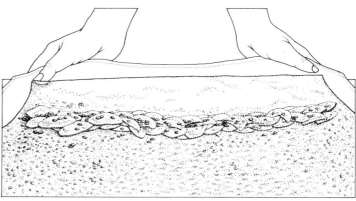

Chocolate nut cake with Ricotta filling

Serves 8
CALORIES PER PORTION: 710 (2972 kJ)
PROTEIN CONTENT PER PORTION: 10 grams
PREPARATION & COOKING TIME: 1 hour
CHILLING TIME: overnight

150 g (5 oz) butter
150 g (5 oz) soft brown sugar
3 eggs
100 g (4 oz) chopped walnuts
150 g (5 oz) wholemeal flour
1 teaspoon baking powder
1 tablespoon cocoa powder
⅛ teaspoon salt
8 tablespoons orange juice
4 tablespoons raspberry jam, heated and sieved
300 ml (½ pint) double cream
about 150 g (5 oz) Ricotta or curd cheese
a few walnut halves

Set the oven at 180°C (350°F) Gas 4. Cream together the butter and sugar until light and fluffy. Add the eggs, one at a time, beating well after each addition. Add the chopped walnuts. Sieve together the flour, baking powder, cocoa and salt. Fold this into the creamed mixture, adding a little more milk if necessary to give a soft dropping consistency.

Divide the mixture evenly between two well-buttered 18 cm (7 in) diameter sandwich tins and bake in the centre of the pre-heated oven for 30 minutes. Turn out on to a wire rack to cool.

Slice each cake in half and sprinkle 2 tablespoons of orange juice over each layer, then spread a thin layer of raspberry jam on three of the layers. Cover and leave in the refrigerator overnight.

A few hours before serving, whip the cream and mix the Ricotta or curd cheese with 2 tablespoons of it; spread this over each layer of raspberry jam. Sandwich the four layers together with the plain one on top; spread the rest of the whipped cream over the top of the cake and decorate with walnut halves. Serve well chilled.

Hazelnut cake

Serves 6
CALORIES PER PORTION: 460 (1930 kJ)
PROTEIN CONTENT PER PORTION: 5.5 grams
PREPARATION & CHILLING TIME: 2½ hours

The cake
4 egg whites
225 g (8 oz) raw brown sugar
½ teaspoon cider vinegar
150 g (5 oz) milled or finely ground hazelnuts
a little melted butter

The filling
50 g (2 oz) plain cooking chocolate, broken into small pieces
2 tablespoons water
300 ml (½ pint) whipping cream

To make the cake: beat the egg whites until stiff enough to stand in peaks, then add the sugar a third at a time, beating well after each addition. Beat in the vinegar, then continue beating until the mixture is completely smooth and stiff. Fold in the hazelnuts.

Set the oven at 180°C (350°F) Gas 4. Line two buttered 20 cm (8 in) diameter round cake tins with non-stick vegetable parchment, then brush the parchment liberally with melted butter. Divide the cake mixture equally between the tins, then bake in the pre-heated oven for 15 minutes.

Reduce the heat to 130°C (250°F) Gas ½ and dry out the meringues for a further 1 hour, or until the top is firm when lightly pressed with the fingertips. Cover the cakes with greaseproof paper or foil if the tops become too brown during baking. Turn the cakes out onto a wire rack, remove the parchment, then leave to cool.

To make the filling: put the chocolate and water in a small, heavy pan and heat very gently, stirring constantly, until the chocolate has melted, then remove the pan from the heat and allow to cool. Whip the cream until thick, then stir in the melted chocolate until evenly mixed.

Spread about three-quarters of the cream filling over one of the cakes, then place the other cake on top and sandwich together. Swirl the remaining cream over the top of the cake, then chill in the refrigerator before serving.

Mille feuilles

Serves 6
CALORIES PER PORTION: 525 (2203 kJ)
PROTEIN CONTENT PER PORTION: 3 grams
PREPARATION & COOKING TIME: 45 minutes
CHILLING TIME: 1 hour

125 g (4 oz) basic Puff pastry (quarter portion of recipe on page 194)
125 g (4 oz) icing sugar
175 g (6 oz) raspberry jam
300 ml (½ pint) whipping cream

Set the oven at 230°C (450°F) Gas 8. Roll out the dough into a 25 cm (10 in) square and cut it in half. Place the two rectangles on a lightly oiled baking sheet and bake in the pre-heated oven for 15-20 minutes or until well risen and golden brown. Remove from the oven and carefully transfer to a wire tray to cool.

Sift the icing sugar into a bowl and gradually stir in just enough water to make a coating icing.

When the pastry is quite cold, cut each rectangle crossways in half. Spread three of the pastry slices with a layer of jam and whipped cream, then carefully lift one on top of the other. Finish with the plain slice of pastry. Spread with the icing and serve chilled.

Chocolate éclairs

Makes about 12
CALORIES PER PORTION: 460 (1920 kJ)
PROTEIN CONTENT PER PORTION: 6 grams
PREPARATION & COOKING TIME: 1½ hours

1 quantity basic Choux pastry (page 194)
300 ml (½ pint) whipping cream
1 tablespoon raw brown sugar
75 g (3 oz) chocolate

Set the oven at 180°C (350°F) Gas 4. Using a 2 cm (¾ in) plain nozzle, pipe 7.5 cm (3 in) fingers of the dough on to well-oiled baking sheets. Use a dampened knife to cut off the dough at the end of each finger and leave about 4 cm (1½ in) between each to allow for rising. Place in the pre-heated oven and increase the temperature to 220°C (425°F) Gas 7. Bake for 20 minutes then check by removing one and breaking it in half. If it is not cooked in the middle, continue baking the rest at the original, lower temperature for 10-15 minutes more.

Remove from the oven, slice halfway through to allow the steam to escape and leave on a wire rack to cool.

When the éclairs are completely cold, whip the cream with the sugar, if used, and pipe into the éclairs. Melt the chocolate in a bowl set over hot water. Coat the tops and allow to set.

Palmiers

Makes 6–8
CALORIES PER PORTION: 110 (457 kJ)
PROTEIN CONTENT PER PORTION: 1 gram
PREPARATION & COOKING: 30 minutes

*125 g (4 oz) basic Puff pastry (quarter
quantity of recipe on page 194)*
*25 g (1 oz) caster sugar, mixed with ½
teaspoon ground cinnamon (optional)*

Sprinkle a marble slab or work surface
lightly with flour and roll out the dough
to a rectangle 30 × 25 cm (12 × 10 in).
Brush it lightly but evenly with water,

then sprinkle over half the sugar mixture
and gently press it in. Fold the edge of
each long side into the centre. Brush again
lightly with water, sprinkle with half the
remaining sugar mixture and press it in
gently. Fold the edge of each long side
into the centre again, making a narrow
rectangle about 30 × 6 cm (12 × 2½ in).
Fold in half and cut crosswise into 12
thick slices.

Set the oven at 200°C (400°F) Gas 6.
Lay each slice flat on the work surface
and roll it out lightly and carefully to
about 5 mm (¼ in) thick, taking care that

the folded layers are spread out by the
pressure of the rolling pin. Place on a well-
oiled baking sheet, leaving about 2.5 cm
(1 in) between each one to allow space for
spreading. Brush the tops lightly with
water, sprinkle with the remaining sugar
mixture and bake in the pre-heated oven
for about 15 minutes, taking care that the
sugar does not burn. If the Palmiers are
not completely crisp after 15 minutes baking, transfer to a wire tray and return to
the oven for a few more minutes.

Serve cold, singly, or sandwiched
together with lightly whipped cream.

Eccles cakes

Makes 12 small cakes
CALORIES PER PORTION: 145 (610 kJ)
PROTEIN CONTENT PER PORTION: 1.5 grams
PREPARATION & COOKING TIME: 45 minutes

25 g (1 oz) unsalted butter
25 g (1 oz) raw brown sugar
25 g (1 oz) finely chopped mixed peel
50 g (2 oz) currants
grated rind and juice of a small lemon
¼ teaspoon ground allspice
*125 g (4 oz) Rough Puff pastry (half
quantity of recipe on page 194)*

Set the oven at 200°C (400°F) Gas 6. Melt
the butter in a small saucepan; add the
brown sugar, peel, currants, lemon rind
and juice and allspice and allow to cool.

Meanwhile, roll out the dough to about
5 mm (a little less than ¼ in) thick and
cut into 7.5 cm (3 in) rounds. Place the
dough trimmings one on top of the other,
re-roll them and cut into rounds as before.
There should be about 12 in all. Divide
the cooled filling between the dough
rounds and, gathering up the edges, form
them into little balls.

Place on an oiled baking sheet with the
joins underneath and flatten them with
gentle hand pressure until they are about
1 cm (½ in) thick. Using a sharp knife,
mark the tops with a lattice pattern, then
chill in the refrigerator for 20 minutes.
Brush the tops with beaten egg and sprinkle with a little caster sugar. Bake for 15-
20 minutes until golden brown and well
risen. Serve hot or cold.

*Eccles cakes, Palmiers sandwiched
with whipped cream and Chocolate
éclairs – why not have one of each?*

To prepare, bake and glaze a flan case

For a really crisp flan, bake the case 'blind' before adding any filling. This also helps eliminate the possibility of the filling breaking through the pastry before it is cooked.

To line the flan ring, roll out the dough into a round, about 4 mm (3/16 in) thick and about 5 cm (2 in) bigger in diameter than the ring. Unless the flan ring has a removable base, place it on a baking sheet. Lift the dough on the rolling pin and gently lay it over the ring. Without stretching it, carefully ease the dough into the ring, pressing it down well so no air gets trapped underneath; this will cause the pastry to rise in bubbles during cooking. Press the dough to the sides, then trim the excess from the edges. Line with a sheet of foil or greaseproof paper and half-fill with dried beans.

To bake the flan case, place in a pre-heated oven 200°C (400°F) Gas 6, and bake for 15 minutes. Remove the baking beans and foil or paper lining. Lower the heat to 180°C (350°F) Gas 4 and bake for a further 10-15 minutes, or until the pastry is crisp and beginning to brown. If bubbles do form in the pastry, prick with a skewer to release the air.

To glaze the flan case, while still hot brush the pastry with egg white for a savoury flan, or with strained, melted apricot jam for a sweet flan.

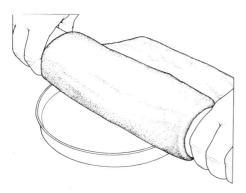

1. Wrap the rolled pastry around the rolling pin to lift it then unroll over the ring or quiche pan.

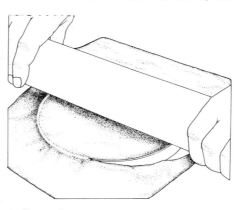

2. Press the pastry into the ring or pan to fit, using a bent forefinger. Roll the pin across to remove excess.

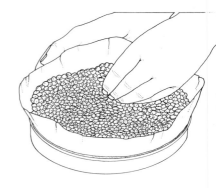

3. Line with foil then dried beans, filling to the sides. Bake first with the lining and then without to crisp it.

Old-fashioned custard pie

CALORIES PER PORTION: 595 (2482 kJ)
PROTEIN CONTENT PER PORTION: 17.5 grams
PREPARATION & COOKING TIME: 1 hour
COOLING & CHILLING TIME: 2 hours

pre-baked 20 cm (8 in) flan case, made with Wholemeal shortcrust pastry (page 194) and glazed with apricot jam
3 eggs
1 egg yolk
50 g (2 oz) raw brown sugar
¼ teaspoon grated nutmeg
¼ teaspoon salt
600 ml (1 pint) milk
½ teaspoon vanilla essence

Set the oven at 180°C (350°F) Gas 4. Place the flan case on a baking sheet. Beat the eggs and egg yolk with the sugar, nutmeg and salt until light and creamy. Bring the milk to the boil and pour it slowly on to the eggs, stirring continuously. Return the mixture to the saucepan and cook, stirring, until the custard thickens to coating consistency. Do not allow it to boil. Stir in the vanilla essence and pour the filling into the flan case. Bake in the pre-heated oven for 30-45 minutes, or until the custard has set. Take care not to overcook the pie, or the custard will become watery. Allow to cool, then chill for 1 hour before serving.

Peanut butter flan

CALORIES PER PORTION: 865 (3617 kJ)
PROTEIN CONTENT PER PORTION: 22 grams
PREPARATION & COOKING TIME: 30 minutes
COOLING AND CHILLING TIME: 1½-2 hours

125 g (4 oz) crunchy unsalted peanut butter
pre-baked 20 cm (8 in) flan case, made with Wholemeal shortcrust pastry (page 194) and glazed with jam
125 g (4 oz) raw brown sugar
3 tablespoons cornflour
½ teaspoon salt
600 ml (1 pint) milk
2 eggs, well beaten
1 teaspoon vanilla essence

Place the flan case on a serving plate. Mix together the sugar, cornflour and salt in a saucepan and gradually stir in the milk. Stir in the peanut butter a teaspoonful at a time. Place the pan over a moderate heat and bring to the boil, stirring continuously. Simmer until the mixture thickens and the peanut butter is well mixed in. Pour slowly on to the eggs, stirring vigorously, then return the mixture to the pan and bring back to the boil, stirring. Lower the heat and simmer the filling for 1 minute. Allow to cool for a few minutes, then stir in the vanilla essence. Pour into the flan case, leave to cool, then chill the flan for about 1 hour before serving.

Pumpkin pie

CALORIES PER PORTION: 542 (2272 kJ)
PROTEIN CONTENT PER PORTION: 13 grams
PREPARATION & COOKING TIME: 1 hour

350 g (12 oz) cooked pumpkin about 550 g (1¼ lb) uncooked
pre-baked 20 cm (8 in) flan case, made with Wholemeal shortcrust pastry (page 194)
¼ teaspoon salt
300 ml (½ pint) milk
2 eggs, well beaten
75 g (3 oz) raw brown sugar
1 teaspoon ground cinnamon
½ teaspoon ground ginger
½ teaspoon grated nutmeg
6 cloves, finely ground, or ¼ teaspoon ground cloves
1 teaspoon grated orange rind

Set the oven at 200°F) Gas 6. Place the flan case on a well-oiled baking sheet. Mix all the remaining ingredients together thoroughly and pour into the prepared flan case. Bake in the preheated oven for 45 minutes until the filling has set, then serve hot or cold.

Linzer torte

CALORIES PER PORTION: 725 (3025 kJ)
PROTEIN CONTENT PER PORTION: 12 grams
PREPARATION & COOKING TIME: 1½ hours

125 g (4 oz) ground hazelnuts
125 g (4 oz) wholemeal flour
½ teaspoon ground cinnamon
¼ teaspoon salt
1 teaspoon grated lemon rind
125 g (4 oz) unsalted butter
50 g (2 oz) raw brown sugar
3 eggs, well beaten
225 g (8 oz) raspberry jam

Set the oven at 180°C (350°F) Gas 4. Mix together the nuts, flour, cinnamon, salt and lemon rind. Cream the butter with the sugar until very soft and fluffy, then gradually add about three-quarters of the eggs, beating thoroughly between each addition. Add the nut mixture and mix to a firm dough, adding a little more egg, if necessary. Put a little less than a quarter of the dough on one side.

Oil a 20 cm (8 in) flan ring and baking sheet and place the larger portion of dough in the centre. Press it out so that it covers the bottom and sides of the ring evenly, and spread it with the raspberry jam. Roll out the remaining dough and cut into strips about 1 cm (½ in) and make a lattice over the jam. Bake in the pre-heated oven for 1 hour, until lightly browned and crisp.

Cool on a wire rack and serve with lightly whipped cream as a dessert, or on its own as an accompaniment to morning coffee.

Pecan pie

CALORIES PER PORTION: 900 (3770 kJ)
PROTEIN CONTENT PER PORTION: 14 grams
PREPARATION & COOKING TIME: 1¼ hours

150 g (5 oz) halved pecans
pre-baked 20 cm (8 in) flan case, made with Wholemeal shortcrust pastry (page 194) and glazed with apricot jam
50 g (2 oz) raw brown sugar
2 eggs, well beaten
50 g (2 oz) melted butter
150 ml (5 fl oz) golden syrup, heated until liquid
¼ teaspoon ground ginger (optional)
¼ teaspoon ground cinnamon (optional)

Set the oven at 180°C (350°F) Gas 4. Place the flan case on a baking sheet. Mix together the sugar, eggs, butter and syrup with the spices, if used. Fold in the nuts, making sure they are thoroughly and evenly mixed. Pour the filling into the flan case, taking care not to spill any over the side as it may run underneath the flan case and burn.

Bake in the pre-heated oven for 45 minutes-1 hour, or until the filling is set and golden brown. Allow to cool slightly before serving, or serve cold.

Strawberry or raspberry shortcake

CALORIES PER PORTION: 675 (2820 kJ)
PROTEIN CONTENT PER PORTION: 12 grams
PREPARATION & COOKING TIME: 1-1¼ hours

generous 350 g (12 oz) hulled strawberries or raspberries
3-4 tablespoons caster sugar
300 ml (½ pint) whipping cream

For the Shortcake
225 g (8 oz) wholemeal flour
½ teaspoon ground cinnamon (optional)
1 tablespoon baking powder
1 teaspoon salt
75 g (3 oz) butter, margarine or shortening
250 ml (8 fl oz) milk

Set the oven at 200°C (400°F) Gas 6. Set aside about 6 whole berries for decoration. Sprinkle the remaining fruit with sugar, crush lightly and then set aside while you make the shortcake.

Sift the flour with the cinnamon, if used, baking powder and salt into a bowl through a coarse sieve to extract the bran. Discard this. Rub in the butter, margarine or shortening until the mixture resembles fine breadcrumbs. Add the milk and mix to a very soft dough. Divide the dough in half, roll it out and line two well-oiled 20 cm (8 in) sandwich tins. Bake in the pre-heated oven for 15 minutes. Remove the shortcakes from the oven and cool for 5 minutes, then turn them out on to a wire rack and allow to cool completely.

Place one shortcake on a serving plate and cover with a layer of crushed fruit. Place the second shortcake on top and cover with the remaining crushed fruit. Decorate with some of the whipped cream and the reserved whole berries and serve immediately with the remaining cream. Alternatively, spread the shortcake layers with whipped cream before covering with fruit and decorate as before.

Apple pie

CALORIES PER PORTION: 610 (2557 kJ)
PROTEIN CONTENT PER PORTION: 8 grams
PREPARATION & COOKING TIME: 1½ hours

700 g (1½ lb) peeled and cored cooking apples
225 g (8 oz) Wholemeal shortcrust pastry (page 194)
150 g (5 oz) raw brown sugar
1 tablespoon wholemeal flour
½ teaspoon ground cinnamon
½ teaspoon grated orange rind
1 tablespoon orange juice
50 g (2 oz) sultanas

Set the oven at 230°C (450°F) Gas 8. Mix the sugar with the flour, cinnamon and grated orange rind. Cut the apples into slices about 1 cm (½ in) thick. Immediately stir them into the sugar mixture to prevent discoloration. Add the orange juice and sultanas.

Roll out three-quarters of the dough and line a 20 cm (8 in) pie dish. Fill with the apple mixture and dampen the edges of the dough. Roll out the remaining dough into a round to fit the top and place this over the apples. Seal the edges well and make two leaf-shaped slits in the top to allow the steam to escape. Bake in the pre-heated oven for 15 minutes then reduce the temperature to 180°C (350°F) Gas 4 and bake for a further 30 minutes.

Serve hot or cold with cream or custard.

Note: if you bake the pie in a flan ring or dish with a removable base, place a dish underneath it to catch any leaking juices.

Wholemeal shortbread

TOTAL CALORIES: 1835 (7680 kJ)
TOTAL PROTEIN CONTENT: 20 grams
PREPARATION & COOKING TIME: 1¼ hours
CHILLING TIME: 1 hour

150 g (5 oz) wholemeal flour
½ teaspoon salt
50 g (2 oz) raw brown sugar
125 g (4 oz) butter
4 tablespoons caster sugar

Mix the flour and salt into a bowl and stir in the brown sugar. Rub the butter into the dry ingredients until the mixture begins to stick together, then press lightly to form a stiff dough. Knead carefully on a floured surface until fairly smooth and then press the mixture into a 20 cm (8 in) diameter loose-bottomed fluted flan tin. Chill for about 1 hour.

Set the oven at 150°C (300°F) Gas 2 and bake the shortbread for 45-60 minutes until firm and just beginning to brown. Remove from the oven and sprinkle the top with half of the caster sugar. Cool in the tin for 5 minutes then turn on to a wire rack and sprinkle the other side with caster sugar. When cold, break into fingers or triangles and store in an airtight tin.

Langue de chat biscuits

TOTAL CALORIES: 750 (3150 kJ)
TOTAL PROTEIN CONTENT: 13 grams
PREPARATION & COOKING TIME: 30-40 minutes

50 g (2 oz) butter or margarine
50 g (2 oz) raw brown sugar
2 egg whites
50 g (2 oz) wholemeal flour
½ teaspoon salt

Set the oven at 180°C (350°F) Gas 4. Cream the butter or margarine and sugar together until soft and fluffy. Whisk the egg whites until they stand in peaks and fold them into the creamed mixture together with the flour and salt.

Using a piping bag fitted with 1 cm (½ in) nozzle, pipe the mixture in 5 cm (2 in) lengths on a baking sheet brushed with melted butter. Keep them about

5 cm (2 in) apart and fairly flat in shape. Bake them in the pre-heated oven for 10 minutes.

Remove the baking sheet from the oven, take off one biscuit and allow it to cool; if it is not completely crisp, return the remainder to the oven, reduce the heat to 130°C (250°F) Gas ½ and cook for a little longer until they are crisp when cold.

Almond or hazelnut biscuits

TOTAL CALORIES: 830 (3470 kJ)
TOTAL PROTEIN CONTENT: 13 grams
PREPARATION & COOKING TIME: 30 minutes

50 g (2 oz) soft butter
50 g (2 oz) raw brown sugar
2 stiffly beaten egg whites
50 g (2 oz) ground almonds or hazelnuts

Set the oven at 180°C (350°F) Gas 4, and line two baking sheets with non-stick vegetable parchment.

Cream together the butter and sugar until light and fluffy, then fold in the egg whites. Stir the nuts lightly into the mixture. Drop teaspoonfuls of the mixture on

to the prepared baking sheets, leaving plenty of space between them, and bake in the pre-heated oven for about 10 minutes, or until they are beginning to turn golden brown around the edges. Remove the biscuits from the oven and allow to cool.

Savoury cheese biscuits

TOTAL CALORIES: 1975 (8250 kJ)
TOTAL PROTEIN: 59 grams
PREPARATION & COOKING TIME: 45 minutes

125 g (4 oz) wholemeal flour
125 g (4 oz) butter
150 g (5 oz) grated Cheddar cheese
salt
freshly ground pepper
cayenne
a well beaten egg

Set the oven at 200°C (400°F) Gas 6. Mix the flour and seasoning together in a bowl and rub in the butter. Add 125 g (4 oz) of the cheese and knead the mixture until it is a smooth paste. Turn out onto a lightly floured board and roll out to about 5 mm (¼ in) thick and cut into squares about 5 cm (2 in) wide and then cut the squares into triangles. Lay them on a well-greased baking sheet and brush lightly with the egg and sprinkle over the remaining cheese and a little cayenne. Bake for 10-15 minutes until golden-brown and firm. Allow to cool slightly before removing from the tin. Serve warm as a cocktail snack or as an accompaniment to soup or casseroles.

Note: if the cheese is dry, it may be necessary to use a little milk to make the paste.

Honey oatcakes

TOTAL CALORIES: 2400 (10050 kJ)
TOTAL PROTEIN CONTENT: 32 grams
PREPARATION & COOKING TIME: 45 minutes

2 tablespoons honey
2 tablespoons golden syrup
75 g (3 oz) butter or margarine
125 g (4 oz) raw brown sugar
250 g (8 oz) rolled oats

Set the oven at 180°C (350°F) Gas 4. Brush a 20 cm (8 in) square sandwich tin with melted butter or margarine and line the base with non-stick vegetable parchment.

Put the honey, syrup, butter or margarine and brown sugar into a saucepan and melt over gentle heat. Add the oats and mix together thoroughly. Turn the mixture into the prepared tin and bake in the pre-heated oven for 20-30 minutes until the oatcake is golden brown. Cut into fingers while it is still warm. Allow to cool in the tin, then turn the oatcakes out. Store in an airtight tin.

Preserving, Pickling and Freezing

There is nothing quite as satisfying as a shining row of jars of home-made jams, jellies, pickles and chutneys glinting on the larder shelves.

Although freezing has become the most convenient way of storing fruit and vegetables straight from the market or garden, the sheer pleasure of opening a jar of fragrant, full-fruit strawberry jam or the first, pungent aroma of your favourite pickle will convince you that nothing can quite take its place. I make my jams when the fruit is at its best – you will find the yields of my recipes vary. Lemon curd, for instance, will not keep well once made, though it is so delicious that the contents will vanish within hours of the jar being opened. Pepper relish is one of my favourite pickles and I like to make lots and lots at a time . . .

I include some basic guidelines on freezing, with instructions on the preparation of fruit and vegetables, and the storing of made-up dishes. Though I prefer to prepare my food fresh for each meal, you will some-times find it convenient to cook ahead of time.

Bottling fruit

Recent research has suggested that the home cook should not attempt to bottle fruit lacking in acid, e.g. dessert apples, ripe peaches, and when bottling suitable ingredients such as gooseberries or rhubarb, a pressure cooker must be used to achieve the correct sterilizing temperatures.

While fruit can be bottled in water, the flavour and colour is better preserved if it is covered in a syrup made by boiling 225 g (8 oz) sugar in 600 ml (1 pint) of water about 2-3 minutes. More sugar may be needed if the fruit is very acid.

Prepare the fruit by washing it carefully and removing any stalks, stems or leaves. Cherries should be stoned, gooseberries should be topped and tailed and rhubarb cut into short, even lengths. Apples and pears should be peeled and cored; peaches and apricots should be peeled and halved and the stones removed. Plums can be left whole, or halved and have the stones removed.

Pack the fruit closely, but do not squash together, in clean, sterilized wide-necked preserving jars and cover with the syrup, releasing any air bubbles with a sterilized spatula or skewer. Leave about 1 cm (½ in) space between the syrup and the top of the jar as the fruit may make some juice and if the jar is filled to the top it may boil out. Check that the seals are in good condition and screw on the lids, then loosen them about half a turn to allow steam to escape during processing.

Put the bottles into a large pressure cooker on top of the trivet and see that they do not touch the sides of the cooker or each other. Pour in water to a depth of 2.5 cm (1 in). Put on the lid, leaving the vent open and bring the water to the boil. Allow steam to escape for a couple of minutes, then close the vent and bring the pressure to whatever the manufacturer recommends and hold it for the time they suggest.

Leave to cool before releasing the pres-sure, otherwise the bottles might burst. Remove the lid of the pressure cooker and fasten down the lids of the jars. Test them after 48 hours cooling to see if the seals have taken. The lids should be firm on the jars; if they are, label and store in a cool, dark place.

Jam-making

One of the most satisfying sights in any larder is a row of home-made jams, jellies, chutneys and preserves. However, as already mentioned, recent research has suggested that one should restrict one's efforts at preserving to tomatoes and the acid fruits and leave most vegetables to the professionals.

Wide-necked jars make the removal of the contents much easier. For preserving, make sure that the jars are not cracked or the top edges chipped. The cover should fit perfectly and the rubber sealing rings should not be perished. Wash the jars in hot water with a little detergent, rinse thoroughly in clean water and drain. For jams, jellies, chutneys and pickles, stand the jars upside down on a baking sheet in an oven set at 130°C (250°F) Gas ½ for 30 minutes before filling them.

Choose ripe but not over-ripe fruit for jam-making. Wash it carefully and remove hulls, stems and leaves where appropriate. Cut out any blemishes or bruised parts, using a stainless steel or silver knife to avoid a metallic taste.

Soft berry fruits such as raspberries and strawberries should be soaked in salt water for 20-30 minutes to remove any insects. Use 15 g (½ oz) salt to every litre (1¾ pints) of water. Rinse the fruit thoroughly under cold running water.

Use an aluminium, stainless steel or tin-lined copper pan and simmer the fruit *before* adding sugar if a soft-textured jam is required, as the sugar can toughen the skin. To make a firm-textured strawberry jam, sprinkle the strawberries with the measured sugar and leave them in a bowl overnight. Always allow the sugar to dis-solve completely, stirring constantly, before allowing the jam to come to a boil, then boil rapidly until setting point is reached. I use lemon juice instead of pectin as an aid to setting.

To test for setting, take a small spoonful of the boiling jam and pour it onto a cold saucer. Chill rapidly and push the jam lightly with a finger tip; if jam wrinkles and a drop picked up on a knife does not run off, the jam is ready. Alternatively, run the edge of a spoon through the middle of the jam on the saucer. If the jam stays divided, it is at setting point. Allow the jam to cool for 20-30 minutes, then stir it to distribute the fruit evenly just before filling the warmed jars. Leave a little over 1 cm (½ in) between the jam and the top of the jar.

Seal the jars as soon as they have been filled and the outsides wiped clean. Lay a disc of transparent or greaseproof paper on the surface of the jam, then cover the top of the bottle with a larger disc of greaseproof paper or a jam top and secure it with string or a rubber-band. Don't forget to label the jar and write on it the date the jam was made.

Preserving

Fruit and tomatoes for preserving should be ripe but firm. Wash the fruit and prepare as for jam. Plums and apricots should be halved and the stones removed. If a few of the stones are cracked open and the kernels added to the fruit, this will give the preserved fruit a faint almond flavour. Peaches should be peeled, stoned and halved; do not include any kernels as their flavour will be too strong.

Fruit should be bottled in a syrup made by dissolving 450 g (1 lb) sugar to each litre (1¾ pints) boiling water. Simmer gently until the sugar has dissolved, stirring constantly, then strain and allow to cool completely before using.

Rinse the washed bottles — there is no need to dry them off in the oven — then pack the fruit in carefully, without

1. Simmer the fruit until tender. Add warmed sugar, stirring until it dissolves.

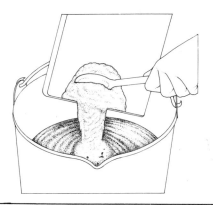

2. Boil at a rolling boil. Test for set on a saucer: jam should stay separated.

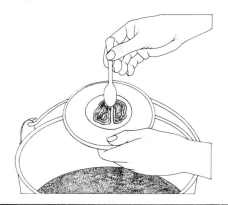

3. When setting point is reached, remove pan from heat and skim off any scum.

quashing it. Leave space of about 2.5 cm (1 in) between the top of the fruit and the rim of the bottle. Pour in enough syrup to come about 1 cm (½ in) above the fruit and use a clean skewer to release any trapped air bubbles.

Tomatoes can be bottled whole, skinned or unskinned, or as a purée. Skin them by dropping them into boiling water for a minute and then transferring them to a bowl of iced water to prevent them continuing to cook. Cut the skin into quarters with a sharp pointed knife and peel off carefully. If the tomatoes are to be bottled unskinned, prick the skins thoroughly to prevent them from bursting. Pack them into the bottles, replacing the sugar syrup with a mild brine made by dissolving 25 g (1 oz) salt in every 1 litre (1¾ pints) of water, releasing any air bubbles with a clean skewer, as for fruit.

To make a tomato purée for bottling, boil coarsely chopped tomatoes, seasoned with salt, pepper and herbs if liked, until reduced to a pulp. Rub through a sieve and pour into warmed jars, as for jam, leaving about 1 cm (½ in) between the purée and the rim of the jar, then seal and label as for jam.

Stand the filled jars on a trivet in a large pressure cooker, put on the rubber rings or seals and follow the manufacturer's instructions for sealing and preserving.

When the bottles are quite cold and properly sealed, store them in a cool, dry, dark, well-ventilated place. If mould appears on jam soon after it has been made, it is generally a sign that the jam was bottled before reaching the setting point, or the fruit was too low in pectin (the substance that makes jams and jellies set). In the case of chutneys or pickles, perhaps it is a sign that the vinegar was not up to strength. Provided the mould has not penetrated below the surface, it can generally be scraped off, but the contents should be eaten up as soon as possible.

Let whole fruit jam stand ½ hour then stir. Pour liquid jam directly into pots.

Apricot jam

CALORIES: 4190 (17530 kJ)
PROTEIN CONTENT: 6 grams
PREPARATION & COOKING TIME: 2 hours

1 kg (2.2 lb) halved and stoned apricots, washed well and any stem ends and leaves removed
juice of 1 large lemon
300 ml (½ pint) water
1 kg (2.2 lb) raw brown sugar

Put the apricots into a saucepan or preserving pan with the lemon juice and the water, bring to the boil and simmer until the fruit is soft. Add the sugar, stir to dissolve and continue boiling, stirring constantly, until setting point is reached. Pour into warmed, sterilized jars and cover with circles of waxed or greaseproof paper. Put in a cool, dry place and cover and tie down securely when cold.

Note: If whole fruit jam is desired, add the sugar at the same time as the fruit, as it will slightly toughen the skin and flesh; take care when stirring the jam not to break the fruit.

A dozen or so kernels from the stones can be added to the jam at the same time as the fruit to give a slightly almond flavour. Blanch them in boiling water for 5 minutes and split them in half before adding them.

Gooseberry jam

CALORIES: 5100 (21340 kJ)
PROTEIN CONTENT: 11 grams
PREPARATION & COOKING TIME: 1¼ hours

1 kg (2.2 lb) topped and tailed gooseberries, washed well
4 tablespoons lemon juice plus the pith and pips of 2-3 lemons
400 ml (¾ pint) water
1.25 kg (2¾ lb) demerara sugar
finely grated rind of 1 large lemon

Tie the pith and pips from the lemons in a small piece of muslin. Put the gooseberries, lemon juice and water into a saucepan or preserving pan, add the muslin bag and bring to the boil. Simmer for 20 minutes, then gradually stir in the sugar with the lemon rind, stirring until the sugar has dissolved. Continue boiling, stirring from time to time, until setting point is reached. Discard the muslin bag, pour the jam into warmed, sterilized jars. Cover with circles of waxed or greaseproof paper and put the jam in a cool, dry place. Cover and tie down when cold. Store in a cool, dry place. Yields about 1.8 kg (4 lb).

Note: Try putting a dozen or so heads of elderflowers into the muslin bag with the lemon. They give the jam a delicate muscatel flavour.

Strawberry jam

CALORIES: 4205 (17590 kJ)
PROTEIN CONTENT: 6 grams
PREPARATION & COOKING TIME: 1½ hours

1 kg (2.2 lb) hulled stawberries, washed well
1 kg (2.2 lb) raw brown or demerara sugar
3 tablespoons lemon juice plus the pith and pips of 3 large lemons

Make sure you have discarded any strawberries that are mouldy or over-ripe. Put the rest into a saucepan, or preserving pan, over moderate heat and bring to the boil, breaking some berries with a spoon to release the juice. Add the sugar and the lemon juice and stir to dissolve. Tie the pith and pips from the lemons in a piece of muslin and suspend this in the boiling liquid. Continue boiling, stirring from time to time to prevent the fruit sticking and burning, until setting point is reached. Discard the muslin bag. Pour the jam into warmed, sterilized jars and cover with circles of waxed or greaseproof paper. Put in cool place; cover and tie when cold.

Note: If whole fruit jam is required, sprinkle the hulled strawberries with the sugar, leave them in a bowl overnight and then put them into a saucepan or preserving pan. Bring them to the boil and follow the recipe, taking care, however, not to break the fruit when you are stirring the jam.

A satisfying variety of fresh-fruit jams and jellies for the store cupboard – choose the best of the season's fruits to enjoy all year round

Raspberry jam

CALORIES: 4190 (17540 kJ)
PROTEIN CONTENT: 9 grams
PREPARATION & COOKING TIME: 1 hour 15 minutes

1 kg (2.2 lb) raspberries
1 kg (2.2 lb) raw brown sugar
2 tablespoons lemon juice plus the pith and pips of 2 lemons

Wash the raspberries by putting them into a bowl of cold water and agitating them gently, then lift them out into another bowl of clean water. By repeating this process with clean water once more, any dust or grit is left behind and the raspberries are not damaged. Discard any that are mouldy or bruised. Put the berries in a saucepan or preserving pan. Stir over gentle heat until the juices begin to run, then follow the method given for Strawberry jam.

Black cherry jam

CALORIES: 3480 (14570 kJ)
PROTEIN CONTENT: 7 grams
PREPARATION & COOKING TIME: 2½ hours

1 kg (2.2 lb) black cherries, washed well and any stems and leaves removed, then stoned
4 large or 6 small lemons, enough to give 200 ml (⅓ pint) of juice
600 ml (1 pint) water
750 g (1¾ lb) raw brown or demerara sugar

Remove the pips and the pith from the lemons before squeezing out the juice and put the pips and pith into a pan with the cherry stones and 400 ml (¾ pint) of the water. Bring to the boil, simmer for 30 minutes, then strain into a clean saucepan, rubbing any pulp through the sieve. Add the rest of the water, the lemon juice and the cherries and bring to the boil. Lower the heat and simmer gently for about 30 minutes. Add the sugar, stir to dissolve, increase the heat and boil, stirring occasionally, until setting point is reached. Pour the jam into warmed, sterilized jars and cover the tops with circles of waxed or greaseproof paper. Put the jam in a cool, dry place, and cover and tie down when cold. Yields about 1.5 kg (3 lb).

Lemon curd

CALORIES: 2065 (8640 kJ)
PROTEIN CONTENT: 30 grams
PREPARATION & COOKING TIME: 1 hour

100 ml (4 fl oz) lemon juice
2 heaped teaspoons finely grated lemon rind
225 g (8 oz) granulated sugar
3 eggs, well beaten
100 g (4 oz) unsalted butter

Put the sugar, lemon juice and rind into a heatproof bowl and stand it in a large saucepan of gently boiling water. Stir until the sugar has dissolved, then stir the beaten eggs thoroughly into the mixture. Divide the butter into four, add one portion to the mixture in the bowl and stir until it melts. Add the rest of the butter piece by piece, stirring all the time and making sure each piece has melted into the mixture before adding the next.

Continue cooking and stirring, scraping the sides and bottom of the bowl from time to time until the curd has the consistency of thick cream, then pour into a warmed, sterilized jar. Allow to cool before covering as for jam and store in a cool, dry place. **Eat within 4 weeks.**

Apple jelly

CALORIES: 5010 (20960 kJ)
PROTEIN CONTENT: 2 grams
PREPARATION & COOKING TIME: 3 hours

1 kg (2.2 lb) cooking apples, washed well and stalks removed
2 litres (3½ pints) water
1.2 kg (2¼ lb) granulated sugar
juice of 1 large lemon

Cut each apple into 8 segments and pu them into a saucepan with the water Bring to the boil, then reduce the heat cover and simmer for 2 hours. Stir occa sionally to break the apples up. When they have cooked to a pulp, rub them through a sieve and pour the purée into a jelly bag. Drain it overnight into a bowl Pour this juice into a clean saucepan, add the sugar and lemon juice and stir to dissolve. Bring to the boil, then reduce the heat and simmer until the jelly reaches setting point. Skim to remove any scum pour into warmed, sterilized jars, and cover with circles of waxed or greaseproo paper, or transparent jam tops. Put in a cool, dry place, and cover and tie down when cold. Store in a cool, dry place.

Blackcurrant jelly

CALORIES: 4220 (17660 kJ)
PROTEIN CONTENT: 9 grams
PREPARATION & COOKING TIME: 1½ hours

1 kg (2.2 lb) blackcurrants, washed well
1 litre (1¾ pints) water
1 kg (2.2 lb) raw brown sugar

Remove any leaves from the blackcurrants but leave the stems. Put them into a saucepan with three-quarters of the water. Bring to the boil and simmer for 20 minutes, stirring occasionally. Strain through a fine sieve into a clean saucepan. Return the pulp to the original pan with the rest of the water and boil for 5 minutes. Strain as before, pressing the pulp gently with the back of a spoon to release any extra juice. Add it to the rest of the juice and bring to the boil. Add the sugar, stir to dissolve and continue boiling until setting point is reached. Pour into warmed, sterilized jars. Cover with circles of waxed or greaseproof paper and put in a cool, dry place, cover and tie down when cold.

This recipe works well for Redcurrant jelly if you use granulated sugar instead of brown.

Three fruit marmalade

CALORIES: 5642 (23580 kJ)
PROTEIN CONTENT: 4 grams
PREPARATION & COOKING TIME: 3½ hours

700 g (1½ lb) mixed citrus fruit (2
*   oranges, 1 grapefruit and 1 lemon)*
1.4 litres (2½ pints) water
1.4 kg (3 lb) raw brown sugar

Scrub the fruit in hot water, cut into quarters and then into thin slices, taking care to save all the juice. Remove the pips and tie them loosely in a piece of muslin. Pour the water into a saucepan, or preserving pan, and add the fruit and juice, suspending the muslin bag containing the pips in the liquid. Bring to the boil, cover the pan and simmer for 1½ hours. Remove the muslin bag and weigh the juice and fruit; if it is much over 1.4 kg (3 lb), return it to the pan and boil rapidly until it is reduced. Weigh the juice and fruit, add the same amount of sugar, return it to the saucepan and stir to dissolve. Boil rapidly until setting point is reached. Skim the marmalade, remove the pan from the stove and leave for 20-30 minutes until it has thickened slightly. Stir to distribute the fruit evenly, then pour into warmed, sterilized jars; cover with circles of waxed or greaseproof paper. Put in a cool, dry place, and cover and tie down when cold.

Chunky marmalade

CALORIES: 8140 (34070 kJ)
PROTEIN CONTENT: 6 grams
PREPARATION & COOKING TIME: 4 hours

1 kg (2.2 lb) Seville oranges
juice, pith and pips of 2 large lemons
2 litres (3½ pints) water
2 kg (4¼ lb) raw brown sugar

Scrub the fruit in hot water to clean them thoroughly. Cut them first into quarters, then into small chunks, taking care to catch all the juice. Remove the central pithy core and pips and keep them on one side. Put the chunks of orange with the lemon juice and water into a saucepan, or preserving pan, with the lemon and orange pith and pips tied loosely in a piece of muslin and suspended in the liquid. Bring to the boil, then reduce the heat and simmer for about 1½ hours until the skin of the oranges is soft and can be pierced easily with a fork. Now add the sugar, stir to dissolve and boil rapidly until setting point is reached. Discard the muslin bag. Skim the marmalade, remove the pan from the stove and leave for 20-30 minutes until the marmalade has thickened slightly. Stir to distribute the fruit evenly and spoon into warmed sterilized jars.

Seville orange jelly

CALORIES: 3665 (15330 kJ)
PROTEIN CONTENT: 3 grams
PREPARATION & COOKING TIME: 4 hours

450 g (1 lb) Seville oranges
1.1 litres (2 pints) water
juice, pith and pips of 2 lemons
900 g (2 lb) granulated sugar

Shred the orange rind into thin strips and tie it in a muslin bag. Peel the white pith off the oranges and keep it on one side; chop the flesh into small pieces, catching all the juice. Remove the orange pips and add them to the pith. Pour the water into a saucepan and add the small chunks of fruit with the orange and lemon juice. Tie the lemon pith and pips in a muslin bag with the orange pith and pips and suspend this in the liquid. Add the other muslin bag containing the shredded rind. Bring the liquid to the boil, reduce the heat, cover the pan and simmer for 2 hours. Discard the muslin bag containing the pith and pips, strain the liquid through a fine sieve, or sieve lined with muslin, and return it to the pan. Add the sugar and the shredded rind from the bag, stir to dissolve the sugar and boil rapidly, stirring occasionally, until setting point is reached. Skim the jelly, remove from the stove and allow to stand for 20-30 minutes until it has thickened slightly. Stir to distribute the rind evenly, then pour into warmed, sterilized jars. Cover with circles of waxed or greaseproof paper, or transparent jam tops. Put in a cool, dry place, and cover and tie down when cold.

Damson cheese

CALORIES: 4280 (17910 kJ)
PROTEIN CONTENT: 4 grams
PREPARATION & COOKING TIME: 1½ hours

1 kg (2.2 lb) damsons, washed well and
*   any stalks or leaves removed, then*
*   stoned*
600 ml (1 pint) water
about 1 kg (2.2 lb) granulated sugar

Put the damsons and the water into a thick-based saucepan and bring to the boil. Reduce the heat, cover and simmer until the fruit is completely soft. Rub through a sieve, weigh the pulp and measure out the same amount of sugar. Pour the pulp into a clean saucepan and boil, stirring constantly, until it has begun to thicken. Add the sugar, stir to dissolve and continue cooking, stirring occasionally until it is a thick purée. Pour the cheese into small warmed, sterilized jars or pots. Cover with circles of waxed or greaseproof paper or transparent jam tops and cool and tie down as for jam.

Orange preserve

CALORIES: 8230 (34430 kJ)
PROTEIN CONTENT: 8 grams
PREPARATION & COOKING TIME: 4 days

1 kg (2.2. lb) oranges
1.4 litres (2½ pints) water
2 kg (4¼ lb) raw brown or demerara
  sugar

Wash the oranges carefully, remove the stem ends and cut the oranges into quarters. Put these into a saucepan with the water and bring to the boil. Cover the pan, reduce the heat and simmer for 2½-3 hours until the skin is soft and can be pierced easily with a fork. Remove from the stove, keep covered and leave overnight. The following morning, add enough boiling water to make up the original quantity of liquid. Bring it to the boil, add the sugar and stir until it has dissolved, then reduce the heat, cover and simmer for 30 minutes, stirring occasionally. Make sure that the orange skins are immersed in the liquid as they are inclined to turn over and float to the top. Remove the pan from the stove, keeping it covered, and leave until the following morning.

Make up the liquid to the original quantity with a little boiling water as before, bring to the boil and simmer for a further 30 minutes, then leave overnight. Repeat the process the following day, simmer for 30 minutes then boil to a syrup just short of setting point. Skim the top and spoon the orange pieces into warmed, sterilized jars. Pour over the boiling syrup and cover with circles of waxed or greaseproof paper, or transparent jam tops. Put in a cool dry place, and cover and tie down when cold.

Note: If you dislike finding the occasional pip, remove them before cooking, tie them in a piece of muslin and suspend them in the liquid during the cooking time.

Spiced pickled peaches

CALORIES: 860 (3610 kJ)
PROTEIN CONTENT: 6 grams
PREPARATION & COOKING TIME: 1 hour

1 kg (2.2 lb) peeled, small, ripe firm
  peaches, halved and stoned
600 ml (1 pint) wine vinegar
1 teaspoon ground allspice
5 cm (2 in) stick of cinnamon, crumbled
1 teaspoon coriander seeds
2 bay leaves, crumbled
100 g (4 oz) raw brown sugar

Put the halved peaches into a saucepan with the vinegar, spices and bay leaves and bring to the boil. Simmer for 10 minutes, or until the peaches are tender, then remove them from the pan with a draining spoon and keep on one side. Add the sugar to the pan, stir to dissolve and return the peaches to the pan. Cook for a further 5 minutes. Remove the peaches from the saucepan with the draining spoon and place them in warmed, sterilized wide-necked jars. Boil the vinegar until reduced by a third and pour this over the peaches, ensuring that it covers them completely. Cover the jars with circles of waxed or greaseproof paper. Put in a cool, dry place, and cover and tie down when cold. Store in a cool, dry place and allow to mature for 1 month. Yields about 1.8 kg (4 lb).

Note: This recipe can also be used to make Spiced pickled apricots, or plums, using the same quantity of the other fruits.

Spiced cherries

CALORIES: 1850 (7740 kJ)
PROTEIN CONTENT: 6 grams
PREPARATION & COOKING TIME: 30 minutes,
  excluding maturing time: 4 weeks

1 kg (2.2 lb) ripe black cherries, well
  washed and stoned
1 litre (1¾ pints) wine vinegar
12 cloves, coarsely crushed
5 cm (2 in) stick of cinnamon, crumbled
2 bay leaves, crumbled
250 g (12 oz) raw brown sugar

Pour the vinegar into a saucepan, add the spices, bay leaves and sugar and bring it to the boil. Stir until the sugar has dissolved before adding the cherries. Bring back to the boil and simmer for 5 minutes then pour the spiced cherries into warmed, sterilized jars and cover with circles of waxed or greaseproof paper, or transparent jam tops. Put in a cool, dry place, and cover and tie down when cold. Store in a cool place for at least a month to mature before using.

Lemon chutney

CALORIES: 3310 (13840 kJ)
PROTEIN CONTENT: 8 grams
PREPARATION & COOKING TIME: 4 hours

700 g (1½ lb) lemons, cut into 5 mm (¼
  in) slices
300 ml (½ pint) wine vinegar
225 g (8 oz) thinly sliced onion
2 cloves of garlic, peeled and thinly
  sliced
5 cm (2 in) stick of cinnamon, crumbled
6 cloves
1 teaspoon cumin seed
2 bay leaves, crumbled
½ teaspoon chilli powder
800 g (1¾ lb) demerara sugar

Put the lemon slices into a pan, cover them with water and bring to the boil. Cover the pan, turn down the heat and simmer for 2 hours, adding a little more water, if necessary, during the cooking time. Measure the liquid and make it up to 300 ml (½ pint) with additional water. Return it to the saucepan with the lemon slices, add the rest of the ingredients, except the sugar, and bring back to the boil. Add the sugar, stirring until it has dissolved, then continue cooking until the juice thickens slightly when a little is put on a cold plate; it should not be quite thick enough to 'jel'. Pour into warmed sterilized jars and cover with circles of waxed or greaseproof paper. Put in a cool, dry place, and cover and tie down when cold. Store in a cool, dry place.

Piccalilli

CALORIES: 450 (1880 kJ)
PROTEIN CONTENT: 12 grams
PREPARATION & COOKING TIME: 2 days

1 kg (2.2 lb) mixed vegetables — small
  sprigs of cauliflower, pickling onions,
  green beans, red and green peppers,
  cucumbers — and unripe pears and
  apples
50 g (2 oz) salt
1½ litres (2½ pints) vinegar
75 g (3 oz) coarsely crushed mustard
  seed
100 g (4 oz) thinly sliced green root
  ginger
50 g (2 oz) garlic, peeled and finely
  chopped
½ teaspoon ground cinnamon
½ teaspoon freshly ground black
  pepper
50 g (2 oz) raw brown or demerara
  sugar
1 tablespoon wholemeal flour

Cut the vegetables into small chunks, sprinkle them with the salt and leave them to drain for 24 hours, stirring 4 times during the draining period. Rinse and dry them thoroughly. Put the vinegar, spices and sugar into a saucepan, bring to the boil and add the vegetables. Bring back to the boil and simmer for 10 minutes, then allow to cool and leave in the pan, covered, for 24 hours. Strain off the vinegar and mix 1-2 tablespoons of it to a smooth paste with the flour. Put this into a saucepan with the rest of the vinegar and bring to the boil, stirring until it thickens. Add the vegetables, bring back to the boil and simmer for 5 minutes. Pour into warmed, sterilized jars and cover with circles of waxed or greaseproof paper. Put in a cool, dry place, and cover and tie down when cold.

Sweet cucumber pickle

CALORIES: 745 (3120 kJ)
PROTEIN CONTENT: 14 grams
PREPARATION & COOKING TIME: 6 hours

1 kg (2.2 lb) coarsely chopped
  cucumbers
350 g (12 oz) thinly sliced onions
225 g (8 oz) halved green peppers
25 g (1 oz) salt
100 g (4 oz) brown or demerara sugar
10 g (½ oz) mustard seed
1 teaspoon ground turmeric
1 teaspoon grated lemon rind
½ teaspoon ground mace
300 ml (½ pint) wine vinegar

Put all the vegetables into a bowl, sprinkle them with the salt and leave for 4 hours. Rinse them and drain thoroughly. Put all the other ingredients into a saucepan and bring to the boil, stirring until the sugar has dissolved. Simmer for 5 minutes before adding the vegetables, then bring back to the boil and cook for 10 minutes, stirring occasionally. Pour into warmed, sterilized jars, cover with circles of waxed or greaseproof paper; cover when cold.

Tomato chutney

CALORIES: 1270 (5310 kJ)
PROTEIN CONTENT: 22 grams
PREPARATION & COOKING TIME: 2½ hours

2 kg (4.4 lb) skinned cored tomatoes
450 g (1 lb) finely chopped onions
300-600 ml (½-1 pint) wine vinegar
1 tablespoon salt
225 g (8 oz) raw brown sugar
5 cm (2 in) stick of cinnamon, crumbled
2 bay leaves
4 cloves of garlic, peeled and chopped
½ teaspoon chilli powder
2 teaspoons ground allspice

Quarter the tomatoes and put them in a stainless steel or enamel saucepan with the rest of the ingredients. Bring to the boil and simmer to a thick purée. Stir occasionally to begin with, and almost constantly towards the end of the cooking time to prevent the chutney sticking and burning. When it is ready, pour into warmed, sterilized jars. Cover with circles of waxed or greaseproof paper. Cover and tie down before storing in a cool dry place.

Note: This recipe can be used for making Green tomato chutney but increase the amount of sugar to 350 g (12 oz).

Pepper relish

CALORIES: 1590 (6640 kJ)
PROTEIN CONTENT: 32 grams
PREPARATION & COOKING TIME: 2 hours

1 kg (2.2 lb) finely chopped red peppers
1 kg (2.2 lb) finely chopped green
  peppers
1 kg (2.2 lb) finely chopped onions
600 ml (1 pint) wine vinegar
225 g (8 oz) raw brown sugar
2-4 cloves of garlic, peeled and finely
  chopped
2 bay leaves, crumbled
1 teaspoon ground allspice
1 teaspoon mustard seed
2 teaspoons salt

Blanch the peppers in enough boiling water to cover them. Drain, put them into a preserving pan with the onions and cover again with water. Bring to the boil, pour off the water, drain the vegetables thoroughly and keep on one side. Put the vinegar into the rinsed out pan and bring to the boil. Add the sugar, garlic, bay leaves, allspice, mustard seed and salt. Stir until the sugar has dissolved, then add the peppers and onions and bring back to the boil. Boil the mixture vigorously for 2-3 minutes, stirring constantly, then pour into warmed, sterilized jars and cover with circles of waxed or greaseproof paper, or transparent jam tops. Put in a cool, dry place, and cover and tie down when cold. Yields about 3.6 kg (8 lb).

Pickled walnuts

CALORIES: 2625 (10980 kJ)
PROTEIN CONTENT: 53 grams
PREPARATION & MATURING TIME: 8 weeks

1 kg (2.2 lb) young green walnuts
350 g (¾ lb) salt
2 litres (3½ pints) water
25 g (1 oz) black peppercorns
25 g (1 oz) small allspice berries
1.5 litres (2½ pints) wine vinegar
½ teaspoon freshly grated dry ginger
5 cm (2 in) stick of cinnamon, crumbled

The walnuts must be freshly picked and should be young enough to be pierced easily with a very thick needle, even through the stem end; the outer covering should be firm and juicy.

Prick the walnuts all over with a carpet needle, holding them in a cloth, or wear rubber gloves, as the juice stains almost indelibly.

Dissolve half the salt in half the water and pour it over the walnuts in a bowl. Do not use a lead-glazed container as the solution and, later, the vinegar will dissolve the lead. If the solution does not quite cover the walnuts then make up a little extra, using the same proportion of salt to water. Cover and leave the nuts for 5 days in a cool place, stirring twice a day to ensure even brining. Drain them, then mix the rest of the salt and water, and any additional brine required, and pour this over the walnuts. Leave for another 5 days, stirring twice a day as before. Drain the walnuts and spread them out in a single layer on a flat dish. Let them dry in the sun until they are black. Crush the peppercorns and allspice berries with pestle and mortar — do not grind them or the flavour will be too strong. Simmer the vinegar with the spices for 15-20 minutes until it is well flavoured. Allow to cool and strain. Fill sterilized wide-necked jars three-quarters full with walnuts and pour in the spiced vinegar, adding extra if necessary to cover the walnuts. Cover securely and leave in a cool place for 6 weeks before using.

Home-made pickles delight the eye and tickle the palate. From left to right: Pepper relish; Tomato chutney; Spiced cherries; more Pepper relish; Pickled red cabbage and Piccalilli – the traditional mustard pickle. Behind: make your own herb vinegars – rosemary, sage and bayleaf – and add their piquancy to salads and vegetable dishes

Pickled red cabbage

CALORIES: 200 (840 kJ)
PROTEIN CONTENT: 2 grams
PREPARATION & MATURING TIME: 6 days

1 kg (2.2 lb) shredded red cabbage
50 g (2 oz) salt
1 litre (1¾ pints) wine vinegar
1 teaspoon ground allspice
1 teaspoon ground cinnamon
2 teaspoons ground coriander
2 bay leaves, crumbled
½ teaspoon ground black pepper

Sprinkle the cabbage with the salt in a bowl, place cover and leave for 24 hours. Rinse and pat dry. Simmer the vinegar with the spices and bay leaves for 10 minutes, then allow to cool. Pack the cabbage lightly into sterilized wide-necked glass jars and strain the spiced vinegar over. Cover the jars and leave for 5 days. The cabbage should now be ready to eat; it softens if kept too long, so use it up in the next 2-3 weeks.

Pickled onions

CALORIES: 230 (960 kJ)
PROTEIN CONTENT: 9 grams
PREPARATION TIME: 30 minutes
SALTING TIME: 24 hours

1 kg (2.2 lb) small pickling onions
4 tablespoons salt
400 ml (¾ pint) wine vinegar
½-1 teaspoon ground allspice
1 teaspoon coarsely ground coriander
¼ - ½ teaspoon ground cloves
½ teaspoon freshly ground black
 pepper
5 cm (2 in) stick of cinnamon, crumbled

Drop the onions into a pan of boiling water, bring the water back to the boil and transfer the onions immediately to a bowl of cold water. Using a sharp knife, top and tail them, cutting just enough of the onion to allow you to remove the outer skin. Put them into a glass bowl and sprinkle with salt, turning them so that they are covered. Cover the bowl and leave for 24 hours, stirring about every 6 hours so that the onions are evenly salted. Rinse and dry them thoroughly.

Pour the vinegar into a saucepan, add the spices and bring to the boil. Cover and allow to cool. Pack the onions loosely into sterilized glass jars and cover with the vinegar, tapping the side of the jar to release any bubbles. Bottle and store in a cool place for 2 months before using.

Note: If a milder flavour and a softer texture is required, put the onions into warmed, sterilized jars, pour the boiling vinegar over them and seal when cold.

Pickled eggs

CALORIES: 1015 (4240 kJ)
PROTEIN CONTENT: 93 grams
PREPARATION & COOKING TIME: 1 hour,
 excluding storage time

12 freshly cooked hard-boiled eggs
1 litre (1¾ pints) wine vinegar
1 teaspoon ground allspice
1 teaspoon ground coriander
½ teaspoon coarsely ground black
 pepper
1 teaspoon salt
5 cm (2 in) stick of cinnamon, crumbled
6 cloves, coarsely ground
2 hot red chillis, or green chillis if a
 milder flavour is preferred
2 bay leaves, crumbled
1 clove of garlic, peeled and finely
 chopped
100 g (4 oz) thinly sliced onion

Put the vinegar into a saucepan with the spices, bay leaves, garlic and onion. Bring to the boil, then reduce the heat, cover the pan and simmer for 10 minutes. Shell the eggs and place them in sterilized wide-necked jars. Allow the vinegar to get cold, then strain it over the eggs — they must be completely immersed. Cover and store for 10 days before using them.

Note: Fresh hens' eggs must be used; the eggs of other birds can be unsafe.

Herb vinegars

CALORIES AND PROTEIN CONTENT: nil
MATURING TIME: 3-4 weeks

Herb vinegars are delicious, so it is worth making the effort to obtain fresh herbs in the required quantity. Use wine or cider vinegar as the basic liquid. You will require approximately the same volume of loosely packed leaves and young stems of tarragon or mint as vinegar — 100-175 g (4-6 oz) to 1 litre (1¾ pints), 4-6 sprigs, 30 cm (12 in) long, of rosemary to 600 ml (1 pint) of vinegar. Carefully wash, dry and bruise the leaves before you immerse in the liquid. Store in screw-topped bottles for 3-4 weeks for the flavours to infuse before using the vinegar in salad dressings or add in small quantities to soups, casseroles or vegetable dishes.

Spiced vinegar

CALORIES AND PROTEIN CONTENT: nil

Add 6 cloves of garlic and 2-4 red chillis, all thinly sliced, with 600 ml (1 pint) of boiling vinegar. Leave to steep for 2 weeks. This makes a fiery and piquant seasoning.

Freezing

The main advantages of freezing are convenience and economy. It allows the busy cook the luxury of planning ahead, preparing and cooking food for future consumption so that it only needs thawing and reheating when required. By buying frozen food in bulk, freezing fresh food when it is plentiful and cheap, and by freezing home-grown fruit and vegetables, a considerable saving can be made.

Choose a freezer best suited to your requirements. A vertical cupboard type takes up less floor area and is easier to load and unload. The horizontal chest-type ones are not so convenient but are generally slightly cheaper. Go to a reputable, specialist dealer and discuss your requirements and available budget, and once you have bought a freezer, make sure that you know what to do if it breaks down. The manufacturer's instruction booklet will help here.

Good quality wire baskets make storage easier and more efficient in top loading freezers, as one does not have to move a lot of individual packages to find a particular item. It is advisable to keep food of one type together in one basket. Choose stainless steel or plastic covered rust-proof baskets.

The inside of the freezer should be cleaned at least twice a year. Run the stocks down beforehand and wrap the rest in layer upon layer of newspaper to prevent them thawing; keep them tightly packed in a cool place — preferably a freezer or refrigerator — while you clean the interior.

Switch off the power supply and leave the doors or lid of the freezer open. You can accelerate the defrosting by standing bowls of hot water on the shelves. Scrape off the frost from the sides, top and bottom, being careful not to damage the surface. Wipe all inside surfaces with a weak solution of bicarbonate of soda or mild detergent and water, or follow the directions of the manufacturer. Rinse the inside surfaces carefully with a clean cloth wrung out in fresh water, dry thoroughly and turn the power back on. Set the temperature control to its lowest setting or quickest freezing rate, or use the fast-freezing switch and reload it with the food as soon as the normal storage temperature of $-18°C$ ($0°F$) is reached. Remember to turn the control back to its normal setting once the correct temperature is reached.

Freeze food in heavy-duty plastic bags or food containers with well fitting lids. Use foil containers, obtainable from freezer shops or counters in the larger department stores, for cooked food that you wish to reheat without removing from the container.

Make sure that all food is hermetically sealed and that as much air as possible is removed to avoid oxidation of the contents. Use a drinking straw to suck the air out of the partially closed bag before sealing. When using rigid containers, cover the surface of the food with waxed paper or freezer foil. Remember that liquids expand by approximately $\frac{1}{10}$ of their volume when they freeze so leave enough head space to allow for this, otherwise you will have accidents. When you freeze casseroles or food in a sauce, ensure that all the food is covered with sauce, then cover the surface with waxed paper or freezer foil. Freeze convenient portions of food in separate containers; it is annoying and wasteful to find that you have to thaw enough soup for 8 when you only require enough for 2. Separate individual rissoles, crêpes, etc. with layers of waxed paper or foil to prevent them sticking together.

Label all food clearly with waterproof ink; record what it is, when it was frozen, and the quantity. It is surprising how the memory can play tricks!

Remember that the quality of the frozen food depends on the quality of the food before freezing. Ensure that all food preparation is done under hygienic conditions and that the food is cooled and frozen as quickly as possible after blanching or cooking.

When freezing pre-cooked food, it is advisable to undercook it slightly to allow for the extra time it will cook for when it is reheated. Be generous with sauces so that the food does not dry out when it is being reheated. Season lightly, adding extra, if necessary, when the food is reheated as freezing can concentrate flavouring. Garlic is inclined to develop a musty flavour so add on reheating the dish. Add cream or egg liaisons when reheating as freezing can make them separate, and you may find you have to thicken flour-based sauces at this point.

The general principle to remember when freezing fresh vegetables is to choose the best available quality of fresh-picked, unblemished produce and blanch and cool it immediately in ice-cold water to prevent enzyme action taking place whilst it is stored.

Fruit in prime condition can be frozen whole, though it is often more convenient to peel it and remove any cores or pips before freezing. If it is at all over-ripe, cook it and then freeze it as pie filling or fruit purée. Strawberries and similar fruit can be frozen spread out on trays before being packed in bags. This ensures that they do not freeze into a clump and can easily be separated on thawing.

Herbs freeze well and should be stripped or chopped and frozen in small containers, or in water in ice cube trays.

Pack the flavoured ice-cubes in polythene bags for storing.

The following charts give more detailed instructions on freezing the more common vegetables, prepared fruits and some cooked foods.

Thawing

The best way to thaw raw frozen food is also the slowest. Take it out of the freezer and leave it in the refrigerator; allow enough time for it to thaw completely; 450 g (1 lb) will take approximately 6-hours. If you are in a hurry, thaw it out at room temperature which will halve the time. Remember that vegetables should be cooked from frozen and not be thawed first. Loaves and cakes can be left to thaw in the refrigerator overnight.

Once the food is thawed, cook it as soon as possible to prevent any growth of bacteria.

Heating and cooking

Frozen casseroles, pies and flans should be heated as rapidly as possible to achieve the best results. Set the oven to 200°C (400°F) Gas 6 and transfer the food to an ovenproof dish if it has not been frozen in a foil container. Put it into the oven when it reaches the correct temperature. A shallow casserole holding 1 litre (1¾ pints) will take about an hour to heat up. Leave the lid off for quicker cooking; as the food thaws, gently separate the pieces.

If the food has a sauce it may be necessary to strain it off and whisk it vigorously to make it smooth. It may also be necessary to mix it together again if it has been separated out, or to thicken a flour based sauce.

Soups and sauces can be thawed from frozen in a saucepan over moderate heat but stir them constantly to prevent them sticking and burning and heat them thoroughly.

Blanching and freezing vegetables

If frozen vegetables are going to be stored for more than 2 months, the raw vegetables should be blanched first to prevent enzyme action changing the flavour. Use a frying basket placed inside a larger pan filled with boiling water for blanching fruit and vegetables. Allow 3.6 litres (6 pints) of boiling water per 450 g (1 lb). See that the heat under the pan is sufficient to bring the boiling water back to the boil within 1 minute of the vegetable being plunged in, and do not attempt to blanch too much at a time. Time blanching from the moment the water comes back to the boil. When the time is up plunge the vegetables immediately into ice-cold water to stop them cooking further. Replace the water and keep adding more ice to ensure that it really is ice cold.

Once the vegetables have cooled — and this should be done as quickly as possible, hence the ice-cold water — drain them. Pack them in heavy-duty polythene bags, freezer foil or rigid, lidded containers and freeze them as quickly as possible. Follow the manufacturer's instructions on how much fresh food your freezer can freeze down and store at a time. The key to successful freezing and the least damaging to nutrition and flavour is *how fast* you can freeze and *how much air you can remove* from the container. Full details for different types of vegetables are given on pages 206–207.

Keeping times

Most vegetables and fruit will keep for up to 12 months, if properly frozen. However, beetroot and onions will keep up to about 6 months; puréed potatoes to about 3 months and blanched new potatoes up to 6 months.

Fruit

Fruit can be frozen after blanching — as for vegetables. It can be frozen separately and packed into bags when frozen, or it can be frozen in syrup, or as a purée. If you are using syrup, ensure that you have enough; allow about 300 ml (½ pint) to every 450 g (1 lb) of fruit. Dissolve 450 g (1 lb) sugar in 1.1 litre (2 pints) hot water and bring to the boil. Allow to cool and then refrigerate before using. Keep the fruit below the surface of the liquid with a piece of non-absorbent paper, waxed or greaseproof paper. Add about ⅛ teaspoon ascorbic acid to the syrup for each 450 g (1 lb) of those fruits which might otherwise discolour. Do not forget to leave room for expansion when using syrup.

Thaw the fruit just before using and keep it submerged in the syrup for as long as possible.

Apples Peel, core and cut into quarters or 1 cm (½ in) slices. Blanch for 1-2 minutes depending on the firmness of the fruit and cool quickly. Pack in rigid containers and cover with syrup. Alternatively, peel and core the apples and cook to a purée with a little sugar and freeze, when cold, in rigid containers.

Apricots Drop them into boiling water, leave for 30 seconds to loosen the skins, then drain and peel them. Cut them in half and remove the stones. Pack in rigid containers and cover with syrup plus ascorbic acid. Cover with waxed or greaseproof paper and the lid and freeze.

Berries Blackberries; blackcurrants; cherries; gooseberries; raspberries; redcurrants; strawberries.

Wash carefully and dry. Pick over the fruit and remove any stems, leaves or hulls; top and tail gooseberries. Freeze by any of the following methods:
1 Freeze separately on trays covered with non-stick paper and pack them together in bags, when frozen.
2 Sprinkle them with sugar, allowing 125-175 g (4-6 oz) to 450 g (1 lb) fruit. Mix well; pack into bags and freeze.
3 Pack into rigid containers, cover with syrup and the surface of the liquid with a piece of non-absorbent, waxed or greaseproof paper.
4 Reduce to a purée in a blender, then sweeten and freeze in rigid containers.

Grapes Freeze seedless grapes whole; seeded grapes should be cut in half and the seeds removed. Pack into rigid containers, cover with syrup and a piece of non-absorbent waxed or greaseproof paper and freeze.

Grapefruit and oranges Peel, removing all the pith; separate into segments and pack in rigid containers. Cover with syrup and a piece of non-absorbent, waxed or greaseproof paper and freeze. Alternatively, squeeze out the juice and strain. Freeze into cubes in an ice tray, putting the cubes into bags when they are frozen.

Lemons and limes Squeeze and freeze the juice as for grapefruit and oranges above, or cut them into thin slices and interleave with non-stick paper. Pack them flat in polythene bags before freezing.

Peaches Peel the peaches, if ripe, without any preliminary immersion in boiling water to loosen the skins, as the heat will cause some discolouration. Cut them in half, remove the stones and pack the peaches as they are, or cut into 1 cm (½ in) thick slices, in rigid containers. Cover with syrup and a piece of non-absorbent, waxed or greaseproof paper and freeze.

Pears These do not freeze as well as other fruits. Choose pears that are slightly under-ripe, poach them in syrup, add ascorbic acid and pack into rigid containers. Cover with the poaching syrup and a piece of non-absorbent waxed or greaseproof paper before freezing.

Plums Wash, cut in half and remove the stones. Pack into rigid containers, cover with syrup plus ascorbic acid and a piece of non-absorbent waxed or greaseproof paper, and freeze.

Rhubarb Wash, trim and cut into 2.5 cm (1 in) lengths. Blanch for 1½ minutes. Cool quickly, pack into rigid containers and cover with syrup to freeze. Use in flans and pies or cook from frozen.

Cream ices and sorbets

The following recipes will serve 4-6 people. It is well worth making them in even larger quantities, however, as they are quite time-consuming to make, but keep well in the freezing compartment of the refrigerator, or in the freezer.

When making cream ices in a domestic refrigerator, turn it to its coldest setting a few hours before required. Remove the cream ice from the freezing compartment before serving and leave to stand for about 30 minutes in the main body of the refrigerator, or for 10-15 minutes at room temperature.

The sugar content of the following recipes is adjusted for making ice cream in a freezing compartment with a 3-star marking; use a little less sugar if your freezing compartment is less cold.

Orange sorbet

Serves 4
CALORIES PER PORTION: 210 (867 kJ)
PROTEIN CONTENT PER PORTION: 2 grams
PREPARATION & COOKING TIME: 4 hours

finely grated rind of 2 oranges
300 ml (½ pint) fresh orange juice
175 g (6 oz) granulated sugar
300 ml (½ pint) water
2 egg whites

Put the sugar and water in a pan and heat gently until the sugar has dissolved, stirring occasionally. Remove the pan from the heat and leave until cold.

Stir in the orange rind and juice, then pour the mixture into a freezing tray. Cover and place in the freezer, or freezing compartment of the refrigerator. Freeze for about 1 hour until the mixture becomes slushy and the edges are solid, then remove from the refrigerator or freezer and stir well. Replace and freeze for another hour. Remove the tray from the freezer or freezing compartment again, stir the mixture well to break up any lumps and mix the frozen parts into the rest of the mixture. Beat the egg whites until stiff enough to stand in peaks, then fold the mixture into them. Return the sorbet to the freezer or freezing compartment and freeze again for 2-3 hours, or until firm and set.

Note: To make Lemon sorbet, substitute lemon rind and juice for the orange.

Raspberry sorbet

Serves 4
CALORIES PER PORTION: 230 (955 kJ)
PROTEIN CONTENT PER PORTION: 2.5 grams
PREPARATION & FREEZING TIME: 3-4 hours

400 g (14 oz) fresh or thawed frozen
*   raspberries*
200 g (7 oz) granulated sugar
200 ml (⅓ pint) water
2 egg whites

Put the sugar and water in a pan and heat gently until the sugar has dissolved, stirring occasionally. Remove the pan from the heat and pour over the raspberries. Leave until cold.

Rub the mixture through a sieve then make the purée up to 700 ml (1¼ pints) with water. Pour the mixture into a freezing tray, cover and place in the freezer or freezing compartment of the refrigerator. Freeze for about 1 hour until the mixture becomes slushy and the edges are set.

Beat the egg whites until stiff enough to stand in peaks. Remove the tray from the freezer or freezing compartment, stir the mixture well to break up any lumps and mix the frozen bits into the rest of the mixture, then fold the mixture into the egg whites. Return to the freezer or freezing compartment and freeze again for 2-3 hours until firm.

Blackcurrant ice

Serves 4
CALORIES PER PORTION: 370 (1547 kJ)
PROTEIN CONTENT PER PORTION: 3.5 grams
PREPARATION & FREEZING TIME: about 5 hours

225 g (8 oz) fresh or frozen
*   blackcurrants*
100 g (4 oz) raw brown sugar
300 ml (½ pint) water
1 teaspoon lemon juice
300 ml (½ pint) whipping cream
2 egg whites

Put the blackcurrants, sugar and water in a pan and heat gently until the sugar has dissolved, stirring occasionally. Bring to the boil, then boil for about 10 minutes or until the blackcurrants are soft. Remove from the heat and leave until cold.

Rub the mixture through a sieve, then stir in the lemon juice. Pour the mixture into a freezing tray, cover and place in the freezer or freezing compartment of the refrigerator. Freeze for about 1 hour until the mixture becomes slushy and the edges are solid.

Whip the cream until thick. Remove the tray from the freezer or freezing compartment, stir the mixture well to break up any lumps, then fold into the whipped cream. Return to the freezer or freezing compartment and freeze again for about 1 hour, until thick.

Beat the egg whites until stiff enough to stand in peaks. Remove the cream ice from the freezer or freezing compartment, then fold into the egg whites. Return to the freezer or freezing compartment and continue freezing for 2-3 hours until the ice is firm and set.

Champagne ice

Serves 4
CALORIES PER PORTION: 790 (3315 kJ)
PROTEIN CONTENT PER PORTION: 3.5 grams
PREPARATION & FREEZING TIME: about 5 hours

600 ml (1 pint) Champagne
150 g (5 oz) granulated sugar
100 ml (4 fl oz) water
juice of 2 oranges
finely grated rind of 2 lemons
juice of 3 lemons
600 ml (1 pint) whipping cream
2 tablespoons brandy

Put the sugar and water in a pan and heat gently until the sugar has dissolved, stirring occasionally then remove from the heat and leave until cold.

Stir in the orange juice, lemon rind and juice and the Champagne, then pour the mixture into a freezing tray. Cover and place in the freezer or freezing compartment of the refrigerator. Freeze for about 1 hour until the mixture becomes slushy and the edges are solid.

Remove the tray from the freezing compartment, stir the mixture well to break up any lumps, and mix the frozen parts well into the rest of the mixture, whip the cream until thick. Fold the frozen mixture into the whipped cream with the brandy. Return to the freezer or freezing compartment and freeze again for 2-3 hours, or until firm and set.

Note: a sparkling white wine such as an Asti spumante will also do.

Vanilla cream ice

Serves 4
CALORIES PER PORTION: 710 (2957 kJ)
PROTEIN CONTENT PER PORTION: 10.5 grams
PREPARATION & FREEZING TIME: about 5 hours

300 ml (½ pint) milk
1 vanilla pod or ½ teaspoon vanilla
*   essence*
3 eggs, separated
100 g (4 oz) raw brown sugar
600 ml (1 pint) whipping cream

Heat the milk gently in a pan with the vanilla pod (if using), then set aside for a few minutes for the flavour to infuse. Whisk together the egg yolks and sugar in a bowl, strain in the hot milk and continue whisking until all the sugar has dissolved. Add the vanilla essence at this stage, if using this instead of the vanilla pod.

Pour the mixture into the rinsed-out pan, return to the heat until the sauce thickens, stirring constantly. Remove the pan from the heat and leave to cool.

Pour the mixture into a freezing tray, cover and place in the freezing compartment of the refrigerator. Freeze for about 1 hour until the mixture looks slushy and the edges are solid.

Whip the cream until thick. Remove the tray from the freezing compartment, stir the mixture well to break up any lumps, then fold in the whipped cream. Return to the freezing compartment and freeze again for about 1 hour, or until the mixture is thick.

Beat the egg whites until stiff enough to stand in peaks, then remove the cream ice from the freezing compartment and fold it into the beaten egg whites. Return to the freezing compartment again and freeze for 2-3 hours until the ice is firm. Serve sprinkled with chopped nuts and Chocolate or Caramel sauce.

Chocolate cream ice

Serves 4
CALORIES PER PORTION: 1000 (4192 kJ)
PROTEIN CONTENT PER PORTION: 13 grams
PREPARATION & FREEZING TIME: about 5 hours

225 g (8 oz) plain chocolate

Follow the basic recipe for Vanilla cream ice, melting the chocolate in half the milk then adding the remaining milk before continuing.

Coffee cream ice

Serves 4

CALORIES PER PORTION: 710 (2980 kJ)
PROTEIN CONTENT PER PORTION: 11.5 grams
PREPARATION & FREEZING TIME: about 5 hours

2-3 tablespoons instant coffee powder

Follow the basic recipe for Vanilla cream ice, dissolving the instant coffee powder in the milk before continuing.

Ices and sorbets make a refreshing interlude between spicy or strongly flavoured dishes at a dinner party. They are not difficult to make in quantity if you have a freezer or large freezing compartment. Top left: Strawberry cream ice. Top right: Lemon sorbet. Bottom left: Champagne ice. Bottom right: a Raspberry ice

Brown bread cream ice

Serves 4

CALORIES PER PORTION: 850 (3547 kJ)
PROTEIN CONTENT PER PORTION: 15 grams
PREPARATION & FREEZING TIME: 5-6 hours

1 portion vanilla cream ice
225 g (8 oz) wholemeal bread, made into crumbs
2 tablespoons castor sugar
½ teaspoon ground cinnamon
2 tablespoons cream sherry

Sprinkle the breadcrumbs with castor sugar and cinnamon, spread them over a baking sheet and put them into an oven at 190°C (375°F) Gas 5 until well browned. Allow to cool. Sprinkle the sherry over them and stir them into the vanilla ice just before folding in the egg whites. Serve with a Caramel or Raspberry sauce (pages 198 and 199).

Praline cream ice

Serves 4

CALORIES PER PORTION: 850 (3547 kJ)
PROTEIN CONTENT PER PORTION: 15 grams
PREPARATION & FREEZING TIME: 5-6 hours

100 g (4 oz) unblanched almonds
50 g (2 oz) granulated sugar

Cook the almonds with the sugar in a thick-based pan over moderate heat until the sugar melts and coats the almonds. Stir constantly to prevent it burning. Continue cooking until the sugar has caramelized slightly, then pour the praline onto an oiled plate, or a large sheet of non-stick vegetable parchment. Leave until cold, then work to a powder in a blender, or crush finely with a rolling pin.

Follow the recipe for Vanilla cream ice, omitting the vanilla pod and using only half the quantity of given sugar. Fold in the praline powder with the cream.

Freezing Prepared and Cooked Food

Food	Storage time	Preparation	Freezing	Thawing and cooking
Note: Do not over-season curries of hot, spiced dishes as flavourings intensify during freezing. You will soon know how much to add.				
Soups and Sauces (except egg-based sauces)	2-3 months	Go carefully with the seasoning.	Freeze in convenient amounts in plastic bags.	Warm bag in winter, then pour sauce into pan. Melt over moderate heat, avoiding burning. Adjust seasoning and add extra liquid if necessary.
Casseroles and food cooked in sauces (except egg-based sauces)	2 months	Season lightly and omit the garlic if the food is going to be stored for the maximum time. Cook for a slightly shorter time to allow for the extra cooking when it is reheated. Allow to cool, then pour into polythene bags lining casserole dishes, or into rigid containers with lids. Make sure the sauce covers the surface of the food, lay a piece of greaseproof paper on top and seal.	Freeze lined casserole dishes until firm; then remove the dish and wrap the frozen casserole in a freezer bag for storage.	Thaw in room for 4-6 hours. Pour into dish, add garlic if required. Bake at 200°C (400°F) Gas 6 for 1 hour, until boiling. Alternatively remove foil and place in original dish. Bake at 200°C (400°F) Gas 6 for 1 hour then 180°C (350°F) Gas 4 for ½ hour. Heat fully. Thicken if necessary.
Crêpes	1-2 months	Add one tablespoon of olive or sunflower oil to every 125g (4oz) flour in the recipe. Cook and allow to cool.	Interleave with lightly oiled greaseproof paper and seal in a freezer bag.	Thaw in refrigerator overnight or in room 2-3 hours. Remove paper, wrap in foil. Bake at 190°C (375°F) Gas 5 for ½ hour. Or roll up with hot filling. Bake in covered dish for ¼ hour.
Croquettes and rissoles (uncooked)	1 month	Make up the mixture.	Wrap mixture in foil or a freezer bag and seal it.	Thaw in room. Mix and form into rissoles. Cook as in recipe.
Pizzas (cooked)	2 months	Bake as usual, and allow to cool.	Wrap cooled pizzas, interleaved with waxed apper and seal in foil or freezer bags to freeze.	Bake from frozen at 200°C (400°F) Gas 6 for 20 minutes, or thaw in room for 2 hours. Reheat for ¼ hour.
Vegetable loaves and terrines (uncooked)	1 month	Season lightly; omit the garlic for maximum storage. Line a loaf tin with foil and pour in the filling.	Freeze until hard, remove the loaf tin. Wrap in more foil, or seal in freezer bag.	Put bag in water until foil loosens. Remove foil and return loaf to original well-oiled tin. Bake as in recipe.
Vegetable loaves and terrines (cooked)	2 months	Cook as in the recipe but season lightly. Omit garlic for maximum storage. Cool completely.	Wrap in foil or a freezer bag and seal.	Thaw in room for 4-6 hours, Serve cold.
Brown rice (cooked)	2-3 months	Cook in 4 times its volume of water for 40 minutes, slightly underdone. Dry well.	Pack in convenient portions in freezer bags for freezing.	Thaw in room. Reheat gently in ovenproof dish covered with foil.
Dried beans and lentils		Cook as usual but err on the slightly underdone side. Drain and fry.	As rice.	As rice.
Biscuit dough	6 months	Shape dough into cylinders, wrap in foil or freezer-grade polythene.	Freeze dough cylinders wrapped in the chosen covering; freeze shapes on non-stick paper, pack in rigid containers.	Thaw in room. Slice and bake as usual. Shaped biscuits can be baked from frozen; allow an extra 5-10 minutes.
Biscuits (cooked)	6 months	Bake as usual and allow to cool.	Pack in rigid containers.	May be crisped when thawed at 180°C (350°F) Gas 4.
Bread	4 weeks	Bake in the usual way and allow to cool.	Freeze, sealed in freezer bags or foil.	Thaw in bag or foil in room; allow 2½-3 hours for small loaf. Make toast from frozen bread slices.
Cakes	4-6 months	Bake as usual and cool. Roll up Swiss rolls with waxed paper inside. Fill and ice cakes after thawing.	Wrap in foil or seal in freezer bags.	Thaw in room; allow sandwich cake layers 3-4 hours, small cakes 1-2 hours, large fruit cake 4-6 hours.
Pastry (dough) Shortcrust: Puff:	3 months 3-4 months	Roll out; trim to fit flan cases, pie liners and tops, or foil dishes. Puff pastry can be made into vol-au-vent cases.	Freeze unwrapped until hard. Leave in foil dishes, or remove the pie dish and interleave pastry with greaseproof paper. Seal in freezer bags.	Thaw in room for 3-4 hours. Fit into oiled or buttered flan or pie dishes. Proceed as for fresh pastry.
Pastry (cooked)	6 months		Allow to cool before freezing with care, sealed in foil or freezer bags.	Thaw unfilled flan cases in room for 1 hour, filled case for 2-4 hours. Reheat at 180°C (350°F) Gas 4 for 15-20 minutes.

Planning a Menu

The first consideration when planning a lunch or dinner party is to choose food that you think will appeal to your guests. Try and find out beforehand whether there are any foods which your guests will not enjoy; nothing spoils an occasion more than if a guest is forced to refuse something the host or hostess has taken a great deal of time and trouble to prepare. Choose the food as far as possible to match the occasion, but remember that the best and most enjoyable meals are often the simplest ones. Never strain your own capabilities or the resources of your kitchen. The best cooking is always done when you are confident and relaxed and not in a state of nervous exhaustion.

Winter Dinner Party for 8

CALORIES PER PORTION: 1925 (8055kJ) approx.
PROTEIN CONTENT PER PORTION: 50 grams approx.

Make double quantity of all the recipes except the
Hazelnut Cake.

Summer Buffet for 12

ALORIES PER PORTION: 3980 (16650kJ) approx.
OTEIN CONTENT PER PORTION: 83 grams approx.

Make double quantity of the soup, both
l-au-vents, and – for guests with a sweet tooth –
two Shortcakes.

Winter Lunch for 4

CALORIES PER PORTION: 1205 (5070kJ) approx.
PROTEIN CONTENT PER PORTION: 37 grams approx.

Barbecue Supper for 4

CALORIES PER PORTION: 2710 (11360kJ) approx.
PROTEIN CONTENT PER PORTION: 70 grams approx.

The method for baking potatoes is given in the
recipe for Stuffed Potatoes on page 50. Wholemeal
Baps are made from the Basic Quick Bread
recipe on page 151.

Indian Supper for 4

CALORIES PER PORTION: 2570 (10750kJ) approx.
PROTEIN CONTENT PER PORTION: 95 grams approx.
We assume you will have a portion of each dish.

Chinese Meal for 4

CALORIES PER PORTION: 2905 (12170kJ) approx.
PROTEIN CONTENT PER PORTION: 71 grams approx.

Chinese Sugar Apples (page 142) would make a delicious dessert for this menu, should one be required; otherwise, serve fresh lychees.

Summer Picnic for 6

For the Pâté menu:
CALORIES PER PORTION: 1530 (6425kJ) approx.
PROTEIN CONTENT PER PORTION: 44 grams approx.

For the Quiche menu:
CALORIES PER PORTION: 1510 (6325kJ) approx.
PROTEIN CONTENT PER PORTION: 43 grams approx.
(not including bread, cheese and fruit)

Basic Recipes

Without basic recipes, no cook can proceed, while the vegetarian cook will want to look again at the staples of the domestic kitchen. In this section you will find not only a Shortcrust pastry made from wholemeal flour, but also successful brown Puff pastry, Rough puff and Choux as well, for delicious light creations.

Sauces are given for all occasions: a Barbecue sauce or a piquant fruit sauce will lend distinction to a meatless main course. There are also sweet sauces for tempting puddings or you could try the original Brown sugar frosting or Peanut butter icing on a Sunday cake.

Yoghurt is easy to make at home – and it is an improvement on the shop-bought curd. If you have not tried sprouting your own seeds, instructions are given for four different types for fresh, vitamin-packed salads. You will also find invaluable information on vegetables: helpful charts giving cooking and serving instructions which preserve the flavour of fresh vegetables. If you want to freeze them to delay the pleasure of eating, you will also find comprehensive freezing instructions.

Wholemeal shortcrust pastry

TOTAL CALORIES: 1720 (7200 kJ)
TOTAL PROTEIN CONTENT: 33 grams
PREPARATION & CHILLING: 40 minutes

225 g (8 oz) wholemeal flour
½ teaspoon salt
125 g (4 oz) unsalted butter
2-3 tablespoons water

Mix the flour and salt in a bowl. Rub in the butter until the mixture resembles fine breadcrumbs. Gradually add the water, with a little extra if necessary, and mix to a firm dough. Knead lightly on a floured surface until smooth, then wrap the dough in aluminium foil or transparent wrap and chill in the refrigerator for about 30 minutes before using.
Note: This recipe makes enough pastry to line a 20 cm (8 in) diameter flan ring with some over for a lattice topping, or a 23 cm (9 in) diameter flan ring.
For a rich shortcrust pastry, increase the amount of butter in the recipe to 150 g (5 oz).

Puff pastry

TOTAL CALORIES: 4905 (20539 kJ)
TOTAL PROTEIN CONTENT: 46 grams
PREPARATION TIME: 2 hours

450 g (1 lb) unsalted butter
450 g (1 lb) unbleached white flour
2 teaspoons salt
300 ml (½ pint) ice-cold water with 2 teaspoons lemon juice added

You should have no difficulty in making puff pastry as long as you realise that success depends on keeping the layers of butter and dough separate. The butter and dough must be of the same consistency. Take care to keep the ingredients and utensils as cool as possible. Use a marble slab for preference when rolling out the pastry.

Knead 400 g (14 oz) of the butter until pliable and shape into a square of about 13 cm (5 in).

Sift the flour and salt into a bowl and rub in the remaining 50 g (2 oz) of butter. Add the water and mix with a knife to a firm dough. Knead lightly on a floured surface until smooth. Roll the dough into an oblong, about 40 cm by 23 cm (16 in by 9 in). Place the butter in the centre and fold over the two sides, slightly stretching the dough to overlap a little in the centre. Dampen the edge of the top layer to seal it. Fold over both ends, completely enclosing the fat, and press very lightly with the rolling pin to seal the layers of dough together. Wrap the dough in aluminium foil or film wrap and chill in the refrigerator for 10 minutes.

On a lightly floured surface, gently roll out the dough into an oblong, about 40 cm by 23 cm (16 in by 9 in). To begin with, gentle pressure with the rolling pin, rather than actual rolling, will prevent the dough splitting and the butter coming through. Fold the bottom third of the oblong up and the top third down, press the edges lightly to seal and turn the top fold to the right-hand side. Repeat the rolling and folding five more times. Wrap the pastry and place in the refrigerator to relax for 20 minutes after the second, fourth and sixth rolling and folding. Use as required or divide into portions and freeze.

Rough puff pastry

TOTAL CALORIES: 2170 (9080 kJ)
TOTAL PROTEIN CONTENT: 25.2 grams
PREPARATION TIME: 1½-2 hours

175 g (6 oz) well-chilled unsalted butter
250 g (9 oz) plain white flour
½ teaspoon salt
150 ml (¼ pint) ice-cold water with 1 teaspoon lemon juice added

Knead the butter until it is pliable but not soft or oily. Sift the flour and salt into a bowl and rub in a quarter of the butter. Cut the remaining butter into cubes. about 2 cm (¾ in) and add to the flour. Toss lightly in the flour with the fingertips until well coated, taking care not to squash them. Add enough of the water and mix with a knife to make a fairly soft dough. Turn out on to a floured surface and flour the dough but do not knead. Shape it into a rectangle about 10 cm (4 in) wide by 15 cm (6 in) long with gentle hand pressure then roll out to a rectangle 30 cm by 13 cm (12 in by 5 in). Fold the bottom third up and the top third down.

Press the edges lightly by hand or with a rolling pin to seal. Turn the top fold to the right-hand side. Repeat the rolling and folding once and then wrap the pastry well and place in the refrigerator for about 30 minutes to chill. Roll and fold twice more and chill it for a further 30 minutes. Use as required.

Choux pastry

TOTAL CALORIES: 1280 (5360 kJ)
TOTAL PROTEIN CONTENT: 37 grams
PREPARATION TIME: 15 minutes

100 g (4 oz) plain white flour
200 ml (⅓ pint) milk
75 g (3 oz) butter
¾ teaspoon salt
3 eggs, well beaten

Sift the flour. Put the milk, butter and salt into a saucepan and place over a moderate heat until the butter melts. Increase the heat and bring to the boil, then remove the pan from the heat and immediately add the flour all in one go, stirring vigorously. Return the pan to the stove and continue stirring until the mixture thickens and comes away from the sides of the pan. Allow to cool very slightly then add the eggs a little at a time, beating very well between each addition. The mixture should be glossy and firm enough to hold its shape and, you may not need to use all the egg. There should be enough mixture to make about 12 Chocolate Eclairs.

Coating batter

TOTAL CALORIES: 660 (2760 kJ)
TOTAL PROTEIN CONTENT: 28 grams
PREPARATION & RESTING TIME: 35 minutes

150 g (5 oz) wholemeal flour
1 teaspoon salt
1 tablespoon melted butter
2 egg yolks, beaten
150 ml (¼ pint) milk
1 egg white

Sift the flour into a bowl with the salt through a medium-meshed sieve. Discard the bran. Mix the butter and egg yolk into the milk and pour this on the flour. Mix thoroughly then stand 30 minutes. Stir in stiffly beaten white and use.

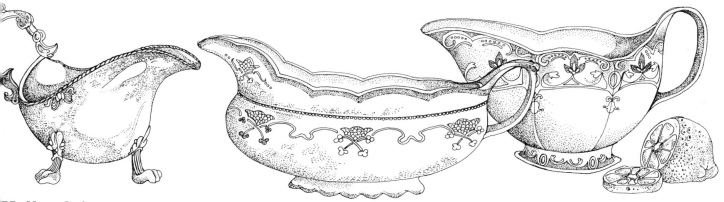

Hollandaise sauce

CALORIES PER PORTION: 225 (1060 kJ)
PROTEIN CONTENT PER PORTION: 2 grams
PREPARATION & COOKING TIME: 10 minutes

2 egg yolks
1 tablespoon lemon juice
125 g (4 oz) unsalted butter
salt

Beat the egg yolks with the lemon juice in a small mixing bowl until they are completely smooth. Stand the bowl over a saucepan of hot water, add about a sixth of the butter and whisk it into the egg yolks. Increase the heat under the saucepan, but never allow the water to boil, otherwise the sauce will curdle. Add another piece of butter and continue beating. Carry on in this way until all the butter has been used up and the sauce has begun to thicken. It should be thick enough to leave a trail when the spoon is moved across the surface.

Remove the bowl immediately from the saucepan and continue beating until the bowl has cooled down slightly and there is no danger that the sauce will go on cooking. (The bowl can be placed in a larger bowl of cold water to hasten the process.) Season very lightly with salt and serve. Hollandaise sauce should be served lukewarm. If it has to be kept, stand the bowl in a saucepan of warm water, but do not let it boil.

Mousseline sauce: Stir 2-3 tablespoons lightly whipped cream in to the basic Hollandaise sauce just before serving.

Butter sauce

This sauce is delicious served with vegetables where the richness of Hollandaise is not required.

CALORIES PER PORTION: 635 (2560 kJ)
PROTEIN CONTENT PER PORTION: 3 grams
PREPARATION & COOKING TIME: 20 minutes

75 g (3 oz) unsalted butter
1½ tablespoon white unbleached flour
300 ml (½ pint) boiling water
1-2 teaspoon lemon juice
a good pinch of grated lemon rind
salt
freshly ground pepper

Melt half of the butter in a saucepan over gentle heat, then remove the pan from the stove and mix in the flour. Pour on the boiling water, stirring vigorously. Do not return the pan to the stove. When the sauce is completely smooth, beat in the rest of the butter in four separate portions; add the lemon juice and rind and season with salt and pepper.

Do not allow this sauce to cook at all, or the flavour will be spoilt.

Béarnaise sauce

CALORIES PER PORTION: 1080 (4510 kJ)
PROTEIN CONTENT PER PORTION: 13 grams
PREPARATION & COOKING TIME: 20 minutes

4 tablespoons wine vinegar
25 g (1 oz) finely chopped onion
1 bay leaf
1 tablespoon finely chopped mixed herbs
6 peppercorns, coarsely crushed
2 large egg yolks
125 g (4 oz) unsalted butter

Put the vinegar, onion, bay leaf, mixed herbs and peppercorns into a small saucepan and simmer it over very, very gentle heat until only 1 tablespoon is left. Strain it into a small mixing bowl, add the egg yolks and mix thoroughly. Stand the bowl over a saucepan of hot water and add about a sixth of the butter. Increase the heat slightly but do not let the water boil and continue whisking until the butter has melted and is mixed into the eggs. Add another sixth of the butter and continue whisking. Carry on in this way until all the butter has been used up and the sauce is thick and foamy.

Béchamel sauce

CALORIES PER PORTION: 120 (500 kJ)
PROTEIN CONTENT PER PORTION: 3.5 grams
PREPARATION & COOKING TIME: 40 minutes

25 g (1 oz) butter
50 g (2 oz) finely chopped onion
25 g (1 oz) wholemeal or unbleached
white flour
300 ml (½ pint) milk
bay leaf
a blade of mace or a pinch of grated
nutmeg
salt
freshly ground black pepper

Melt the butter over gentle heat and fry the onion until transparent. Stir in the flour and cook for a few moments longer, stirring all the time. Remove the pan from the heat and gradually add the milk, stirring well after each addition. Return the pan to the stove, add the bay leaf and mace or nutmeg and bring the sauce to the boil, stirring until it thickens. Transfer it to a double boiler, cover with a piece of buttered greaseproof paper and simmer for 30 minutes. Strain the sauce and thin with a little hot milk if necessary. Adjust the seasoning and serve.

Béchamel sauce is the basis of a number of other sauces:

Cheese sauce: Add 50 g (2 oz) of strongly flavoured grated Cheddar cheese to the Béchamel sauce before straining. Stir until it has melted into the sauce, then strain as above and adjust the seasoning, adding a pinch of cayenne if liked.

Onion sauce: Cook 100 g (4 oz) finely chopped onion in a tablespoon of butter until just transparent and add to the sauce before it is put into the double boiler. Rub some of the purée through the sieve with the sauce if you like a stronger onion flavour.

Parsley sauce: Stir 2 tablespoons of finely chopped parsley to the sauce after straining it and add a little lemon juice as well, if liked.

Caper sauce: Add 2-3 tablespoons finely chopped capers and a little wine or cider vinegar, or some of the vinegar from the capers, if liked, after straining the sauce.

Polonaise sauce: Add 1-2 tablespoons freshly grated horseradish, after straining. Then stir in 2 tablespoons double cream and a little lemon juice, if liked.

Mustard sauce: Stir in 1-2 teaspoons prepared French mustard and a little wine, or cider, vinegar after straining.

Sauce allemande: Stir a little of the basic Béchamel, after straining, on to 2 well-beaten eggs in a bowl. Mix well, pour in the rest of the sauce and return it to a clean saucepan. Sprinkle with a pinch of grated nutmet and add a teaspoon of lemon juice and stir well. Reheat the sauce, taking care that it does not boil or the eggs will curdle, and serve.

Lyonnaise sauce: Cook 100 g (4 oz) finely chopped onion in 2 tablespoons melted butter until golden brown, then add them, with the butter in which they have been cooked, to the Béchamel sauce after straining.

Brown sauce

CALORIES PER PORTION: 140 (590 kJ)
PROTEIN CONTENT PER PORTION: 3.5 grams
PREPARATION & COOKING TIME: 30 minutes

125 g (4 oz) finely chopped onion
2 tablespoons olive or sunflower oil
2 coarsely chopped tomatoes
1-2 tablespoons wholemeal flour
300 ml (½ pint) brown vegetable stock
a pinch of dried thyme
bay leaf
50 ml (2 fl oz) red wine
1 teaspoon yeast extract
salt
freshly ground pepper

Fry the onion in the oil until golden brown; add the tomatoes and continue cooking, stirring constantly, until all the liquid has evaporated and they have started to brown. Sprinkle over the flour, stir it well, then pour on the stock and bring to the boil, stirring all the time until the sauce thickens. Add the thyme, bay leaf, red wine and yeast extract and simmer the sauce for 20 minutes, stirring occasionally. Strain into a clean pan, adjust the seasoning, reheat and serve.

The following sauces are based on Brown sauce.

Mushroom sauce: Cook 100 g (4 oz) finely chopped mushrooms in 2 tablespoons melted butter until soft and shiny and add them to the brown sauce after straining it. If a smoother textured sauce is required, add the mushrooms before straining the sauce and rub them through the sieve. Season well with pepper and a little cayenne, if desired.

Paprika sauce: Add 2 tablespoons of fresh paprika to the basic Brown sauce recipe with the flour. A little wine vinegar or lemon juice can also be added, if liked.

Madeira sauce: Add 2-4 tablespoons well-flavoured dark Madeira to the basic Brown sauce after straining. Adjust the seasoning and serve as it is, or simmer for 5-10 minutes to evaporate the alcohol.

Piquant sauce: Pour 3 tablespoons wine vinegar into a saucepan with 3 coarsely crushed peppercorns, a bay leaf and a sprig of thyme or rosemary. Reduce it to 1 tablespoon, then strain into the finished sauce. Add 1 tablespoon very finely chopped pickled cucumber or gherkins.

Tomato sauce

CALORIES PER PORTION: 60 (247 kJ)
PROTEIN CONTENT PER PORITON: 1.5 grams
PREPARATION & COOKING TIME: 40 minutes

450 g (1 lb) coarsely chopped tomatoes
50 g (2 oz) finely chopped onion
1 tablespoon olive or sunflower oil
1 tablespoon wholemeal flour
150 ml (¼ pint) water
1 bay leaf
1 clove of garlic, peeled and finely
chopped (optional)
salt and freshly ground pepper

Fry the onion in the oil until transparent, stir in the flour, then add the water. Stir well, then put in the tomatoes with the bay leaf and garlic, if used. Bring to the boil, stirring all the time, then simmer for 30 minutes, stirring from time to time. Rub the sauce through a sieve, adjust the seasoning and reheat before serving.

For a more piquant sauce, add 1 tablespoon wine or cider vinegar to the water and stir ½ tablespoon finely chopped capers into the sauce after straining.

Bigarade sauce: Add the thinly pared and sliced rind of 2 Seville oranges, with their juice, to the basic Tomato or Brown sauce. If liked, you can add it to a blend of the two.

Catalane sauce

CALORIES PER PORTION: 130 (540 kJ)
PROTEIN CONTENT PER PORTION: 3 grams
PREPARATION AND COOKING TIME: 20 minutes,
  using prepared basic sauces

150 ml (¼ pint) Brown sauce
150 ml (¼ pint) Tomato sauce
50 g (2 oz) finely chopped red peppers
1 tablespoon melted butter
1 tablespoon lemon juice
½ teaspoon grated orange rind
½ clove of garlic, peeled and finely
  chopped

Heat up the two sauces together. Fry the peppers in the butter over moderate heat until they are soft; add the lemon juice, orange rind and garlic and cook for a few minutes, then pour on the sauces. Stir well and simmer for a further 5 minutes before serving with vegetable loaves.

Barbecue sauce

CALORIES PER PORTION: 145 (610 kJ)
PROTEIN CONTENT PER PORTION: 2 grams
PREPARATION & COOKING TIME: 20 minutes

150 g (5 oz) finely chopped onion
2 tablespoons sunflower or olive oil
300 ml (½ pint) Tomato sauce
1 clove of garlic, peeled and finely
  chopped
125 g (4 oz) canned pineapple, finely
  diced
125 g (4 oz) pickled cucumber, finely
  diced
2 tablespoons wine vinegar
salt
freshly ground pepper
a pinch of cayenne

Fry the onion in the oil until transparent then add all the other ingredients except the salt, pepper and cayenne and simmer for 5 minutes. Adjust the seasoning and serve the sauce hot or cold.

Piquant cherry sauce

CALORIES PER PORTION: 47 (195 kJ)
PROTEIN CONTENT PER PORTION: 1 gram
PREPARATION & COOKING TIME: 45 minutes

225 g (8 oz) stoned morello cherries
6 tablespoons wine vinegar
2 tablespoons finely chopped onion
150 ml (¼ pint) water
grated rind and juice of 1 orange
salt
freshly ground pepper
½ teaspoon freshly ground allspice
¼ teaspoon ground cinnamon

Spiced apricot sauce

CALORIES PER PORTION: 115 (485 kJ)
PROTEIN CONTENT PER PORTION: 1.5 grams
PREPARATION & COOKING TIME: 10 minutes

350 g (12 oz) cooked or canned apricots
150 ml (¼ pint) Brown vegetable stock
  (page 34)
½ teaspoon ground cinnamon
½ teaspoon ground ginger
a dash of Tabasco sauce
3 tablespoons cream sherry
salt
freshly ground pepper

Rub the apricots through a sieve or Mouli mill into a saucepan and thin the purée with some of the stock.

Add the rest of the ingredients, season well with salt and pepper and bring the sauce to the boil over moderate heat, stirring constantly to prevent it from sticking. Lower the heat and simmer for another 5 minutes stirring occasionally. Pour into a jug and serve.

The sauce can also be served cold.

Put the vinegar and onion into a small saucepan and simmer over gentle heat until the liquid is reduced by half. Add the cherries, water and the orange rind and juice and increase the heat slightly. Simmer until the cherries are soft, about 15-20 minutes, then remove from the stove and rub them through a sieve. Adjust the seasoning and reheat the sauce, if necessary, before serving.

Horseradish sauce

CALORIES PER PORTION: 175 (725 kJ)
PROTEIN CONTENT PER PORTION: 1 gram
PREPARATION TIME: 10 minutes

2-3 tablespoons peeled horseradish,
  freshly grated
1 teaspoon wine vinegar or lemon juice
150 ml (¼ pint) double cream
salt

Mix together the horseradish and vinegar or lemon juice. Lightly whip the cream, then fold in the horseradish and season with salt.

For a change, try using cultured sour cream instead of double cream.

Green gooseberry sauce

CALORIES PER PORTION: 110 (460 kJ)
PROTEIN CONTENT PER PORTION: 1 gram
PREPARATION & COOKING TIME: 30 minutes

175 g (6 oz) halved green gooseberries
50 g (2 oz) butter
1 tablespoon wholemeal flour
200 ml (⅓ pint) water
1 tablespoon white wine
salt
freshly ground pepper

Cook the gooseberries in very little water until they are tender, about 10-15 minutes. then rub them through a sieve. Melt the butter in a pan over gentle heat and stir in the flour, then remove the pan from the heat, pour on the water and mix until smooth. Return the pan to the heat, bring to the boil and simmer the sauce for 10 minutes, stirring occasionally to prevent it burning. Add the gooseberry purée and wine and mix well. Adjust the seasoning if necessary, and cook for a few minutes longer before serving.

Herb butter

CALORIES PER PORTION: 100 (412 kJ)
PROTEIN CONTENT PER PORTION: nil
PREPARATION & CHILLING TIME: 1 hour

100 g (4 oz) unsalted butter
4 tablespoons finely chopped herbs,
  such as parsley, tarragon, chervil or
  watercress, or a mixture

Beat the herbs into the butter. Form the herb butter into a roll and chill well before cutting it into 4 slices, one for each portion.

Clarified butter

CALORIES PER PORTION: 415 (1472 kJ)
PROTEIN CONTENT PER PORTION: 0.25 grams
PREPARATION TIME: 10 minutes

225 g (8 oz) butter

Put the butter into a small pan and stand it over gentle heat until it has melted and begun to bubble. Continue cooking until the bubbling subsides, but do not allow the sediment at the bottom of the pan to colour. Strain the melted butter through a fine cloth or muslin-lined sieve and store in a covered jar. Discard the milk solids that are left after straining. This quantity should give about 175 g (6 oz) of clarified butter.

Montpelier butter

CALORIES PER PORTION: 100 (412 kJ)
PROTEIN CONTENT PER PORTION: nil
PREPARATION & CHILLING TIME: 1 hour

1 clove of garlic, peeled and cut in half
1 tablespoon chopped chervil
1 tablespoon chopped tarragon
1 tablespoon chopped chives
2 tablespoons chopped watercress
1 teaspoon finely chopped capers
1 teaspoon finely chopped pickled
  gherkin
100 g (4 oz) unsalted butter

Rub the inside of a small bowl with the cut clove of garlic. Put in the herbs, watercress, capers and gherkin and mix well. Beat in the softened butter and form it into a roll. Chill well before cutting into 4 portions for serving.

Sweet Sauces

The sweet sauces have been chosen to complement the cakes, puddings, ices and desserts in this book.

These are followed by one or two of my favourite icings, frostings and fillings for cakes.

Chantilly cream

CALORIES PER PORTION: 335 (1465 kJ)
PROTEIN CONTENT PER PORTION: 4 grams
PREPARATION TIME: 5 minutes

300 ml (½ pint) whipping cream
3 tablespoons soft brown sugar
1 egg white, stiffly beaten

Lightly whip the cream with the brown sugar until it just holds its shape, then fold in the stiffly beaten egg white.

Butterscotch sauce

CALORIES PER PORTION: 157 (660 kJ)
PROTEIN CONTENT PER PORTION: 0 gram
PREPARATION & COOKING TIME: 20 minutes

2 tablespoons golden syrup
25 g (1 oz) butter
75 g (3 oz) raw brown sugar
1½ tablespoons cornflour
300 ml (½ pint) water

Put the syrup, butter and sugar into a pan and cook over medium heat until the sugar has started to caramelize; mix the cornflour to a cream with a little of the water, then add the rest of the water and mix well. Remove the pan from the heat and pour the cornflour mixture onto the caramel. Stir well, return the pan to the heat and cook, stirring until it is well blended and the sauce has thickened.

If a richer sauce is required, use half milk and half water.

Caramel sauce

CALORIES PER PORTION: 185 (780 kJ)
PROTEIN CONTENT PER PORTION: 0 gram
PREPARTION & COOKING TIME: 20 minutes

1 tablespoon cornflour
300 ml (½ pint) water
75 g (6 oz) granulated sugar

Mix the cornflour to a cream with a little of the water and then add the rest. Melt the sugar in a thick-based pan, stirring continuously, and continue cooking until it has turned a rich golden brown. Take the pan off the heat and gradually stir in the water and cornflour mixture, taking care that the hot sugar does not spatter onto your hand. Return the pan to the stove and cook stirring well until the caramel has dissolved and the sauce has thickened. Pour it into a jug and serve hot or cold.

Custard sauce

CALORIES PER PORTION: 210 (872 kJ)
PROTEIN CONTENT PER PORTION: 5 grams
PREPARATION & COOKING TIME: 40 minutes

50 g (2 oz) butter
25 g (1 oz) wholemeal or unbleached
  white flour
300 ml (½ pint) milk
25 g (1 oz) raw brown sugar
1 vanilla pod
1 egg, well beaten

Melt the butter in a saucepan over gentle heat, stir in the flour and cook for a few moments without allowing the flour to colour. Remove the pan from the heat and stir in the milk. Return the pan to the stove, add the sugar and bring the sauce to the boil, stirring until it thickens. Add the vanilla pod, pour the sauce into a double boiler, cover it with a piece of buttered greaseproof paper and let it simmer over boiling water for about 30 minutes. Remove from the heat and allow to cool slightly before pouring it slowly onto the egg, stirring vigorously as you do so. Strain the sauce and thin with a little extra milk, if necessary, to make it up to 300 ml (½ pint).

Tipsy custard

CALORIES PER PORTION: 210 (872 kJ)
PROTEIN CONTENT PER PORTION: 5 grams

Follow the recipe (left), but add 1-2 tablespoons of brandy before straining the sauce.

Raspberry sauce

CALORIES PER PORTION: 250 (1045 kJ)
PROTEIN CONTENT PER PORTION: 1 gram
PREPARATION & COOKING TIME: 30 minutes

450 g (1 lb) raspberries
225 g (8 oz) raw brown sugar

Put the raspberries into a saucepan with the sugar and place over gentle heat. Break some of the fruit with a wooden spoon to release some of the juice, and simmer over gentle heat for about 20 minutes. Rub the sauce through a sieve and serve hot or cold.

Chocolate sauce

CALORIES PER PORTION: 265 (1115 kJ)
PROTEIN CONTENT PER PORTION: 1.5 grams
PREPARATION & COOKING TIME: 15 minutes

200 g (7 oz) raw brown sugar
25 g (1 oz) butter
200 ml (⅓ pint) water
2 tablespoons cocoa powder

Put the sugar, butter and water into a pan and bring to the boil stirring continuously. Simmer until all the sugar has dissolved, then sift in the cocoa powder and continue stirring. Boil until the sauce thickens slightly when a drop is put onto a cold plate. If it is boiled for too long it will turn into toffee.

For a special occasion add 1 teaspoonful of brandy just before serving. The above recipe will make about 200 ml (⅓ pint) of sauce.

Brown sugar frosting

TOTAL CALORIES: 2520 (10540 kJ)
TOTAL PROTEIN CONTENT: 7 grams
PREPARATION & COOKING TIME: 30 minutes

125 g (4 oz) raw brown sugar
3 tablespoons boiled water
2 egg whites, stiffly beaten
½ teaspoon vanilla essence

You need a sugar thermometer to make this frosting successfully.

Put the sugar and water into a very clean, small, thick-based saucepan and bring to the boil over fairly high heat. Boil until the temperature reaches 110°C (225°F). As soon as the syrup reaches the correct temperature, pour it slowly into the egg whites while whisking vigorously. Add the vanilla essence and continue whisking until the frosting is thick enough to coat the top and sides of a cake.

If the syrup goes grainy as it gets near to the correct temperature, it shows that the saucepan was not quite clean and grease-free or perhaps that the sugar was not of good enough quality. Try not to let any sugar crystallise around the edges of the pan as it will encourage graining.

Chocolate frosting: Add 3 teaspoons of sieved cocoa powder towards the end of whisking.

Coffee frosting: Add 1-2 teaspoons of instant coffee powder towards the end of whisking.

Orange frosting: Add 1-2 teaspoons finely grated orange rind towards the end.

Brown sugar butter cream

TOTAL CALORIES: 2565 (10740 kJ)
TOTAL PROTEIN CONTENT: 4 grams
PREPARATION & COOKING TIME: 20 minutes
   plus cooling time

125 g (4 oz) butter or margarine
150 g (5 oz) raw brown sugar
125 ml (4 fl oz) milk
250 g (generous 8 oz) sifted icing sugar

Put the butter or margarine, sugar and milk into a saucepan over a moderate heat and stir until the sugar has dissolved. Allow to cool a little before stirring in the icing sugar. Stand the saucepan in a bowl filled with ice cubes and stir briskly until the icing is cold and the consistency thick enough to coat the top and sides of a cake. If the consistency is still too soft when the icing is quite cold, beat in more sugar.

Vanilla flavoured cream: Add ½ teaspoon vanilla essence with the butter.

Chocolate flavoured cream: Add 2-4 teaspoons cocoa powder to the butter, sugar and milk while the sugar is dissolving.

Coffee flavoured cream: Add 2-4 teaspoons of instant coffee powder to the butter, sugar and milk in the pan.

Peanut butter icing

TOTAL CALORIES: 2225 (9300 kJ)
TOTAL PROTEIN CONTENT: 32 grams
PREPARATION TIME: 10 minutes

125 g (4 oz) peanut butter
1 teaspoon lemon juice
350 g (12 oz) sifted icing sugar
125 ml (4 fl oz) milk

Soften the peanut butter, if necessary, by standing the container in a pan of warm water. Mix in the lemon juice and icing sugar, then add just enough milk to give a coating consistency. There will be enough icing to cover the top and sides of a 20 cm (8 in) diameter sandwich cake.

Almond paste

TOTAL CALORIES: 3320 (13900 kJ)
TOTAL PROTEIN CONTENT: 61 grams
PREPARATION TIME: 10-20 minutes

300 g (11 oz) ground almonds
225 g (8 oz) sifted icing sugar
150 g (5 oz) caster sugar
1 whole egg and 1 egg yolk
1-2 teaspoons rose water (optional)
1 tablespoon lemon juice

Mix together 150 g (5 oz) of the icing sugar, the caster sugar and the almonds in a bowl. Whisk the eggs with the rose water, if used, and lemon juice and pour into the dry ingredients. Mix thoroughly and turn out on to a board or work surface. Knead until smooth, adding more of the icing sugar if necessary to make a firm paste. Use as required.

Yoghurt

Yoghurt makes a pleasantly sour sauce for fresh or cooked fruit. Mixed with honey and served chilled it makes a refreshing dessert.

CALORIES PER PORTION: 165 (695 kJ)
PROTEIN CONTENT PER PORTION: 9 grams
PREPARATION TIME: 12 hours

1 litre (1¾ pints) milk
2 tablespoons fresh live yoghurt or commercial yoghurt culture (follow the maker's instructions)

Make sure that the yoghurt is genuine *natural* yoghurt and that it contains live culture; it is important to ensure that all your utensils and equipment you use are spotlessly clean.

Bring the milk to boiling point and scald it for 5 minutes. Allow to cool to just above blood heat. Meanwhile, thoroughly clean a large container, pour in the warm milk, add the live yoghurt and mix thoroughly. Cover the bowl and keep warm, at a temperature a little above blood heat, for 8-12 hours or until the yoghurt has set. Allow to cool and then use as required. Retain a couple of tablespoons of this yoghurt with which to start the next batch, but do not keep it longer than a couple of days. Store in the refrigerator, where it

will keep fresh for 2-3 days.

When the yoghurt begins to lose its strength, it will be necessary to start again with a fresh lot of live yoghurt, or a dried culture.

When making yoghurt it is much easier to use sterile UHT or long life milk; there is also less chance of undesirable organisms invading the culture.

Fat-free yoghurt is made by using dried skimmed milk made up with sterile warm water that has been brought to the boil and allowed to cool.

Note: There are a number of very efficient commercial yoghurt makers available on the market and it may be worth investing in one of these.

Chhana

Makes 275 g (10 oz) cheese

CALORIES PER PORTION: 130 (545 kJ)
PROTEIN CONTENT PER PORTION: 12.5 grams
PREPARATION TIME: 12 hours

1 litre (1¾ pints) freshly made yoghurt

Line a strainer or colander with a scrupulously clean piece of muslin and stand it over a bowl. Pour the yoghurt into the muslin-lined strainer, cover it and leave it to drain overnight in a cool, insect-free, airy place. Turn the cheese out of the cloth, keep it in the refrigerator and use

as required. It is slightly more acid than normal curd cheese, but is very good to eat with wholemeal bread or salads.

Use the whey as the cooking liquid in casseroles or for making stock; the slight acidity gives a pleasing piquancy to the finished food.

Panir

CALORIES PER PORTION: 130 (545 kJ)
PROTEIN CONTENT PER PORTION: 12.5 grams
PREPARATION TIME: 12¼ hours

Panir is a chhana which has been pressed; you can improvise a press quite easily if you have two cake tins of 15 cm (6 in) diameter with removable bases. Use the outside tin and both bases.

Place a base inside the tin and line the base with 6 layers of absorbent kitchen paper, leaving a small space around the edge for the liquid to drain away during pressing. Line the inside of the tin with a layer of muslin and on this spread the chhana. Wrap the muslin firmly round the chhana, or put another layer of muslin over the top. Add 6 more layers of absorbent kitchen paper, then the second cake tin base and place a weight of approximately 2 kg (4.4 lb) on top. If the chhana begins to ooze out straightaway, try a

slightly lighter weight. After about 4 hours the weight can be increased to about 3 kg (6.6 lb) and, after 4 more hours, this weight can be doubled to about 6 kg (13 lb). Leave for a further 4 hours, then carefully dismantle the press and remove the cheese. Strip off the muslin and cut it into cubes.

To cook panir: arrange the cubes in a well-buttered non-stick baking dish and brush the tops with melted butter. Bake towards the top of the oven at 200°C (400°F) Gas 6 for 30-40 minutes until they are golden brown but not dried out. Turn the pieces over about half way through the cooking time.

Note: It is easier to bake home-made panir than to fry it, as it tends to disintegrate in the frying pan. Add it to casseroles for extra protein, or eat with salads.

Garam masala

Indian cooking depends for its subtlety of flavour on the fact that Indian cooks mix their own spices for each dish. Commercially-made curry powder can be used instead, of course, but the difference in flavour if you blend your own cannot be compared.

The base
3 parts green cardamons
2 parts cinnamon
1-2 parts cumin seeds

For coriander-based
add 2 parts coriander seeds

For clove-based
add ¼-½ part cloves

For fennel-based
add ½ part of fennel seeds

Mix together all the ingredients and grind them to a fine powder either in a pestle and mortar or a small mill.

Sprouting beans and seeds

One of the great attractions of sprouting is that anyone with enough space to stand a bottle or jar of ½ -2 litres (1-3½ pints) can grow appetising and nutritious supplement to their diet. Many varieties of beans and seeds are now sold solely for sprouting and are readily available from wholefood shops.

There are various methods of sprouting seeds; if one keeps the basic requirements of germination in mind, it is easy to find the simplest method. Seeds require moisture to germinate and, as they are being grown in greater concentration than in nature, certain waste products need to be dispersed.

There are commercially available sprouting trays with special draining systems and some people recommend ordinary kitchen sieves. I found that when I used a sieve, the roots grew straight through the holes in the mesh and were difficult to disentangle, and the commercially designed trays took up too much space — so I now use the simplest method, and in my opinion, the best.

Choose a wide necked bottle of about ½ litre (1 pint) capacity for smaller seeds and a 2 litre (3½ pint) bottle for growing larger seeds and for production in quantity. You will also need a piece of nylon gauze or net of a mesh size smaller than any seed you intend sprouting and a piece of thin string or an elastic band to keep it in place over the top of the jar.

The seeds you intend to sprout must be of edible quality. That is why it is advisable to buy them from a wholefood shop, particularly if you tell them what you are using them for, as some seeds will not sprout if they are too old and the shop should know the state of their stock. Do not use horticultural seeds unless they are being sold for sprouting as they might otherwise be treated with insecticides, chemical retardants or fungicides.

Select good-quality, undamaged seeds and discard any that are split, chipped or blemished in any way as they will not germinate; worse, they might rot and taint the rest of your crop. Spread them out on a tray for inspection and pick out any bad ones. Most seeds expand to about eight times their original volume; 25 g (1 oz) will give 225 g (8 oz) of sprouts, enough for 2 servings. As a general rule, the smaller the seed the greater they increase in size.

Put them into a sieve or fine strainer and rinse them under cold running water. Then transfer them gently to the bottle, taking care not to damage them. Cover them with water, fasten the straining net securely over and leave them to soak overnight. The following morning, pour off the water, re-fill the bottle and immediately pour the off again so that the seeds have just the moisture which is clinging to them. Do not leave any excess water in the bottom of the jar. Stand it in a cupboard or on a shelf at room temperature. In the evening, fill the jar with water again and drain it off, and repeat this routine again last thing at night. Continue this daily ritual until the shoots are the length you require, about 5-7 days, depending on the warmth of the atmosphere and the type of sprout. Never leave the seeds standing in water or they will rot. and take care to remove any seeds that have not sprouted within 36 hours of the first germination. Take out any that show signs of going mushy, then double-rinse the jar before using again.

Alfalfa

Delicious in salads, the sprouts cook almost instantly. Use them on their own, or with a light salad dressing, or as a garnish to vegetable dishes.

Mung beans

These have a flavour similar to very young raw peas and will be recognized as an essential ingredient in many Chinese dishes. Use them when the root is 4-6 cm (1½ -2½ in) long. Stir fry them for 2-3 minutes.

Mustard and cress

This is grown in a totally different way, but is so easy that it has to be included. Put a layer of cotton wool in a shallow waterproof dish and moisten it lightly. Sprinkle the seeds sparsely over the surface and place the dish on a light window sill but not in full sunlight. Keep the surface covered with a piece of card until the seeds germinate. If you want to harvest both mustard and cress at the same time, plant the mustard seed four days after the cress.

Soya beans, lentils, chickpeas, wheat and many other seeds can be sprouted, so I suggest you find a specialist book on the subject. I hope the examples above will whet your appetite.

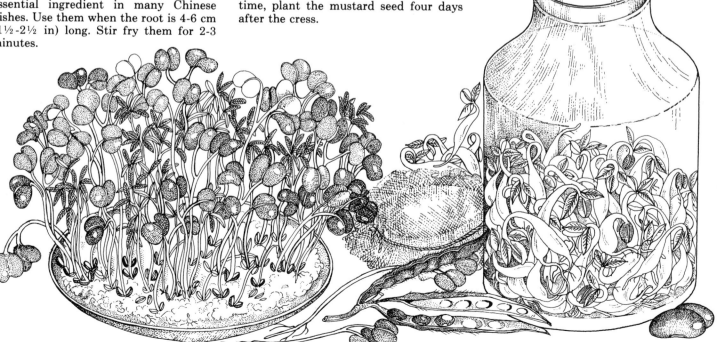

Preparation of accompanying vegetables

Vegetable	Quantity for 4	Preparation	Cooking instructions	Serving instructions
Brassicas & leaves				
Broccoli (calabrese, purple and white)	450 g (1 lb)	Remove any large leaves and cut off any fibrous stem. Divide large heads into florets. Rinse well.	Boil 10-15 minutes; steam 10-15 minutes.	Serve with a knob of butter and a dash of pepper; or with Hollandaise sauce; or sprinkle with grated cheese and finish off under the grill.
Brussels sprouts	450 g (1 lb)	Remove outer leaves and ends of stems. Leave whole. If sprouts are large and stems are thick, cross-cut to ¼ way up.	Boil 8-10 minutes; steam 10-20 minutes, depending on size.	Serve buttered with pepper; or buttered with lemon juice and chopped oregano; or browned in butter with chopped onion and boiled chestnuts.
Chinese cabbage	450 g (1 lb)	Remove outer leaves. Tear the inner leaves into 5 cm (2 in) squares and wash well.	Stir-fry 5-10 minutes.	Serve straight from the pan; or add a little shredded orange rind and juice.
Green winter cabbage (Savoy)	450 g (1 lb)	Remove bruised or damaged outer leaves and watch for caterpillars. Chop coarsely or shred finely after removing hard core.	Boil 10-15 minutes.	Serve with a knob of butter and a dash of pepper.
Red cabbage	450 g (1 lb)	As green winter cabbage.	Braise with onions, garlic and/or apple, raisins, brown sugar, spices (shown right) and with vinegar. Cook in oven 2½ hours, on stove 1½.	Flavour with pickling spice, cloves or caraway seeds to taste.
White cabbage	450 g (1 lb)	As green winter cabbage.	Shred for serving. Boil 5-10 minutes; stir-fry 5-10 minutes; steam 5-10 minutes.	As green winter cabbage; or try putting ½ teaspoon caraway seeds in to flavour the water, if boiling.
Cauliflower	1 medium head or 450 g (1 lb)	Remove outer leaves and any discoloured curd; leave whole or break into florets. Cut out part of the centre core if leaving whole.	Boil whole 20 minutes; boil florets 5-10 minutes, depending on size.	Serve buttered; or with lemon and butter; or with a Béchamel or Cheese sauce.
Kale	600 g-1 kg (1¼-2 lb)	Discard all damaged or discoloured leaves. Watch for insects. Rinse well.	Boil in just enough water to cover; young leaves 5-10 minutes, older leaves 10-15 minutes. Steaming is not advisable.	Serve buttered and sprinkled with herbs; or with chopped onion; or with a chili sauce. Mask them in a rice Cream sauce or Cheese sauce, and finish off under the grill for a few moments.
Spinach	600 g-1 kg (1¼-2 lb)	Discard all damaged or discoloured parts of leaves. Watch for insects. Wash leaf by leaf under cold running water. Remove all stems.	Cook in just the water clinging to the leaves. A little butter or oil on the bottom of the pan prevents them sticking; young leaves 5-10 minutes; older leaves 10-15 minutes. Steam for about 15 minutes; stir-fry 5-10 minutes.	Serve buttered; with chopped onion; in a Cream or Cheese sauce and browned under the grill; or puréed and made into a soufflé (page 68).

Other greens

Note: Cook all greens uncovered for the first 5 minutes to preserve their colour. Keep any remaining liquid for use in stock. Keep some tender young leaves for use in salads.

Mild-flavoured greens				
Beet tops, Dandelion, Endive, Lettuce, Spinach beet, Spring cabbage, Watercress	600 g-1 kg (1¼-2 lb)	As spinach.	As spinach.	As spinach.
Strong-flavoured greens				
Mustard greens		As kale.	As kale; or cook stems as a separate vegetable; boil 20-25 minutes; steam 30 minutes.	As kale.
Swiss chard (Seakale beet)		As kale.	As mustard greens.	As kale.
Turnip tops		As kale.	As mustard greens.	As kale.

Preparation of accompanying vegetables—continued

Vegetable	Quantity for 4	Preparation	Cooking instructions	Serving instructions
Stalks and shoots				
Asparagus	450 g-1 kg (1-2 lb)	Break off base of stem as low down as possible – it should break cleanly; otherwise, cut off the lower woody part. Scrape off any remaining tough skin from the base of the stem.	Cook vertically, tied in bunches, for 15-25 minutes, with only the lower part of the stems in the water. The tips will cook in the steam.	Serve with melted butter or Hollandaise sauce.
Cardoons	450 g (1 lb)	Remove old or wilted stems. Break the rest into 7 cm (3 in) pieces. Remove all strings. Trim heart and cut in half.	Boil for 1-2 hours in vegetable stock with added lemon juice.	Serve with the reduced, thickened stock; or with Béchamel sauce.
Celery	450 g (1 lb)	Cut off roots and leaves and remove all strings. Separate the stalks and break into 5-7 cm (2-3 in) lengths. Rinse well.	Boil 10 minutes; steam 12-15 minutes; stir-fry 10 minutes.	Serve buttered; or with a warm Vinaigrette sauce; or a Cheese sauce with a little cumin seed added.
Celtuce	450 g (1 lb)	Remove outer layer and root; cut into small pieces. Rinse well.	Cook stalks as celery and leaves as kale.	Use young leaves in salads; or serve as kale; serve stalks as celery.
Chicory	450 g (1 lb)	Cut off root plate and remove any outer discoloured leaves. Leave whole or chop.	Braise whole for 1¼ hours. Stir-fry chopped leaves 5-10 minutes.	Serve raw chopped leaves in orange Vinaigrette.
Florence fennel	450 g (1 lb)	Cut off root base and top leaves. If large, cut bulb into quarters; if small, cut in half.	Boil 10-15 minutes or, cook separated 'leaves' as celery.	Serve buttered, or with a mild cheese sauce.
Globe artichokes	1 per person	Break off the stem as this pulls out more fibres than cutting will. Soak in salted water for 30 minutes to get rid of any insects. Trim off the points of the leaves.	Boil in salted water coming ½ way up the artichoke, for 30-45 minutes; they are done when a leaf pulls out easily.	Serve hot with melted butter or Hollandaise sauce. Serve cold with Vinaigrette dressing or Mayonnaise.
Seakale	450 g (1 lb)	Remove roots and keep leaves for salads.	Boil stems 20-25 minutes in acidulated water; steam 30 minutes.	Serve buttered; or with a Hollandaise or Béarnaise sauce.
Pods and seeds				
Broad beans	1.4 kg (3 lb) unshelled	Remove beans from pods.	Boil 10-30 minutes depending on age and size. The cooked beans should not be mushy.	Serve buttered, or with a herb sauce.
Garden peas	1.4 kg (3 lb) unshelled	Shell immediately before cooking.	Boil 10-15 minutes; add some of the pods for extra flavour. Stir-fry 10-15 minutes.	Serve buttered; or with butter and chopped herbs. Use mint very occasionally – it is monotonously associated with peas.
Mangetout (Sugar peas)	450 g (1 lb)	Top and tail and remove any strings.	Steam 5-10 minutes; stir-fry 5 minutes.	Serve with the cooking juices; or with a little butter.
Okra	450 g (1 lb)	Cut off stems and discard any discoloured pods. Leave whole or cut into 1 cm (½ in) lengths. Rinse well.	Boil 10-15 minutes.	Serve with a little lemon juice; or in Tomato sauce.
Runner beans (Green; French; haricots verts)	450 g (1 lb)	Top and tail and remove any strings. Leave whole or cut diagonally into thin strips or straight across into 2 cm (1 in) lengths. Rinse well.	Boil very young beans 5-10 minutes, older ones 15-20 minutes; steam 10-25 minutes; stir-fry young beans 5-10 minutes. Try flavouring the cooking water with a little savory.	Serve with butter, butter and lemon juice; or a herb butter.
Sweetcorn	1 cob per person	Remove outer husk and silk. Either leave kernels on cob or strip them off.	On the cob, boil in unsalted water for 10-20 minutes; off the cob, boil 5-10 minutes. Or parboil for 5 minutes, brush with butter and grill for 10 minutes.	On the cob, buttered with salt and pepper. Off the cob, with butter or cream, salt and pepper.

Preparation of accompanying vegetables—continued

Vegetable	Quantity for 4	Preparation	Cooking instructions	Serving instructions
Roots				
Beetroot	450 g (1 lb)	Do not peel and take care not to break the skin, otherwise the colour will bleed. Trim off leaves 5 cm (2 in) above the bulb.	Boil 2-3 hours, depending on size. Best flavour and colour is achieved by baking; wrap in foil and bake at 150°C (300°F) Gas 2 for 2-3 hours.	Serve with butter and lemon juice; or Béchamel sauce and a little grated nutmeg.
Carrots	450 g (1 lb)	Remove stem tops and scrape off skin if necessary. Scrub well and leave whole if very small, or split in half lengthways. Slice into rounds or shred coarsely.	Boil young small carrots for 10 minutes; whole large roots for 20-30 minutes. Stir-fry if shredded for 5 minutes. Try cooking young carrots in Indian tonic water; or with a small piece of orange rind added.	Serve buttered, with chopped parsley or other herbs; mash or purée older carrots with cream or butter and parsley.
Celeriac	450 g (1 lb)	Trim off leaves and stem without peeling. Scrub well. Alternatively, peel and shred or peel and cut into 2 cm (1 in) cubes. Put into acidulated water.	Boil for 30-60 minutes if whole; 10-15 minutes if cubed. (It should still be slightly crisp).	If cooked whole, peel and mash with butter or an equal quantity of potatoes. Add a little Dijon mustard and lemon juice. Serve cubes buttered.
Kohlrabi	450 g (1 lb)	Cut the roots and leaves off very young ones, about 2-4 cm (1-1½ in) diameter, and leave whole. Older ones need peeling, slice or dice.	Boil for 20-30 minutes; braise older ones for 30-60 minutes in well-flavoured stock.	Serve young ones with butter; or in Béchamel sauce. Mash old ones with plenty of butter, soured cream or yoghurt.
Parsnips	450 g (1 lb)	Cut off stem top and spindly root. Peel and dice, slice or cut into quarters or strips; remove fibrous core from old ones.	Boil 10-15 minutes, depending on whether sliced or quartered; bake at 180°C (350°F) Gas 4 for 30-45 minutes; or roast.	Serve boiled parsnips buttered; or in Béchamel sauce. Mash them, deb the top with butter and brown under the grill.
Radishes	225 g (8 oz)	Cut off the tops and spindly roots. Leave whole, or slice.	Boil 10-15 minutes; stir-fry slices for 3-5 minutes.	Add some melted butter or sprinkle over a little soy sauce.
Salsify, Scorzonera	450 g (1 lb)	Cut off tops and tapering root. Peel and immerse in acidulated water. Cut into 2-5 cm (1-2 in) lengths.	Boil for 15-20 minutes then finish in butter for 5 minutes over moderate heat.	Serve straight from the pan with the butter poured over; or with Hollandaise sauce.
Swedes	450 g (1 lb)	Peel and remove any fibrous core. Rinse well, then slice, dice or cut into strips.	Boil 15-30 minutes. Drain well and dry off in warm oven.	Toss in butter or mash with cream of butter; or serve in Béchamel sauce.
Turnips	450 g (1 lb)	Peel. If very young, leave whole; large ones can be sliced, cut in quarters or diced.	Boil whole ones 10-30 minutes. Drain and dry off in warm oven. Diced turnips need about 10 minutes.	Toss in butter with a little parsley; serve in a Béchamel sauce with a little lemon rind added.
Tubers				
Jerusalem artichokes	450 g (1 lb)	Peel thinly, using a small knife to get between the knobs. Slice, leave whole or dice.	Boil 15-20 minutes if whole; 10 minutes if sliced. Stir-fry thin slices for 5-10 minutes.	Serve with butter and a sprinkling of nutmeg; or masked in Béchamel sauce. Try stir-fried while still crisp; they taste like a strong flavoured water chestnut.
Potatoes	450 g-1 kg (1-2 lb)	Scrub well and remove any eyes or discoloured patches. Leave skins on whenever possible, otherwise scrape off as thinly as possible. Leave whole, or cut in halves or quarters. New potatoes should only be scrubbed. **For chips** Cut the potatoes into 1 cm (½ in) slices and then cut the slices into strips of about the same thickness, leave in acidulated water until required. Dry them thoroughly before frying. **For wafer chips** Cut the potatoes into slices about 20 mm (¹/₁₀ in) thick.	Boil new potatoes in their jackets for about 15-25 minutes; or cook in a covered casserole for 30-40 minutes at 200°C (400°F) Gas 6, after brushing with oil or butter. Boil whole maincrop potatoes 30-40 minutes; cut ones, 15 minutes. Brush the skin with oil or butter, sprinkle with salt, cut a small cross on top to allow the steam to escape and bake for 1-1½ hrs at 180°C (350°F) Gas 4. Fry chips in deep oil at 180°C (350°F) until golden brown and cooked through. Fry wafers at 180°C (350°F) keeping separate.	Serve boiled potatoes with melted butter and parsley or, after boiling, sauté in butter or oil until golden brown. It is essential to heat the milk to almost boiling point when mashing potatoes; 200 ml (⅓ pint) of milk to 400 g (1 lb) potatoes is about the correct proportion. Add the milk and 1 tablespoon of butter, mash with a wooden spoon, then rub through a sieve and season to taste; return to the saucepan to re-heat but do not allow to burn.
Sweet potatoes, Yams	450 g-1 kg	Scrub the skins. Peel after boiling or baking.	Boil for 30-40 minutes; bake at 180°C (350°) Gas 4 for 45-60 minutes.	Serve peeled and mashed with butter and a dusting of cinnamon.

Preparation of accompanying vegetables—continued

Vegetable	Quantity for 4	Preparation	Cooking instructions	Serving instructions
Vegetable fruit				
Aubergine	700 g-1 kg (1½-2 lb)	Cut off stem and flower ends; cut into slices about ½-1 cm (¼-½ in) thick. Sprinkle with salt and leave to drain for 30-45 minutes. Rinse and pat dry before frying. Leave whole with both ends if baking.	Fry in a little olive oil for 5-10 minutes each side; fry in coating batter (page 194); bake 40-60 minutes at 180°C (350°F) Gas 4.	Straight from the pan; if baked, with a little fresh or soured cream pour on and well seasoned with salt and pepper.
Cucumber	450 g (1 lb)	Peel (or not, as you wish). Cut lengthways into halves or quarters, then into 5-7 cm (2-3 in) chunks.	Blanch, refresh, then cook very gently in butter for 5-10 minutes.	Serve with a little parsley or fresh dill sprinkled over; or masked with Hollandaise sauce.
Courgettes	450-700 g (1-1½ lb)	Trim off stem and blossom ends; leave whole, cut in half lengthways, or slice. Sprinkle with salt and leave to drain for 30-45 minutes to remove bitter juices. Rinse and pat dry before cooking.	Boil for 4-15, minutes. Stir-fry slices for 10 minutes with a little chopped onion, herbs, or garlic; or stir-fry with tomatoes and garlic.	If boiled, serve from the pan, or mashed with butter; if stir-fried, serve from the pan.
Marrow, Winter squash (Banana, hubbard, butternut, acorn, des Moines, table queen).	450-700 g (1-1½ lb)	Peel, if desired. Leave whole; or cut in half or slices, if large.	Boil 20-30 minutes depending on size, or bake marrow with appropriate stuffing (page 88). Bake halves of smaller squash on an oiled baking sheet, skin uppermost, at 180°C (350°F) Gas 4 for 40-60 minutes; turn over at half time and put a pat of butter on top.	Serve buttered, or scoop out the insides and mash with cream and fresh herbs and fill the shells with the purée. Sprinkle grated cheese over mashed marrow and brown under the grill.
Peppers (green & red)	450 g (1 lb)	Remove stems, seeds and fibrous cores; leave whole for stuffing, or cut into ½-1 cm (¼-½ in) slices, or dice.	Parboil whole peppers for 5 minutes; then stuff and bake for 25-30 minutes. Stir-fry sliced or diced peppers for 5-10 minutes.	Serve straight from the pan; or sprinkled with a little lemon juice or wine vinegar.
Pumpkin	450-700 g (1-1½ lb)	Cut off required section and remove pips and fibrous centre. Peel and cut into chunks about 7 cm by 5 cm (3 by 2 in) by the thickness of the pumpkin.	Boil 25-30 minutes; or roast.	Mash with butter and season well with salt and pepper or cinnamon. Make into fritters by adding a well-beaten egg, seasoning and a little wholemeal flour; then fry in shallow oil on both sides.
Summer squash (white, yellow, light or dark green)	450-700 g (1-1½ lb)	Trim off stem and blossom ends; leave whole or cut in half, quarters or slices. Remove any large pips and fibrous core.	Boil for 10-30 minutes, depending on size. Stir-fry slices for 10-15 minutes. Bake round squash for 30-60 minutes; test with a skewer.	As courgettes.
Tomatoes	700 g-1 kg (1½-2 lb)	Wipe skins; cut in half; brush with melted butter and sprinkle with salt and pepper, if grilling; dip into seasoned wholemeal flour, if frying.	Grill 10-15 minutes depending on size; fry 5 minutes cut side down, then turn and continue cooking until the juice starts boiling out.	Serve as they are cooked; vary by sprinkling with a little chopped basil or onion.
Mushrooms				
Button mushrooms	450 g (1 lb)	Wipe with a damp cloth; leave whole or cut in slices parallel to the stem.	Stir-fry in butter for 5-10 minutes. Add salt and pepper at half times.	Serve with the reduced juice.
Large mushrooms (field or commercially-grown)	450 g-1 kg (1-2 lb)	Rinse gently, then peel (if wild) and check for insects. Leave whole or cut into quarters, halves or slices parallel to the stem.	As button mushrooms; or grill, for 5-10 minutes under moderate heat. Baste with oil or butter.	Serve as buttom mushrooms; or with finely-chopped fried onion. Add a little cream before serving and sprinkle with chopped parsley.

Preparation of accompanying vegetables—continued

Vegetable	Quantity for 4	Preparation	Cooking instructions	Serving instructions
Onions				
Pickling onions	450 g (1 lb)	Blanch, top and tail them, then remove coloured skins.	Boil 15-20 minutes.	In a Béchamel sauce.
English, Spanish, large Italian onions or Shallots		Remove tops and root plates, then peel. (Wearing spectacles or peeling under running water helps prevent the tears). Leave whole or slice into rings with a sharp knife.	Boil small onions for 15-20 minutes; large ones 20-40 minutes. Bake large ones at 180°C (350°F) Gas 4 for 45-60 minutes. Finish in butter so they are just coloured. Stir-fry sliced onion for 10-15 minutes. Finish stir-frying in a little white wine for a treat. Dip separated rings in batter and deep-fry.	Straight from the pan; or in a Béchamel sauce.
Spring onions	450 g (1 lb) (4 bunches)	Trim off the roots and any discoloured outer leaves. Leave about 7 cm (3 in) of green stem above the white part; total length should be about 20 cm (8 in).	Stir-fry for 5-10 minutes in butter or oil over gentle heat.	Straight from the pan.
Leeks	450 g (1 lb)	Cut off roots. Discard discoloured leaves and 5 cm (3 in) of the tops above the white part. Cut in half lengthways, taking care that the leaves do not come apart. Wash well under a running tap to get rid of all the grit trapped between the leaves. Leeks can also be cut across the stem and separated into 2 cm (1 in) rings.	Boil for 10-15 minutes; braise, covered, in well-flavoured stock for 40-60 minutes. Stir-fry in oil for 10-15 minutes. The cross-cut strips will cook in 5-10 minutes if the leeks are young.	Serve with a knob of butter or mask with Béchamel or Mornay sauce.

Freezing Fresh Vegetables

Vegetable	Preparation	Blanching time	Cooking time and method
Roots			
Beetroot	Choose young tender beets about the size of golf balls: if larger, cut into halves or quarters. Blanch, cool, peel and pack into freezer bags.	5-10 minutes	Cook from frozen in boiling salted water for 1 hour.
Carrots	Choose young tender roots; top and tail; if very young, leave the skins on, otherwise scrape them. Slice if very large. Blanch, cool and pack in freezer bags.	3-5 minutes	Cook from frozen in boiling salted water for 5-8 minutes; alternatively, sauté them in butter for 8-10 minutes.
Celeriac	Wash, peel and cook; then purée. Pack in foil containers.		Reheat in the container or in a foil-covered oven-proof dish, or in the top of a double boiler with a little cream or butter.
Jerusalem artichokes	Peel, cook with added lemon juice and purée them; pack in rigid containers.		Use for soups.
Kohlrabi	Choose small roots, a little larger than golf balls. Top, tail and peel. Blanch, strain, cool and pack in freezer bags.	2 minutes	Cook in boiling salted water for 10-15 minutes.
Parsnips	Peel and dice: drain and cool. Pack into freezer bags.	2 minutes	Cook from frozen in boiling salted water for 5-10 minutes.
Swedes and turnips	Peel and dice: blanch, cool and pack in freezer bags. Alternatively cook and purée.	2¼ minutes	Cook from frozen in boiling salted water for 10 minutes. Reheat purée in the top of a double boiler with a little butter or cream.
Tubers and onions			
Onions	Peel and finely chop or thickly slice. Blanch, cool and pack in freezer bags or rigid containers. Put in a second bag for safety. Small onions can be peeled, then blanched whole.	chopped or sliced: 2 minutes small, whole: 4 minutes	Use as required in the recipe.
Potatoes and sweet potatoes	Cook and purée, then prepare as croquettes or duchesse potatoes and pack in rigid containers. Young, small, new potatoes can be frozen but lose flavour. Wipe, blanch, cool and pack in freezer bags.	3-5 minutes	Put croquettes or duchesse potatoes into a cold oven, set to 200°C (400°F) Gas 6 and cook for 20-30 minutes. Cook new potatoes for 15 minutes in boiling salted water.

Freezing Fresh Vegetables — continued

Vegetable	Preparation	Blanching time	Cooking time and method
Vegetable fruits			
Aubergines	Wash and cut into 2cm (¾in) thick slices. Blanch and cool on kitchen paper. Interleave with paper, in rigid containers.	4 minutes	Use from frozen in recipes as required, but take care as they are very soft and can easily disintegrate if overcooked.
Courgettes	Choose small ones. Wash, top and tail and cut into 15mm (¾in) thick slices. Blanch, drain and cool; pack in bags interleaved with paper.	1 minute	Cook from frozen to a little boiling salted water for 3 minutes or thaw and saute in butter.
Marrow	Peel, cut into slices and remove the seeds. Blanch, drain, cool and pack as courgettes.	2-3 minutes	Thaw and sauté in butter, or use in a casserole dish.
Peppers	Wash, cut in half and remove core, pips and pith. Blanch, drain, cool and pack separately. Or slice or dice, then blanch, cool, drain and bag.	halved: 3 minutes sliced or diced: 1½ minutes	Thaw halved ones and use as required in recipes. Diced or sliced ones can be used in casserole dishes.
Tomatoes	Cook and purée; pack in convenient portions in foil or rigid containers.		Heat in the top of a double boiler. Add to sauces and casserole dishes.
Brassicas and leaves			
Brussels sprouts	Choose small firm heads. Remove and loose outer leaves; wash thoroughly. Blanch, cool, drain well and then pack in freezer bags.	2-3 minutes	Cook from frozen in boiling salted water for 6-8 minutes.
Broccoli	Choose young spears. Cut off any woody stem or tough outer leaves. Divide into sprigs and wash. Blanch, cool and drain. Pack in single layers or interleave with paper in rigid containers.	small sprigs: 3 minutes thick sprigs: 4 minutes	Cook from frozen in boiling salted water for 5-8 minutes.
Cabbage, green or red	Discard outer leaves and cut out core; wash and shred finely. Blanch, cool, drain and bag.	1½ minutes	Cook from frozen in a little boiling salted water.
Cauliflower	Choose firm white heads. Cut off any tough stem; separate heads into small florets. Wash carefully and blanch in water with 2 teaspoons of lemon juice added to each 600ml (1 pint). Cool, drain and pack in layers, interleaved with non-stick paper in rigid containers.	3 minutes	Cook from frozen in boiling salted water for 5-8 minutes.
Spinach	Discard any bruised or blemished leaves; cut out any fibrous stems. Wash very carefully under cold running water. Blanch a little at a time and drain thoroughly. Pack in rigid containers.	2 minutes	Cook from frozen in a little butter and its own juice for 5 minutes. Take care that it does not stick and burn.
Stems and shoots			
Asparagus	Remove woody base of stems; wash carefully, blanch and cool. Pack in layers interleaved with non-stick paper in rigid containers.	thin stems: 2 minutes thick stems: 3-4 minutes	Cook from frozen in boiling salted water for 5-8 minutes.
Celery	Wash carefully and remove any strings. Cut into 1cm (½in) strips; blanch, cool and drain and pack into bags. (It will only be suitable for use in cooked dishes.)	3 minutes	Cook from frozen in boiling salted water for 10 minutes, or add to casserole dishes.
Fennel	Trim and cut the bulb in half, or separate the fronds. Blanch, cool and pack in freezer bags.	halved: 5 minutes leaves: 3 minutes	Cook from frozen in boiling salted water for 5-8 minutes.
Globe artichokes	Remove the stems; wash carefully. Trim off the sharp points of the leaves. Blanch in water with 2 teaspoons lemon juice added to each 600ml (1 pint). Cool rapidly, drain upside down; pack individually and freeze in freezer bags.	8-10 minutes depending on size	Cook from frozen in boiling salted water for about 8 minutes or until a leaf will pull out easily.
Pods and seeds			
Beans	Top and tail runner, French or green beans and trim off the sides if they are stringy. Slice runner beans into 3cm (1½in) pieces. Broad and other large beans should be shelled. Wash, blanch, cool, drain and pack in freezer bags.	2-3 minutes	Cook from frozen in boiling salted water; green beans for 5 minutes and broad beans and other large beans for 7-8 minutes.
Peas	Shell the peas, blanch cool and pack in freezer bags.	1 minute; stir to ensure even blanching	Cook in boiling salted water for 4-7 minutes.
Mangetout (sugar peas)	Top and tail; blanch and cool. Pack in freezer bags or rigid containers.	1 minute	Allow to thaw at room temperature. Cook in a little butter for 1-2 minutes.
Sweetcorn	Choose young cobs and remove husks, silk and stem. Blanch, cool, and wrap individually.	2-6 minutes	Cook from frozen in boiling salted water for 20-30 minutes.

Nutrition

Good nutrition is a matter of eating adequate but not excessive amounts of all the nutrients necessary for maintaining the body in good health. These nutrients can be divided for convenience into five main groups — protein, carbohydrate, fat, minerals and vitamins — each of which has a different function in the body and in maintaining good health. Proteins are required for building and repairing the body's tissues, carbohydrate and fat are the major energy sources, and minerals and vitamins are needed for regulating the body's chemical or metabolic processes. Water and a certain amount of fibre are also essential for the body to function correctly — and produce a feeling of fitness. Most of the foods we eat are a mixture of these different nutrients, yet no one food is complete in itself. A balanced diet made up of a variety of foods is therefore necessary for us to obtain an adequate amount of all the nutrients. In a vegetarian diet, there are fewer foods to choose from, but the idea of eating mixtures of a variety of foods still applies. The strict vegetarian or 'Vegan' will eat no animal produce whatsoever, and must obtain all his necessary nourishment from vegetables, fruit, nuts and cereals. Vegetarians who allow themselves to eat dairy produce such as milk, yoghurt, cheese, butter, eggs and cream in addition to the foods mentioned above are called Lacto-vegetarians, and for them the régime is not so strict. Many factors affect the choice of the foods we eat. They may be traditional, cultural or religious factors, prices, or such things as seasonal availability and our personal likes and dislikes. Everyone has his preferences for certain kinds of food and there is no need to eat foods which we find unpleasant simply because they are 'good for you'. On the whole, a balanced diet can be achieved by choosing foods which are varied, appetising and satisfying without being excessive in quantity. It is unwise as well as wasteful to eat more food than you need.

What are our needs?

One person's requirement for any nutrient can vary considerably from another's even then, the needs of the individual will vary from day to day. Your age, level of activity, general state of health, sex and your own particular metabolism all have an effect on the body's needs. A young person who is still growing will need more nutrients than a less active, fully-grown adult. Similarly, a sick person needs more nutrients — to repair damaged tissues and fight infection — than a healthy person. For these reasons, then, it is not easy to lay down precise needs.

Table 1, which has been compiled from statistical information on a large number of people, gives *average* daily requirements for protein and energy, and this can be used as a guide. The Tables beginning on page 212 give the protein and energy content of most of the foods usually available for inclusion in a vegetarian diet. These, too, can be used as a guide when planning your meals and ensuring you have the correct balance of nutrients in your diet. The values for every single nutrient have not been included because, in general, when the body's requirements for protein and energy are satisfied, the other nutrients have also been taken in the same foods.

ENERGY

Energy is what we need to keep us alive. Its gradual release in the body is controlled by special protein substances

TABLE 1
AVERAGE DAILY REQUIREMENTS OF PROTEIN AND ENERGY

	PROTEIN grams	ENERGY Mega Joules	Calories
Infants birth up to 1 year	20	3.3	800
Infants 1 up to 2 years	30	5.0	1200
Children 2 up to 5 years	35–40	5.9– 6.7	1400–1600
Children 5 up to 9 years	45–53	7.5– 8.8	1800–2100
Children 9 up to 12 years	58–63	9.6–10.5	2300–2500
Teenagers 12–18 years	58–75	9.6–12.6	2300–3000
Adult women	55–63	9.2–10.5	2200–2500
Adult men	68–90	11.3–15.1	2700–3600
Elderly people	48–59	8.0– 9.8	1900–2350

* Recommended Intakes of Nutrients for the U.K.
Department of Health & Social Security, 1970.

208

called enzymes. All the main nutrients such as carbohydrate, fat and protein can provide us with energy. Another source is the alcohol in alcoholic drinks; this however, like sugar, has only energy and supplies no other nutrients. We need energy even when the body is at rest to maintain basic activities such as breathing and the maintenance of body temperature. Extra energy is required as soon as the body starts to move, and those indulging in strenuous activities such as sports or heavy manual work, are obviously going to require a lot more energy for activity than someone who sits at a desk all day and gets very little exercise. Extra energy is also needed by growing children, mothers who are breast-feeding and by invalids.

Unfortunately, your body never lets you know when it's time to stop eating. If you eat or drink foods which provide more energy than you need for first of all keeping alive and then your daily activities, some of this will be converted into body fat and your body weight will increase as this fat is stored in the tissues. Continuous over-indulgence will soon become apparent around the waistline and in order to lose this fat, you must simply take in less energy than you are likely to use in a day. You can eat less (i.e. go on a low-calorie diet), or increase your level of physical activity — or combine both, after your doctor's advice has been sought. The amount of energy supplied by any item in the diet is now measured in units known as Megajoules; this unit replaces the more familiar term of Calorie (1 Megajoule = 1000 Kilojoules = 240 Calories).

THE NUTRIENTS

Energy is vital to life, but we need more than just energy. We need nourishment from the foods we eat — and some foods are more nourishing than others. Some knowledge of the nutritional values of different foods and how to cook and process foods without destroying all the valuable nutrients they contain is useful, and will help you when working out a healthy eating pattern — whatever your diet. How do you select food for its nutritional value and not simply for its energy content? The following information will help and a summary of the main functions and main sources of each nutrients is given in Table 2.

Carbohydrate

Carbohydrates, usually present as starches and sugars, are our main sources of energy. *Starch* is found predominantly in the storage part of plants, for example in the tuber of the potato and the seeds of cereals — the grains. Thus we obtain starch from all cereals and their products, including flour, bread, pasta, cakes and

TABLE 2

Nutrients	Main Functions	Main Sources
PROTEIN	Provides materials for growth and repair of body tissue, and for the regulation of metabolic processes.	Eggs, cheese, milk, yoghurt, cereals and cereal products, pulses, nuts and vegetables.
CARBOHYDRATE	Provides energy for bodily activities and for maintaining body temperature.	Cereals and cereal products such as bread, pasta, biscuits and cakes; fruit, vegetables, sugar, sweets, mineral drinks.
FAT	Provides a concentrated source of energy. Contains fat soluble vitamins A D E and K.	Butter, margarine, vegetable oils, cream, cheese.
VITAMINS		
Vitamin A	For vision in dim light and the maintenance of healthy skin and body tissues.	Butter, margarine, green vegetables, carrots, milk.
Vitamin B complex B_1, B_2, biotin, nicotinic acid	For the gradual release and utilisation of energy.	Fortified breakfast cereals, bread, flour, potatoes, eggs, milk.
B_6, B_{12}, folic acid	For protein metabolism and the formation of red blood cells.	Eggs; whole cereal and vegetables for B_6 and folic acid. **NB** B_{12} is only found in dairy produce and this will be limiting in the Vegan diet.
Vitamin C	Maintains healthy tissues and aids healing of wounds. **NB** The claims that large doses of vitamin C can prevent or cure colds are controversial. There is little scientific evidence to support them.	Citrus fruits, green vegetables, potatoes, rosehip and blackcurrant fruits and syrups.
Vitamin E	As an antioxidant.	Cereals and cereal products, eggs, vegetable oils.
Vitamin K	For normal blood clotting.	Cereals and cereal products, vegetables. Also synthesised in the body itself.
Vitamin D	For calcium metabolism and bone development.	Milk, cheese, eggs, butter, margarine. Also synthesised in the skin by the action of sunlight.
MINERALS Calcium	For bone and tooth formation, blood clotting and muscle contraction.	Milk, cheese, white and brown bread and flours.
Phosphorus	For bone and tooth formation and the release and utilisation of energy.	Present in nearly all foods.
Iron	For the formation of haemoglobin—the red blood pigment responsible for the transport of oxygen around the body.	White, brown and wholemeal bread and flour; potatoes, green vegetables, eggs.
Sodium & Chlorine	As sodium chloride (salt)—for maintaining water balance. Sodium maintains muscle and nerve activity.	Salt, bread and cereal products, vegetables, milk.
Potassium	For water balance in the body tissues.	Vegetables, fruit, milk.
Magnesium	For utilisation of energy.	Widespread, especially in foods of vegetable origin.
Fluorine	Associated with the structure of bones and teeth and protects against tooth decay.	Tea, drinking water (fortified areas only).

biscuits as well as from vegetables. Naturally occurring *sugars* are found in milk (lactose), honey (fructose) and fruits (glucose). However, by far the largest part of the sugar we take in is in the form of sucrose, either on its own, or as an ingredient in a wide variety of foods, including confectionery and soft drinks. Sucrose is a pure form of energy and contains no other nutrients. Furthermore, it is a direct cause of tooth decay. For these reasons, sugar-based foods are not a good choice for inclusion in the diet.

Fibre

This is another form of carbohydrate found in the diet and is commonly called roughage, but it produces a negligible amount of energy because we are unable to digest it. It is necessary, however, as it adds bulk and assists the passage of food through the digestive system. Fibre is found in whole cereals, bran, fruit and vegetables.

Fats

Fats and oils provide us with a concentrated source of energy in the diet, giving more than twice the amount of energy as that given by either proteins or carbohy-

drates. They also make an important contribution to the texture of foods, improving their flavour and making them more appetising. Furthermore, because it is digested comparatively slowly, foods rich in fat have a high satiety value.

Fats are also a source of certain essential vitamins and they provide a reserve store of energy in the insulating layer of fat under the skin. We can readily recognise a great deal of the fat we eat, for example, in butter, margarine and vegetable oils, but some of our fat intake is less obvious, such as that found in milk, cheese, nuts, chocolate, cakes, biscuits and ice cream.

It is widely believed that a high fat intake has an undesirable effect on health over a number of years. The high energy value of fats and oils can easily cause weight gain if eaten in excess of the body's needs, and their rôle as a contributory factor in heart disease is a matter of considerable debate at the present time. Almost all the different fats found in foods contain substances called fatty acids. These are of two main types i.e. saturated and polyunsaturated, which differ slightly in their chemical structure.

Fats containing saturated fatty acids generally come from animal sources and

are contained in butter, cream, cheese and of course, meat; and polyunsaturated fatty acids are contained in fats of vegetable origin, for example corn oil and sunflower seed oil. Cholesterol is another form of fat which is found in foods of animal origin; this and saturated fat have both been implicated in the causation of heart disease. There is some indication that polyunsaturated fats have a protective effect, although we usually recommend that fats in general should only be eaten in small quantities in any case. These small amounts are better obtained from vegetable sources where possible — polyunsaturated margarine and vegetable oils instead of butter.

Proteins

Proteins are an essential part of all living cells and the daily requirement for protein provides material for the growth and repair of body tissues. If you consume more than you need, any extra will be lost from the body, or used as an expensive source of energy — which may be stored as fat.

Proteins are made up of a complex combination of substances called *amino acids*. Some of these amino acids cannot be made in the body, but need to be provided in the diet. These are called the essential amino acids and they can be obtained from both animal and vegetable sources. The important protein-providing foods for a Lacto-vegetarian are cereals, nuts, pulses, eggs, milk and cheese. The Vegan who eats no animal produce, has to rely solely on the first three groups. As the body cannot store large quantities of amino acids, you should make sure you eat a mixture of protein foods at each meal, and since each foodstuff provides a different combination of amino acids — and may even be lacking in one or more of the essential ones — a good mixture of vegetable proteins is always necessary. A combination of cereals and pulses is particularly good (e.g. baked beans on toast or lentil curry and rice).

During periods of growth, the body's protein requirements are increased. In childhood and adolescence, a child who is deprived of protein will not grow as well as he should; extra protein is also required during pregnancy and lactation. In illness — whether this is in the healing of a wound or building up muscles that have become weak due to infection — protein intake should be stepped up to help repair the body tissues.

Vitamins and minerals

Vitamins and minerals are found in minute amounts in most foods. However, they are essential to the body for its growth, repair and general functioning of the metabolic processes. If you make sure

you eat a good and varied diet, you will take in enough of these substances as a matter of course and it should not be necessary to resort to commercial vitamin tablets or supplements, except where these are prescribed during periods of growth, or deficiency due to illness or exhaustion. Vitamins A, D, E and K are soluble in fat and can therefore be stored in the fatty tissues of the body. Vitamin C and those of the B group are water-soluble and cannot be stored in the tissues, so it is important that they are supplied daily.

Similarly all the necessary minerals are readily available in a sensible and appetising mixed diet. They are needed to maintain body structure and for various metabolic processes. The main functions and sources of vitamins and minerals are summarised in Table 2. In addition to those listed, there are certain other substances that are required in very small amounts and these are known as *trace elements*. They include cobalt, copper, chromium, iodine, manganese and zinc and dietary deficiencies of these are most unlikely to occur.

Deficiencies of vitamins or minerals only tend to happen in unusual circumstances such as among those people who eat food from a single source, or a limited number of sources, or among alcoholics. The former group need not include Lacto-vegetarians or Vegans if they follow the golden rule of eating adequate amounts of a wide variety of different foods from within each of the food groups: cereals, nuts, pulses, fruit, vegetables and — for all except Vegans — dairy produce.

Vitamin B_{12} is found only in animal foods, so that Vegans are at risk of developing some deficiency. Yeast extract is a good source of some of the B vitamins and also has a small but useful amount of B_{12}. It should be included daily in the Vegan diet. There are also certain groups of people who may be susceptible to vitamin or mineral deficiencies at certain times of life, because their needs are increased for various reasons. A woman needs more iron and folic acid during pregnancy — if these nutrients are not present in adequate amounts in the diet, she may develop anaemia.

It is dangerous to take large doses of the fat-soluble vitamins over a long period of time as they can gradually accumulate in the body to a poisonous level. This would only occur in unusual circumstances — by taking commercial vitamin supplements to excess, or by drinking carrot juice every single day. This is quite the opposite of a sensible, balanced diet and should be avoided!

Water

Although water is not strictly a nutrient it is essential for our survival. We obtain water not only from drinks but also from solid food. About two-thirds of the body's weight is comprised of water and this is the medium in which most body processes take place.

Alcohol

Alcohol, like sugar, contains energy, but no useful nutrients. Alcoholic drinks such as beer contain a significant amount of B vitamins — riboflavin and nicotinic acid, but spirits contain no vitamins. Varying amounts of carbohydrate may also be present in wines and beers and this provides additional energy.

The effects of processing and cooking on nutritional value

The nutritional value of proteins, fats, carbohydrates and fat soluble vitamins usually remain unaltered by normal cooking conditions. By contrast, though, the water-soluble B group vitamins, vitamin C and minerals largely provided by cereals, vegetables and fruits are very sensitive and easily lost in processing, preparation and cooking. After peeling or shredding vegetables, Vitamin C is rapidly destroyed. Its loss can be minimised by preparing vegetables just prior to use and by plunging them into boiling water to destroy the enzymes which cause this vitamin loss. Potatoes contain vitamin C just under the skin and there is less loss of vitamin C if they are not peeled, but cooked in their skins. During cooking, the vitamins and minerals from vegetables and fruits are either destroyed by heat or lost into the cooking water, so it makes sense to cook vegetables in the very minimum of water and subsequently using this water for making stock. It is also a good idea not to allow your vegetables to overcook. Do not keep them waiting but serve them as soon as they are cooked, as keeping them hot for long periods will increase the loss of vitamin C. Green vegetables and fruits are especially valuable when eaten raw as they suffer no cooking losses. Dried fruits do not contain any vitamin C as it is destroyed by the drying process.

The nutritional value of cereals depends on the extent of the processing before they reach the shops — whole grains and wholemeal products are obviously the wisest choice. The distribution of nutrients within the wheat grain is not uniform and the concentration of protein, minerals, and vitamins is higher in the germ and outer layers. These layers are lost during the milling of white and brown flours, or when polishing rice. The fibre content of cereals is also affected. After processing, the nutritional value of cereals is largely unchanged (except for some destruction of thiamin) by cooking.

ORGANIC AND HEALTH FOODS

Any food derived from plants or animals is organic and all of these foods provide nourishment. Eaten as part of a balanced diet, they are conducive to good health. The term 'organic foods' tends to be associated with foods grown using organic fertilisers, without chemical pesticides and which are either processed or not, but *without the use of additives*. Their nutritional value is largely determined by the species of plant or animal from which they came.

A key to healthy eating

It is wise to have one main meal each day, one light meal — and breakfast. Each meal should include a number of protein sources such as cereals, nuts, pulses and for the non-Vegan, eggs, milk and cheese. Starchy foods — cereals, for example — will help satisfy hunger, but do not use too much fat. Aim to eat some fresh fruit or vegetables *at least once a day* and drink as much fluid (preferably unsweetened), as you like. Children and adults too should be discouraged from eating sweets and chocolates between meals as they will decrease the appetite for the next main meal. All man's nutritional requirements — with the exception of vitamin B_{12} can be met by a diet composed entirely of plant foods, but to do so it must be carefully planned and a wide variety of foods must be included. A mixture of plant proteins from cereals, legumes, pulses and nuts will provide sufficient protein of good quality. Lacto-vegetarians will also include milk, cheese and eggs as their protein sources. Vegans need to take special care to ensure that sufficient energy, calcium, iron, riboflavin, vitamin B_{12} and vitamin D are also included — refer, again, to Table 2. Vegetarians need to have an awareness of the nutritional value of the food they eat. A weekly review of your diet should give you some idea of what may be lacking, or taken in excess, but it is possible to eat healthily and well without being obsessive over every single meal.

It does no harm to have a fling occasionally if you are eating out or entertaining. Too much cream, butter or chocolates, for example, is definitely to be avoided, but their rôle in cooking, particularly for the gourmet, cannot be ignored when entertaining. Use them in judicious amounts and balance your diet by having simple meals on the days when you do not need to entertain — or be entertained. Eat slowly, enjoy your food and remember — there is nothing more tedious than a discussion of dietary habits and preferences to those who are not interested in the principles of good and healthy eating. A fit and healthy person is the very best of examples!

The tables on the following pages give counts for individual foods. Guide lines to the different types are given here.

DAIRY PRODUCTS

Milk is high in nutritional value, being one of the most complete of all foods. It contains nearly all the constituents of nutritional importance to man and is a particularly valuable source of good-quality protein, calcium and riboflavin (Vitamin B_2). It is comparatively deficient in iron and vitamins C and D but contains some carbohydrate in the form of milk sugar (lactose).

Bottled milk should not be exposed to the sun for prolonged periods since a substantial amount of the riboflavin will be destroyed after one hour.

Dried milks contain all the nutrients of the original whole (or skimmed) milk apart from the B vitamins, which are destroyed by the drying process.

The nutritional value of *yoghurt* will be similar to that of the milk upon which it is based — either skimmed or whole.

Cream is derived from fresh milk and is the separated-off fatty layer. The energy value of different types of cream vary with the fat content; single cream contains 18% by weight as milk fat, double cream 48%, and whipping cream 35%. Cream will contain the fat-soluble vitamins found in milk — particularly vitamin A and the remaining skimmed milk will contain most of the protein, calcium and B vitamins.

Butter is made by churning cream in order to separate fat globules from the liquid buttermilk. The butter must not by law (in the U.K.) contain less than 78-80% milk fat. It contains the fat-soluble vitamins A and D — the exact amounts depending on the milk content.

Cheese is made by coagulating the milk proteins to form a curd which is then treated in a variety of ways to produce many different cheeses (see page 28). The curd contains most of the protein, fat and fat-soluble vitamins and most of the calcium from the milk. Lactose and the B vitamins are lost in the discarded whey.

Cottage cheese is made from skimmed milk and therefore contains very little fat, whereas cream cheese has a particularly high fat content.

Eggs are useful sources of good-quality protein, vitamin D, vitamin A (retinol) riboflavin, and iron. The amount of iron absorbed from eggs is dependent on other dietary factors; for example, a source of vitamin C such as fruit juice taken with eggs will aid absorption. The colour of egg shells is not related to nutritional value — only the breed of hen. Similarly, the differences in the colour of the yolks are not important. Free range, battery and deep litter eggs are of similar composition, although free range contain more vitamin B_{12} and folic acid.

PULSES

Pulses or legumes are rich in protein, and provide more energy and B vitamins than either green or root vegetables. Fresh peas and broad beans contain vitamin C, but this is lost when they are dried. Soaking

Vegetables:

Energy values of the following foods are given in calories and kilojoules, per 100g and per oz. Protein values are given in grams, per 100g and per oz.

Food	Description	per 100 g Energy Units kcal	kJ	Protein (grams)	per oz Energy Units kcal	kJ	Protein (grams)
Artichokes, Globe	Base of leaves and soft inside parts; boiled	15	62	1.1	4	18	0.3
Artichokes, Jerusalem	Flesh only; boiled	18	78	1.6	5	22	0.5
Asparagus	Soft tips only; boiled	18	75	3.4	5	21	1.0
Aubergine	Flesh only; raw	14	62	0.7	4	18	0.2
Beans, French	Pods and beans; boiled	7	31	0.8	2	9	0.2
Beans, runner	Pods trimmed; raw	26	114	2.3	7	32	0.7
Beans, runner	Pods trimmed; boiled	19	83	1.9	5	23	0.5
Beansprouts	Canned; drained	9	40	1.6	3	11	0.5
Beetroot	Flesh only; raw	28	118	1.3	8	33	0.4
Beetroot	Flesh only; boiled	44	189	1.8	12	54	0.5
Broccoli	Tops; raw	23	96	3.3	7	27	0.9
Broccoli	Tops; boiled	18	78	3.1	5	22	0.9
Brussels sprouts	Inner leaves only; raw	26	111	4.0	7	31	1.1
Brussels sprouts	Inner leaves only; boiled	18	75	2.8	5	21	0.8
Cabbage, red	Inner leaves; raw	20	85	1.7	6	24	0.5
Cabbage, savoy	Inner leaves; raw	26	109	3.3	7	31	0.9
Cabbage, savoy	Inner leaves; boiled	9	40	1.3	3	11	0.4
Cabbage, spring	Inner leaves; boiled	7	32	1.1	2	9	0.3
Cabbage, white	Whole cabbage; raw	22	93	1.9	6	26	0.5
Cabbage, winter	Inner leaves; raw	22	92	2.8	6	26	0.8

Food	Description	per 100 g Energy units kcal	kJ	Protein (grams)	per oz Energy units kcal	kJ	Prote (gram
Cabbage, winter	Inner leaves; boiled	15	66	1.7	4	19	0.5
Carrots, old	Flesh only; raw	23	98	0.7	7	28	0.2
Carrots, old	Flesh only; boiled	19	79	0.6	5	22	0.2
Carrots, young	Flesh only, boiled	20	87	0.9	6	25	0.3
Carrots	Canned; drained, heated	19	82	0.7	5	23	0.2
Cauliflower	Flower and stalk; raw	13	56	1.9	4	16	0.5
Cauliflower	Flower and stalk; boiled	9	40	1.6	3	11	0.5
Celeriac	Flesh only; boiled	14	59	1.6	4	17	0.5
Celery	Stem only, raw	8	36	0.9	2	10	0.3
Celery	Stem only; boiled	5	21	0.6	1	6	0.2
Chicory	Stem and young leaves; raw	9	38	0.8	3	11	0.2
Courgettes	Flesh only; raw	16	69	0.6	5	20	0.2
Courgettes	Flesh only; boiled	7	29	0.4	2	8	0.1
Cucumber	Flesh only; raw	10	43	0.6	3	12	0.2
Endive	Leaves only; raw	11	47	1.8	3	13	0.5
Fennel	Leaves only; raw	28	117	2.8	8	33	0.8
Horseradish	Flesh of root; raw	59	253	4.5	16	72	1.3
Leeks	Bulb only; raw	31	128	1.9	8	36	0.5
Leeks	Bulb only; boiled	24	104	1.8	7	30	0.5
Lettuce	Inner leaves; raw	12	51	1.0	3	14	0.3
Mushrooms	Whole; raw	13	53	1.8	4	15	0.5
Mushrooms	Whole; fried	210	863	2.2	59	244	0.6
Mustard & Cress	Leaves and stems; raw	10	47	1.6	3	13	0.5
Okra	Whole; raw	17	71	2.0	5	20	0.6

dried peas and beans can result in some loss of the water soluble vitamins and minerals into the soaking water.

NUTS

Nuts are rich in fat and protein and therefore a good and concentrated source of energy. They also contain B vitamins. They do not, however, contain any vitamin A or C.

FRUIT

Most fruits contain a little sugar and small amounts of mineral and B vitamins, but they are an important source of vitamin C. The vitamin content of fruit will vary with the type of fruit and will be lower in cooked fruit than fresh fruit. Blackcurrants, strawberries and soft fruits, oranges, grapefruit and natural fruit juices (*not* squash or cordial) are the richest fruit sources of vitamin C.

Dried fruits provide energy principally as sugar, but contain no vitamin C. Dried prunes and apricots are also sources of B-carotene.

CEREALS

Cereals contribute energy, protein, carbohydrate, iron, calcium, nicotinic acid and thiamin (vitamin B₁) to the diet. There is more protein, minerals and vitamins in the germ and outer layers of cereal grains and these are lost when the grains are milled. White flours are therefore lower in nutritional value than brown flours, particularly wholemeal. The latter will also contribute fibre to the diet if not sifted. As already mentioned, similar losses of nutrients will result from polishing rice. The cooking and processing of cereals may also destroy some of the thiamin content.

SUGARS AND PRESERVES

White sugar provides energy but no other nutrients. Similarly, brown sugars only contain insignificant quantities of minerals and vitamins in addition to energy. Some preserves contain vitamin C, and chocolate contains iron, but the primary function of these items in the diet is to improve palatability.

VEGETABLES

Vegetables contain 80-95% water but also provide valuable vitamins — particularly vitamin C — minerals and small amounts of protein and energy. They are also a major source of dietary fibre. Green vegetables are good sources of vitamin C, B carotene (which is converted to vitamin A in the body), folic acid, iron and other minerals.

Whenever possible, eat vegetables raw. Wilted and cooked green vegetables contain less vitamin C than the raw vegetables. Cooking may also result in some loss of folic acid and minerals. Root vegetables are the storage parts of plants and contain more energy-providing starches and sugars than most green vegetables. Turnips, swedes, parsnips and potatoes are comparatively good sources of vitamin C, and carrots are particularly rich in B carotene. The care needed in preparing and cooking vegetables in order to preserve their nutrient content has already been mentioned (page 106).

Food	Description	per 100 g			per oz		
		Energy units		Protein	Energy units		Protein
		kcal	kJ	(grams)	kcal	kJ	(grams)
Onions	Flesh only; raw	23	99	0.9	7	28	0.3
Onions	Flesh only; boiled	13	53	0.6	4	15	0.2
Onions	Flesh only; fried	345	1425	1.8	98	404	0.5
Parsley	Leaves; raw	21	88	5.2	6	25	1.4
Parsnips	Flesh only; raw	49	210	1.7	14	59	0.5
Parsnips	Flesh only; boiled	56	238	1.3	16	67	0.4
Peppers, red	Flesh only; raw	31	130	1.4	9	37	0.4
Peppers, red	Flesh only; boiled	26	109	1.2	7	31	0.3
Peppers, green	Flesh only; raw	15	65	0.9	4	18	0.3
Peppers, green	Flesh only; boiled	14	59	0.9	4	17	0.3
Plaintain, green	Flesh only; boiled	122	518	1.0	35	147	0.3
Plaintain, ripe	Flesh only; fried	267	1126	1.5	76	319	0.4
Potatoes, old	Flesh only; raw	87	372	2.1	25	105	0.6
Potatoes, old	Flesh only; boiled	80	343	1.4	23	97	0.4
Potatoes, old	Flesh only; baked in skins	105	448	2.6	30	127	0.7
Potatoes, old	Flesh only; shallow roasted	157	662	2.8	44	188	0.8
Potatoes, old	Flesh only; deep fried chips	253	1065	3.8	72	302	1.1
Potatoes, new	Flesh only; boiled	76	324	1.6	22	92	0.5
Potatoes, new	Flesh only; canned, drained	53	226	1.2	15	64	0.3
Potatoes, instant	Powder; reconstituted	70	299	2.0	20	85	0.6
Potatoes, crisps	Plain and flavoured	533	2224	6.3	151	630	1.8

Food	Description	per 100 g			per oz		
		Energy units		Protein	Energy units		Protein
		kcal	kJ	(grams)	kcal	kJ	(grams)
Pumpkin	Flesh only; raw	15	65	0.6	4	18	0.2
Radishes	Flesh and skin; raw	15	62	1.0	4	18	0.3
Seakale	Stem only; boiled	8	33	1.4	2	9	0.4
Spinach	Leaves; boiled	30	128	5.1	8	36	1.4
Spring greens	Leaves; boiled	10	43	1.7	3	12	0.5
Spring onions	Flesh of bulb; raw	35	151	0.9	10	43	0.3
Swedes	Flesh only; raw	21	88	1.1	6	25	0.3
Swedes	Flesh only; boiled	18	76	0.9	5	22	0.3
Sweetcorn	On-the-cob; kernels only; raw	127	538	4.1	36	152	1.1
Sweetcorn	On-the-cob; kernels only; boiled	123	520	4.1	35	141	1.1
Sweetcorn	Canned; kernels	76	325	2.9	22	92	0.8
Sweet potatoes	Flesh only; raw	91	387	1.2	26	110	0.3
Sweet potatoes	Flesh only; boiled	85	363	1.1	24	103	0.3
Tomatoes	Whole; raw	14	60	0.9	17	17	0.3
Tomatoes	Whole; shallow fried	69	288	1.0	20	82	0.3
Tomatoes	Whole; canned, drained	12	51	1.1	3	14	0.3
Turnips	Flesh only; raw	20	86	0.8	6	24	0.2
Turnips	Flesh only; boiled	14	60	0.7	4	17	0.2
Turnip tops	Leaves; boiled	11	48	2.7	3	14	0.8
Watercress	Leaves and stems, raw	14	61	2.9	4	17	0.8
Yam	Flesh only; boiled	119	508	1.6	34	144	0.5

Fruit

Food	Description	per 100 g Energy units kcal	kJ	Protein (grams)	per oz Energy units kcal	kJ	Protein (grams)
Apples, eating	Flesh only, raw	46	196	0.3	13	56	0.1
Apples, eating	Whole; raw	35	151	0.2	10	43	trace
Apples, cooking	Flesh only; raw	37	159	0.3	10	45	0.1
Apples, cooking	Flesh only; stewed, no sugar	32	136	0.3	9	39	0.1
Apricots	Fresh; stoned; raw	28	117	0.6	8	33	0.2
Apricots	Fresh; whole; raw	25	108	0.5	7	31	0.1
Apricots	Fresh; stoned; stewed; no sugar	23	98	0.4	7	28	0.1
Apricots	Dried; stoned; raw	182	776	4.8	52	220	1.4
Apricots	Dried; stoned; stewed; no sugar	66	288	1.8	19	65	0.5
Apricots	Canned; stoned fruit & syrup	106	452	0.5	30	128	0.1
Avocado pears	Flesh only; raw	223	922	4.2	63	261	1.2
Bananas	Flesh only; raw	79	337	1.1	22	96	0.3
Bananas	Whole fruit; raw	47	202	0.7	13	57	0.2
Bilberries	Whole fruit; raw	56	240	0.6	16	68	0.2
Blackberries	Whole fruit; raw	29	125	1.3	8	35	0.4
Blackberries	Whole fruit; stewed; no sugar	25	107	1.1	7	30	0.3
Cherries, eating	Stoned; raw	47	201	0.6	13	57	0.2
Cherries, eating	Whole; raw	41	175	0.5	12	50	0.1
Cherries, cooking	Stoned; raw	46	196	0.6	13	56	0.2
Cherries, cooking	Whole; raw	39	165	0.5	11	47	0.1
Cherries, cooking	Stoned; stewed; no sugar	39	165	0.5	11	47	0.1
Cherries, glacé		212	903	0.6	60	256	0.2
Cranberries	Whole fruit; raw	15	63	0.4	4	18	0.1
Currants, black	Whole fruit; raw	28	121	0.9	8	34	0.3
Currants, black	Whole fruit; stewed; no sugar	24	103	0.8	7	29	0.2
Currants, red	Whole fruit; raw	21	89	1.1	6	25	0.3
Currants, red	Whole fruit; stewed; no sugar	18	76	0.9	5	22	0.3
Currants, white	Whole fruit; raw	26	112	1.3	7	32	0.4
Currants, white	Whole fruit; stewed; no sugar	22	96	1.1	6.2	27	0.3
Currants, dried	Whole fruit	243	1039	1.7	69	294	0.5
Damsons	Stoned; raw	38	162	0.5	10	46	0.1
Damsons	Whole; raw	34	144	0.4	10	41	0.1
Damsons	Stoned; stewed	32	136	0.4	9	39	0.1
Dates	Dried; stoned	248	1056	2.0	70	299	0.6
Dates	Dried; whole	213	909	1.7	60	258	0.5
Figs	Green; whole fruit	41	174	1.3	12	49	0.4
Figs	Dried; whole fruit; raw	213	908	3.6	60	257	1.0
Figs	Dried; whole fruit; stewed no sugar	118	504	2.0	33	143	0.6
Gooseberries	Fresh; topped & tailed; raw	17	73	1.1	5	21	0.3

Food	Description	per 100 g Energy units kcal	kJ	Protein (grams)	per oz Energy units kcal	kJ	Protein (grams)
Gooseberries	Fresh; topped & tailed; stewed; no sugar	14	62	0.9	4	18	0.3
Grapes, black	Flesh only; raw	61	258	0.6	17	73	0.2
Grapes, black	Whole fruit; raw	51	217	0.5	14	61	0.1
Grapes, white	Flesh only; raw	63	268	0.6	18	76	0.1
Grapes, white	Whole fruit; raw	60	255	0.6	17	72	0.1
Grapefruit	Flesh only; raw	22	95	0.6	6	27	0.1
Grapefruit	Canned; fruit & syrup	60	257	0.5	17	73	0.1
Grapefruit	Juice; canned; unsweetened	31	132	0.3	9	37	0.1
Greengages	Stoned; raw	47	202	0.8	13	57	0.2
Greengages	Whole; raw	45	191	0.7	13	54	0.2
Greengages	Stoned; stewed; no sugar	40	170	0.6	11	48	0.1
Lemons	Whole	15	65	0.8	4	18	0.2
Lemons	Fresh juice	7	31	0.3	2	9	0.1
Limes	Whole	28	117	0.7	8	33	0.2
Loganberries	Whole fruit; raw	17	73	1.1	5	21	0.3
Loganberries	Whole fruit; stewed; no sugar	16	67	1.0	5	21	0.3
Lychees	Flesh only; raw	64	271	0.9	18	77	0.3
Lychees	Canned; fruit & syrup	68	290	0.4	19	82	0.1
Mandarins	Canned; fruit & syrup	56	237	0.6	16	67	0.2
Mangoes	Flesh only; raw	59	253	0.5	17	72	0.1
Mangoes	Canned; fruit & syrup	77	330	0.3	22	93	0.1
Melons, Canteloupe	Flesh only; raw	24	102	1.0	7	29	0.3
Melons, Canteloupe	Whole; raw	15	63	0.6	4	18	0.2
Melons, Honeydew	Flesh only; raw	21	90	0.6	6	25	0.2
Melons, Honeydew	Whole; raw	13	56	0.4	4	16	0.1
Melons, water	Flesh only; raw	21	92	0.4	6	25	0.1
Melons, water	Whole; raw	11	47	0.2	3	13	0.1
Mulberries	Whole fruit; raw	36	152	1.3	10	43	0.4
Nectarines	Stoned; raw	50	214	0.9	14	61	0.3
Nectarines	Whole; raw	46	198	0.9	13	56	0.3
Olives, black	Whole; raw	129	540	1.1	37	153	0.3
Olives, green	Whole; raw	116	485	1.4	33	137	0.4
Oranges	Flesh only; raw	35	150	0.8	10	42	0.2
Orange juice	Fresh	38	161	0.6	11	46	0.2
Orange juice	Canned; unsweetened	33	143	0.4	9	41	0.1

Food	Description	per 100 g Energy units kcal	kJ	Protein (grams)	per oz Energy units kcal	kJ	Protein (grams)
Passion fruit	Skinned; raw	34	147	2.8	10	42	0.8
Paw paw	Canned; fruit & juice	65	275	0.2	18	78	0.1
Peaches	Fresh; stoned; raw	37	156	0.6	10	44	0.2
Peaches	Fresh; whole; raw	32	137	0.6	9	39	0.2
Peaches	Dried; stoned; raw	212	906	3.4	60	257	1.0
Peaches	Dried; stoned, stewed, no sugar	79	336	1.3	22	95	0.4
Peaches	Canned; fruit and syrup	87	373	0.4	25	106	0.1
Pears, eating	Flesh only; raw	41	175	0.3	12	50	0.1
Pears, eating	Whole; raw	29	125	0.2	8	35	0.1
Pears, cooking	Flesh only; raw	36	154	0.3	10	44	0.1
Pears, cooking	Flesh only; stewed, no sugar	30	130	0.2	8	37	0.1
Pears	Canned; fruit and syrup	77	327	0.4	22	93	0.1
Pineapple	Canned; fruit and syrup	76	325	0.3	22	93	0.1
Plums, eating	Stoned; raw	38	164	0.6	11	46	0.2
Plums, eating	Whole, raw	36	153	0.5	10	43	0.1
Plums, cooking	Stoned; raw	26	109	0.6	7	31	0.2
Plums, cooking	Stoned; stewed; no sugar	22	92	0.5	6	26	0.1
Pomegranate	Flesh only; raw	63	264	0.5	18	75	0.1
Prunes	Dried; stoned; raw	161	686	2.4	46	194	0.7
Prunes	Dried; whole; raw	134	570	2.0	38	161	0.6
Prunes	Dried; stoned; no sugar; stewed	82	349	1.3	23	99	0.4
Prunes	Dried; whole; stewed; no sugar	74	316	1.1	21	90	0.3
Quinces	Flesh only; raw	25	106	0.3	7	30	0.1
Raisins	Dried; stoned	246	1049	1.1	70	297	0.3
Raspberries	Whole fruit; raw	25	105	0.9	7	30	0.3
Raspberries	Canned; fruit and syrup	87	370	0.6	25	105	0.2
Rhubarb	Stems only; raw	6	26	0.6	2	7	0.2
Rhubarb	Stems only; stewed; no sugar	6	25	0.6	2	7	0.2
Strawberries	Whole fruit; raw	26	109	0.6	7	31	0.2
Strawberries	Canned; fruit and syrup	81	344	0.4	23	97	0.1
Sultanas	Dried; whole fruit	250	1066	1.8	71	302	0.5
Tangerines	Flesh only; raw	34	143	0.9	10	41	0.3

Pulses

Food	Description	per 100 g Energy units kcal	kJ	Protein (grams)	per oz Energy units kcal	kJ	Protein (grams)
Beans, baked	Canned in tomato sauce	64	270	5.1	18	76	1.4
Beans, broad	Fresh; beans only; boiled	48	206	4.1	14	58	1.2
Beans, broad	Dried; raw	338	1414	25.1	95	401	7.1
Beans, butter	Dried, raw	273	1162	19.1	77	329	5.4
Beans, butter	Dried; boiled	95	405	7.1	27	115	2.0
Beans, haricot	Dried, raw	271	1151	21.4	77	326	6.1
Beans, haricot	Dried; boiled	93	396	6.6	26	112	1.9
Beans, mixed	e.g. white, black eye, brown; raw	340	1423	22.3	96	403	6.3
Beans, mixed	as above; boiled	118	494	7.8	33	140	2.2
Beans, mung	Dried; raw	231	981	22.0	65	278	6.2
Beans, mung	Dried, cooked	106	447	6.4	30	127	1.8
Beans, red kidney	Dried; raw	272	1159	22.1	77	328	6.3
Beans, soya	Dried; raw	403	1686	34.1	114	478	9.7
Chick peas	Dried; raw	320	1362	20.2	91	386	5.7
Chick peas	Dried; cooked	144	610	8.0	41	173	2.3
Lentils	Raw	304	1293	23.8	86	366	6.7
Lentils	Boiled	99	420	7.6	28	119	2.2
Peas	Fresh, peas only; raw	67	283	5.8	19	80	1.6
Peas	Fresh, peas only; boiled	52	223	5.0	15	63	1.4
Peas	Frozen; peas only; raw	53	227	5.7	15	64	1.6
Peas	Frozen; peas only; boiled	41	175	5.4	12	50	1.5
Peas	Canned; garden	47	201	4.6	13	57	1.3
Peas	Canned; processed	80	339	6.2	23	96	1.8
Peas	Dried; raw	310	1318	21.6	88	373	6.1
Peas	Dried; boiled	118	503	6.9	33	142	2.0
Peas	Split, dried; raw	320	1362	22.1	91	386	6.3
Peas	Split, dried; boiled	144	610	8.3	41	173	2.4

Dairy Produce

Food	Description	per 100 g Energy units kcal	per 100 g Energy units kJ	per 100 g Protein (grams)	per oz. Energy units kcal	per oz. Energy units kJ	per oz. Protein (grams)
Butter	Unsalted or salted	740	3041	0.4	210	861	0.1
Camembert-type	e.g. Camembert, Brie	300	1246	22.8	85	353	6.5
Cheddar-type	e.g. Cheddar, Cheshire, Gruyère, Emmenthal.	406	1682	26.0	115	476	7.4
Danish Blue-type	e.g. Danish Blue, Roquefort, Dolcelatte	355	1471	23.0	101	417	6.5
Edam-type	e.g. Edam, Gouda	304	1262	24.4	86	358	6.9
Parmesan		408	1696	35.1	116	480	9.9
Stilton		462	1915	25.6	131	542	7.3
Curd or cottage cheese		96	402	13.6	27	114	3.9
Cream cheese		439	1807	3.1	124	512	0.9
Cream, soured		212	876	2.4	60	248	0.7
Cream, single		212	876	2.4	60	248	0.7
Cream, double		447	1841	1.5	127	522	0.4
Cream, whipping		332	1367	1.9	94	387	0.5
Eggs, hens'	Whole	147	612	12.3	42	173	3.5
Eggs, hens'	Yolk only	339	1402	16.1	96	397	4.6
Eggs, hens'	White only	36	153	9.0	10	43	2.5
Milk	Fresh; whole and long life	65	272	3.3	18	77	0.9
Milk	Fresh; skimmed	33	142	3.4	9	40	1.0
Milk	Condensed; whole; sweetened	322	1362	8.3	91	386	2.4
Milk	Dried; whole	490	2051	26.3	139	581	7.5
Milk	Dried; skimmed	355	1512	36.4	101	428	10.3
Buttermilk	Fluid; cultured	36	151	3.6	10	43	1.0
Yoghurt	Natural, low fat	52	216	5.0	15	61	1.4
Yoghurt	Fruit-type, low fat	95	405	4.8	27	115	1.4

Cereals

Food	Description	per 100 g Energy units kcal	per 100 g Energy units kJ	per 100 g Protein (grams)	per oz. Energy units kcal	per oz. Energy units kJ	per oz. Protein (grams)
Barley	Pearl; raw	360	1535	7.9	102	435	2.2
Barley	Pearl; boiled	120	510	2.7	34	144	0.8
Bran	Wheat	206	872	14.1	58	247	4.0
Cornflour		354	1481	0.6	100	420	0.2
Cornmeal		355	1485	9.2	101	421	2.6
Flour, wholemeal	(100%)	318	1351	13.2	90	383	3.7
Flour, brown	(85%)	327	1392	12.8	93	394	3.6
Flour, white	Plain (72%)	350	1493	9.8	99	423	2.8
Flour, white	Self-raising (72%)	339	1443	9.3	96	409	2.6
Oatmeal		401	1698	12.4	114	481	3.5
Rice, white	Raw	361	1536	6.5	102	435	1.8
Rice, white	Boiled	123	522	2.2	35	148	0.6
Rice, brown	Raw	360	1506	7.5	102	427	2.1
Rice, brown	Boiled	119	498	2.5	34	141	0.7
Sago	Raw	355	1515	0.2	101	429	0.1
Semolina	Raw	350	1489	10.7	99	422	3.0
Wheat, grains	Raw; hard red winter	330	1381	12.3	93	391	3.5

Cereal Products

Food	Description	per 100 g Energy units kcal	per 100 g Energy units kJ	per 100 g Protein (grams)	per oz. Energy units kcal	per oz. Energy units kJ	per oz. Protein (grams)
Bread	Wholemeal	216	918	8.8	61	260	2.5
Bread	Brown	223	948	8.9	63	269	2.5
Bread	Buck wheat, dark	333	1393	11.7	94	395	3.3
Bread	White	233	991	7.8	66	281	2.2
Breakfast cereal	Cornflakes	368	1567	8.6	104	444	2.4
Breakfast cereal	Muesli	368	1556	12.9	104	441	3.7
Breakfast cereal	Puffed wheat	325	1386	14.2	92	393	4.0
Breakfast cereal	Rice Krispies	372	1584	5.9	105	449	1.7
Biscuits	Chocolate-coated type	524	2197	5.7	148	622	1.6
Biscuits	Cream cracker type	440	1857	9.5	125	526	2.7
Biscuits	Crispbread	388	1642	45.3	110	465	12.8
Biscuits	Crispbread; rye	321	1367	9.4	91	387	2.7
Biscuits	Digestive	471	1981	9.8	133	561	2.8
Biscuits	Semi-sweet	457	1925	6.7	129	545	1.8
Biscuits	Water biscuits	440	1859	10.8	125	524	3.1
Custard powder		354	1508	0.6	100	427	0.2
Pasta	Cannelloni lasagne, macaroni, ravioli squares (unfilled), spaghetti, stelletti, tagliatelle	378	1612	13.6	107	457	3.9
Porridge oats	Cooked in water	44	188	1.4	12	53	0.4

Nuts and Seeds

Food	Description	per 100 g Energy units kcal	kJ	Protein (grams)	per oz. Energy units kcal	kJ	Protein (grams)
Almonds	Shelled	565	2336	16.9	160	662	4.8
Almonds	Whole	210	865	6.3	59	245	1.8
Brazil nuts	Shelled	619	2545	12.0	176	721	3.4
Brazil nuts	Whole	277	1142	5.4	78	324	1.5
Cashew nuts	Shelled	561	2347	17.2	159	665	4.9
Chestnuts	Shelled	170	720	2.0	48	204	0.6
Chestnuts	Whole	140	595	1.6	40	169	0.5
Cob or hazel nuts	Shelled	380	1570	7.6	108	445	2.2
Cob or hazel nuts	Whole	137	567	2.8	39	161	0.8
Coconut	Fresh	351	1446	3.2	99	410	0.9
Coconut	Milk	21	91	0.3	6	26	0.1
Coconut	Desiccated	604	2492	5.6	171	706	1.6
Peanuts	Fresh; shelled	570	2364	24.3	161	670	6.9
Peanuts	Fresh; whole	394	1631	16.8	112	462	4.8
Peanuts	Roasted; salted	570	2364	24.3	161	670	6.9
Peanut butter	Smooth	623	2581	22.6	176	731	6.4
Pecan	Shelled	525	2166	10.6	149	614	3.0
Pecan	Whole	336	1388	6.8	95	393	1.9
Pine nuts, pignolios		552	2310	31.1	156	654	8.8
Pistachio nuts	Shelled	594	2485	19.3	168	704	3.7
Sesame seeds	Dry; whole	563	2356	18.6	159	667	5.3
Sunflower seeds	Dry	560	2343	24.0	159	664	6.8
Walnuts	Shelled	525	2166	10.6	149	614	3.0
Walnuts	Whole	336	1388	6.8	95	393	1.9
Water chestnuts	Chinese; raw	79	331	1.4	22	94	0.4

Sugar and Preserves

Food	Description	per 100 g Energy units kcal	kJ	Protein (grams)	per oz Energy units kcal	kJ	Protein (grams)
Chocolate	Cooking	525	2197	4.7	149	622	1.3
Corn syrup		290	1213	0	82	344	0
Golden syrup		298	1269	0.3	84	359	0.1
Honey	Clear, thick, light or dark	288	1229	0.4	82	348	0.1
Jams and marmalade		261	1115	0.5	74	316	0.1
Maple syrup		252	1054	0	71	299	0
Molasses	Black treacle	257	1096	1.2	73	310	0.1
Sugar	Caster, icing, raw brown, granulated	394	1681	trace	112	476	trace

Oils and Fats

Food	Description	per 100 g Energy units kcal	kJ	Protein (grams)	per oz. Energy units kcal	kJ	Protein (grams)
Butter	salted and unsalted	740	3041	0.4	210	861	0.1
Margarine	spreading and cooking	730	3000	0.1	207	850	trace
Vegetable oil	e.g. olive, sunflower, walnut, peanut etc	899	3696	trace	255	1047	trace

Beverages, Soft Drinks, Alcoholic Drinks

Food	Description	per 100 g Energy units kcal	kJ	Protein (grams)	per oz Energy units kcal	kJ	Protein (grams)
Chocolate powder	sweetened	397	1683	5.5	113	479	1.6
Cocoa powder		312	1301	18.5	88	369	5.2
Coffee	Ground, roasted	287	1203	10.4	81	341	2.9
Coffee	Instant	100	424	14.6	28	120	4.1
Tea		0	0	0	0	0	0
Coca cola		39	168	trace	11	48	trace
Lemonade		21	90	trace	6	25	trace
Orange squash	Undiluted	107	456	trace	30	129	trace
Blackcurrant cordial	Undiluted	229	976	0.1	65	276	trace
Yeast extract		179	759	41.1	51	215	11.7
Brown ale	Bottled	28	117	0.3	8	33	0.1
Bitter	Draught or canned	32	132	0.3	9	37	0.1
Lager	Bottled	29	120	0.2	8	34	trace
Stout	Bottled	37	156	0.3	10	44	0.1
Cider	Dry	36	152	trace	10	43	trace
Cider	Sweet	42	176	trace	12	50	trace
Wine	Red	68	284	0.2	19	80	trace
Wine	Rosé	71	294	0.1	20	83	trace
Wine	White-medium	75	275	0.1	21	78	trace
Champagne		76	315	0.3	22	89	0.1
Sherry	Medium	118	489	0.1	33	139	trace
Liqueurs	e.g. cherry brandy	255	1073	trace	72	304	trace
Spirits	70% proof e.g. gin, whisky	222	919	trace	63	260	trace

Index

Note: bracketed numbers refer to
a picture when this is not on the
same page as the recipe.

BIBLIOGRAPHY
Janet BARKAS, *The Vegetable Passion*,
Routledge and Kegan Paul Ltd., 1975 (UK)
Elizabeth DAVID, *French Provincial
Cooking*, Michael Joseph Ltd., 1960;
Penguin Books Ltd., 1964 (UK)
Elizabeth DAVID, *Italian Food*,
Macdonald, 1954; Penguin Books Ltd.,
1963 (UK)
Auguste ESCOFFIER, *A Guide to Modern
Cookery*, William Heinemann Ltd.,
1907 (UK)
Auguste ESCOFFIER, *Ma Cuisine*,
The Hamlyn Publishing Group Ltd.,
1978 (UK)
Ellen Buchman EWALD, *Recipes for a
Small Planet*, Ballantyne Books/Random
House Inc., 1973 (USA)
Walter and Jenny FLEISS, *Modern
Vegetarian Cookery*, Penguin Books Ltd.,
1964 (UK)
Rosemary HEMPHILL, *The Penguin Book
of Herbs and Spices*, Penguin Books Ltd.,
1966 (UK)

Alan HOOKER, *Vegetarian Gourmet
Cookery*, Pitmans Publishing Ltd.,
1976 (UK)
Dorothea van Gundy JONES, *The Soybean
Cookbook*, Arco Publishing Company/The
Devin Adair Company, 1963 (USA)
Frances Moore LAPPE, *Diet for a Small
Planet*, Ballantyne Books/Random House
Inc., 1971 (USA)
Kenneth LO, *Chinese Vegetable and
Vegetarian Cooking*, Faber and Faber Ltd.,
1974 (UK)
Marie LOVEJOY, *International Vegetarian
Cuisine*, Quest Books, 1978 (USA)
W.P.K.FINDLAY, *The Observer's Book of
Mushrooms, Toadstools and Other Common
Fungi*, Frederick Warne Ltd., 1978 (UK)
Martha H. OLIVER, *Add a few Sprouts*,
Pivot Original Health Books/Keat
Publishing Inc., 1975 (USA)
Claudia RODEN, *A Book of Middle Eastern
Food*, Thomas Nelson Ltd., 1968; Penguin
Books Ltd., 1970 (UK)

Jack SANTA MARIA, *Indian Vegetarian
Cookery*, Rider and Company, London,
1973 (UK)
George SEDDON and Helena RADECKA,
Your Kitchen Garden, Mitchell Beazley
Ltd., 1975 (UK)
Anna THOMAS, *The Vegetarian Epicure*,
Vintage Books, 1972 (USA); Penguin
Books Ltd., 1974 (UK)

ACKNOWLEDGEMENTS
*The Publishers would like to thank the
following people who very kindly lent
cooking and other equipment used in the
photographs in this book:*
*Elizabeth David Ltd., Bourne Street,
London SW1*
*Dickins and Jones (Harrods) Ltd.,
Regent Street, London W1*
*Divertimenti Cooking and Tableware,
Marylebone Lane, London W1*
*Leon Jaeggi and Sons Ltd., Tottenham
Court Road, London W1*
*John Lewis and Company Ltd., Oxford
Street, London W1*
*Harvey Nichols and Company Ltd.,
Knightsbridge, London SW1*